THE ACCUMULATION OF CAPITAL

THE ACCUMULATION
OF CAPITAL

BY

JOAN ROBINSON

Third Edition

MACMILLAN

ST MARTIN'S PRESS

First edition June 1956
Reprinted October 1956, 1958
Second edition 1965
Reprinted 1966
Third edition 1969
Reprinted 1971

Published by
THE MACMILLAN PRESS LTD
London and Basingstoke
Associated companies in New York Toronto
Dublin Melbourne Johannesburg and Madras

SBN 333 07205 7 (hard cover)
333 04643 9 (paper cover)

Printed in Great Britain by
REDWOOD PRESS LIMITED
Trowbridge & London

PREFACE

ECONOMIC analysis, serving for two centuries to win an understanding of the Nature and Causes of the Wealth of Nations, has been fobbed off with another bride — a Theory of Value. There were no doubt deep-seated political reasons for the substitution but there was also a purely technical, intellectual reason. It is excessively difficult to conduct analysis of over-all movements of an economy through time, involving changes in population, capital accumulation and technical change, at the same time as an analysis of the detailed relations between output and price of particular commodities. Both sets of problems require to be solved, but each has to be tackled separately, ruling the other out by simplifying assumptions. Faced with the choice of which to sacrifice first, economists for the last hundred years have sacrificed dynamic theory in order to discuss relative prices. This has been unfortunate, first because an assumption of static over-all conditions is such a drastic departure from reality as to make it impossible to submit anything evolved within it to the test of verification and, secondly, because it ruled out the discussion of most of the problems that are actually interesting and condemned economics to the arid formalism satirised by J. H. Clapham in 'Of Empty Economic Boxes'.[1]

Keynes's *General Theory* smashed up the glass house of static theory in order to be able to discuss a real problem — the causes of unemployment. But his analysis was framed in terms of a short period in which the stock of capital and the technique of production are given. It left a huge area of long-run problems covered with fragments of broken glass from the static theory and gave only vague hints as to how the shattered structure could be rebuilt.

[1] *Economic Journal*, September 1922.

v

In recent times the centre of interest has returned to the classical problems of the over-all growth of the economy. A leading example of this change is R. F. Harrod's *Towards a Dynamic Economics*. In order to discuss dynamic problems in a simple manner Harrod dismisses the whole problem of relative prices and sets out an analysis of the over-all development of an economy without paying attention to the theory of value. The present work follows his example.

The revival of interest in the classical questions brings a revival of the classical theory. Much in the following pages will be startlingly familiar to learned readers. I did not myself arrive at these ideas by studying the classics. The problem presented itself to me as the generalisation of the *General Theory*, that is, an extension of Keynes's short-period analysis to long-run development. But I was very much illuminated by Piero Sraffa's Introduction to Ricardo's *Principles*.

ACKNOWLEDGMENTS

My debt to Keynes, Wicksell and Marshall is the debt we all owe to our progenitors, and will be sufficiently obvious in the following pages. I have referred to them at particular points for the reader's convenience, not by way of acknowledgment of their legacies. Michal Kalecki, though a contemporary, comes into the same category. In this connection I should like also to mention Gunnar Myrdal's *Political Element in Economic Theory*.

My first attempt at setting out an analysis of accumulation was inspired by Harrod, and I must repeat once more my gratitude for his most fruitful provocation. My debt to Harrod goes back much earlier, for it was under his influence that I first formulated the concept of neutral technical progress that we have both made the centre of our analysis.[1] As so often, it was R. F. Kahn who saw the point that we were groping for and enabled us to get it into a comprehensible form.

[1] See 'The Classification of Inventions', *Review of Economic Studies* (February 1938).

A problem which Harrod left completely open was the reconciliation of secular growth at a constant ratio of capital to output with the notion embodied in Wicksell's production function, or what F. von Hayek called the 'Ricardo effect' — the relation of real wages to the most profitable 'length of the period of production'. On this subject, as well as on the whole question of accumulation, my ideas were formed in a long series of debates with Nicholas Kaldor, going back to the time when we disputed with Erwin Rothbarth the theory put forward in his posthumous article : 'Causes of the Superior Efficiency of U.S.A. Industry compared with British Industry'.[1]

In discussions of this sort it is impossible to evaluate the contribution of one party. I only know that my borrowings from Kaldor have been very great though he did not always approve the use to which I put them.[2]

The production function was a very tough nut to crack. In this undertaking I had invaluable help from R. F. Kahn, who, once more, found the essential clue to rescue the argument from the tangle into which I had ravelled it. D. G. Champernowne came to our aid with the heavy artillery of his mathematical expertise. I am especially indebted to him for his part in the formulation of the problem of the value of invested capital, and he and Kahn (with the consent of the editors of the *Review of Economic Studies*) have kindly allowed their joint note on this subject to be republished herewith.

An alternative method of solution was independently evolved by C. A. Blyth.

I am also indebted to Champernowne for his extension of the argument to the problem of accumulation with two factors of production (land and labour in fixed supply with capital

---

[1] *Economic Journal* (September 1946).

[2] His published works bearing on the subject of our debate are: 'The Recent Controversy on the Theory of Capital', *Econometrica* (July 1937); 'On the Theory of Capital', A Rejoinder to Professor Knight, *Econometrica* (January 1938); 'Capital Intensity and the Trade Cycle', *Economica* (February 1939); 'Professor Hayek and the Concertina Effect', *Economica* (November 1942); 'Mr. Hicks on the Trade Cycle', *Economic Journal* (December 1951); 'The Relation of Economic Growth and Cyclical Fluctuation', *Economic Journal* (March 1954); and the article on the Theory of Distribution in *Chambers's Encyclopaedia*.

investment going on) [1] and for much help (even when he did not agree with me) in the formulation of the theory of accumulation in a given state of technical knowledge.

I have also had much assistance from discussions with R. Goodwin, D. Bensusan-Butt, R. Matthews, H. G. Johnson, Ruth Cohen, J. Knapp and L. Tarshis. E. F. Jackson read a large part of the proofs and made many helpful suggestions.

PLAN OF WORK

Book I contains some discussion of the concepts and categories required for the analysis of accumulation. Its general theme is that it is of no use framing definitions more precise than the subject-matter to which they apply. In this connection I would like to cite the following passage from K. R. Popper, *The Open Society and Its Enemies*.[2]

'The view that the precision of science and of scientific language depends upon the precision of its terms is certainly very plausible, but it is none the less a mere prejudice. Rather, the precision of a language depends just upon the fact that it takes care not to burden its terms with the task of being precise. A term like "sand-dune" or "wind" is certainly very vague. (How many inches high must a little sand-hill be in order to be called a sand-dune? How quickly must the air move in order to be called a wind?) However, for many of the geologist's purposes, these terms are quite sufficiently precise; and for other purposes, when a higher degree of differentiation is needed, he can always say "dunes between 4 and 30 feet high" or "wind of a velocity of between 20 and 40 miles an hour". And the position in the more exact sciences is analogous. In physical measurements, for instance, we always take care to consider the range within which there may be an error; and precision does not consist in trying to reduce this range to nothing, or in pretending that there is no such range, but rather in its explicit recognition.'

[1] 'The Production Function and the Theory of Capital: A Comment', *Review of Economic Studies*, vol. xxi (2), No. 55 (1953–4).
[2] Vol. ii, p. 18.

Economic concepts such as wealth, output, income and cost are no easier to define precisely than wind. Nevertheless these concepts are useful, and economic problems can be discussed.

Book II, 'Accumulation in the Long Run', contains the central part of the work. Its strategy is to proceed step by step from the most severely simple assumptions towards greater complexity, squeezing out all that can be learned at each step before proceeding to the next. Section I of Book II, 'Accumulation with One Technique', contains the most important propositions set out in this way, and the rest of the book may be regarded as complications and qualifications surrounding this central core. One simplification used in this section is the assumption of rigid technical coefficients at any given stage of development, so that, when the pattern of consumption is given, the ratio of labour to equipment (at capacity) is given irrespective of the level of wages and profits. In Chapter 9 technical progress, both neutral and biased, is treated under this assumption.

In Section II this assumption is removed and the influence of the level of wages on the choice of technique is brought into the argument. This problem is extremely intricate, and the difficulty of the analysis is out of proportion to its importance. It seemed necessary, however, to treat it at some length, both because it has some importance in reality and because it occupies (under the guise of the conception of a production function) a large place in traditional economic doctrine.

In Section III the analysis of technical progress is recombined with the analysis of the influence of wages on technique.

Chapter 18 summarises the propositions which have been deduced so far.

Book III deals with the evolution of an economy in which uncertainty prevails and expectations about the future are overweighted by current experience. This state of expectations gives rise to short-period fluctuations in activity. The relation between fluctuations in the rate of investment from year to year and its trend over the long run is discussed in Chapter 22.

Book IV treats of finance and the monetary system. In this department of economic life the particular form of institutions (such as Central Banks) and legal rules (such as laws regulating the issue of currency) play a large role; no attempt is here made to account for or to assess the particular forms that institutions and rules have taken in actual economies. The description of their operation is set out in a generalised and therefore highly stylised form.

So far, the argument has been conducted under the assumption that there is no consumption out of profits. Book V introduces the rentier. We then have to retrace our steps and consider how the argument already set out has to be modified to allow for consumption out of profits. This arrangement is perhaps troublesome to the reader, but (I believe) less so than would be the introduction of rentiers into the first model.

Up to this point scarcity of land has been assumed away. In Book VI rent is introduced, and once more we have to retrace the earlier argument to show what complications are required in it to allow for scarcity of land. Much of this analysis could be modified to apply to problems presented by a multiplicity of factors of production, for instance skilled and unskilled labour.

The last chapter of this Book ('Increasing and Diminishing Returns') and the remaining Books ('Relative Prices' and 'International Trade') map out in a very sketchy manner well-trodden ground which occupies a large space in current economic teaching; they are appended in order to show the connection between this territory and the terrain of the problem of accumulation rather than to contribute anything fresh to the topics discussed.

The whole argument is set out, as far as possible, as an analytical construction, with a minimum of controversy.

Some Notes are added on a variety of topics in order to defend the concepts used and to show their connection or divergence from some other methods of analysis. These Notes are not intended to provide a survey of current economic doctrines. They are offered only to assist the reader to see in what respects the argument of this work conflicts with certain lines of thought with which he is likely to be familiar.

The discussion of one point, the concept of marginal productivity of investment, is both so important and so perplexing that it seemed best to promote it to a place in the main text. It appears as a 'Digression' after Chapter 30.

The diagrams illustrate those propositions in the text which are susceptible to treatment in two dimensions.

The final Note by D. G. Champernowne and R. F. Kahn provides a formula, on certain simplifying assumptions, for the element of interest in the cost of capital goods.

JOAN ROBINSON

CAMBRIDGE, 1955

AUTHOR'S NOTE TO THE SECOND EDITION

SOME corrections have been made to the text of the first edition, principally to remove the errors referred to in the preface to *Essays in the Theory of Economic Growth*.

JOAN ROBINSON

CAMBRIDGE, 1964

CONTENTS

BOOK III

THE SHORT PERIOD

BOOK IV

FINANCE

BOOK V

THE RENTIER

Contents

BOOK I
INTRODUCTION

Chapter i

THE CLASSES OF INCOME

THE economic life of a robin is simpler than that of a man. Most of the year a robin's work consists in finding and eating food. He occupies a certain area of ground, and other robins behave as though they recognised his right of property in it, for each appears to fight with a good heart to defend his own territory and to be feeble and easily intimidated when invading a neighbour's. In the spring he is joined by a wife who, in addition to the work of feeding herself, undertakes capital construction, finding materials and building a nest. He does some extra work to feed her while she is sitting, and both do extra work to feed their young.[1]

Some human economies are only slightly more complicated than the robin economy ; in a free peasant society each family owns an area of land and produces from it almost all that they consume, with a minimum of trade with other families. But in working (and, unfortunately, in fighting) a number of individuals who specialise and co-operate produce far greater results than the sum of their independent efforts, and consequently human economies develop into enormously intricate complexes of specialised activities. The method of distribution of the product of interlocking activities then becomes important.

WORK AND PROPERTY

The robin swallows the caterpillar that he finds ; for him production and consumption are completely integrated. A man in a developed economy lives by consuming a part of the joint product of the whole society ; there is no bit of it which

[1] See David Lack, *The Life of the Robin*.

is obviously his own, and the sharing of the product has to be carried out according to some sort of rules of the game. Moreover, the robin eats as he goes, whereas most kinds of human production consist of processes which take time to complete. The flow of consumption goods becoming available to-day is the result of work which was done in the past and with the aid of tools and equipment that may have been constructed very far in the past. These must be looked after and controlled in an orderly manner, not allowed to be grabbed or cut about by all comers. Thus in human economies there must be property in capital goods — equipment and work-in-progress — as well as in territory. Work without property can produce nothing, and property without work is soon consumed. The rules of the game are largely concerned with the manner in which work and property are combined in production and with the rights that they give to shares in the proceeds.

In a slave economy there is no income from work. The consumption of the slaves is part of the upkeep of capital goods. The whole of the proceeds of production accrue to the owners of property (if some give their slaves more than the necessary minimum for subsistence and reproduction, this is outside the rules of the game, for the slaves have no rights, and should be regarded as an indulgence of the owners rather than as earnings by the slaves). An artisan, who owns his own tools and organises his own work, shares in the flow of consumable output by exchanging his products for others; for him income from work and income from property are fused in one. In a thorough-going socialist economy property is owned collectively, work is organised collectively; income is distributed partly in the form of free services (education, medicine, etc.) and partly as an allocation to each individual according to some formula based upon the work that he contributes. In a capitalist economy property is owned by a small number of individuals who hire the labour of a large number at agreed wage rates and organise their work (directly or through hired managers). The excess of the product over the wages bill then appears as income from property.

No actual economy conforms to a pure type, and economies which are predominantly capitalist contain many elements of production for home consumption, many elements of artisan production and many elements of socialism. These simple categories, however, are useful, provided that we remember innumerable complications that have to be reintroduced before abstract analysis can be confronted with reality.

THE ENTREPRENEUR

Under the capitalist rules, anyone who commands sufficient purchasing power, or *finance*, and knows how to set about it, can become an employer of labour or *entrepreneur*. In the typical case he provides a place to work — a factory — some equipment and some materials to work on. The workers whom he takes on lend him work, but since they have little or no property and must live from their earnings, the amount of work he can borrow from any one man is limited, and usually he pays off the loan at the end of a week by disbursing wages from his fund of finance (salaried employees may lend him their services for a month or a quarter of a year). By the time the first cycle of production and sales is completed (the length of the cycle depending on the period that it takes to put materials through the process of production and to market the product) he has recovered (if his operations are successful) the cost of materials and outlay on wages, so that proceeds from the first cycle are available to finance the second, and so on, as long as production and sales continue successfully. The cycle of utilisation of plant is normally very much longer than the cycle of production ; to have finance available to renew plant when it has reached the end of its useful life the entrepreneur must accumulate an amortisation fund out of proceeds while it is working. Provided that he does so, and that his operations continue to be successful, an investment of finance, once made, creates a stock of capital goods which continues to exist indefinitely. The investment, however, involves a risk, for there is no guarantee that operations will be successful, and if they are not, say because the market for the type of production concerned shrinks unexpectedly, the value of the capital goods falls or vanishes completely. The entrepreneur then wishes he had committed his original fund of finance to some other line, where it would not have been lost. The first requirement for being a successful entrepreneur consists in choosing lines of production where this does not happen.

In the early days of capitalism the typical entrepreneur was an individual who had invested his own finance in a business which he managed himself and bequeathed to his heirs as a going concern. There are still great numbers of such entrepreneurs, but the advantages of large-scale production (both in technical economies and in strategic power) and the development of financial arrangements to make large-scale business possible, have brought into existence great departmentalised companies operated by cadres of managers. The managers are then formally the employees of owners of property, but their knowledge of the detail of the business gives them a good deal of independence which often amounts in effect to complete control. 'The entrepreneur' in modern conditions is a very amorphous conception; all the same, decisions concerning the conduct of a business must get themselves taken, whether by individuals or by interaction between individuals, and it is, perhaps, legitimate to think (with due reservations) of a decision-taking entity, embodying the policy of a firm, and, by an anthropomorphic turn of speech, to refer to 'him' as an entrepreneur.

The capitalist rules of the game foster large-scale production and the use of elaborate techniques. It is hard for independent artisans to co-operate, for each 'likes to be his own master', whereas propertyless men are perforce amenable to discipline. Entrepreneurs can organise large masses of workers, bringing about economies of division of labour; their command of finance makes it possible for each to provide the workers whom he employs with complicated equipment, and he is impelled to do so by the competitive struggle to undersell others; this raises output per man (for standardised products) much above what an artisan can achieve. Consequently the control of production, once it has been concentrated, is prevented from becoming widely diffused, and this set of rules of the game is kept in force.

THE RENTIER

The capitalist rules of the game are favourable to establishing property in debts. *A* borrows the command over purchasing power from *B*, on terms usually including a pledge of security for repayment and a promise to pay interest at an agreed rate, and gives him an acknowledgment. This *B* is free to sell, or to use as security for a loan to himself; the debt is his property. The titles to debts are called by various names, according to their terms. Mortgages are secured on land, bills are of short currency (debts repayable at an early date), bonds of longer currency (or of no specified date) and so forth.

In pre-capitalist economies the most frequent cause of borrowing (apart from warlike operations) was to finance consumption, either by spendthrifts or by families which had fallen into misfortune. Public opinion was hostile to lenders, who were making a usurious income out of vice and misery, and the rules of the game surrounding dealings in debts were not favourable to promoting such transactions.

Where a profit is to be made by investing finance in capital goods and employing labour in productive processes, the situation is quite different. The borrower confidently expects to be able to pay interest out of the proceeds of his activity, and the lender, far from battening on the misfortunes of others, is assisting in a process which (apart from ill-judged or purely competitive investment) leads to an increase in the productive resources of the economy as a whole. Lenders are then regarded with favour, and elaborate legal provisions are made to facilitate lending and borrowing in a great variety of forms, and to facilitate dealings in second-hand debts.

The development of modern financial techniques has brought into existence an important type of property — ordinary shares — which is intermediate between debts (such as those represented by bonds) [1] and finance owned by the entrepreneur who controls the business in which it is invested.

---

[1] We are using an eclectic terminology for the sake of its convenience and perspicuity; we use the American term *bonds*, instead of the English *debentures*, and the English term *shares* instead of the American *stock*.

Legally, a shareholder is a part owner of any business whose shares he holds, but the institution of limited liability and of facilities for dealing in shares at second hand (the Stock Exchange) has brought about a divorce between ownership and control which makes many shareholders, in effect, much more like lenders than like entrepreneurs. The shareholders may be roughly divided into *insiders*, who have large and permanent holdings in a particular business and take an active interest in its affairs, and *outsiders*, whose wealth is distributed amongst a number of businesses and who have no continuing interest in any one of them. Insiders fulfil some of the functions of the entrepreneur, while the relation of outsiders to a particular business is very similar to the relations of its creditors (bond holders). In some cases a business may be owned entirely by a floating population of outside share-holders who leave the managers entirely free to run it as they think best. The legal owners of the business then have no smack of the entrepreneur about them.

We have borrowed from the French the term *rentier* to mean an individual whose income is derived from owning debts (that is, from interest on bonds). It is convenient to include all who derive income from financial property under this title, though some rentiers (when the term is used in this extended sense), in so far as they are inside shareholders, are at the same time partly entrepreneurs.

It is convenient also to borrow from France the term *placement* to mean the purchase of titles to debts or shares, whether out of new savings recently made or from the proceeds of selling some other property. The term *investment* can then be confined to the sense of using finance to cause capital goods to be created.[1] By extension we may use the term placements to mean financial property of all kinds, that is, things which are of no use in themselves, either for consumption or production, but are valuable because they constitute a store of purchasing power that can be used by their owner at any time, if he chooses, to buy or hire whatever goods and services are available in the economy of which he forms

---

[1] There may also be investment in purely financial business (see below, p. 46).

a part. Placements, then, mean things like bank deposits, which represent debts owed by a bank to an individual (of this more anon); bonds and bills, which represent debts owed by corporate bodies of various kinds to individuals; shares, which represent part-ownership of companies; and so forth. The term rentier, as we shall use it, is then co-extensive with the category of owners of placements.

Like all economic categories, the concept of placements is vague at the edges. Shares are desired partly as a means of control over the companies concerned. Land (with or without buildings on it) is sometimes a pure placement, as when the title-deeds are held by an owner who has no interest in them except as a source of money return or potential selling value, but much of land is partly a consumption good or an instrument for production as well as being a store of purchasing power to its owner. Stocks of commodities are held both for use in production and as a speculation. Whether a particular physical object (say a house) is most like a consumption good, a capital good or a placement depends on the habits and state of mind of its owner. At the two extremes the distinction is clear. A holding of Old Consols is nothing but a placement, and a soft-boiled egg is nothing but a consumption good. As always with economic categories, we must rely on rough common-sense distinctions, not on scholastic definitions of words more precise than the concepts to which they apply.[1]

FINANCE

The chief ways in which an entrepreneur can provide himself with finance are: calling in loans which he has made in the past, for instance by drawing on a bank deposit; selling some property which he owns; or borrowing, in which case he may pledge property that he owns as security directly (as when land is mortgaged) or appeal to the knowledge that he does own property (which could be used to meet his liability to repay in case the investment he is making goes wrong) to get himself good terms. (A lender who makes ill-secured loans exacts a high rate of interest, thus causing his good

[1] Cf. above, p. viii.

debtors to reimburse him for losses that he makes on transactions with those who fail.) He may also acquire finance by selling shares in his business as a going concern, or if it is already a joint-stock company, by making a new issue of shares.

External finance (as opposed to finance provided from property owned by the business) is supplied by owners of wealth who wish to receive a return on their property without themselves taking an active part in business. In the case of shareholders, however, this (as we have seen) is a matter of degree, for their legal status as part owners gives them certain rights over the control of the business which may or may not be exercised in effect.

The need for finance arises because one lot of people (active entrepreneurs) see opportunities for profitable investment beyond what they can finance themselves, while another lot (partly or completely passive owners of wealth) are willing to have their command over purchasing power turned to profitable use for them by others.

The activity of bringing lenders and borrowers together, and of dealing in second-hand debts and in shares, provides an opportunity for business in which, also, finance can be invested, and has given rise to a host of specialised professions — stock jobbing and broking, accepting bills, underwriting new issues and speculating on changing values of obligations in the second-hand market. There is also an important class of business which deals in debts by providing lenders on the one hand and borrowers on the other with terms convenient to them and making a profit out of the margin between the rate that the lender is willing to take and the rate that the borrower is willing to pay. (Insurance houses, for instance, accept loans, in the form of premiums, to be repaid in case of accidents, sudden death, survival to old age, etc., and relend on bonds repayable at a definite date, or saleable in the market, so that lenders can be repaid when their need arises without inconvenience to borrowers.)

In this class of business banks occupy a special place. They accept loans (deposits) repayable on demand or at short notice, and lend for specified periods (advances) or by holding readily marketable obligations. The most convenient way for an owner of wealth to make use of his command over purchasing power is to transfer his rights in loans that he has made (by drawing a cheque on his bank account). Loans made to one individual reappear as deposits in the accounts of others to whom he has made payments. Thus as well as taking part in the business of supplying finance to borrowers, the banks provide a convenient medium of exchange for settling debts, making payments, making other kinds of loans and dealing in property of all kinds.

The incomes earned and the speculative profits realised in all these transactions do not correspond to any particular bit of the process of production which can be earmarked as due to them; the whole structure, by providing security and convenience to lenders, helps to mobilise finance and put it at the service of entrepreneurs, thus contributing indirectly to building up the real productive resources of the economy. But since the prices of placements of all kinds are liable to vary, as a whole and relatively to each other, the main art of being a successful placer consists in buying ones which will rise and eschewing ones which will fall. This involves a utilisation of finance, and an expenditure of brain power and nerves, which are quite out of proportion to any contribution that they make to the productivity of the economy.

PROFESSIONAL INCOME

The distinction between income from work and income from property is not clear-cut. The executives of large concerns may be paid partly by salaries and partly by a share in the profits of the business. Amongst the professions, a lawyer, who sells his services in the market, has something in common with an artisan (his tools being his knowledge of the law); a teacher, employed on a salary, has more in common with a worker, but his income also is partly a return on capital invested in his own education.

From the point of view of an individual an investment in acquiring earning power, by paying to be trained, may be alternative to holding income-yielding property, but it is different in an important respect; under the capitalist rules of the game it cannot be bought and sold (though to a minor extent it can be insured and borrowed against) so that the present capital value of future personal earning power has a metaphorical, not an actual financial meaning.

From the point of view of the economy as a whole, the similarity is more important than the difference. The stock of teachers, doctors and trained workers of all kinds has to be maintained, by devoting resources to education, in much the same way as the stock of machinery has to be maintained by the engineering industry, and to increase the stock of trained personnel requires investment, just as much as to increase the stock of physical capital goods.

LAND

Territory, as a means of production, differs from capital goods in various respects. The rules of the game concerning land tenure differ in different capitalist countries. In some, property in land is much like any other kind of property, but in most the landowners, whether peasants, yeomen or aristo-crats, form a distinct class, with social habits and political interests different from those of capitalists. A transfer of wealth from one to the other — say a rise in the price of agri-cultural products relatively to manufactures — has different consequences from those of a transfer from one group of capitalists to another. For this reason, the rent of land has to be treated, for many questions, as a category of income distinct from profits on capital.

Land differs from the general run of capital goods in technical as well as social characteristics. This is not because land is a 'free gift of nature' whereas capital goods are man-made. Each generation finds itself born into a world provided with means of production, and there is no significance (apart from historical interest) in the distinction between mere space and the hedges and ditches found on it, or in inquiring whether a roadway was made by the ancient Romans or by a freak of geology. But some land provides exhaustible resources (mineral deposits) which are destroyed in being used, while land in general shares with certain other means of production, such as railway embankments, bridges and (to a lesser extent) buildings of all kinds, the characteristics that it can be kept permanently in good order by a relatively small expenditure of resources on running repairs (hedging and ditching), and that it can be put to a wide variety of uses, so that it is not much subject to the wear and tear and the obsolescence due to changes in demand for its services that limits the useful life of machinery. At the same time, in a settled country, it is very expensive, if not physically impossible, to increase the supply of land (as, for instance, by draining fens or irrigating deserts). Consequently, the supply of land varies much less than the supply of most kinds of capital goods in response to changes in the income that can be got by owning it.

On the other hand, where there is new land to be brought into use (for instance by improving transport facilities) a great addition may be made to productive resources by a relatively small investment. And land is often subject to a kind of negative obsolescence, as when the development of a new crop, such as rubber, turns formerly useless jungles into rich productive resources. It is in this connection that the notion of free gifts of nature (or free loot of conquest) is highly significant.

INCOMES AND CLASSES

The sources of income in a capitalist economy are traditionally divided between the categories : wages, rent, interest and profits. Wages (including salaries) represent contractual payments for work of all kinds, rent is a contractual payment for the hire of land and buildings, and interest a contractual payment for the loan (at first or thousandth hand) of finance. Profit is not such a simple concept. We shall use the expression *quasi-rent* [1] to mean the excess of proceeds over running-costs of a business ; and *profit* to mean the excess of quasi-rent over rent and the amortisation required to maintain the capital of the business. Interest is regarded as paid out of profit, along with dividends and the allocations made to their households by entrepreneurs who own their own businesses. The

[1] For the origin of this term see Marshall, *Principles*, 7th ed., p. 74 See also below, p. 289, note.

excess of profit over these payments is retained by the entrepreneur as the property of the firm. Entrepreneurs, according to this way of looking at things, have no personal income. The income of individuals fulfilling the function of entrepreneurship is made up of salaries (in the case of hired managers) and of personal allocations of profits, interest and dividends which they receive in their capacity as rentiers.

One individual may draw income from sources belonging to several categories, but in the main the category of wages corresponds to the income of the large class of individuals who have a negligible amount of property, and live by selling their work. Rent goes to a more or less distinct class of landowners; and interest and dividends to a class of rentiers (using that term in our extended sense), some of whom are doubling the role of rentier with that of entrepreneur.

The middle class of salaried workers and independent experts who sell their services piecemeal (lawyers, doctors in private practice, etc.) generally own some property and derive part of their incomes from it. For them interest is the most convenient way of drawing an income from property without having to be distracted from their own speciality by problems of management, but some may own land, and many are outside shareholders.

Thus the classes of society do not correspond exactly, though they do in the main, to the broad categories of income.

CHAPTER 2

THE MEANING OF WEALTH

WEALTH, as the copy-book maxims tell us, is not necessarily a source of satisfaction. There are two ways of satisfying desires : one is to get more and the other to want less. Moreover human beings do not pursue satisfaction in a direct and consistent manner ; they are constantly going a long way out of the way to torment themselves. But, taken by and large, as individuals, groups and nations, they do pursue wealth, and the very fact that human beings are interested in wealth justifies some of them (called economists) in talking about it, without being obliged to take a view on the wisdom or folly of the race.[1]

EXPENDITURE AND CONSUMPTION

Economic wealth is not a very precise idea and we must be content with a rough definition of it.[2] Broadly, economic wealth is the command over goods and services that are desired, or consuming power for short. The significance of production lies in the consumption which it makes possible. Under the capitalist rules of the game the major part of production is for sale, not for consumption. The motive of each individual is to get command over money, and a flow of goods and services suitable to meet human wants emerges as a by-product of their efforts to do so. At any moment, also, a large part of production is devoted to maintaining and increasing the stock of capital goods to be used in future production. But an economy in which the processes of production did not provide for consumption would not be viable, so that looking

[1] Cf. D. H. Robertson, *Utility and All That.*
[2] Cf. above, p. viii.

at the economy as a whole we may say that the significance of production, though not the motive for it, lies in consumption. (Production for purposes of what is euphemistically called defence does not fit into this way of looking at things; the present discussion is confined to civilian goods and services.)

Consumption is very much an individual affair. The archetypal act of consumption is swallowing a mouthful of food (though the desires and the satisfactions of individuals are not independent of the society in which they live; the need for calories is individual, but the kind of food a man eats and the psychological pleasure that accompanies eating are influenced by the traditions of his forebears and the habits of his neighbours). Consumption may be carried out collectively; a symphony concert, for instance, is a collective consumption good, but individuals partake of it in twos and threes. At the same time, individuals identify their own consumption with that of others. A mother is more interested in what the children eat than in what she eats herself; a man is more interested in what his wife is wearing than in his own clothes. A family is, in a sense, a consuming entity, and something like family feeling is extended by individuals to all sorts of groupings within an economy such as religious sects, social classes and, above all, nations. Thus we can talk about the consumption of a class or of a nation, as well as of an individual or a family.

But a group of human beings is a very loosely organised sort of entity. There are conflicts of economic interest even within a family. The more consuming power is exercised by a man in the pub the less his wife can exercise on the groceries. A nation is made up of groups and classes with conflicting interests. The only example of a human society without internal conflicts was Robinson Crusoe, and even he may have suffered from ambivalence. An economy is an entity consisting of groups with conflicting interests held together by rules of the game. When the conflicts become so acute that the rules are unplayable, the economy ceases to be viable, and explodes or changes into a different entity. Thus it has, as long as it survives, a kind of individual existence which at the same time is partly dividual. When we are talking about

the consuming power of a family, a class, or a nation, as though
of an individual, we must never forget to pose at the same
time the detective-story question, *cui bono?* which is often
mistranslated : What's the use? but properly means, Who
gets the swag?

What kinds of goods and services does economic wealth
command? Consuming power cannot be identified with
purchasing power — the command over things which have a
price and to which the 'measuring rod of money' can be
applied. Even the most highly developed capitalist societies still
contain important areas of strictly economic life which are
unpriced. There is a great deal of production for direct
consumption, within the house and garden of a family, which
is concerned with material welfare at its most material — how
many calories can be got from a pound of potatoes? Domestic
work can be given a notional money value, but it is somewhat
artificial to do so. How assess the relative success of an English
and a French housewife with the problem of potatoes? A
very important part of the natural resources of a nation is
unappropriated. A deer forest and a moor where hikers roam
at will are much alike in every respect except that one commands a rent and the other does not. One has as good a claim
as the other to be treated as economic wealth. And a very
important part of national property — in particular the road
system — is most conveniently operated, not under socialist
but under communist rules of the game : to each according
to his need and from each according to his taxable capacity.
Thus purchasing power is not co-extensive with consuming
power.

Economic analysis is very much easier to apply to purchasing power than to total consuming power. The technique
of the subject, as it has been developed, is best suited to that
part of production and consumption which consists of goods
and services that are exchangeable, and so have value or
purchasing power over each other. Exchangeable goods and
services designed for consumption may be called *commodities*
for short. Commodities disappear from the statistician's ken
at the moment of sale ; consumption takes place in the privacy
of households. It is a temptation, therefore, to identify the

purchase of commodities with consumption simply because purchases can be measured and consumption cannot. But this is a very inaccurate way of describing even that part of consumption which is catered for by purchases of commodities. Consumption takes time and only begins at the moment of purchase. It is true that for certain kinds of goods — a very old book or a very new hat — the mere act of buying is a specific pleasure in itself, quite apart from the subsequent enjoyment of the property, but with most things the only motive for buying them is to enjoy their services over a shorter or longer period of future time.[1]

Yet so ingrained is the habit of thinking of purchasing as consumption that it affects the attitude of the plain man, as well as the arguments of economists. When clothes rationing was introduced in Great Britain it seemed to everybody perfectly fair and egalitarian to allot coupons at so much per head, without any regard to the unequal distribution of consuming power represented by stocks.[2] This habit of thought is misleading in theory ; and in practice it fosters the bias (unconscious or cynical) of producers who, under the capitalist rules of the game, can make more profit from frequent sales of goods which disintegrate quickly than by trying to provide purchasers with the maximum consuming power technically possible for a given outlay.

There is another way in which the use of the measuring rod of money is liable to mislead. For many capitalists, marketing their output is more troublesome than producing it, and a large part of the price which a consumer pays for physical objects covers the costs, not of physical production and technically necessary transport and storage, but of persuading him to buy. This means that if we think of a consumption good, naïvely, as something solid and comfortable, the measuring rod of money does not always measure what we think.

But when all is said, it remains true that great changes

---

[1] Cf. K. E. Boulding, *A Reconstruction of Economics*, p. 135.
[2] Mr. W. B. Reddaway, who was concerned with the administration of the scheme, remarked that it was like rationing the pence and taking no notice of the pounds.

do take place in the mass of solid goods and useful services consumed, and that the purchasing power of individuals and groups is the major influence on their consuming power, so that the command over purchasing power is a subject worth discussing.

PURCHASING POWER AND EXPENDITURE

Purchasing power must be examined, so to say, in two layers — the command of an individual or group over money, and the command given by a unit of money over goods and services.

The purchasing power in terms of money that an individual commands at any moment is not a very precise quantity. It certainly is not confined to cash in the house or in his current account at the bank. Nor does it consist only in his placements (assets of a purely financial nature).[1] An overcoat, though generally desired simply as a consumption good, is also a store of purchasing power that can be tapped by selling or pawning it. Nor is purchasing power bounded by property; it may include borrowing power, or credit. Overdraft facilities are just as good a source of purchasing power as a bank balance. Moreover the separate stores of purchasing power of individuals (which give each one of them a comfortable feeling that he could spend if he wished) cannot be made to add up for the economy as a whole. If everyone tried to exercise his purchasing power at once, the economy would explode in a hyper-inflation.

In normal times, however, individual owners of purchasing power have fairly regular habits about how they exercise it, and the behaviour of an economy depends on the exercise of purchasing power, not its existence. Thus the vagueness of the concept of purchasing power in terms of money does not undermine the possibility of conducting economic analysis. We can measure the total amount of purchasing power exercised by a family or a group over a certain period, that is, their expenditure for, say, a week or a year. What is commonly called National Income is a sum of the expenditures

[1] See above, p. 8.

made in a year by all the families composing the nation (*plus* expenditure on investment for new capital goods and the balance, positive or negative, of exports over imports). Expenditure is an interesting subject in itself, for it makes the market for goods and services, and keeps the economy running. In the present context we are interested in expenditure as a (very imperfect) guide to the consumption of the individuals or groups concerned.

MEASURING PURCHASING POWER

The purchasing power in real terms of a sum of money consists in a list of all the possible goods and services that it might buy. Here we strike down to a lower level of analysis and come upon a fresh layer of problems.

The human mind is naturally poetic and thinks in terms of mystic essences. The proposition, that everything is what it is and not another thing, has to be accepted, but it goes against the grain. It is far easier to think of economic wealth as a quantity of *value* that has been put into it by labour or a quantity of *utility* that can be got out of it by consumption, than to recognise that it consists of an enormous who's who of miscellaneous items that can be treated as a quantity only when it is measured according to some more or less arbitrary convention.

The absolute purchasing power of money (at a given point in time and space) is an elusive concept. But for the purposes of analysing the sort of problems of which economics treats — the conditions governing the production of wealth by individuals, groups, nations or the human race, and the distribution between them of its consumption — we are mainly interested in changes in quantities or shares in totals, rather than absolute quantities. Thus we are interested in making comparisons of purchasing power rather than in trying to measure absolute purchasing power.

To compare the real value of different money outlays involves comparing different who's whos of goods. Suppose that we want to compare purchases by a group of consumers at two different points in time, taking a straightforward case in which there are recognisable items (eggs, overcoats, symphony concerts, etc.), with definite specifications as to their physical properties, age, durability, etc., examples of each being found in both lists ; the only difference between the two lists is then in prices and quantities.

The simplest method of comparison is to evaluate both sets of commodities at one of the sets of prices. Thus if we are comparing purchases at an earlier and a later date we may take each item in the second list and enter it up at its price in the first list. We then, by an illogical but convenient use of language, call the proportionate difference in the totals so arrived at the change in *volume* of purchases.

By using the prices in the first list, we are liable to flatter the volume of purchases at the second date if the proportions in which various commodities are purchased has altered. Some commodities which appear in the first list at high prices may be in plentiful supply at lower prices at the second date, and, according to this method of calculating, their weight, or influence over the resulting index of volume, is partly a reflection of a high value due to scarcity in the first position which has ceased to be relevant.[1]

On the other hand, a calculation based on the quantities at the first date at both sets of prices gives a conservative account of the benefit which each individual in a group of purchasers enjoys from a given volume of expenditure, when relative prices have altered between the two dates. A consumer is free to get the best bargain for himself that he can with his purchasing power, and is likely to buy the goods that, in each situation, are cheaper relatively to the desire that he feels for them ; thus he adapts the composition of his purchases to the pattern of prices, and however much he is deluded by the wiles of advertisers or swayed by the ambition to impress his neighbours, the very fact that (in a typical case) he survives and raises a family shows that there is a solid core of correspondence between his desires and his needs. Thus he gets

[1] For example, if the first list consisted of 60 loaves of bread costing a total of £1 and 1 ounce of caviare costing £1, while the second list consists of 48 loaves and 5 ounces of caviare, an index number constructed by this method would show the volume of purchases as having risen in the ratio of 290 to 100.

a greater benefit after a change of relative prices from what would be shown by the calculation as an equivalent amount of real purchasing power.[1]

To estimate the possible extent of these biases due to using the first set of prices or quantities, the calculations are made backwards, evaluating the items in the first list at the prices obtaining in the second period, and vice versa; this gives a conservative estimate of an increase in volume and flatters an increase in purchasing power.[2]

There is no target of a Platonic Ideal index number which lies somewhere between these bracketing shots (or which could be found by more refined methods of calculation). *The* volume of output and *the* purchasing power of money are metaphysical concepts.[3] All we can say is that the actual facts of the two positions are more accurately described by a bracket of pairs of index numbers than they would be by either pair taken singly.

Moreover, a difference in relative prices in two situations means that the purchasing power of money has altered differently from the point of view of different consumers. From the point of view of a particular consumer, many of the commodities in the list are of no interest whatever either because he has no taste for the goods or because his income does not permit him to think of buying them. A teetotaler has no practical interest in the price of whisky, or a bicyclist in the price of petrol. (Certain groups in society are composed

---

[1] Suppose that in the second position bread still costs 4d. a loaf, while caviare now costs 2s. an ounce. A purchaser who, in the first period bought bread and caviare in the proportion of 60 loaves to 1 ounce would be regarded, according to the index number calculation, as being given the same command over real purchasing power by £1 : 2s. in the second position as by £2 in the first position; but now he is consuming more caviare (unless he bought it in the first place in response to a snob appeal that it has since lost) and getting more benefit from what is shown by the index number as a constant amount of real purchasing power.

[2] Then the change from 60 loaves and 1 ounce of caviare to 48 loaves and 5 ounces is exhibited as a rise in the volume of purchases in the ratio of 26 to 22, so that the index rises from 100 to 118 (instead of to 290), and the fall in the price of caviare from £1 to 2s. per ounce is shown as a rise in the purchasing power of money in the ratio of 116 to 26. Thus while the first index grossly flatters the change in volume of purchases, the second grossly flatters the rise in purchasing power.

[3] Keynes, *Treatise on Money*, vol. i, p. 87

of individuals who have a list more or less in common. A cost-of-living index, for instance, is generally intended to represent the list of prices relevant for an ordinary working-class family.)

Changes in expenditure are normally accompanied by changes in relative prices and in the composition of sales, so that we can never expect to be free from the gap between the bracket of index numbers, or from differences in changes in purchasing power for different classes of consumers.

When a change in total expenditure takes place rapidly over a short period, the output of some commodities responds less readily than of others, and consequently their prices alter more. In particular, the rate of output of manufactures can be changed (when it is profitable to do so) more rapidly than of agricultural commodities, so that there is normally a rise and fall of agricultural relatively to manufactured-good prices over the course of a boom and slump in trade. Since food occupies a larger proportion of the budgets of poorer than of richer families such a change in relative prices is a change in the distribution of real income between classes.

Over the long run, a change in productivity due to capital accumulation and technical progress affects different commodities differently. In particular, a gradual rise in output per man-hour normally causes a gradual fall in prices relatively to money-wage rates, and so makes goods progressively cheaper relatively to services. The adaptation of the pattern of purchases to the pattern of prices, particularly for middle-class families, then gradually alters the whole complex of consumption habits (more electric gadgets and less employment of domestic servants ; more pairs of shoes, and less soleing and heeling by cobblers) and this is liable to make the gap between the index-number brackets extremely wide.

All these ambiguities arise even when there is no difference in the who's whos of goods except in quantities and prices. In reality qualities of all kinds, including the very important quality of durability (which gets overlooked when purchases are equated with consumption), vary with the rate of output and with the passage of time. Moreover, totally new kinds of goods appear in the lists and old ones vanish   This introduces a difference in purchasing power that cannot be expressed in numbers. (Consider the difference in the command over goods and services given by a sum of money, say, in London, in Paris and in the Outer Hebrides ; over the long run qualitative differences quite as great emerge in a single economy.)

The pattern of consumption reacts upon the character of the consumers. The mistress of servants is a different kind of human being from a gadget-minded working housewife, and a car-driver is a different human being from a horse-rider. A comparison between two different patterns of consumption, in which different groups of consumers have grown up, cannot be made in numerical terms. If a consumer from either group is dropped into the life of the other, he feels himself (according to temperament) in a desert of privation or in a paradise of unaccustomed delights.

Economics is the scientific study of wealth, and yet we cannot measure wealth. This seems a sad state of affairs. But it is not altogether desperate. When large changes are taking place in purchases over relatively short periods, for groups of consumers who are not rapidly changing their tastes and habits, the indications given by a bracket of index numbers make it possible to describe what is happening at least in a broad way. And even over the long run such indications are not entirely useless. Humans of all ages and climes have needs in common, for food, shelter and amusement ; the economist's method of description can still be used (provided it is applied with a proper sense of its limitations) to contribute something valid and important to a general account of the changes in society.

CHAPTER 3

THE MEANING OF MONEY

ONE of the purposes of economic theory is to look through the veil of money [1] to the realities behind it. The plain man rarely looks through the veil. To him money means wealth. When he says: Money is not everything, he means (in the economist's language): A command over goods and services is not the same thing as happiness. He does, however, take a glance through the veil when he says: Money is not what it was. Then he means that the purchasing power of a unit of money over goods and services has fallen in the more or less recent past.

MONEY AND PURCHASING POWER

The reason why the plain man concentrates upon money is that he can hope (according to his personal circumstances) by working, saving, speculating, employing labour, demanding a rise in pay, to increase his command over money, whereas the purchasing power over goods and services that a unit of money represents is something arising out of the total operation of the economy, which he can do nothing about.

Moreover, it is a necessary condition for the operation of a capitalist economy (or, indeed, of any economy much more complicated than that of the robins) that its members should think in terms of money rather than purchasing power. For, if they are highly purchasing-power conscious, then, when they expect a rise in money prices they all become speculators, buying goods not for use but for a rise in value, and this itself causes prices to rise, so that, unless there are powerful checks

[1] Cf. A. C. Pigou, *The Veil of Money*.

25

in operation, the monetary system explodes itself in hyper-inflation. Or when they expect a fall in prices, each tries to sell at second hand anything he can, and refrains from buying except for inescapable immediate needs, so that the productive process seizes up. It is necessary, to keep the system running, that the plain man should act as though he thought that, as he quaintly puts it : A shilling is a shilling, even when he is vaguely aware that it is not.

The economist, however, has to be purchasing-power conscious, for his concern is with the total of wealth and its distribution. In order to try to disentangle the relations between money and wealth, it is tempting to imagine a non-monetary world, where all transactions are conducted in real terms. But it is misleading to apply conclusions drawn from such an imaginary case to a capitalist economy. We can imagine an artisan economy in which trade takes place in the form of direct barter, or in which simple triangular transactions are made in kind. Every exchangeable commodity represents both itself and a certain amount of purchasing power over other commodities ; the basket-maker may sell his wares to the blacksmith for nails which he does not propose to use but to exchange later on for something else. But the degree of specialisation and trade that would be possible in these conditions would be very limited, and in fact we know that money, in the sense of a generally acceptable medium for making payments, emerges very early in the development towards complexity in human economies. In particular, a wage economy requires money. An employer who is starting in business has to pay his workers before he has anything to sell, so that he must have a stock of purchasing power (finance) in some form or other before he begins (where workers wait to be paid a share of proceeds, they are co-operators, not employees ; this entails quite different rules of the game from those which prevail in a capitalist economy). And for a business which is already a going concern, it would be most inefficient to pay the workers with their own product (unless it happens to be one which is a convenient medium of exchange), for if workers have to engage in barter trade to exchange their product for packets of all the various things they want to consume, they have little time or energy to work.[1] (Moreover, they would be taking on themselves the risks of the business, which again entails a different set of rules of the game.) Thus a society which had not succeeded in inventing money could not develop a capitalist economy.

The robin economy is non-monetary, because there is no specialisation and exchange between families (the robin does not trade caterpillars for worms, and he acquires his territory by conquest or occupation, not by purchase), while within the family duties and rights are laid down by strict rules of the game (working through inborn instincts) which do not involve any payments. The hen needs no finance to build the nest because she feeds herself at the same time. And the food which the cock later fetches for her is not a payment to induce her to sit, but a means to keep her alive when the rules prevent her from leaving the eggs. A large section of human economic life is subject to similar intra-family rules which do not involve money. But for the larger human economic organisations money, in some form or other, is a *sine qua non*. Thus money, regarded as an institution, is built into the system which we are peering through the veil of money values to see.

Though it is impossible to imagine a non-monetary capitalist economy without falling into contradictions, it is an instructive exercise to imagine an economy in which the various functions of money are carried by different vehicles. Suppose that debts are settled and payments made with nails, that values are expressed in ounces of silver and the wage contract is made in bushels of wheat. Then an employer pays a worker by handing to him a quantity of nails that has the same value in terms of silver as the agreed quantity of wheat. The profitability of a business is largely governed by the wheat price of its products, for this determines how much of his own product the employer must give for a man-hour of labour, and so (given output per man-hour) governs the quasi-rent per man employed. The price of nails affects his cost of production in much the same way as the cost of a raw material, for he has to have a supply of nails (replaced by purchases

[1] Something like this was seen in Western Germany between the end of the war and the currency reform.

each week) just as he has to have a supply of materials (replaced over the course of the cycle of production) to keep the business running. In this system there are three money-price levels : the prices of all commodities expressed in silver, in nails and in wheat. Of these the most important is the price level in terms of wheat, for this (given the wheat-wage rate) both expresses the share of wages and quasi-rents in total proceeds and governs the real wage of the workers, in the sense of what their nail-pay packets enable them to buy. Thus it is wheat (in which the wage contract is made) that is money *par excellence*, though nails provide the medium of exchange and silver the unit of account.

In an economy where there is a particular medium of exchange that has become standardised (because it is generally acceptable, like gold, or because it has been constituted legal tender, like Bank of England notes) it is expressed as a quantity of the unit of account (say, the pound sterling, which, in itself, is just a word) and the wage contract is made in terms of it. All the characteristics of money are then fused into one.

The price level in terms of money has considerable importance, for many contracts besides the wage bargain are made in terms of money, and changes in the purchasing power of money bring about opposite changes in the real benefit and the real cost of the payments concerned so long as the contract holds. But in the long run all contracts are revised, so that a change in the real value of money becomes just a change in words. Over the long run the important price level is the price level in terms of labour time, for this, as we have seen, expresses the distribution of the total product of the economy between work and property.

MONEY AND PROPERTY

So far we have been considering money in relation to the process of production and distribution going on through time. We must also consider it in connection with the stock of property in existence at a moment of time.

A durable object may be desirable partly for its direct usefulness, partly for its power to assist production, partly

for the rent it can command if hired out, and partly because
it provides its owner with a store of purchasing power which
he can release when he likes, by selling the object and using
the purchase price to buy goods and services, to make a new
loan, or buy a second-hand debt, a piece of land or a share
in a business. Different kinds of property offer these various
attractions in different degrees. An ordinary arm-chair has
little to offer except direct use, for its second-hand price is
small (in normal times) and it detracts from rather than increases productive activity. A period piece, however, may be
desirable as a store of value or as a speculation as well as for
use. Specialised productive machinery has no direct use to
its owner, and, in itself, it is (like the arm-chair) not a store
of value ; but as part of a going concern it may be saleable
(through an issue of shares) or may provide security for a
loan. Land and buildings may be used by their owner or
rented out. In either case they represent at the same time a
store of value. Property in placements is of no use, and makes
no contribution to production (though shares may be desired
partly for the rights of control that they offer in a business).
It is desired for the interest that the debtor is obliged to pay
(in the case of shares, the dividends that it is hoped the directors
of the company will vouchsafe to distribute) and as a store
of value.

For any kind of property the store of value aspect is very
much affected by expectations about its future price. If it is
expected to lose value over its lifetime (like the ordinary
arm-chair) it obviously has little attraction as a store of value.
If it is generally and confidently expected to rise in value in
the future, its price to-day is adjusted accordingly, so that there
is no more to be expected from holding it than can be got by
holding interest-yielding debts. If its future value is thought
to be liable to erratic movements, or if it is very uncertain
how its future value will behave, it is attractive to those of a
speculative temperament, to those who want to make up a
mixed bag of risks of various kinds in their holding of wealth,
or to someone who happens to take a more favourable view
of its future value than that reflected in its present price. In
general, however, it is less eligible as a store of value than

something which is believed to be predictable, for though uncertainty cuts both ways (it may go up or may go down) for most property owners the fear of loss outweighs the hope of gain. And even if it is confidently expected to have ups as well as downs, an owner fears that it may be going through one of its bad patches just at the moment when he has an urgent need to sell it to get some purchasing power for consumption or investment, or just when he sees an attractive opportunity for placement in some other kind of property, Thus assets of this type, in order to get themselves owned, must offer good attractions in the form of the yield which they promise, to make up for their low scores in the store-of-value competition.

There is another characteristic which different kinds of property have in varying degrees, connected with their quality as a store of value, but not identical with it ; that is, marketability. Land may score very well in the predictable-future-value competition, but a piece of land is an individual unstandardised thing, and the chance of making a good sale at any particular moment depends very much on someone turning up who wants just this piece ; moreover, there is cost and trouble involved in carrying out the transaction. By contrast, a debt which is gilt-edged (in the sense that the debtor is well known and not considered to be liable to default); in which there is a wide market, so that buyers are coming forward all the time ; and for which there are well-established, convenient and not too costly facilities for dealing (as in a well-conducted financial centre) gains very high marks in the marketability competition. Consequently such assets can get themselves owned when offering a lower yield than less marketable types which offer equal security of future value.

The two qualities — certainty of future value and easy marketability — blend together in the quality of *liquidity*.

Now, any durable object which represents a store of value is a potential medium of exchange, but those with the greatest liquidity are most useful for this purpose. An owner of wealth (including one who is going to own it only from this Friday till next Thursday) requires a balance that he can draw upon to make payments and replenish from receipts, and a seller (whether of goods and services or pieces of property) requires to be paid with something that he can readily use for purchases or placements. A debt of a well-known and safe debtor, carrying a guarantee of repayment of its face value in terms of the unit of account in the near future, is highly liquid; still better, a debt repayable on demand. Its future value in terms of money (not, of course, of purchasing power over goods and services) is as nearly perfectly certain as anything can be in our uncertain life, and its marketability is so perfect that to call it marketability becomes forced — acceptability is a better term. It is then highly eligible for service as a medium of exchange. Finally, if it takes the form of a bank-note expressed in terms of the unit of account and endowed with the status of legal tender (which makes it completely acceptable, as long as there is confidence in the whole set up) then it is completely liquid. It *is* money, and the mysterious words 'Promise to pay the bearer on demand the sum of one pound' written upon it are only an historical allusion to the time when there was something still more liquid in terms of which the debtor promised to redeem it.

Bank-notes score so well in the liquidity competition that they have no need to offer interest. A loan repayable on demand to a well-respected bank (a current account) provides such convenience (safety from robbers, power to make payments of any denomination with a small piece of paper) that owners of wealth are even prepared to pay the borrower (bank charges). A loan repayable at short notice (a deposit account) offers interest to overcome a small defect in liquidity. Other kinds of debts — bills, bonds, etc. — are driven out of the sphere of operating as a medium of exchange by the competition of these more perfectly liquid kinds of property, and, to get themselves owned, have to yield interest.

GOLD

Commodities used as a medium of exchange, such as gold, silver and cowrie shells, have played a great part in the development of money. Originally they were commodities like any others, required for use (though for beauty and pride rather than any material purpose), but properties making them peculiarly serviceable as a medium of exchange — durability, standardisation, divisibility (and, perhaps, a mystic aura clinging round them since primitive times) — led to their becoming established as money, and the stock in existence then became mainly absorbed in liquid balances, so that their capacity as commodities became quite secondary.

Gold, being of all commodities the most easily marketable, is very attractive to produce, but, the supplies provided by geology being limited, the stock above ground did not grow nearly as fast as the demand for liquid balances, and banks came into existence to supplement the supply. The transition from gold to bank-notes and deposits as the leading form of money was bridged by the banks holding reserves of gold and offering to redeem their debts in gold on demand. This established confidence in their obligations, and gave them liquidity. Nowadays the boot is on the other leg, and the value of gold is maintained largely by the fact that certain Central Banks are prepared to buy it in exchange for their national currencies.

The provision of a convenient and reliable medium of exchange is so important for the successful working of a complicated economy that national monetary authorities, such as Central Banks, have been set up in all important capitalist countries, and elaborate legal and customary requirements have been established to secure the credit of profit-seeking banks and to regulate the supply of national currency. The international monetary system, however, is still in a primitive state of development.

CHAPTER 4

CAPITAL AND INCOME

THE distinction between capital and income is rooted in moral ideas. Morality is neither rational nor irrational; it operates, so to say, in a different dimension. It is irrational to burn incense to idols in order to improve the crops, for observation shows that free-thinkers, with their scientific methods, get better crops. But it is not irrational to burn incense because it is right and seemly so to do. It is irrational to allow one's conduct to be influenced by the thought of the pleasure that one will derive from being famous a hundred years hence, but it is not irrational to feel a sense of obligation to the future inhabitants of the earth. 'We must preserve our national heritage for the sake of future generations' and 'What should we do for posterity? They have never done anything for us' are expressions of two opposite moral ideas, and neither one is more rational than the other.

But we can look at an economy from the outside, as a going concern, and observe that its viability depends upon the moral ideas of its inhabitants, and the extent to which they live up to them. (Even with the robins, instinct, or whatever it is, that makes them recognise each other's territorial rights, works like a code of morality ensuring the viability of the species.)

MORALITY AND VIABILITY

The morality of a peasant, who gathers his crops according to the rhythm of the seasons, is to put back into the soil what he takes out of it, and to set aside seed from each harvest, so as to preserve productive capacity for the future, not only for his lifetime, or his children's lifetime, but for the future as such. It is this morality which produces the conception of

33

capital and income. Income consists in the kindly fruits of
the earth, and capital in the fertility of the soil. Animal and
human economies can flourish for a time by mining the soil,
creating deserts, or by preying upon other economies, but to
be viable over a long run, in peaceful conditions, an economy
must be impregnated with the peasant's morality; this is
pre-eminently true of an industrial economy whose productive
capacity consists largely in a stock of long-lived equipment
which must be maintained by repairs and renewals, and which
can function only in an environment in which the rules of the
game in respect to property, trade and the financial system are
accepted and maintained in working order.[1]

An individual peasant family is both a consuming and a
producing entity. A nation can be regarded as a consuming
entity only in a very vague sense, but (though interdependent
in many ways with the whole world economy) it can be regarded as a producing entity. Its labour power consists in the
brain, muscle and diligence of its citizens ; its capital in natural
resources, training and education, and physical goods ; its
organisation is partly directed consciously by accepted authorities and partly emerges from the operation of the rules of the
game.

For a nation, the distinction between capital and income
is real but far from precise and the peasant's morality applies
to it very imperfectly. Its production consists partly in mining
in the literal sense. It may also consist partly in mining in
the metaphorical sense of exploiting natural or inherited resources without maintaining their productive power for the
future ; partly in preying upon other economies (by conquest
or cunning) ; partly in exploiting external markets in a manner
which impairs their future profitability. All this is shocking
to the morality of the nation in a rather vague way, for the
concern of the nation with its heritage is vaguely felt. In the
main the preservation of its productive resources depends upon
the concern which individuals and groups within it feel in
maintaining the particular parts of the total with which they
are concerned.

[1] Cf. Keynes, *The Economic Consequences of the Peace*, p. 17.

RENTIER'S CAPITAL

Some types of individual property have no connection at all with the productive capacity of the economy in which they exist. This is true, in particular, of placements in National Debt. The finance was borrowed long ago and expended in blowing things to bits. The debt corresponds to no element in productive capacity and is secured merely on the credit of the government—that is, on the belief that the government will arrange for payment of the agreed interest and undertake redemption on the agreed terms out of tax receipts or new borrowing. The nominal interest (five per cent War Loan, two and a half per cent Consols, etc.) reflects the price of finance at various times in the past when governments borrowed. The effective rate of interest, or yield, which a rentier could get by making a placement now, depends upon the price at which the bonds stand in the general market for placements. Bonds or shares of industrial concerns represent finance that (in the typical case) was expended in creating real capital goods, but their price in the market is subject to many influences quite unconnected with productive capacity. Differences in yield between one and another depend partly upon their liquidity, and the whole level of yields (the level of interest rates) depends upon the demand for liquid placements in relation to the supply made available by the banking system. (These matters will be discussed later.)[1] Thus the relation between the yield and the capital value of placements is very loosely connected with the relation between output and productive capacity for the economy. But for the individual rentier the analogy between the yield of placements and the yield of the soil is quite close.

The typical rentier has been brought up in conceptions which echo the morality of the peasant. He feels that he has a right to spend his income, but feels guilty if he draws purchasing power from his stock of capital. When he spends less than his income he gives himself good marks for saving and adding to his stock. His capital, however, is not identifiable except as a quantity of value. The value of money may

[1] See Book IV.

be changing, or may be expected to change in the future ; but in the present context we will assume that the general price level is sufficiently stable to make it reasonable for the rentier to think in terms of money value only. Now, a year rarely goes by without the value (in the sense of purchasing power in terms of money) of particular placements altering. How, then, is the rentier to say what has been his income over a year ? He may have kept his placements unchanged, so that identical pieces of paper have lain in his safe all the year. He can then regard them as his capital, and the payments he has received as his income. Or, when he changes the identity of his placements, he may keep a separate capital account, and pay interest and dividends into an income account. But this is merely a convention that he chooses to observe. For an individual there is no logical distinction between interest and capital appreciation. For instance, when the market composed of placement holders as a whole is expecting a fall in the general level of interest rates over the next year or two, long-dated bonds (which promise certain sums per annum for many years ahead) are more valuable than short-dated (for when the debt is paid off the money can be re-placed only at a lower yield) and their relative prices are adjusted (by the interplay of supply and demand in the market) in such a way that interest on the short bonds is more or less equal to the interest *plus* expected appreciation on the long bonds.[1] Or borrowers may have issued bonds at a discount (that is, with an undertaking to repay at some future date larger sums of money than are initially received) in order to have to pay less annual interest. There is no logic in regarding whatever happens to be called interest as income. The logical procedure for the individual rentier is to make a periodic valuation and deduct from the interest received over a period the depreciation, or add the appreciation, of the selling value of his pieces of paper in order to say what his income for the period has been, and to make estimates of what such valuations will show, in order to say what income he expects in the future. If he has been successful in the guessing game (on the advice of his broker or backing his own fancy) and made placements

[1] Keynes, *General Theory*, p. 168.

which have risen in price so that his capital has appreciated, he has to debate with his conscience whether he has a right to realise the appreciation and spend it, and his decision turns very much upon whether he may expect similar gains in the future, so that they are properly to be regarded as a continuing income.

If the value of his holdings has risen, not because of his personal skill as a placer, but because of a general fall in the level of interest rates which is expected to be permanent, he is faced with a different problem. For the time being his receipts are unchanged and the value of his placements has risen, but, unless all his holdings are in very long-dated bonds, or in shares in whose future capacity to pay dividends the market has great confidence, he will later have to re-place money at a lower return, so that his prospect of future income has fallen. How should this react upon his present rate of spending ? He may decide to regard his income now as the permanent yield over an indefinite future (at the new level of interest rates) of the present value of his placements. It would certainly not be legitimate to include a rise in capital value of placements in the income of a year during which interest rates happen to have fallen. Nor need he feel obliged to restore the value of his holdings (by a heroic effort of saving) during a year in which the interest rates happen to have risen. A change in the level of interest rates means a change in the terms on which income can be obtained by owning wealth (similar to the change in the ease or difficulty of obtaining income from work which occurs when the level of wages alters) and the rentier may decide to accept the change in income, and adjust his views of what it is legitimate to spend accordingly. But since changes in the general level of interest rates are mixed up with changes in the relative yields of different types of placements it is by no means a simple matter for any individual rentier to decide what he should properly consider his income to be.

The conventions which the conscientious rentier observes may be important for the economy as well as for himself. If he has in any case a margin of saving, and keeps his expenditure at a steady level, it does not make any practical difference what he chooses to call his income and his rate of saving. But if his expenditure is related to what he considers his income to be, then his demand for goods and services (and consequently sales by other members of the economy) are influenced by the conventions that he observes (as well as by his strength of mind in living up to whatever conventional rule he has adopted). Thus, while the definition of rentier income is a subject for logic chopping, the views that rentiers act upon are an operative element in an economy.

The conventions observed by tax collectors as to what is and what is not income are also a matter of practical importance for individuals and for the economy as a whole.[1]

RECEIPTS AND COSTS

The application of the peasant's conception of income to the affairs of an entrepreneur is even more difficult than its application to those of a rentier. The income of a firm is its profit, that is the excess of receipts over costs, but neither receipts nor costs are at all simple ideas.

First, the receipts attributable to a year's sales are not quite definite. Credit terms vary, so that payments do not bear a regular relation to sales (and bad debts may be encountered). Second, part of proceeds accrues to the firm in kind. This happens when equipment is made in the firm's own shops, and when there is an accretion of stocks of partially processed goods. The value of these to the firm lies in the future (there is all the difference in the world between an increment of work-in-progress due to an expectation of increased sales in the near future, and an increment due to silting up when sales have recently fallen off) and the equivalent in terms of receipts is a matter of judgment.

There are still greater difficulties in giving precision to the notion of costs. Even a year's wages bill is not quite a definite quantity. Such payments as contributions to the firm's pension fund or a subsidy to the canteen may be regarded either as a supplementary wage cost or as a kind of bonus to the workers out of profits. Salaries to some extent overlap with profits.[2]

[1] Cf. N. Kaldor, *An Expenditure Tax*, p. 67.   [2] See above, p. 11.

Materials have to be bought some time before they are sold, and since their prices are variable there is an element of profit or loss which can be treated as greater or less according to the date at which valuations are made.

The amount of payments for rent and the part of profit that has to be paid as interest are a matter of historical accident, depending upon how far the firm has been financed by borrowing and whether it happens to own its own sites.

These are relatively minor points, however. The main difficulty is connected with long-lived plant. Plant loses value over the course of its life in three distinct ways: by wear and tear due to using it, which would be saved if it were laid up; by the physical ageing due to the mere passage of time, exposure to risks from fire and so forth; and by loss of profitability of the markets which its output supplies, due to changes in running costs or in demand on the part of customers or to the invasion of the market by rival sellers. The cost of the plant is shared by the whole output over its lifetime; how much should be attributed to the output of any one period? The amount of amortisation appropriate to allot to the output of any one year largely depends upon the expected future earning life of the plant. The shorter the future life the larger this year's share in costs and consequently the smaller the year's profit. (The calculation is further complicated by the interest that can be earned by using an amortisation fund to hold placements, or the profit that can be earned by using it to finance investment.) Thus both receipts and costs are not definite sums of money, but contain many elements of notional valuation.

THE ENTREPRENEUR'S CAPITAL

The morality of the entrepreneur echoes that of the peasant in a more extreme form. For the entrepreneur the purpose of earning profits is not to indulge in consumption but to preserve and expand his business. Thus morality demands that in case of doubt he should adopt conventions that make costs appear as high as possible and profits as low as possible (in this the entrepreneur is continually at loggerheads with the tax-collector). It is true that entrepreneurs, incarnate as family-business men, managing directors and inside shareholders, do in general enjoy a much more expensive level of consumption than, say, the workers whom they employ, but this is because no human being fully lives up to his own moral code (and they excuse themselves by pointing out that it is necessary to appear prosperous for the sake of the firm's credit). The morality of the entrepreneur demands (in the case of a family business) that he should put business before family, and (in the case of a managerial concern) that he should distribute only so much of profit as will keep the shareholders in a good humour and prevent them from exercising their legal right to wind up the business and gouge the capital out of it or sell it to some other entrepreneur who will treat them better, and as will keep the shares at a good price in the placement market, so as to facilitate the raising of new finance when further expansions of the business can be made. As much profit as possible should be invested in increasing productive capacity, and to be on the safe side, the amount of quasi-rent regarded as absorbed by costs should be set as high as is at all plausible.

The habit of ploughing profits into the firm is partly due to the pressure of competition, for any business which is not constantly struggling to expand is liable to shrink and collapse. But it is mainly to be accounted for by the adherence of entrepreneurs to an exacting code. Some, it is true, are content to manage a small business and positively prefer a comfortable and untroubled life, but they are regarded as eccentrics, and certainly, if all had been like them, the capitalist system would not have grown and flourished as it has.

Profits are made by sales, not by creating wealth, but, as we have already observed, there must be a solid core of correspondence between purchases and the satisfaction of consumers' needs. Thus the paradoxical-seeming pursuit of profit for its own sake has led to the development of an economic system which has proved not only viable but remarkably productive of wealth.[1]

---

[1] Cf. Keynes, *Economic Consequences, loc. cit.*

CHAPTER 5

CONSUMPTION AND INVESTMENT

FOR the goods which are being sold to-day, costs of production were incurred some time in the past (bread was baked last night; the field where the wheat was sown was ploughed last autumn). Sales are out of stock, and current production is replenishing stocks with a view to future sales. Thus from the point of view of a very short period all production is investment, and sales disinvestment. But when a regular cycle of production is being carried out and everything is going according to expectations, the greater part of current cost of production is being provided for out of current sales, and for this part it is a legitimate simplification to speak of the sales value of production week by week as though it was the same thing as actual sales week by week. Normally some of the production, in any week, is not merely replacing last week's sales, but is directed to increasing the rate of output in the future. When entrepreneurs are in course of expanding their activities they are expending finance over and above the costs of current output, and investing in capital goods, including additions to work-in-progress. (When the rate of output is running down they are expending less than current sales proceeds, and disinvesting.)

GROSS AND NET INVESTMENT

How should we regard outlays upon replacements of worn-out equipments? If no new investment was being made, or technical changes taking place, and if output of every kind had long been at a steady rate, and was planned to remain at that rate over a long future, all production would consist in a continual repetition of an identical cycle, so that whenever we took a snapshot of the economy it would look exactly the same. This situation entails that the age composition of all stocks of long-lived goods is balanced, so that it remains constant through time and at any moment new capital goods are being completed and beginning to work at just the same pace as old goods of each kind are being scrapped. Every worker is contributing to producing the flow of final output and to keeping the stock of capital goods intact, and there is no point in separating the consumption-good wages bill from the capital-good wages bill for the system as a whole.

It is not necessary to imagine that each firm operates an outfit of equipment of balanced age composition. Consider a firm which owns a single plant that is an integrated whole, with a certain definite service life. At a particular date it is brand new and its whole life lies in the future. Over its life the firm accumulates an amortisation fund out of the quasi-rents that it earns, and at the end of its life replaces it by a replica of its original self. The system as a whole being in balance, the rate of reinvestment of accumulated amortisation funds just absorbs the current rate of accumulation of funds.

In reality such a balance is never to be found. New investment is normally going on and at the same time the composition of output and techniques of production are changing. A worn-out plant is rarely replaced by an exact replica of its original self, and when the physical specification of the replacement, or its expected future life, is different, or the market conditions in which it will operate are different, there is no precise and unambiguous criterion by which to judge whether it is exactly equivalent to what it replaces. We cannot then draw a clear line between replacements and new investment, though firms must adopt accounting conventions to make the distinction between amortisation and profit.

Moreover, amortisation quotas, though they reflect the element in cost of production due to wearing out plant and to its loss of earning power through the mere passage of time, are not tied to the flow of current production in the same way as current costs. If the output being sold this week is not being replaced by work-in-progress, or if running repairs of plant are not being carried out, production will shortly come to a stop. But if amortisation quotas are deficient, nothing happens except that the firms in question are making less profit than they reckon, or, at worst, experiencing a loss of capital which will become obvious only when the plant is worn out ; and if they are excessive, nothing happens except that the firms are saving and acquiring capital at a greater rate than they permit themselves to believe. (The accounting practices of firms may, however, be important if they influence policy in regard to the distribution of dividends, which may affect expenditure on consumption by rentiers. This is particularly important when prices are changing, so that if inventories — stocks and work-in-progress — are valued at historic cost there is an illusory profit or loss due to a departure of reproduction cost from book values.)

Net investment and profit are, therefore, elusive concepts, and for many purposes it is best to lump amortisation allowances in with retained profits and to include replacements of long-lived plant in *gross investment*. An important class of border-line cases then exists when periodical replacements of shorter-lived elements, such as particular machines, are necessary in order to keep a whole plant in going order. Any reasonable line can be drawn through these cases. If a particular replacement is counted as part of current cost, then quasi-rent is by so much the less, and, if it is counted as part of gross investment, then quasi-rent and retained profit are both so much the greater.

INVESTMENT AND SAVING

Having drawn the line in any reasonable way, we may allocate the total wages bill between current production and gross investment. If we assume, in the first instance, that workers spend the whole of their wages as they receive them from week to week, then the wages bill for commodities (consumption goods) being currently produced is exactly covered by sales to the workers engaged on producing them. Workers engaged on investment and rentiers (including the households of entrepreneurs) are also buying commodities. This makes it possible for the selling value of commodities to exceed their wages costs. Looking at the same thing in another way, if the sales value of commodities were no greater than their wages cost, no one except the workers engaged in producing them could consume anything at all. The gap between sales value and wages costs prevents these workers from buying the whole of their own output and obliges them to share it with other consumers.

The excess of the sales value of commodities over their wages cost is equal to the wages bill for gross investment *plus* expenditure on consumption out of profits. This excess is the quasi-rent earned by production of commodities. The distribution of the quasi-rent between entrepreneurs is complicated by the fact that they buy materials, power and equipment from each other — one firm's costs are partly other firms' quasi-rents — but for the system as a whole this comes out in the wash and aggregate sales value can be divided into aggregate wage bill and aggregate quasi-rent.

For some purposes it is necessary to treat professional people as a separate class, but in the present context we may fit them into our broad scheme of categories of income by regarding salaried employees of all kinds as workers and independent experts as entrepreneurs selling an output of their own services.[1]

In so far as workers are spending less than their wages, their savings partly offset the wages bill for investment, and the gap between sales value and wages bill for commodities is *pro tanto* reduced.

Taking any arbitrary period of time, say a year, the increment of capital goods made during the year accrues in kind to the firms who are going to use them.[2] Their value lies in the future quasi-rents that they are expected to earn, and they are entered in the books of the firms either at the price which was paid for them, if they have been bought from other firms, or at a notional value covering their actual cost of production *plus* a notional margin.

For the economy as a whole, there has been an addition to wealth equal to the outlay on gross investment *minus* the value

[1] Cf. above, p. 11.
[2] Unfinished capital goods in the pipe-line of production of a firm producing equipment for sale to other firms count as part of its working capital.

of capital goods used up during the year. The additional wealth has accrued partly to outside savers, such as rentiers, and partly to the firms as an addition to their own capital. Saving means an excess of receipts by the public (as wages, interest, rent and dividends) from entrepreneurs over payments to entrepreneurs (for the purchase of commodities) and therefore an increase of the aggregate debt of entrepreneurs to the public. The excess of the value of gross investment over the increment of debt is the retained profit and amortisation allowances of the firms. From the point of view of the firms' balance-sheets there has been an addition to their liabilities to banks or rentiers from whom they have borrowed, or to their own shareholders, and an addition to their assets equal to the notional value of new capital goods *minus* the loss of value of old capital goods.[1]

[1] The following numerical illustration shows the consolidated accounts for all firms for, say, a year. Workers are assumed to spend the whole of wages, and there is no rent for land or buildings.

	Consumption Sector	Investment Sector	Total
Value of output	80	20	100
Wages bill	40	10	50
Quasi-rent	40	10	50
Interest and dividends	28	7	35
Rentier expenditure	24	6	30
Rentier saving	4	1	5
Retained Profit (including amortisation)	12	3	15

The sales value of consumption goods (80) is made up of expenditure by workers (50) *plus* expenditure by rentiers (30). Quasi-rent from consumption goods (40) is made up of expenditure by workers in the investment sector (10) *plus* expenditure by rentiers (30). The gross investment of the year (20) is matched by rentier saving (5) *plus* undistributed profit, including amortisation (15). The entrepreneurs' debt to the rentiers has increased by the amount of the latter's saving (5). The value of gross investment contains a notional element since part of it consists of capital goods produced by firms for their own use. The division of gross investment between replacements and net investment is partly a matter of convention or estimation. The division of retained profits between amortisation and addition to value of assets is also a matter of convention. The notional elements in the values are concentrated in the quasi-rent in the investment sector and retained profits. All the other values correspond to actual transactions between rentiers, entrepreneurs and workers, each taken as a whole.

CATEGORIES OF INVESTMENT

There are some elements in investment which do not fit into this simple scheme and must be discussed separately.

Financial Business. Finance may be invested in purely financial business — say the reserve of a bank. This kind of investment leads to no expenditure on wages and no increment of capital goods. The buildings of a bank and its equipment with ledgers, pens and blotting-paper is an investment in concrete capital goods and for some purposes must be counted in with industrial investment, but the commitment of finance to purely financial operations is excluded from investment in the sense in which we shall be using this term.

Cost of Sites. A large scheme of investment in new capital equipment, such as a new factory or railway line, may require some purchases of pre-existing means of production, in particular, sites. Outlay of this kind uses up finance from the point of view of the entrepreneur who makes it, but it does not generate income. The individual who sells the site is simply altering his placements. (A particular individual may be doing so in order to blue the proceeds on purchases for consumption, or to finance investment, but, if so, the income which is generated by his expenditure must be attributed to his outlay, not to that of the entrepreneur who bought the site from him.) Thus expenditure of finance of this kind does not enter into current quasi-rents, and is excluded from investment in our sense, though in some contexts the absorption of finance in transactions of this kind must be borne in mind (for instance, in the case of additions to the National Debt due to compensating landlords for the sites of aerodromes).

Cost of Borrowing. Part of the cost of a scheme of investment consists in the expenses connected with raising finance, such as commissions to underwriters who guarantee the flotation of an issue of securities. From the point of view of the firm concerned this is a capital cost, and involves expenditure of finance, while from the point of view of the recipient it is part of current gross receipts, covering both the wages for his employees and his professional earnings. From the point of view of the firm's balance-sheet, the notional value of the new capital goods to be acquired by expending the finance must cover these charges as well as the costs of production or purchase price of the physical capital goods. Thus it is best to regard these charges as part of the outlay on investment. Their importance lies in the fact that (other things equal) a firm financing investment from its own reserves (say by selling placements that it has been holding or drawing on its bank balance) will get somewhat more physical goods from a given outlay than a firm which has borrowed or issued shares to raise the finance.

Houses. An individual who buys a house for his own family is acting partly as a purchaser of consumption goods, partly as a rentier making a placement and partly as an entrepreneur investing finance in a capital good. When he buys an existing house the rentier aspect is dominant and when he has a house built, the entrepreneur aspect. Hire-purchase of durable consumption goods is similar, and so is the provision by businesses of amenities for their employees, such as tennis courts for the workers or marble halls for the directors. These all require an investment of finance which is not intended to yield quasi-rents, and none of them fit neatly into our categories ; for the categories have been developed to deal with transactions for the market. The measuring rod of money can be applied to consumption [1] only by the artificial device of attaching a money value to a stream of satisfaction. It is easy enough to say that a future subjective income of satisfaction expected from living in the house, using a washing-machine instead of a tub or enjoying board meetings in sumptuous surroundings must be at least equivalent to the interest on the finance expended. (The tennis court is a slightly different case, for the satisfaction of the workers may be expected to yield a money return to the firm.) But this does not really advance the argument. In a kind of economy where such transactions were the rule and investment for a money return the exception, different categories would be appropriate and different habits of thought would have been developed. Instead of trying to squeeze square facts into round categories

[1] Cf. above, p. 17.

it is better to treat them frankly as exceptions and to bring them into analysis in their own right in cases where they are likely to be important.

THE INFLATION BARRIER

A higher proportion of investment-wages to consumption-wages entails a higher ratio of quasi-rent to wages bill in the sales of commodities, and a higher share of quasi-rent is likely to give rise to a higher level of consumption expenditure out of profits, which, in turn, entails a higher share of quasi-rent. Thus each entrepreneur is better off the more investment his colleagues are carrying out. The more the entrepreneurs and rentiers (taken as a whole) spend on investment and consumption, the more they get as quasi-rent.[1]

But there is a limit to the possible maximum proportion of quasi-rent to wages, which is set by what we may call the *inflation barrier*. Higher prices of consumption goods relatively to money-wage rates involve a lower real consumption by workers. There is a limit to the level to which real-wage rates can fall without setting up a pressure to raise money-wage rates. But a rise in money-wage rates increases money expenditure, so that the vicious spiral of money wages chasing prices sets in. There is then a head-on conflict between the desire of entrepreneurs to invest and the refusal of the system to accept the level of real wages which the investment entails ; something must give way. Either the system explodes in a hyper-inflation, or some check operates to curtail investment.

The more conservative firms are in distributing profits and the more thrifty is the public (including entrepreneurs in their capacity as family men), that is, the less they spend upon consumption goods, the further out does the inflation barrier lie, and the higher is the proportion of investment to production of consumption goods that the system is capable of standing.

How is the inflation barrier related to full employment of labour ? Where workers are strongly organised in trade

[1] See M. Kalecki, *Essays in the Theory of Economic Fluctuations*, p. 76 *The Theory of Economic Dynamics*, p. 46.

unions and are highly purchasing-power conscious, an irresistible demand for higher money-wage rates may set in even when there is a considerable margin of unemployment in the system. The fact that it is quite common to make wage contracts in terms of a cost-of-living index (the money-wage rate rising in some agreed manner with the index number of the money value of some conventionally accepted who's who of goods) shows that the notion is prevalent that real wages ought not to fall below a level that has been established in the past.[1] If this view is general, and if the bargaining power of the workers is strong enough to enforce it, an inflation barrier is set up at whatever level of real wages has been experienced recently, and, over time, the barrier moves with the level of real wages experienced, so that it puts a ratchet behind any change in the level of real wages that actually occurs.

At the other extreme, in an economy where labour is unorganised and there is a mass of permanent quasi-unemployment among landless peasants or younger sons of small traders who are living on their families, the inflation barrier is reached when the level of real wages is so low as to impair the efficiency of workers, so that employers themselves offer a rise in money wages to counteract a rise in prices. Peasants can support life (more or less) when living in their villages at a lower level of consumption than is required for the bare physiological minimum of an industrial worker. Thus the inflation barrier may be encountered long before all available labour is in employment.

In the intermediate case which is normal in modern industrial economies, the level of real wages is some way above the physiological minimum, while the bargaining power of workers is not strong enough to check a fall in real-wage rates while there is considerable unemployment, but is very strong in a situation in which nearly all workers are already employed. The inflation barrier then operates only in conditions of full employment.

---

[1] On the other hand, in times of high demand for labour the great national trade unions may exercise a restraining influence and prevent money-wage rates from rising as fast as they would in an unorganised labour market.

Both the conception of full employment and the conception of the inflation barrier, like all economic categories, are not clear cut; each is rather a matter of degree. But, whether it is encountered gradually or with a sudden supersonic bang, there is somewhere an upper limit to the proportion of investment to total output that entrepreneurs can succeed in establishing.

SHORT-PERIOD LIMITS TO INVESTMENT

There are a number of checks upon the rate of investment which may operate, in given conditions, some way inside the inflation barrier.

Finance. A business will not embark upon a scheme of investment unless it is sure of having enough finance to complete it. It is of no use, with six months' wages bill in hand, to start a process of production which will not yield any sales for a year, or to begin building a ship with means to pay for only half the cost. The amount of finance which an entrepreneur can command at any moment is limited by the reserves of his firm (in money and placements), the property, such as sites, that can be mortgaged, and his borrowing power. Borrowing power depends partly upon his reputation (or plausibility) and partly on the ratio of the interest payments that he is already committed to making to the prospective earning power of the firm.[1] Moreover, the amount that anyone can borrow depends partly upon how much finance others are trying to raise at the same time, for the first in the field tap the most willing lenders, and successive appeals (within a short period of time) for bank advances, or successive batches of new securities offered on the placement market, involve the promise of higher interest rates or meet a total lack of response.

The amount of finance available limits the value of investment plans that can be organised, not the rate of investment. It circumscribes, so to speak, a lump of future investment, not the pace at which investment schemes, once organised, can be carried out. Even in the absence of bottle-necks (which will be discussed in a moment), there are, however, technical

[1] See M. Kalecki, *The Theory of Economic Dynamics*, p. 92.

limits to the rate at which a given scheme of investment can be carried through. Whatever our school sums used to say, it is not true in real life that if a hundred men could dig a trench in ten days a thousand men could dig it in one day, or eight thousand in one hour. The rate of investment at any moment may be limited by the extent of investment plans and so, at one remove, by the amount of finance that it has been possible to organise in the recent past.

This limit acts as a check upon the extent to which the rate of investment can rise above what it has been in the past, but it does not set a limit to the level of investment that can be maintained over the long run. Assuming that investments made in the past have (by and large) been successful, so that profit expectations have been realised, and that the ratio of outside saving to acquisitions of own capital by firms, during any period, is no greater than the ratio of rentier claims as a whole to entrepreneurs' property, so that the ratio of profits to firms' obligations to outsiders has not fallen, the borrowing power of entrepreneurs, after one lot of finance has been expended and turned into earning assets, is no less than before the finance was raised. Thus a high rate of investment creates conditions (as far as finance is concerned) for investment to continue high, and a gradual rise in the rate of investment gradually pushes the finance limit outwards. It is a large and rapid *rise* in the rate of investment, not a *high* rate of investment, which the finance limit prevents.

Capacity. In a highly developed industrial economy the physical rate of output of capital equipment is limited by the capacity of certain specialised capital-good industries. (This is not the case in undeveloped countries where investment is carried out by employing large numbers of workers, say on road building or the construction of dams, using only simple tools.) Some of the industries producing capital equipment, such as shipyards, cater for a narrow range of types of product, but others, such as iron and steel, engineering and building, cover the provision of equipment for a wide range of industries. Their capacity, at any moment, is limited partly by the amount of plant and partly by the availability of labour with the special skills required (for instance bricklayers). The

limit set by capacity upon the rate of output of capital goods
may operate through prolonging delivery dates, so that investment plans have to queue up and await completion, or by
high prices of new equipment, which (unless it is accompanied by correspondingly high prospects of future quasi-rent)
causes some investment plans to be cancelled or postponed.

In such a situation, however, the investment industries
themselves are enjoying high quasi-rents, and are likely to be
expanding their capacity by laying down new plant and training a larger labour force. Thus this check, like that set by
finance, limits the possible rise in the rate of investment above
what it has been in the past, but can put a permanent restraint
upon the rate of investment only in so far as there are permanent bottle-necks (such as a limited number of estuaries
convenient for shipbuilding) in the industries concerned.

Money. A higher level of transactions (a high wages bill
in particular) compared to a lower level, entails a larger demand
for liquid balances and (other things equal) a correspondingly
lower demand for illiquid placements. It is therefore associated
with a higher yield of placements and this is likely to mean that
new finance can be obtained only at a correspondingly higher
rate of interest. Thus when the rate of investment actually
being carried out is high, a drag is set upon plans for further
investment by the raised cost of finance.

If the economy has entered into the foothills of the inflation
barrier, and money-wage rates and prices are rising, the requirement for liquid balances is being further increased and
the rate of interest tends to be pushed up; this may be a
sufficient check to prevent the economy from moving nearer
to the barrier.

In the long run the supply of media of exchange adapts
itself to requirements. If one form of money (say Bank of
England notes) is limited in supply, others (say bank deposits)
will be developed. The liquidity bottle-neck, like the capacity
bottle-neck, may limit the extent to which the rate of investment can rise over a short period of time, but does not limit
the level at which the rate of investment can be maintained over
the long run.

For a closed system the inflation barrier, set by the level

to which real wages can be squeezed down, is the only permanent upper limit to the ratio of investment to production for consumption.

The Balance of Payments.   For a particular country there is another element in the situation.   The value of imports of a particular country cannot for long exceed the value of its exports *plus* the net inflow of finance from abroad (from new loans and sales of second-hand placements to foreigners), for an excess of the deficit on the trading account over net borrowing is settled by net payments through internationally acceptable media of exchange, such as gold, and a continual one-way flow would sooner or later exhaust the country's reserves.   (Similarly, an individual whose receipts on income account and from the sale of placements have fallen short, over any period, of his purchases of commodities and placements has reduced his cash balance.)

A high ratio of home investment to home production of consumption goods is likely to entail a high level of imports of consumption goods, and capital goods for the investment schemes may also require to be imported.   Thus countries may often find themselves in a situation where the position of their international accounts puts obstacles in the way of home investment.   (Indeed, apart from countries which are particularly attractive to foreign lenders or whose industries happen to be in a highly favourable competitive position *vis-à-vis* those of the rest of the world, the operative limit to the ratio of home investment to home production is normally the balance of payments.)

THRIFT AND ENTERPRISE

The rentier morality which inculcates thrift and the acquisition of safe placements partly supports and partly frustrates the morality of entrepreneurs, which inculcates the accumulation of an ever-increasing productive capacity.

In any given situation, the lower the level of expenditure on consumption by rentiers the further out the inflation barrier lies, and the higher the rate of accumulation that is possible. When entrepreneurs, taken as a whole, are aiming at a high rate of accumulation, and are held in check only by the inflation barrier, the more thrifty everyone is the better it suits them.

On the other hand, if the system is in any case running well within the inflation barrier, the higher the level of rentier expenditure the better the entrepreneurs are pleased, for it increases the amount of commodities that can be sold at any given ratio of prices to wages costs, and makes profits easier to obtain.

An abrupt increase in thrift leading to a decline in outlay on consumption goods is acutely distressing to entrepreneurs ; some find themselves unable to make the sales in expectation of which their productive capacity was built up, and if, in consequence, they dismiss workers or curtail investment plans, others also suffer a shrinkage of markets.

A gradual increase in thrift, leading to a gradual fall in the ratio of outlay on consumption to outlay on investment would do no harm if the amount of outlay on investment gradually increased to the corresponding extent. But there is no reason to expect this ever to happen, for there is (apart from an exception to be discussed in a moment) no co-ordination between the decisions of entrepreneurs affecting investment and the decisions of rentiers affecting expenditure.

The exception concerns a section of the economy for which the two sets of decisions may be geared together ; this consists of individuals who combine the role of entrepreneur and rentier in respect to the same business, such as owners of family firms or inside shareholders who actively control joint-stock companies. For them a relatively low rate of outlay on consumption may be induced by good prospects of profit from investment ; they may reduce the share of profits they hand over to their families in order to have more funds to put into the business. But this connection between enterprise and thrift does not seem likely to work in reverse. When prospects of profit are poor and investment unattractive entrepreneur morality does not favour lavish expenditure. Rather the families of such entrepreneurs are likely to be asked to economise because business is bad. (By doing so, they make it all the worse.)

There is also a more subtle way in which rentier thriftiness reacts upon the position of entrepreneurs. At any moment the larger the proportion of all property that is owned by outside rentiers the harder it is likely to be to raise finance, both because a high ratio of rentier property is likely to mean a high proportion of fixed interest obligations to profit, and because rentiers, in general, prefer safe placements and are disinclined to finance risky investment schemes. At any time, the more thrifty have rentiers been over the past, the larger is the proportion of debts to assets for entrepreneurs as a whole, and the harder or more expensive it is likely to be to raise new finance. As time goes by, if the ratio of rentier saving to investment outlay exceeds the initial ratio of rentier property to the total value of capital, finance is likely to be growing progressively harder to raise.

Thrift, in short, makes possible a high rate of accumulation and yet sets obstacles in the way of achieving it. This paradoxical operation of the capitalist rules of the game is one of the main subjects which we hope to be able to elucidate by economic analyses.

THE ACCUMULATION OF CAPITAL

Within the limits imposed by the inflation barrier and by international finance, decisions of the entrepreneurs, taken as a whole, to carry out investment determine the rate of accumulation of capital that the system will achieve. The inner limits, set by capacity, finance and the monetary system, crystallise around the rate of investment that has been established and so build buffers in front of the inflation barrier, preventing the rate of investment from rising rapidly above an established level. But as to what governs the level at which it gets itself established we know very little. We know that it varies widely from period to period and from country to country, but any attempt to identify causes of variation in such influences as a tradition of vigorous competition among entrepreneurs (as opposed to a lethargic spirit of live and let live), a rapid rate of technical progress or a high propensity to retain profits (amassing reserves to finance investment without external borrowing) is in danger of confusing symptoms with causes. On the other hand, it is not very satisfactory to have to rely for an explanation upon a 'capitalist spirit' due to Protestantism or goodness knows what. Economic analysis requires to be supplemented by a kind of comparative historical anthropology which is still in its infancy as a scientific study. Meanwhile economic analysis has by no means completed its own task of clarifying the consequences, and the proximate causes, of differences in, and changes in, the rate of accumulation.

Chapter 6

THE MEANING OF EQUILIBRIUM

The word equilibrium, in ordinary speech, describes a relation between bodies in space. The scales of a balance are in equilibrium when the balance is at rest. If we throw a handful of coppers into the right-hand scale the balance wobbles for a short time and comes to rest again in a new equilibrium position with the bar tilted further to the right than before. If we are continually throwing coppers at random into either scale, the balance is continually wobbling and never reaches equilibrium; but, at any moment, there is a definite equilibrium position which it would quickly reach if, from that moment, we left it alone.

The metaphor of equilibrium can be applied to economic affairs only with great caution. In some conditions a system may be said to be in equilibrium, as a balance is when it is stationary. For instance, the market for placements may be said to be in equilibrium when all owners of property are content with their holdings, at the ruling prices, and the only transactions taking place are ins and outs due to personal reasons, not motivated by price differences. Such an equilibrium position, however, is likely to be temporary and to contain within itself causes of change which will operate as time goes by (as though the balance were to grow restless and begin to shift without any change in the weights). The prices of bonds, for example, may be in equilibrium for a time at a level which is higher than the average experienced over the recent past. An upward movement was recently checked and brought to rest by the expectation of the market that the high prices will not last. A number of placement owners are holding cash or very short-dated bonds at low yields in the expectation of being able to buy long bonds cheaper in the near future.

But if this position remains in force for a considerable time, expectations begin to be revised, the bears grow bored and begin to buy bonds without waiting any longer. Thus the very fact that yields have remained low for a time causes them to fall.

Again, a market for commodities may be said to be in equilibrium when a regular rate of sales at steady prices is taking place. But this rate of sales is yielding certain profits to entrepreneurs, and they are likely to be making plans to increase their outputs (if the profits are satisfactory) or to be allowing productive capacity to shrink (if they are making losses) so that, without any external event (like coppers thrown into the scales), the position in the market will begin to alter.

When a market reacts to a change in circumstances, we cannot liken it to the reaction of the balance to a once-for-all change in the weights. However the balance wobbles about, it will come to rest in exactly the same position ; but in most economic reactions the path the market follows, while it is adapting itself to a change, has a long-persisting effect upon the position that it reaches. Thus, if a sudden increase of demand makes a particular market very profitable, many entre-preneurs (each ignoring the other's action) enlarge their plant (or set up fresh businesses) and in a short time the increase in supply of the commodity concerned over-shoots the increase in demand and causes the market to become exceptionally unprofitable. Plant once built, however, cannot readily be switched to other markets, so that for a long time (if demand remains unchanged at its new level) the market continues to be over-supplied ; prices are low, or the volume of sales is not sufficient to utilise all the capacity now in existence. It is true that if the market continues to be unprofitable, a gradual shrinkage in capacity will take place ; but the extent of the overshoot in the first place determines how much shrink-age will follow and so has an influence for a long time after it occurred (as though the balance were liable to get lodged on a nail if one of its wobbles is too violent).

Nor can we apply the metaphor of a balance which is seeking or tending towards a position of equilibrium though prevented from actually reaching it by constant disturbances. In economic affairs the fact that disturbances are known to be liable to occur makes expectations about the future uncertain and has an important influence upon any conduct (which, in fact, is all economic conduct) directed towards future results. For instance, placement owners (and their professional advisers) are always on the look-out to buy what will rise in value. A belief that a particular share is going to rise causes people to offer to buy it and so raises its price. Similarly, a belief that placements as a whole are going to rise makes them rise (and yields fall). This element of 'thinking makes it so' creates a situation where a cunning guesser who can guess what the other guessers are going to guess is able to make a fortune.[1] There are then no solid weights to give us an analogy with a pair of scales in balance. Similarly, a belief that markets are going to be profitable causes entrepreneurs to make investment, thus increasing employment and incomes, and causing for the time being the prosperity they foresaw.

The metaphor of equilibrium is treacherous, but it is true that some economies are less disturbed than others (the age reflected in Marshall's *Principles* was much less disturbed than our own) and it is convenient to have an expression to describe an absence of disturbance. We may speak of an economy in a state of *tranquillity* when it develops in a smooth regular manner without internal contradictions or external shocks, so that expectations based upon past experience are very confidently held, and are in fact constantly fulfilled and therefore renewed as time goes by. In a state of perfect tranquillity the prices ruling to-day, in every market, are those which were expected to rule to-day when any relevant decisions were taken in the past; the quantities of goods being sold, costs, profits and all relevant characteristics of the situation are turning out according to expectations; and the expectations being held to-day about the future are those that were expected in the past to be held to-day. A state of tranquillity corresponds to the position of a balance which has long since got over wobbling, and is not liable to have its weights changed for some time.

[1] See Keynes, *General Theory*, p. 156.

It is difficult to imagine such a state of confident expectations if beliefs about the future are at all complicated, but it does not necessarily entail a stationary situation. An economy can be imagined to expand in a state of tranquillity, with all relevant quantities (flows of output, stocks of capital, rates of consumption) expanding in step with each other.

We may describe as a condition of *lucidity* a state of affairs in which everyone is fully aware of the situation in all markets, and understands the technical properties of all commodities, both their use in production and the satisfaction that. they give in consumption. In such a situation there would be no scope for salesmanship, and profits could be made only by meeting the needs of consumers.

Finally, we may describe as *harmony* a situation in which the rules of the game are fully understood and accepted by everyone, in which no one tries to alter his share in the proceeds of the economy, and all combine to increase the total to be shared.

An economy which existed in a state of tranquillity, lucidity and harmony would be devoted to the production and consumption of wealth in a rational manner.

It is only necessary to describe these conditions to see how remote they are from the states in which actual economies dwell. Capitalism, in particular, could never have come into existence in such conditions, for the divorce between work and property, which makes large-scale enterprise possible, entails conflict ; and the rules of the game have been developed precisely to make accumulation and technical progress possible in conditions of uncertainty and imperfect knowledge. Yet too much disturbance, deception and conflict would break an economy to pieces. The persistence of capitalism till to-day is evidence that certain principles of coherence are imbedded in its confusion.

BOOK II
ACCUMULATION IN THE LONG RUN

CHAPTER 7

A SIMPLE MODEL

THE processes leading to the production and distribution of wealth which are going on around us to-day are intricate and the connections between various elements in the economy are interwoven with each other in a highly complicated manner. It is impossible to reduce economic theory to a set of simple hypotheses which can each be tested separately, like hypotheses about, say, the cause of a disease or the effects of a constituent of diet upon growth. Moreover, since human beings do not live, like the robins, in a timeless present, but plan their actions with a view to future consequences, most causal elements in economic life lie partly in the beliefs and expectations (often vague and emotional) of the actors and are very hard, if not impossible in principle, to pin down by any scientific observation. For these reasons it can be plausibly maintained that economics is not and never will be a serious scientific discipline, and that it properly belongs to the class of subjects, such as theology or aesthetic criticism, which use words to play upon sentiment rather than to investigate reality.

Against this view, however, it can be argued that economics, as it has been developed, does throw light on particular problems, such as the causes of price movements, the effects of taxation upon the distribution of wealth, and the effects of national policies designed to maintain employment or to maintain solvency in the international transactions of a country. The purpose of economic theory, of the generalised kind set out in the book, is to provide a framework within which such particular questions can be usefully discussed.

The method of analysis which has been developed in economic theory is to set up a highly simplified *model* of an economy, which is intended to bring into an orderly scheme

63

of ideas the main movements that may be expected to occur in reality, while ruling out innumerable detailed complications. By thinking about the behaviour of such a simplified model we hope to be able to disentangle the broad movements and so gain insight into the behaviour of the actual, complicated, economy. (It is important to remember, however, what complications have to be reinserted before conclusions drawn from a model can be confronted with evidence from reality.)

THE ASSUMPTIONS

I. The first type of simplification, to make our problem manageable, is to visualise an imaginary economy in which the problem of index numbers would cause no difficulty. As we have seen, any category of the kind in terms of which economic analysis is conducted — a class; a factor of production; a level of costs, of prices or of incomes; a stock of capital goods or of placements — is highly complex, consisting of elements which vary relatively to each other as the total changes. An accurate statement of changes in such multi-dimensional quantities which is simple enough to be useful is necessarily rough and can be expressed only in terms of limits. Any precise simple statement is necessarily inaccurate. We escape from this dilemma by abstracting from relative movements, so that we can conduct our argument in terms of simple quantities.

The main part of our argument will be conducted in terms of an imaginary economy in which the following assumptions are fulfilled :

1. All workers are alike, so that we can reckon work simply in terms of man-hours of standard labour time. The money wage per man-hour is always the same for all workers.

2. The commodities purchased for consumption do not alter through time (a loaf is always a loaf, or a shirt a shirt) and they are consumed in fixed proportions, so that, in effect, the output of consumption goods consists of units of a rigid composite commodity. (This assumption is relaxed in Book VII.)

3. A given technique of production requires equipment (factory buildings, machinery, etc.) of specific quantities and designs, and a specific time-pattern in the cycle of production in the sense that each process, on a particular batch of goods, requires a definite time, and different processes are applied, in parallel or in sequence, in a definite manner, so that, at any moment, the stock of capital goods, including equipment, work-in-progress, technically necessary stocks of materials, etc., required to produce a given flow of output is rigidly determined by the technique in operation. Since commodities are produced in rigid proportions, the stock of equipment of all kinds must be in appropriate proportions. The same rule applies to equipment required to produce equipment, so that a given flow of consumption *plus* increase in the stock of capital goods requires a definite outfit of capital goods. In the special case where no positive or negative accumulation is going on, all final output is being consumed, equipment is being continuously renewed as it wears out and the stock of capital goods remains constant through time.

4. A *short-period* situation is one in which the stock of equipment is given. The rate of output and the amount of employment of labour may vary in the short period with given plant in existence, but it is assumed that the proportions in which individual commodities are sold remain rigid.

II. In reality, in capitalist economies, technical change is always taking place; indeed we might say that the *raison d'être* of the capitalist rules of the game is that their development was favourable to technical progress. It would therefore be absurd to rule technical progress out of our model. But actual technical change largely consists in altering the nature of consumption goods (by substituting one kind for another — say cotton for linen, or rayon for cotton, or by introducing new kinds of goods such as motor-cars or television sets). Thus any realistic treatment of technical change is beset by index-number ambiguities, and is inconsistent with the above assumptions.

We can evade this difficulty by introducing into the model an abstract conception of technical progress which consists in improvements in methods of production without any changes in the composite commodity representing the output of consumption goods.   Thus if technical progress occurs in the production of particular consumption goods, the cost of the composite commodity is *pro tanto* reduced but its composition is not affected.

III. In order to separate long-run from short-run influences it is a useful device to imagine an economy developing in conditions of tranquillity, and to postulate that the expectations about the future, held at any moment, are in fact being fulfilled. This yields results equivalent to assuming correct foresight, without raising any metaphysical problems about free will and predestination.   But this device works only when it is assumed that the development of the economy is in fact going to follow an unvarying course.   To postulate correct foresight of any complicated developments involves considerable difficulties. A general expectation that something will happen may cause it to happen (even if the expectation has no objective basis). For instance, an expectation of rising prices in the future causes demands to be increased in the present and supplies to be withheld, so that in fact prices do rise.   On the other hand, expectations may cause avoiding action to be taken.   For instance, an expectation that an increase in the output of a particular commodity is going to precipitate a fall in its price may cause a monopoly to be set up which restricts the increase in output.   Thus correct foresight involves highly sophisticated expectations which take account of the influence of the expectations themselves upon the course of events.

There is another difficulty.   An expected downward trend in future quasi-rents affects different items in an outfit of capital goods differently, being greatest for those with the longest life, which will live into the period of lowest quasi-rents. Thus there ceases to be a uniform rate of expected profit for different types of investment.   In these conditions correct planning would require a high level of mathematical training for entrepreneurs, and a correct account of the values of capital goods would involve for economists an index-number problem of a formidable character.

Far from simplifying analysis, the postulate of correct foresight (except in conditions of tranquillity with a constant rate

of profit) makes it completely intractable.   And it can claim
no merit as being realistic, for a situation in which complicated
developments are known to be liable to occur is one in which
the future is clouded by uncertainty.   We shall therefore
conduct our analysis (except when otherwise stated) on the
assumption that at every moment entrepreneurs expect the
future rate of profit obtainable on investment to continue
indefinitely at the level ruling at that moment; that they
expect the rate of technical progress (which may be nil) to be
steady; and that they fix amortisation allowances for long-
lived plant accordingly.   When something occurs which causes
a change, we assume that expectations are immediately adjusted,
and that no further change is expected.

IV. The endowment of natural resources enjoyed by an
economy is obviously of the highest importance, but at the
first stage of our argument we shall leave this factor out of the
picture, in order to put aside the complexities which arise
because of the special characteristics of land both as a form
of productive equipment and as the source of income of a
particular class.   To eliminate these complications we assume
that all equipment is produced and reproducible.   This means
that we abstract not only from the existence of scarce natural
factors of production such as mineral deposits but also from
territory.   It is impossible to visualise an economy of any
degree of complexity in which there is not property in land,
but we can imagine an economy, like that of the robins, which
can spread freely over space (the economic quality of land being
perfectly homogeneous) so that the area of operations depends
upon the amount of labour employed, and land commands no
price.   This highly artificial assumption is made purely to
separate out one layer of the argument, and problems connected
with land will be introduced in Book VI.

V. How should demographic changes be treated ?   In reality
the supply of labour and the accumulation of capital are not
independent of each other, but the inter-connections between
them cannot be reduced to any simple formula.   In many
cases a great increase in population, and therefore in the
labour force, has come about through a drop in a death rate
which was formerly high, balancing a high birth rate.   This

may be a consequence of increasing wealth resulting from accumulation, but it depends partly upon factors (such as the growth of medical knowledge and its diffusion) which are very loosely connected with the growth of wealth, and even when it can clearly be attributed to a growth of wealth it may lead to a change of numbers quite out of proportion to the development of productivity which set it going. The drop in the birth rate which has frequently followed after a fall in the death rate, so as to slow down or reverse the growth in population, is clearly connected with the rise in the standard of life and the change in mental attitudes that accompanies industrialisation, but, again, it follows laws of its own, which are by no means perfectly understood, and which cannot be reduced to a simple function of changing productivity.

The closest connection between accumulation and the growth of population is seen (as, for instance, in North America or Malaya) where the development of industry in sparsely populated territory attracts immigration. But the recruitment of labour may run ahead or fall short of the pace of accumulation, and in any case it depends upon the existence of other parts of the world where the population has been increasing relatively to opportunities for employment. Thus it seems best to treat accumulation and growth in the labour force as two independent factors which may or may not be in harmony with each other.

VI. As we have already remarked, the class structure of a modern economy is highly complex. We shall simplify the picture in a drastic manner. At the first stage (which includes Books II-IV) we operate a two-class model consisting only of workers and entrepreneurs. The workers (whom we assume all alike) own no property beyond some supplies of consumption goods (the clothes they stand up in). The entrepreneurs are abstract impersonal figures who take the decisions relevant to the conduct of firms. They own property in the capital of their firms and may borrow finance from each other, but we abstract entirely from their consumption. They have no life outside of office hours.

When (in Book V) we introduce rentiers (that is, owners of financial property), individuals who carry out the functions

of entrepreneurship may be regarded as also being rentiers
and their households are consumers, but then an individual
who plays two parts is regarded as keeping them distinct. He
has one life in the office, where he is concerned with the fortunes of his firm, and another at home, where he is concerned
with the consumption and saving of his family.

Intermediate classes such as artisans and professional
experts are not introduced into the model.

VII. In our imaginary economy the capitalist rules of the
game are well established and have long been played. Because
of the economies of division of labour the minimum size of
each type of productive enterprise is fairly large. It is impossible for independent artisans to compete with capitalist
enterprise. The size of individual firms (above the minimum)
is not strictly determined. Each entrepreneur, with patriotism
for his own firm, is continually struggling to enlarge his
business, and new firms are being launched from time to
time. Competitive conditions entail that their struggles have
kept each other in check so that large numbers of independent
sellers supply the market for each commodity. Where competition for a particular market has left few, or only one,
survivor, there is oligopoly or monopoly. There may also be
monopolistic conditions established by agreements between
erstwhile competitors.

VIII. Strict *laisser-faire* prevails. Governments play no
part in economic affairs.

IX. To rule out important groups of complications which
cannot be tackled at the first stage of the argument we
assume :

1. The economy is a closed system existing in isolation.
It can best be visualised as a single large nation without foreign
trade. (This assumption is removed in Book VIII.)

2. There are no economies due to the total scale of production of particular commodities or of the economy as a
whole, so that (with free land) costs of production in the long
run (but not in the short period with given equipment) are
independent of the rate of output. (Some consequences of
removing this assumption are considered in Chapter 33 and
in Book VII.)

The formal argument will be conducted upon these highly abstract assumptions, but at certain points we shall consider how the propositions drawn from it should be interpreted to apply to actual situations.

THE LONG-RUN PROBLEMS

With the aid of this model we shall examine the problems of accumulation over the long run, leaving the manner in which they express themselves through short-period movements for later treatment. Our chief concern is with the relation between wages and profits, and the argument is conducted in terms of (1) the relations of the stock of capital to the available labour force, (2) the influence of competition, and (3) the technique of production.

Since we treat accumulation and the growth of the labour force as independent of each other, an important part of the argument is concerned with the relations between them. At each layer of the analysis we consider positions in which they are in harmony and positions in which there is a tendency to a surplus or a scarcity of labour in relation to capital.

Competition plays an important part in the argument because a growth of monopoly may reduce real wages (by raising prices relatively to money-wage rates) without increasing profits (because lower real wages reduce demand).

Changes in technique are considered in two separate categories, those which arise from inventions and discoveries and those which are due to changes in wages relatively to profits in a given state of technical knowledge. The separation is somewhat artificial, for in reality the two types of change are inextricably mingled, but for analytical purposes the distinction is helpful. We shall find the first type of change (technical progress) easier to discuss than the second, for it is possible to discuss the first on the basis of a constant rate of profit, which makes the measurement of the stock of capital simple, whereas the second necessarily involves changes in the rate of profit and leads us into the problem of the meaning of a stock of capital (discussed in Chapter 11) which no simplifying assumptions can make easy.

Throughout the argument it is necessary to distinguish *differences* from *changes*. The effect of having had in the past, and continuing to have, say, a higher rate of accumulation or a higher degree of monopoly, is not the same as the effect of a rise in the rate of accumulation or of an increase in monopoly. The analysis is therefore conducted in terms both of a comparison between economies with permanently different characteristics and of a single economy in which a change takes place at a moment of time.

As an analytical device it is useful to distinguish the conditions required for harmonious development with full employment of labour (neither scarcity nor surplus) in order to be able to discuss the influences which cause an economy to fail to achieve harmony or to fall out of it.

When we descend into short-period problems (in Book III) we find that every such influence tends to be exaggerated and subsequently reversed because of the short-period reactions that it sets up.

SECTION 1

ACCUMULATION WITH ONE TECHNIQUE

CHAPTER 8

ACCUMULATION WITH CONSTANT
TECHNIQUE

In our model economy there are no inhabitants except workers who spend their wages (and nothing but their wages) currently as they receive them, and entrepreneurs whose consumption is negligible and whose sole function and aim is to organise production and accumulate capital. These assumptions pare off all complications and enable us to examine the mere essence of the capitalist rules of the game.

WAGES AND PROFITS WITH ONE TECHNIQUE

For the purpose of this chapter we assume that only one technique of production is known. A given rate of output of each type of product requires a specific outfit of capital goods, a specific time-pattern of production and a specific flow of man-hours of work per annum. When our story begins, a capitalist economy has long been established and there is in existence a stock of productive equipment appropriate to the known technique, with all its pipe-lines full of work-in-progress. The amount of employment is governed by the stock of equipment in existence. We will first assume that entrepreneurs have always found as much labour available as they wanted to employ. (We may imagine that the capitalist economy exists side by side with a self-subsistence peasant economy with which it does not trade, but from which it can recruit labour as required.)[1]

In the dark backward and abysm of time, capitalism emerged from some pre-existing type of economy where labour was

---

[1] Cf. W. A. Lewis, 'Economic Development with Unlimited Supplies of Labour', *Manchester School* (May 1954).

performed by serfs or by artisans and free peasants. The level of wages, in terms of consumption goods, that the capitalists had to pay to get work done was set by the existing standard of life of workers (or, at worst, by the physiological minimum that would enable them to work and raise families). Since then a process of historical evolution has brought the wage rate and the level of employment to what it is to-day. The difference between the wage bill, so established, and the total product, say of a year, which depends upon the technique of production in use, is the increment of capital accumulated over the year (the pre-existing stock of capital goods being maintained intact), and since we are assuming no consumption out of profits, this is the same thing as the total profit on the year's operations.[1]

Entrepreneurs specialise on the production of particular commodities or items of capital equipment, but they are free to switch from one line to another so that a uniform rate of profit is established throughout the system.[2]

There is no difference in principle between an investment in equipment and in an increase in work-in-progress or in retailers' stocks, but it is easiest to visualise what is happening if we think of capital goods which are different in kind from consumption goods, so that we can say that, at any moment, a certain number of workers are engaged on producing consumption goods, and a certain number on producing capital goods which are added to the stock of capital or replace items that have reached the end of their useful life. We shall refer to capital goods as machines or plant; but it must be remembered that each machine put into service (provided that it is being utilised at capacity) requires a particular investment in work-in-progress to go with it and a particular volume of stocks in the pipe-lines of commerce.

The demand for consumption goods (and therefore their rate of output) depends on the relations between (1) the number

[1] Cf. N. Kaldor, 'The Recent Controversy on the Theory of Capital', *Econometrica* (July 1937), and J. von Neumann, 'A Model of General Economic Equilibrium', *Review of Economic Studies*, vol. xiii (1), No. 33, (1945–6).

[2] The manner in which the rate of profit enters into the cost of investments of different time-patterns is discussed below, p. 104.

of workers engaged in producing capital goods, (2) the real wage
per man-year, (3) the ratio of output of consumption goods
per man-year, with the prevailing technique, to the real-wage
rate.   The entrepreneurs in effect (though of course they are
not acting on any conscious concerted plan) are employing a
certain number of workers to produce capital goods and whatever further number of workers is required to provide wage
goods for all the workers employed.   In money terms, given
the money-wage rate, the sales value of commodities per annum
is equal to the wages bill for consumption-goods output, plus
the wages bill for capital goods, and quasi-rent obtained from
the sale of consumption goods is equal to the wages bill for
capital goods.

If W_1 is the wages bill in the investment sector and W_2
in the consumption sector and Q the quasi-rent from the sale
of consumption goods, the sales value of consumption goods
is equal to $W_2 + W_1$ or to $W_2 + Q$.   The ratio of employment
in the investment sector to employment in the consumption
sector is equal to Q/W_2, which is the ratio of quasi-rent per
man employed in the consumption sector to the wage, quite
irrespective of quasi-rent in the investment sector.[1]

Outlay on a machine bought from a specialist producer
exceeds its wages cost, thus providing quasi-rent in the investment sector.   Capital goods produced by an entrepreneur for
his own use are valued at a price exceeding their wages cost
by a notional profit margin.   Thus total profit for a year exceeds quasi-rent in the consumption sector, net of amortisation,
by an amount equal to the excess of the value of the increment
of capital made during the year over profit in the consumption
sector.   The excess of a year's output of capital goods over the
year's wastage is equal to the excess of total quasi-rent over
amortisation, that is, to the year's profit.

[1] All production being divided into two sectors, investment and consumption, output per man in the consumption sector is, say, twice the real
wage per man ; total employment is then twice employment in the investment sector.   Or if the wage rate is two-thirds of output in the consumption
sector, total employment is three times employment in the investment
sector.   Thus : wages bill in investment sector : 100 ; wages bill in consumption sector : 200.   Value of sales of consumption goods : 300.   Quasi-
rent in consumption sector : 100.

PROFITS AND ACCUMULATION

The relation between profits and accumulation is two sided. For profit to be obtainable there must be a surplus of output per worker over the consumption per worker's family necessary to keep the labour force in being. But the existence of a potential technical surplus is not a sufficient condition for profits to be realised. It is also necessary that entrepreneurs should be carrying out investment. The proposition that the rate of profit is equal to the ratio of accumulation to the stock of capital (when no profit is consumed) cuts both ways. If they have no profit, the entrepreneurs cannot accumulate, and if they do not accumulate they have no profit.

Suppose that, with existing techniques, the output of commodities produced by the workers employed in the consumption sector exceeds a bare subsistence wage by only just enough to provide subsistence wages for the workers required to keep the existing stock of equipment in being (by replacements of items wearing out). Then there is no room within the inflation barrier for net investment and no accumulation can take place.

Now consider a case in which real wages are comfortably above the subsistence level, so that there is a technical surplus available for accumulation, and in which the workers are not so strongly organised and so price-conscious as to set up an inflation barrier against a fall in real wages. Accumulation is possible. But it may happen that each entrepreneur individually is satisfied with the amount of capital that he has already accumulated. Collectively, they employ only enough labour to keep the stock of capital intact. Consequently quasi-rents are equal only to amortisation, and there is no profit.

Set out in terms of our austere assumptions both these cases may seem unnatural, but they illustrate a point of the greatest importance which remains true when overlaid with all the complications of reality. There are two opposite kinds of stagnation to which capitalist economies may be subject — stagnation due to technical poverty and stagnation due to satiety.[1]

---

[1] A third kind of stagnation, due to defects in the financial and monetary mechanism, is discussed in Chapter 24, and a fourth, due to consumption of profits, in Chapter 26.

MONOPOLY AND REAL WAGES

The level of real wages, on our assumptions, is uniquely correlated with the ratio of the rate of accumulation per unit of time to the stock of capital, but it would be misleading to say that one determines the other, for the relationship between them involves a long past history.

The point can be most easily seen if we imagine that we can compare two economies alike in every respect except that in one of them, Beth, the real-wage rate is (and always has been) lower than in the other, Alaph. The technique of production is the same in both, the money-wage rate is the same, and we have caught them at a moment in their respective histories when the amount of employment is the same in both. In Beth profit margins per unit of output are higher than in Alaph, whether because the trade unions in Beth are weaker, or the entrepreneurs are more monopolistic, or simply because a different conception prevails there of what is the right and proper level of margins. Prices are thus higher in Beth than in Alaph and the real-wage rate lower. Since total employment is the same in each, the demand for consumption goods and their rate of output is higher in Alaph, and the amount of employment in the consumption sector, with the appropriate equipment, is larger; the investment sector is consequently smaller and the rate of accumulation and the rate of profit lower. (This requires that recruitment of labour is proceeding at a correspondingly lower rate in Alaph than in Beth.)

Now let us suppose that the Alaph entrepreneurs begin to form themselves into rings and raise prices. We will suppose that the process takes place gradually, so that the economy is not subject to a violent shock. As prices rise, with constant money wages, the volume of sales of consumption goods gradually falls (or rather fails to rise at its former rate). Workers become unemployed, and the utilisation of capital equipment in the consumption sector falls below capacity. (To avoid complicating the story we will suppose that the redundant workers retire into the neighbouring self-subsistence economy.) Initially employment in the investment sector is unaffected, and the quasi-rent in the consumption sector is therefore initially unchanged ; quasi-rent per man employed has risen in the proportion in which employment per unit of capital has fallen. But with redundant equipment in the consumption sector the demand for replacements falls off, there is unemployment in the investment sector and a fall in the rate of profit. We may suppose that after passing through a period of disinvestment, accumulation recovers to its former level (though there is no necessary reason why it should do so). If, now, real wages are the same as they were in Beth when the story began, the ratio of accumulation to the stock of capital is now the same in Alaph as it was in Beth, but this ratio has become established by a reduction in the stock of capital (and in the labour force) so that it now bears the low, Beth, ratio to the low, Alaph, level of accumulation.

Contrariwise, if competition broke out in Beth, and gradually raised real wages there to the original Alaph level, a burst of extra accumulation (and immigration of labour) would establish the stock of capital at the high, Alaph, ratio to the high, Beth, rate of accumulation.

This illustrates an essential paradox of capitalism. Each entrepreneur individually gains from a low real wage in terms of his own product, but all suffer from the limited market for commodities which a low real-wage rate entails.

SURPLUS OF LABOUR

We now remove the assumption that the supply of labour adapts itself to the demands of the entrepreneurs for workers. The capitalist economy is self-contained and depends for labour upon its own population.

So far we have seen that, provided that the ratio of profit margins to wages costs does not alter (there is no change in the intensity of competition or the bargaining power of trade unions) then, so long as the ratio of accumulation to the stock of capital is constant (gross investment per annum rises through time at the same rate as the stock of capital) the rate of profit on capital (which is equal to that ratio, because of the assumption that there is no consumption out of profits) is constant, and so is the rate of real wages.

Accumulation can go on indefinitely at a steady rate pro-vided that population is increasing at about the same rate as capital is accumulating. There is then (we may suppose) a margin of unemployed labour, and the system is riding along some way within the inflation barrier. The ratio (which may be quite small) of the number of unemployed to the number of employed workers remains more or less constant as time goes by. Unemployed workers and their families are supported by friends and relations who are earning.

What would happen if the population were increasing at a faster rate than capital was accumulating and no emigration of labour was possible?

Sooner or later the existence of a swollen reserve of unem-ployed labour leads to a fall in money-wage rates. The workers' power to resist a cut in wage rates has been weakened, and each group of employers thinks to gain an advantage by reducing wages costs.

The manner in which the situation develops depends upon how entrepreneurs react to the fall in wages. If they maintain a constant rate of accumulation in physical terms, so that employment in the investment sector is unaffected, the wage bill in that sector, and consequently quasi-rents in the con-sumption sector, falls in the same ratio as the wage rate. In competitive conditions prices are reduced in the same propor-tion, so that, in spite of the weak position of the workers, the real wage remains constant. Since the rate of accumulation has failed to respond to the increase in the surplus supply of labour, the reserve of unemployed workers continues to increase and the ratio of unemployment to employment to rise.

If the imperfection of competition makes prices sticky so that they fail to fall in proportion to money wages, the situation is still worse, for with a lower real-wage rate and the same employment in the investment sector, the demand for con-sumption goods falls and there is a reduction of employment in the consumption sector. Accumulation is retarded while the now redundant equipment in the consumption sector is digested, and consequently employment for a time falls still further. This repeats the story of Alaph, where real wages were lowered by the setting up of monopolistic rings.

All this follows from the assumption that employment in the investment sector remains constant when money wages fall. Alternatively, we may assume that entrepreneurs think in terms of the value of capital rather than in its physical quantity, and that the rate of accumulation tends to be maintained constant in terms of money outlay, or at any rate to fall in a smaller proportion than costs.[1]

In that case, employment in the investment sector increases when the money-wage rate falls and the wage bill in that sector falls in a smaller proportion than the money-wage rate. Prices of commodities are then lower than before the cut in wages occurred in a smaller proportion than wages, and the real wage is lower. Employment in the consumption sector is rising through time with the stock of machines, and since accumulation of machines is now going on more rapidly than before, the demand for labour has, at least partially, responded to the increase in available supply.

A once-for-all fall in wages, however, would produce only a once-for-all increase in employment. The inertia of investment in money terms would become re-established at a lower level; the economy would relapse into the former rate of accumulation and the surplus of labour would begin to grow again, as fast as before. On the other hand, repeated falls in wages would set up expectations that would tend to retard accumulation.

SCARCITY OF LABOUR

What happens in the contrary case, where capital is accumulating faster than available labour? As the stock of machines gradually increases, any reserve there may have been of unemployed workers is drained and entrepreneurs begin to find difficulty in getting more hands to man new equipment. They begin to compete with each other for workers, and offer higher money wages. Once more the manner in which the situation develops depends upon the reaction of investment. If entrepreneurs in the investment sector refuse to part with labour, and raise their wages in competition with those in the

---

[1] The relation of the prices of capital goods to their wages costs is discussed below, p. 120.

consumption sector, prices rise as fast or faster than money wages, the real-wage rate fails to rise and the economy is in an impasse.[1]

But if money outlay on investment does not increase sufficiently to maintain the physical rate of output of capital goods, the consumption sector wins in the scramble for labour. Employment in the investment sector falls and so releases labour to man the new equipment which is coming into use in the consumption sector. The wages bill in the investment sector has then increased in a smaller proportion than the money-wage rate, and prices in the consumption sector have risen in a smaller proportion. The real-wage rate has increased, and consumption increases as the new productive equipment in the consumption sector yields its output.

The rate of accumulation has now fallen. If it is still going on faster than new labour is becoming available, the scarcity of labour emerges again, and the whole process is repeated until the two are brought into harmony.

The mechanism by which the rate of accumulation is adjusted to the rate of increase in the supply of labour is thus reliable when what is required is a reduction in the rate of accumulation, not when a rise is required : it is only too easy for a surplus of labour to grow, relatively to the stock of capital, while investment fails to increase and the economy sinks into stagnation ; whereas entrepreneurs will not accumulate and maintain redundant capital, so that when the rate of accumulation is too high (relatively to the labour force) one way or another it is certain to be cut down.

In the special case where the total labour force remains constant it is evidently impossible, with a single technique, for accumulation to continue indefinitely. In such a case the mechanism may be conceived to work to its logical conclusion. If accumulation is going on, a scarcity of labour will sooner or later emerge. A rise in the real-wage rate and a fall in accumulation draws labour out of the investment sector. The rate of accumulation falls, but if it is still positive the scarcity of labour will sooner or later emerge again ; a further rise in wages will further reduce the rate of accumulation, and so on, until

---

[1] Monetary reactions are discussed below, p. 238.

A.C.—D

replacement absorbs the whole of gross investment, and the stock of capital ceases to increase.[1] All labour is then employed on producing consumption goods and maintaining capital, wages absorb the whole net product of industry, and the rate of profit is zero.[2]

---

[1] The age composition of the stock of capital will gradually become adjusted from that appropriate to a growing stock to that appropriate to a constant stock, and redundant plant in the investment sector will be abandoned.

[2] To make a simple numerical example we assume that machines are perfectly durable, we ignore working capital, and take no account of the equipment in the investment sector which is destined to become redundant and be scrapped. The labour force consists of 100 teams of men (each team of an equal number).

First Position

	Consumption Sector	Investment Sector
Labour	80 teams	20 teams
Machines	50 outfits	..
Product per annum	100 units of commodities	5 outfits of machines

Real wage per team-year : 1

One year later

	Consumption Sector	Investment Sector
Labour	88 teams	12 teams
Machines	55 outfits	..
Product per annum	110 units of commodities	3 outfits of machines

Real wage per team-year : 1·1

This transition may have come about by several routes, which all reach the same result in real terms while entailing different movements of money wages and prices.

(1) If the money-wage bill in the investment sector is unchanged, the money-wage rate has risen by approximately 66 per cent and prices by 50 per cent.

(2) The monetary authorities (whose behaviour will be discussed in Book IV) may, in order to check the threatened rise of prices, have induced a fall in investment sufficient to reduce employment in that sector to the required extent. Prices of commodities are then constant, and the money-wage rate has risen 10 per cent.

(3) The consumption sector got in first with a rise of wages, attracting 8 teams of labour to man the new machines, and the investment sector acquiesced, allowing its labour force to fall and raising the wage rate for those that remained in line with the rise in the consumption sector. In

This is not properly to be described as a state of stagnation, but rather as the *state of economic bliss*,[1] since consumption is now at the maximum level which can be permanently maintained in the given technical conditions.[2]

SUMMARY

The foregoing argument may be concisely stated: In an economy with only one technique, and no consumption out of profits, when the supply of labour adapts itself to demand, starting from any given situation (produced by past history), the future rate of accumulation is limited:

(1) By the technical surplus available above subsistence wages for the workers employed.

(2) Within that limit, it is limited by the surplus above the level of real wages that the workers are willing to accept and

---

this case money wages and prices are indeterminate; the money wage has risen 10 per cent more than prices.

The first route involves (on our assumption of durable machines) the absurdity that money wages must rise to infinity when the output of machines is zero. The second requires an impossible degree of skill and foresight on the part of the monetary authorities. The last route is therefore the easiest to visualise. Whatever route is followed in the final position we have:

	Consumption Sector	Investment Sector
Labour Machines Oputut	100 teams 62·5 outfits 125 units of commodities	nil

Real wage per team-year : 1·25

Assuming that full employment is maintained from the moment when scarcity of labour is first felt, the time taken by the whole process is independent of the scale of the transition. It depends on the time that men in the investment sector take to produce the machines required to offer them employment in the consumption sector. The larger is the investment sector in the first instance, the larger is the transition to be made and the faster the pace at which it is carried out.

[1] Cf. Keynes, *Treatise on Money*, vol. ii, p. 163. The reference to Frank Ramsey's article in the *Economic Journal* is wrongly given. It should be December 1928.

[2] Even then it is not easy to define a unique state of bliss, for the amount of work done by a given labour force is not technically determined. There may be different blisses in the same technical conditions with different ratios of consumption to leisure.

able to enforce (by creating an inflation barrier against a fall in real wages).

(3) Within that limit, accumulation is limited by the energy with which entrepreneurs carry it out.

(4) When the size of the labour force is independent of the entrepreneurs' demand for workers, a maximum is set to the possible rate of accumulation by the rate of increase of the labour force. When accumulation fails to reach this rate there is growth of long-period unemployment.

Many of our conclusions will have to be extensively modified as the assumptions of one technique and no rentier consumption are relaxed, but we shall find that the argument holds good in all essential respects, and provides a picture of the basic characteristics of accumulation under the capitalist rules of the game.

Chapter 9

TECHNICAL PROGRESS

We must now introduce technical progress into the picture. At present we continue to assume that corresponding to each state of technical knowledge there is only one possible method of production for each type of commodity and of equipment (a spectrum of technical possibilities, entailing different ratios of labour to capital in a given phase of knowledge will be discussed in the next chapter).[1]

THE DIFFUSION OF INNOVATIONS

As time goes by entrepreneurs are continually introducing improvements in methods of production.[2] Some are more active than others, and in each line there are some progressive firms, who are the first to make innovations, while the rest follow only when compelled to do so by the pressure of competition (those who are obstinately conservative, or who cannot raise funds to make the investments required by new methods are finally driven out of business and their space in the economy is taken up by other men).

The speed at which new methods are diffused throughout the economy depends partly upon the physical life of capital goods. When worn-out equipment is being replaced the new capital goods installed embody the latest devices to which the entrepreneur has access. Innovations which save working capital by speeding up the processes of production are very rapidly diffused (unless kept secret or protected by patents taken out by their first discoverers) for the capital goods

[1] At this stage we assume that a new method is superior to all older ones at every level of wages.

[2] Changes in products are ruled out (see above, p. 66).

embodied in work in progress are being continuously replaced as production goes on. With durable equipment a continual game of leap-frog is being played. Suppose that ten years is the profitable life of plant in a particular industry; then a nine-year-old plant has the highest costs and yields the lowest profits; next year it is replaced by new plant with all the improvements that have been made over the past ten years. Nine years hence it will again be high-cost plant, having lost its lead gradually as each year's entry of new plant has jumped ahead.

Where equipment has a potentially long life (it is physically durable) the rate at which it is superseded by improved plant depends to a large extent upon the degree of competition between entrepreneurs. A progressive entrepreneur who has installed new plant which reduces the cost of production of a particular commodity may decide to continue selling it at the same price as before, being content with a more or less constant share of the market and enjoying higher profits. In that case unprogressive entrepreneurs are not put under any pressure to become progressive, old plant is no less profitable than before and will live out its natural life, being replaced (if the new methods are accessible) by the improved plant at the time when it would in any case have been due for renewal.

When the progressive entrepreneur prefers to take advantage of lower costs to expand his share of the markets that he serves (or fears that if he does not expand, others will) he cuts prices somewhat to attract customers and raises wage rates to get more labour. To defend themselves entrepreneurs with old plant competing with him have to follow suit, and this goes on until the wage rate in terms of the particular product has risen to the point when old plant no longer yields quasi-rent. Then the old plant is scrapped, and the entrepreneurs concerned either yield their place in the market to the progressive firm or install new plant to hold their own. The leap-frog game is then speeded up, and the economic life of plant is shorter than its potential physical life.

When the speed of diffusion of innovations is very rapid, progressive entrepreneurs get little benefit from their progressiveness, for the excess profits due to having lower costs are rapidly competed away by imitators. An entrepreneur who has a new idea which requires to be embodied in a heavy investment in equipment is on the horns of a dilemma. He does not want to install it unless he can be sure of recovering from it enough quasi-rent to amortise the investment and yield at least the ruling rate of profit. If other entrepreneurs will soon be installing even better plant the high-yielding period of this plant will be short, and its total quasi-rent over its life inadequate. But if he does not install it, and his competitors make some equivalent improvement, he will suffer a fall of prices without having enjoyed the reduction of costs. He would prefer no one to make the improvement, but if anyone is to make it he would prefer it to be himself. This leads to what we may call the paradox of patents. A patent is a device to prevent the diffusion of new methods before the original investor has recovered profit adequate to induce the requisite investment. The justification of the patent system is that by slowing down the diffusion of technical progress it ensures that there will be more progress to diffuse. The patent system introduces some of the greatest of the complexities in the capitalist rules of the game and leads to many anomalies. Since it is rooted in a contradiction, there can be no such thing as an ideally beneficial patent system, and it is bound to produce negative results in particular instances, impeding progress unnecessarily, even if its general effect is favourable on balance. In many lines of production legal patents are unimportant and the same essential paradox shows itself rather in the jealous guarding of 'know how' by the progressive firms.

THE CONDITIONS FOR STABILITY

An increase in output per head at an even pace equal in all lines of production is equivalent, from the point of view of potential output, to an increase in the labour force at the corresponding rate. To simplify exposition we will assume that the population is constant, so that we can confine the analysis to an increase in potential output coming only from increasing productivity. Now, when the system is working in such a way that productive capacity increases at the same pace as output per head, there is steady employment of the given labour force over the long run. The division of the labour force (and of productive capacity of capital goods) between the investment sector and the consumption sector then remains unchanged as time goes by. A given number of workers in the investment sector produce plant (for both sectors) of an ever increasing productive capacity, and a given number of workers in the consumption sector operate it to produce an ever increasing output. Real wages rise with output per man, and the rate of profit remains constant.

As the standard of life of the workers rises, hours of work may be falling, or the amount of labour provided by a given population may be reduced by a rise in the age of entry into industry, a fall in the age of retirement, or less employment of women. This does not disturb the smooth development of the economy, provided that it affects both sectors equally. It merely means that total output rises less fast than output per man-hour,[1] and that workers are receiving part of the benefit of increasing productivity in the form of leisure instead of commodities.

When productivity alters, the relations between the values of money, labour, commodities and capital goods are changed. When the real wage rises with output per head (and the rise in output per head is evenly distributed through the economy)[2] the cost of capital goods in terms of commodities is constant. The money-price level then depends upon the money-wage level. For instance, if money wages are constant, the money price of commodities falls as output per head rises, and so does the cost of machines. If money wages rise with output per head money prices are constant. When we introduce rentiers into the model, changes in the money prices of commodities will assume great importance. Meanwhile they need not concern us. The prices which are important for this layer of the analysis are the cost of labour in terms of commodities — that is the real wage per man-hour — and the cost of machines in terms of commodities, which is governed by the

---

[1] It must be observed, however, that with single-shift working, a shorter day reduces the productive capacity of given plant, and increases the ratio of capital to labour with a given technique of production. This point is discussed below, p. 170.

[2] And the time pattern of the processes of production is unchanged.

real-wage rate and the productivity of labour in the investment sector.

The first essential condition for smooth development of a progressive economy is that the stock of machines (in terms of productive capacity) [1] is growing at the rate appropriate to the increase in output per man that is taking place, while competition ensures that prices move relatively to money-wage rates in such a way as to keep equipment working at normal capacity, that is, in such a way as to cause the level of real wages to rise with output per man, so that sufficient demand always exists to absorb the ever-growing output of the ever-growing stock of equipment.

Secondly, to preserve a stable level of employment it is necessary that any chance discrepancy between available labour and equipment should be quickly eliminated. This occurs provided that when there is surplus labour the real-wage rate rises less fast than output per head but at the same time outlay on the investment sector is maintained in such a way that accumulation in terms of productive capacity is speeded up in the manner discussed in the last chapter. When there is scarcity of labour money wages rise relatively to prices, the real wage rises by more than output per man and the rate of accumulation is slowed down. When this mechanism is operating the supply of capital goods is continuously adjusted to the supply of labour, and any tendency to surplus or scarcity of labour is promptly corrected.

It is only necessary to set out the conditions required for stability to see how precarious the preservation of stability is under the capitalist rules of the game. In what follows we will discuss situations in which the conditions break down because : (1) the rate of technical progress alters unexpectedly ; (2) the competitive mechanism becomes clogged ; (3) accumulation tends to vary relatively to the rate of increase of productivity ; (4) technical progress fails to be spread evenly throughout the system.

---

[1] For the time being we assume that increasing productivity is brought about without requiring any change in the time pattern of the processes of production. A more general treatment of technical progress must be deferred until we have discussed the problem of measuring capital.

THE PACE OF PROGRESS

The more rapid is the rise of output per head due to technical progress the faster will real wages rise (with a given amount of employment), but the more rapid is the rate of technical progress which the economy has come to expect, the lower is the level of real wages at any moment. This proposition can be unravelled by means of another comparison between Beth and Alaph. The labour forces in the two economies are alike and at the moment when the comparison is made they are in the same phase of technical development. It has been reached in Alaph by a longer and slower 'process, and the Alaph entrepreneurs expect a slower rate of development in the future than those in Beth ; they are carrying on a smaller rate of investment.

Since the rate of accumulation is higher in Beth, a larger part of the labour force (with appropriate equipment) is occupied in producing replacements and a smaller proportion engaged on producing consumption goods. Real wages are lower in Beth. In money terms, if the money-wage rate is the same in each, the price level is higher in Beth, and entrepreneurs there recover the initial cost of plant out of quasi-rent over a shorter period.

If full employment is maintained, the real-wage rate in Beth will rise more rapidly as time goes by and sooner or later it will surpass the level in Alaph.

It does not follow that if the pace of innovation in one economy changed to that of the other, the difference between them would quickly disappear, for the situation in each is moulded by a long past history.

Let us suppose that in Beth the rate at which innovations are being introduced falls to the pace obtaining in Alaph (whether because inventiveness dries up or because competitive pressure slackens and the rate of diffusion of inventions slows down). The immediate effect is that entrepreneurs with old-fashioned plants are pleasantly surprised to find that they are still earning after the date when it was expected that they would have to be scrapped. But if, as a result of this, orders for replacements fail to be made there is unemployment in the investment sector. Consequently there is unemployment also in the consumption sector and slump conditions prevail. The economy may take a long while to recover from this shock and it may sink into a long period of stagnation.

Contrariwise, if the pace speeds up in Alaph to the original Beth rate, some capital goods have to be scrapped before their initial cost has been fully recovered. The entrepreneurs who have installed new low-cost plant find that there are expanding potential markets at a level of prices just below the least that the high-cost producers will accept, and they set about expanding their productive capacity to take advantage of the situation. There is a rush to invest, which draws labour out of the consumption sector and causes real wages to fall. If the workers in Alaph are strongly organised they may set up an inflation barrier at the level of real wages to which they have become accustomed, so that the attempt to increase investment is frustrated. The entrepreneurs then make speeches to the workers pointing out their short-sighted folly — if only they would permit real wages to be reduced for a time they will rise far higher in the future. But lectures may not be sufficient to check inflation.

In each case there is a path which it is possible for the economy to follow to a new line of smooth development. Suppose that in Beth the entrepreneurs who find themselves with redundant amortisation funds promptly set about investing them in more equipment of the type already in use. A condition of scarcity of labour then develops (assuming that there was more or less full employment in the first instance) the real-wage rate rises and the rate of accumulation is slowed down in the manner that we have already analysed. When the wage and the rate of accumulation strike the level obtaining in Alaph (and the stock of capital goods has been appropriately adjusted) the Beth economy can proceed along the Alaph line without further perturbations.

In Alaph, when the rate of progress speeds up, the level of real wages would be held constant if labour from the consumption sector were drawn off just at the (now faster) pace at which output per man is rising, until the proportion of labour (with appropriate equipment) in the investment sector was raised to the original Beth ratio. From then on, Alaph can follow the Beth path from the point that Beth would have reached when wages there had just caught up with the Alaph level.

In each case such a gradual transition to a changed pace of progress is technically possible, but there is no mechanism provided by the capitalist rules of the game that can be relied upon to steer the economy on to the appropriate course. A prolonged slump in Beth and a sharp boom in Alaph are much more probable than a smooth adaptation to the change in the pace of technical progress, and each would have disturbing consequences for a long time after it occurred.

UNDER-CONSUMPTION

The mechanism which ensures that actual output expands more or less in step with the rise in potential output due to technical progress is the competition which keeps prices in line with costs, and so raises the real-wage rate with productivity. This mechanism tends to grow weaker as the economy progresses, for the more vigorous is competition between entrepreneurs the more rapidly do the strong swallow up the weak, so that the number of separate sellers in each market tends to fall as time goes by.[1]

Let us consider an extreme case of atrophy of the competitive mechanism. Money-wage rates are constant, and prices have ceased to fall with costs ; in so far as competition is still going on, it takes the form of advertising and salesmanship. (We assume for simplicity that advertising employs a negligible amount of labour, so that advertisers are, in effect, taking a share of the profits of productive entrepreneurs.) Once competition in selling has taken root, entrepreneurs whose production costs are falling (as output per man rises, with constant wages) find that they need increasing margins to cover

[1] At the same time fresh opportunities are created for 'small men' in specialised chinks of markets and in the interstices between the giants, but this does little to keep competition alive, for the small men find it more profitable to operate in the shelter of the giants' price policy than to stir up trouble by challenging them to competition.

increasing selling costs, so that (even without overt monopolistic agreements) price-cutting seems to be out of the
question.

Now, if the real-wage rate is constant the total volume of
output of commodities is constant. If, in the first instance,
money outlay on the investment sector is maintained, productive capacity tends to increase at a rising rate, for machines
of a given productive capacity are falling in cost as output per
head rises in the investment sector. But with a constant output
of commodities there is no use for more machines. (The
under-utilisation of plant fails to bring down prices because
of the atrophy of competition.) Moreover, employment in
both sectors is falling as output per man rises, and consequently the sales of commodities and the outlet for investment
are not only failing to expand, but actually shrinking. The
whole process goes on slowly, for in these conditions the
diffusion of innovations is sluggish (output per head may be
rising at, say, less than one per cent per annum) and the
strongest entrepreneurs may still be making profits, which they
invest in buying up the businesses of weaker colleagues, so
that no one notices that total output is shrinking and the
situation does not present itself to the entrepreneurs as a crisis
until the gradually increasing volume of unemployment creates
a political problem for them.

The socialist writers of a hundred years ago [1] who pro-
claimed that this extreme form of under-consumption (due to
the constancy of the real-wage rate) was an inescapable consequence of the capitalist rules of the game were evidently
exaggerating, but in a mild form it is an ever present menace
to the prosperity of a technically progressive economy (all the
more so to-day when a kind of remedy has been found in
accumulating armaments instead of productive capital).

When it is present in only a mild form, so that real-wage
rates are rising somewhat, though less than enough to keep
the economy at stretch, the corrective of reducing hours of
work may come into operation. When wages per man-hour
are rising, but jobs growing harder to find, the workers may
succeed in obtaining a reduction of hours of work without a

---

[1] *E.g.* Sismondi, *Nouveaux principes d'économie politique.*

reduction of real income per family, thus turning unemployment into leisure and improving their standard of life without increasing physical consumption. This keeps the growth of unemployment within bounds and an appearance of harmony is preserved in the stagnant economy.

The main defence against the tendency to stagnation comes from pressure by trade unions to raise money-wage rates. When they succeed, the stickiness of prices tells in their favour, for entrepreneurs may prefer (within limits) to accept a cut in margins rather than to alter their price policy. In so far as this occurs, real-wage rates rise. If by this means real wages can be made to rise as fast as output per man the root of the trouble is cut, and the economy can accumulate capital and increase total product at the rate appropriate to the pace at which technical improvements are being introduced, just as though competition were still active.

It may then happen that the most progressive entrepreneurs become the allies of the trade unions for, even with rising wages, their costs are lower than those of their competitors, and the rise in wages speeds up the rate at which high-cost producers are squeezed out of existence. Self-interest, humanitarianism and political *savoir-faire* join in generating the philosophy of 'the economy of high wages', and the trade unions, in turn, may become the allies of the progressive monopolists. A kind of live-and-let-live system is then established, and provided that real wages are rising somewhat (over the long run) no one is concerned to inquire if they might be made to rise faster by a more rapid rate of accumulation.

ACCUMULATION AND TECHNICAL PROGRESS

Accumulation weak. When the rate of accumulation fails to keep productive capacity expanding as fast as output per man-hour is rising, employment in terms of man-hours of work is falling. Harmony may still be preserved if hours of work are being reduced at the same time (by shortening the working week, or the working lifetime). Where this relief is not operating (or is operating too weakly), increasing output per man reduces the number of men employed (population being constant). This is commonly called *technological unemployment*, for on the surface it appears to be the direct consequence of the increase in productivity which is taking place, but in essence it is of the same nature as the unemployment which follows from a failure of accumulation to keep pace with an increase in population.

The appearance of surplus labour checks the rise of real wages, which causes surplus capacity to appear in the consumption sector. This further weakens the pressure to accumulate and generates all the more unemployment and surplus capacity. But technical progress, at the same time, itself tends to be slowed down. With growing unemployment the workers develop a Luddite resistance to increasing productivity, and, with hands always available, the entrepreneurs have little motive for bothering about introducing improvements. In short, when accumulation tends to be slower than the rate which technical progress makes possible, growing unemployment tends to pull it down ; at the same time the weight of its own sluggishness drags back the rate of technical progress.

Accumulation strong. The same mechanism works on the opposite tack, when accumulation is running ahead of technical progress.

With a given labour force and given technique, an upper limit is set to the possible rate of accumulation at any moment by the inflation barrier. When technical progress is going on and the competitive mechanism is working, the real-wage rate is tending to rise as time goes by. The inflation barrier is then moving outwards like the horizon of a traveller, for it is a fall in real wages below what they have been in the past rather than below what they might be in the present that brings it into operation. Consequently it is possible for the rate of accumulation (in terms of the growth of productive capacity) to rise progressively (the falling tendency of real wages due to an increasing rate of accumulation pressing against the rising tendency due to technical progress, without outweighing it). Thus it is possible for the rate of accumulation to accelerate up to a certain point (provided that entrepreneurs are sufficiently active to make it do so) without encountering the inflation barrier.

But accumulation cannot permanently continue (with a given labour force) at a faster rate than technical progress. When it has been faster for a time a condition of scarcity of labour begins to emerge, as the increment of new capital goods requiring man-power grows from month to month, just as it does when accumulation is running ahead of the growth of population with constant technique. (All the more so if the supply of labour per family is falling as working hours per lifetime are reduced.) Real wages tend to rise faster than output per head, the rate of profit tends to fall, and the increased demand for consumption goods tends to draw labour out of the investment sector, so that the rate of accumulation tends to be slowed down to the pace of technical progress.

But at the same time technical progress is being speeded up to keep step with accumulation. The rate of progress is not a natural phenomenon that falls like the gentle rain from heaven. When there is an economic motive for raising output per man the entrepreneurs seek out inventions and improvements. Even more important than speeding up discoveries is the speeding up of the rate at which innovations are diffused. When entrepreneurs find themselves in a situation where potential markets are expanding but labour hard to find, they have every motive to increase productivity; and the experience of wage rates rising with output overcomes the reluctance of the workers to assist them to do so.

In short, the capitalist rules of the game produce the most flourishing results when the available supply of labour is tending to shrink [1] (population is increasing little, if at all, and hours of work are falling) and the available supply of capital tending to grow, so that a rise in real wages (due to scarcity of labour) is constantly threatening a fall in the rate of profit, which technical progress is constantly fending off. In these conditions the economy is most highly productive (though not necessarily most agreeable in other ways).

---

[1] According to the basic assumptions of our model, the labour force is in any case large enough to ensure *constant returns*, that is to say, there are no economies of large-scale total production which lead to an increase of output per head merely because total output is increasing. This question is discussed below, Chapter 33.

BIASED TECHNICAL PROGRESS

So far we have assumed technical progress to be evenly distributed throughout the economy. How does the system develop when one sector is more strongly affected than the other? Let us first examine the situation when inventions and discoveries have been fully digested into the stock of capital. In Beth and Alaph the labour forces are alike; and the rate of output of commodities, the real-wage rate and the rate of profit on capital are all the same in each. The only difference between the two economies is that, owing to a bias in technical progress in the past, Alaph has a higher rate of output of commodities per man in the consumption sector and a lower rate in the investment sector, reckoning output in the investment sector in terms of machines of given productive capacity. A larger proportion of the labour force is employed in the investment sector in Alaph than in Beth and the cost of machines (of given capacity) in terms of commodities is higher. Looking at the situation from the point of view of a worker in the consumption sector, his output is higher in Alaph, but he has to part with a larger proportion of his output to get himself provided with equipment. From the point of view of an entrepreneur, quasi-rent per man employed in the consumption sector is higher (for output per man is higher and the real wage the same) but the cost of the outfit of capital goods per man employed is correspondingly higher, and the rate of profit is the same.[1] The technique of production in Alaph may be said to have a *capital-using bias*, compared to that in Beth, or the technique in Beth a *capital-saving bias* compared to that in Alaph.

Now let us suppose that technical progress in an economy takes on a capital-using bias — that is to say, innovations are

---

[1] For example, suppose that in each economy stationary conditions obtain, with zero profits. In each, 100 teams of men are employed, 100 units of commodities and 5 outfits of machines (of given capacity) are produced per annum. The stock of machines in use consists of 40 outfits in the consumption sector and 10 in the investment sector. 10 per cent of machines are replaced every year. In Beth, 80 teams are employed in the consumption sector and 20 in the investment sector. In Alaph, 75 and 25. In Beth, 4 outfits of machines are sold by the investment sector to the

made which raise output per man-hour faster than before in the consumption sector and more slowly in the investment sector. For simplicity we will suppose that for a time there are no improvements at all in the investment sector, so that a constant amount of labour is required to produce a machine of given productive capacity while a bout of inventions occurs in the consumption sector. The immediate effect of the innovations that are now introduced is a fall in employment in the consumption sector, for initially new productive capacity is coming forward at the same rate as before, while each new outfit of machines that comes into use in the consumption sector requires less labour to man it than that which it replaces. Unemployment checks the rise in real wages, but at the same time it is possible for the rate of accumulation to be speeded up. If this happens, at least some part of the labour expelled from the consumption sector finds employment in the invest-ment sector. The real-wage rate has risen (if at all) less than output per head in the consumption sector, and the rate of profit for the time being is higher than before. The situation presents itself to the entrepreneurs as an investment boom, though it took its origin in an outbreak of unemployment. After a time the stock of equipment becomes adjusted to the new technical situation and (if no further disturbances occur) the rate of accumulation and the rate of profit may return to their former level.

Conversely, if a bout of inventions are made which raise output per man in the investment sector, while leaving it unchanged in the consumption sector, the rate of increase of productive capacity is temporarily speeded up; scarcity of labour develops in the consumption sector, the real-wage rate rises (while output per head in that sector is constant) and the

---

consumption sector for 20 units of commodities (the wages bill of the investment sector). The value of an outfit of new machinery is therefore 5 units of commodities, and the value (neglecting interest) of the park of 50 outfits of machines of balanced age composition is $\frac{1}{2}(50 \times 5) = 125$. In Alaph 4 outfits are sold for 25 units of commodities and the value of the park is $\frac{1}{2}(50 \times 6\frac{1}{4}) = 156\frac{1}{4}$. Quasi-rent (in terms of commodities) per outfit of machines in the consumption sector is $\frac{1}{2}$ in Beth and $\frac{5}{8}$ in Alaph. In the investment sector the quasi-rent on 10 outfits of machines is one outfit, which is worth 5 units of commodities in Beth and $6\frac{1}{4}$ in Alaph.

rate of profit falls, until sufficient labour has been drawn out of the investment sector into the consumption sector to restore the balance.

THE GOLDEN AGE

When technical progress is neutral, and proceeding steadily, without any change in the time pattern of production, the competitive mechanism working freely, population growing (if at all) at a steady rate and accumulation going on fast enough to supply productive capacity for all available labour, the rate of profit tends to be constant and the level of real wages to rise with output per man. There are then no internal contradictions in the system. Provided that political events cause no disturbances, and provided that the entrepreneurs have faith in the future and desire to accumulate at the same proportional rate as they have been doing over the past, there is no impediment to prevent them from continuing to do so. As long as they do, the system develops smoothly without perturbations. Total annual output and the stock of capital (valued in terms of commodities) then grow together at a constant proportionate rate compounded of the rate of increase of the labour force and the rate of increase of output per man. We may describe these conditions as a *golden age* (thus indicating that it represents a mythical state of affairs not likely to obtain in any actual economy).

If we conceive the rate of technical progress and the rate of growth of population as given by nature then we may say that the golden age appropriate to the given conditions represents a state of economic bliss, since consumption is then increasing at the maximum technically feasible rate which is compatible with maintaining that rate of increase.[1] But this is not a very enlightening way of looking at the matter, for technical progress is not a natural phenomenon, and there is no limit to human ingenuity. Whatever rate of progress is being maintained, in a golden age, it would always be possible to progress faster. If the rate of accumulation were speeded

[1] In the language of Mr. Harrod's *Towards a Dynamic Economy* the *natural*, the *warranted* and the actual rate of growth of national income are all equal.

up (or the rate of growth of population were to decline, or the available supply of labour to be reduced by shortening hours, while accumulation went on as fast) the pressure of scarcity of labour, driving up wage rates, would induce more inventions to be made and hasten the diffusion of improvements already known, so that the level of real wages would rise all the faster. The limit to the rate of growth of wealth, over the long run, is set not by technical boundaries but by the lethargy which develops when the goad of competition and rising wage rates is blunted.

THE TECHNICAL FRONTIER

CHAPTER 10

THE SPECTRUM OF TECHNIQUES

IF there were only one method of production available for each kind of output in a given phase of technical development, an entrepreneur who had decided upon a scheme of investment (whether to create new productive capacity or to replace equipment which had ceased to be profitable) would have no doubt as to what kind of capital goods to install. We must now take account of the fact that in any state of knowledge a great variety of methods are technically feasible, offering different rates of output per man with different types of equipment, and that the choice between them depends upon their relative profitability at the ruling levels of costs and prices. This very much complicates the foregoing analysis without altering its broad implications.[1]

THE CHOICE OF TECHNIQUE

When an entrepreneur is planning an investment he wants to be sure, first of all, of not losing any capital (he must be confident of recovering the cost of an initial outlay from quasi-rent over the earning lifetime of equipment) and, secondly, he wants to obtain the maximum possible profit from the investment. In competitive conditions the price of his product, the money-wage rate and the prices of all kinds of capital goods are given, and (assuming a reasonable degree of tranquillity) he can calculate the rate of profit to be expected from investments appropriate to various techniques. Each

---

[1] The reader is warned that the argument of this and the following chapters is difficult out of proportion to its importance. After a long excursion we shall return to conclusions substantially the same as those of the last chapter. See below, p. 416, for diagrams illustrating the argument of this section.

available technique requires a particular outfit of machines and pipe-line of work-in-progress, a particular amount of labour to operate it, and yields a particular output per man employed. With given prices and wages, quasi-rent per man is greater the greater is the rate of output per man. A greater rate of output per man is offered by a greater investment in capital goods, that is to say, the higher is the *degree of mechanisation* of the technique the greater is the quasi-rent per man employed, and the greater also is the cost of the required investment per man. If a certain sum of money were invested in the equipment for a particular technique, say Beta, it would offer a certain rate of return. If the same sum were invested for a more mechanised technique, Alpha, less labour would be employed, total output would be less (this must be the case, for if Beta, with a larger wages bill, offered a smaller product than Alpha it would not be under consideration as a feasible technique) and the wages bill would be less.[1] If the deficiency in product is greater than the saving on the wages bill, Beta is preferred. Similarly, with a less mechanised technique, Gamma, employment (for a given sum invested) is greater and the product is greater. If the excess in the wages bill is greater than the excess in product, Beta is preferred. Looking at the same thing the other way round : to employ a given number of men with Beta technique requires a certain investment of capital, and yields a certain rate of return per unit of capital. To employ the same number of men with Gamma technique requires a smaller investment and yields a smaller return. If the deficiency in the return is more than in proportion to the saving on the investment, Beta is preferred. To employ the same number of men with Alpha technique requires a larger investment and yields a larger return. If the excess of the return is less than proportional to the excess in the investment, Beta is preferred.

Where the difference in profit per man employed is exactly proportional to the difference in investment per man employed

---

[1] In so far as the greater cost of the capital goods required for Alpha technique is due to their having a longer life, the greater productivity of Alpha technique shows itself in requiring less labour to maintain a given stock of equipment, and a correspondingly lower annual allowance for amortisation for capital goods of a given value.

two techniques yield the same rate of profit on investment and the entrepreneur is indifferent between them.

THE RATE OF PROFIT AND THE COST OF INVESTMENT

To compare the profitability of different techniques in this way it is necessary to know the cost of the outfit of capital goods required for each. This is by no means a simple matter, for the cost of equipment and work-in-progress to an individual entrepreneur does not depend only upon the sums that have to be paid in wages to get the work done, but also upon the length of time taken to produce it, and the value of equipment depends upon the manner in which its future earnings will be spread through time.

Anyone who commands purchasing power is at liberty to acquire a share in a business which is already a going concern, and so to begin immediately to get a profit on his money. Investment in new capital goods involves a delay between making outlays and receiving the return on them ; the loss of potential profit over the waiting period is part of the cost, from the point of view of an individual entrepreneur, of acquiring capital goods. Different schemes of investment involve different periods of delay, and different time patterns of future outlays and receipts, and in comparing the advantages of one with another this element of cost has to be taken into account. Thus the rate of return on investment itself enters into the calculation of the cost of any particular outfit of capital goods.

For this reason an unambiguous measure of the cost of capital goods requires a definite and universally applicable expected rate of profit. This could exist only, first, in conditions of perfect tranquillity, when future costs and quasi-rents are believed to be known, and, second, in conditions where the degree of competition and the ease of entering different lines of production are everywhere the same, and have established a uniform rate of profit throughout the system.

Such conditions, of course, are never found in reality, but we can set out the layer of the analysis with which we are now concerned by imagining them to exist. We postulate, then, that there is a uniform rate of profit ruling throughout the economy, which has been ruling for some time in the past and is confidently expected to continue into the future. We then employ a notional interest rate, equal to this rate of profit, in calculating the cost of capital goods.

Interest enters into the cost of capital goods both in respect of the period of gestation when equipment is being constructed and the pipe-line of work-in-progress filled up, and in respect of the period of the earning life of equipment.

First, consider the gestation period. An entrepreneur contemplating a scheme of investment normally reckons to buy some of the ingredients (materials or ready-made equipment) from other firms. For these he pays actual prices which include an allowance for profits at the ruling rate for the entrepreneur from whom he buys them. Another part of the cost is incurred directly in his own workshops. To both types of outlay he must add a notional interest charge, to arrive at the cost of the investment, and reckon this interest, in turn, as part of the costs incurred. Thus the cost of the investment exceeds the sum of the actual outlays made by the amount of compound interest on each outlay from the moment when it was made to the moment when quasi-rent begins to be earned.

Now consider the calculation in respect to the period of time over which capital goods are earning quasi-rent. Each investment, once made, is regarded as permanent (for even if a particular entrepreneur does not expect to remain in business indefinitely he requires to be able to recover an amount of capital at least equal to his initial investment when he winds his business up). The investment represented by work in progress is continuously maintained (as long as production goes on) by refilling the pipe-line out of the proceeds of current sales, so that once the investment has been built up it remains at the same level. Plant which requires periodical renewals, on the other hand, represents an investment which fluctuates over time. The entrepreneur reckons to collect an amortisation fund out of the quasi-rents that the plant will earn, to be re-invested when it requires to be replaced (whether by an exact replica of the original plant, or by plant embodying improvements that have been developed meanwhile). The amount of finance committed to the investment will therefore alter over the lifetime of the plant. When it is brand new and just beginning to earn, the whole initial cost is committed. When the capital is fully amortised the whole of the finance will be available in a liquid form ; when a renewal takes place it is once more committed ; and so on over an indefinite future. If plant is expected to earn quasi-rent at an even rate over its life then half-way through the lifetime of one incarnation of the capital it will have been half amortised, and the commitment of finance (without reckoning interest) will then be half the initial cost. The average commitment (without interest) over an indefinite future, is half the initial cost of the capital goods.

How does interest come into the calculation ? In practice firms often hold amortisation funds in a liquid form or place them in safe securities yielding a rate of interest much less than the ruling rate of profit. But this is because the world in reality is far from tranquil, and uncommitted reserves represent an insurance against possible losses. In our imaginary ideal conditions all finance can earn the ruling rate of profit. Thus amortisation funds (for the purpose of our calculation of the cost of investment) must be credited with interest equal to the ruling rate of profit. During each successive incarnation of the investment the commitment of finance is larger over the earlier than over the later years and the amortisation fund is larger over later than over earlier years. Therefore, calculating at compound interest, the notional interest on the finance committed exceeds the return on the amortisation fund. For this reason, the average commitment of finance, which constitutes the cost of the investment, is somewhat more than half the initial outlay on the brand-new outfit of capital goods (the difference being greater the higher the rate of interest). The excess over a half rises with the length of life of the plant. In the limiting case where the plant is expected to have an indefinitely long earning life, the cost of the investment is equal to the initial cost of the plant.[1]

[1] See *The Value of Invested Capital* by D. G. Champernowne and R. F. Kahn, reprinted below, p. 429.

If annual quasi-rent is expected to fall over the lifetime of each incarnation of the investment, either because more running repairs or greater current costs per unit of output are required as the plant grows old or because the prices of its products are expected to fall (or the difficulty of selling them to increase) as it meets competition from improved equipment, a larger part of the amortisation fund must be recovered from the earlier stages of its life, and the ratio of the cost of the investment which it represents to the initial cost of the plant is correspondingly less.

The mathematics involved in an ideally correct calculation of the relative costs of investment in outfits of capital goods with different prospective life patterns is no doubt too complicated to be serviceable to entrepreneurs, who in any case have to make their decisions in a fog of uncertainty; but the accounting procedures which they adopt give a more or less close approximation to it, according to the degree of sophistication to which they feel it worth while to carry them.

THE HIERARCHY OF TECHNIQUES

In any given phase of development the entrepreneurs contemplating investment (whether to increase productive capacity or to replace old plant) find themselves so to speak at a mechanisation frontier. When the available techniques, Alpha, Beta, Gamma, etc. are arranged in a hierarchy, according to the rate of output per man, the technique with a higher rate of output requires a larger investment per man (calculated in the above manner) and the frontier lies at the technique which offers the highest rate of profit on investment at the ruling wage rate, or between the two techniques which are equally profitable at that wage rate.[1]

The position of the frontier depends upon the ruling level of real wages. For each entrepreneur the choice of technique depends upon the wage rate and the cost of capital goods in terms of his own product. A rise in the real-wage rate (with

[1] In the following illustration wide differences in techniques are assumed for the sake of clarity. To avoid the complications associated with profit as an element in the cost of capital goods we ignore working capital and

given output per head) entails a rise in the wages bill in terms of their own product for entrepreneurs in the consumption sector,[1] and (in competitive conditions) prices in the investment sector tend to be such as to yield the same rate of profit

profit in the investment sector. We assume that equipment takes a very short time to build and has an indefinitely long earning life.

NUMBER OF MEN EMPLOYED: 50

Wage Rate	1			1·1		
Technique	Gamma	Beta	Alpha	Gamma	Beta	Alpha
Cost of plant	25	50	100	27·5	55	110
Product	55	60	65	55	60	65
Wage bill	50	50	50	55	55	55
Profit	5	10	15	0	5	10
Rate of profit	20%	20%	15%	0	9%	9%

INVESTMENT: 100

Wage Rate	1			1·1		
Technique	Gamma	Beta	Alpha	Gamma	Beta	Alpha
Employment	200	100	50	182	91	45·5
Wage bill	200	100	50	200	100	50
Product	220	120	65	200	109	59
Profit	20	20	15	0	9	9

When the wage rate is 1, an additional investment of 25 required to employ the same amount of labour with Beta rather than Gamma technique adds 5 to profit (the marginal return on investment is equal to the rate of profit, 20 per cent). An addition to employment of 100 men due to using Gamma technique with the same investment of capital adds 100 to product and to the wages bill (the marginal return on labour employed is equal to the real wage). Beta and Gamma techniques are therefore equally profitable. Similarly, at a wage rate of 1·1 Beta and Alpha techniques are indifferent. As between Beta and Gamma at the wage rate of 1 (or between Alpha and Beta at the wage rate of 1·1) a smaller employment of labour with the same investment reduces output and the wage bill equally; a larger investment with the same amount of employment produces an increment of output which bears the same ratio to the increment of capital as the rate of profit. (The relation between the marginal return on investment or employment to an individual entrepreneur and the marginal products of investment and of labour to the economy as a whole is discussed below, p. 307).

[1] This follows from the assumptions of our model. Where there are some commodities (luxuries) sold only to rentiers, whose prices move differently from those of goods bought by workers, the wage rate in terms of their own product for entrepreneurs producing the former does not move exactly with the real-wage rate.

as is obtainable in the consumption sector. Thus, for the economy as a whole the degree of mechanisation of the investment plans being carried out, in a given phase of technical knowledge, is governed by the level of real wages.

WAGES AND TECHNIQUE

If the body of technical knowledge with which an economy is endowed in a given phase of development contained a continuous range of techniques, each small difference in investment per man employed leading to an appreciable difference in output per head, every small difference in the level of wages in terms of product would bring a fresh technique over the frontier of profitability. Where there are wide gaps (which seems in general more likely to be the case, if we neglect minor adaptations) there is a certain range of wages over which each technique is the most profitable.[1]

Let us call the wage rate at which Beta and Gamma techniques are equally profitable the Gamma-Beta wage rate. Then there is a certain range of higher wage rates — the Beta range — at which Beta technique remains the most profitable. At successively higher wages within this range the rate of profit is lower, but Beta is still the best technique to use. At a higher, compared to a lower, wage the rate of profit obtainable with Beta technique is reduced by more than that obtainable with Alpha, for a given rise in wages reduces the *difference* between costs per man and proceeds per man in a smaller proportion for larger than for smaller proceeds per man.[2] Therefore as we ascend the series of wage rates there comes a point, at the Beta-Alpha wage, where Alpha technique is no less profitable than Beta. Similarly there is a Gamma range of wage rates, below the Gamma-Beta wage rate, and an Alpha range above the Beta-Alpha wage rate.

At one critical wage rate there is not only one possible technical position. At, say, the Beta-Alpha wage rate all labour may be employed with Beta technique, all with Alpha, or with

---

[1] Cf. Wicksell, *Lectures*, vol. i, p. 177.
[2] Cf. numerical illustration, p. 107 above, note.

any mixture of the two. Starting from a position in which only Beta technique is used, there is a continuous range of positions with successively larger amounts of capital per head, higher rates of output per head, and a larger proportion of Alpha to Beta equipment in the stocks of capital goods, up to the point at which only Alpha technique is in use. In all these positions the level of wages and the rate of profit are equal. Similarly there is a range of possible positions at the Gamma-Beta wage rate.

A CURIOSUM

As a general rule the degree of mechanisation of the technique brought over the frontier by a higher wage rate is higher than that corresponding to a lower wage rate, but it is possible that within certain ranges there may be a perverse relationship.[1] This occurs because of the element of notional interest cost, which, as we have seen, enters into the price of capital goods. If we compare outfits of equipment for, say, Gamma and Beta techniques, each employing the same number of men, then at the Gamma-Beta wage rate, the cost of the Gamma plant (with appropriate work-in-progress) is less than that of the Beta plant in the same ratio as its profit is less (it is this relationship which identifies the Gamma-Beta wage at which they are equally profitable). If we compare the costs at a higher wage rate, each is raised in a smaller proportion than the wage rate, since the rate of profit (and the notional interest rate that enters into the cost of plant) is now lower. Each type of plant has its own time pattern, and its cost reacts differently to the change in the notional interest rate. If the Gamma plant has a longer gestation period or length of life than the Beta plant it reacts more strongly to the difference in interest, and this effect may be so great that the Gamma plant is cheaper at some wage rate, relatively to Beta, in a greater proportion than its output is less. In such a case, as we ascend the list of wage rates, Gamma becomes more profitable than Beta, and the

---

[1] This was pointed out to me by Miss Ruth Cohen. The following paragraphs are concerned with a somewhat intricate piece of analysis which is not of great importance.

rise in wages moves the frontier from Beta to Gamma instead of from Beta to Alpha.[1]

It seems on the whole rather unlikely that cases of this kind should be common, for more mechanised techniques usually require heavier and longer-lived plant, so that the sensitiveness of the cost of equipment to differences in the interest rate is likely to be greater for more than for less mechanised techniques, and where this is the case the perverse relationship between wages and mechanisation cannot arise. We may therefore take it as a general rule that a higher degree of mechanisation is associated with a higher, not a lower, level of wages in terms of product.

SPECIAL CASES

Particular entrepreneurs may be subject to particular conditions which deflect them from using the technique that (at the ruling wage rate) yields the highest obtainable rate of profit on capital.

Finance. Where the minimum technically feasible investment in the equipment for the most profitable technique is large, entrepreneurs who do not command sufficient finance to embark on it may use less mechanised techniques and be content with a lower rate of profit, rather than lose their independence.

Management. An individual entrepreneur may lack capacity or inclination for managing a business of more than a certain size. This does not necessarily affect the technique chosen, but for the same reason as above it is likely to be associated with a relatively low degree of mechanisation.

Monopoly. When an entrepreneur enjoys a monopoly in a particular market he may make a higher rate of profit on capital invested for the production of the commodity concerned than is obtainable in the general run of industry, but the amount of the commodity which it pays him to produce is

[1] There are then three Gamma-Beta wage rates. As the wage rises from a low level the frontier moves from Gamma to Beta in the 'normal' manner. Then from Beta to Gamma in the 'perverse' manner. Then from Gamma to Beta again in the 'normal' manner. See below, p. 417, for a diagrammatic illustration.

limited, for, beyond a certain point, he could sell a larger quantity only by cutting price (or undertaking selling costs) to an extent that would reduce his total profit from the market. The choice of technique then depends upon what other possibilities are open to him. If he is not interested in producing anything except the speciality in which he has a monopoly, it pays him to invest in mechanising production up to the point where the saving on wages compensates the cost of the additional capital, that is, the extra interest he has to pay (or which he forgoes by not lending to other entrepreneurs) on the difference between the cost of capital goods for a more rather than a less mechanised technique. If he is in a favourable position to borrow, the rate of interest that he has to pay may be considerably less than the generally prevailing rate of profit [1] (and if he has capital to spare he may prefer investment in his own business to the interest he can get outside it) so that it pays him to make use of a more mechanised technique than that generally prevailing.[2] But if (as is more usual) it is open to him to invest (when he has exhausted the possibilities of his sheltered market) in other lines of production, where he meets competition but enjoys the same opportunities for making profit as anyone else, he has no motive for increasing mechanisation beyond the point where the marginal return on investment in his speciality is equal to the general level of the rate of profit.

Monopsony. A particular entrepreneur may be able easily to recruit a limited number of workers while it is impossible (or more expensive) to get more. Then if he can command

---

[1] See below, p. 230.

[2] In our numerical illustration, when the wage rate is 1 :

Technique	Output per Man	Capital per Man	100 Units of Output require approximately:	
			Labour	Capital
Alpha	1·3	2	77	155
Beta	1·2	1	83	83
Gamma	1·1	0·5	90	45

Beta is preferred to Gamma at any rate of interest less than 20 per cent, Alpha to Gamma at less than 12 per cent and Alpha to Beta at less than 8 per cent.

finance and wishes to increase his output he can do so by raising the degree of mechanisation. It pays him to invest up to the point where the additional product from the given number of workers covers the interest (paid or forgone) on the additional investment.[1]

Even in these special cases the generalisation that a higher level of real wages tends towards a higher degree of mechanisation still holds good. A rise in the level of real wages wipes out firms that cannot mechanise and leaves those that can in possession of the field. A fall in real wages makes it easier to survive, though it may be that a fall in the real-wage rate permits some small entrepreneurs to climb up to a higher level of mechanisation, so that there is a cross current running against the main tide.

A monopolist is likely to press mechanisation further in his special field when the profit obtainable outside is lower, and the monopsonist (unless he has such a powerful hold over his corner of the labour market as to be immune from a general rise in wages) has a greater motive to raise the product of his limited labour force. Therefore the existence of these special cases (and of the innumerable particular circumstances of individual entrepreneurs) does not destroy the validity of the broad generalisation that the degree of mechanisation is governed by the level of real wages.

RISK AND MECHANISATION

Except in conditions of perfect tranquillity a more flexible investment plan is to be preferred to a more rigid one. This tells in favour of techniques which require short-lived equipment and productive capacity which is divisible, so that in case of need part can be abandoned without the whole becoming worthless. In general (but not necessarily in every case) a

---

[1] In our illustration to raise 50 men from Gamma to Beta technique requires an additional investment of 25 (when the wage rate is 1) and yields an additional product of 5 (a marginal return of 20 per cent, which is equal to the ruling rate of profit). To raise them from Beta to Alpha technique requires an investment of 50 and adds 5 to product (10 per cent). From Gamma to Alpha, an investment of 75, and an addition to product of 10 (13·3 per cent).

more mechanised technique involves a larger amount of durable equipment and more highly integrated productive capacity, so that there is a tendency to prefer less mechanised techniques in uncertain conditions.

This phenomenon is of very great importance in an untranquil world, and accounts for the success of many small businesses using simple techniques in competition with highly mechanised giants.

Note. The argument of this chapter is illustrated and amended in the postscript on p. 426.

CHAPTER 11

THE EVALUATION OF CAPITAL

In the perfect tranquillity of a golden age, with a constant
rate of profit, expectations about the future are definite and
confident, so that the earning power of capital goods is believed
to be known, and their value has a precise meaning.

At first sight, therefore, it might appear quite a simple
matter to compare the ratio of capital to labour at different
positions of the mechanisation frontier, provided that the
conditions of a golden age obtain at each; but in fact we
shall find that such comparisons raise a number of perplexing
problems. We think that we know what 'output', 'profit'
and 'capital per head' mean until we begin to try to formulate
a precise and simple definition.

OUTPUT, CAPITAL AND LABOUR IN A GOLDEN AGE

The problem may be discussed in terms of a comparison
between separate economies, isolated from each other, each
enjoying a golden age appropriate to its own circumstances.
In each economy there is a different wage rate, or if wages in
two economies are at the same critical level (Beta-Alpha or
Gamma-Beta) the mixture of techniques in use is different.
A different wage rate implies a different rate of accumulation,[1]
and the conditions of a golden age require that the rate of
growth of population shall be in harmony with the rate of
accumulation, or that there is just the right rate of neutral

[1] This follows from the assumption that there is no consumption out of
profits. If we assumed that part of profit is consumed, we could compare
economies with different wage rates and the same rate of accumulation,
provided that the thriftiness of the capitalists was different in a compensating manner. See below, p. 259.

technical progress going on. Each economy, then, has a certain rate of output combined with a particular rate of growth of output, and part of its production is devoted to increasing the stock of capital, that is, to net investment. Since the ratio of net investment to the output of commodities is different for each economy these outputs cannot be compared as simple quantities in physical terms.

One set of difficulties flows from this difference in the composition of output in the different economies. Another set of difficulties flows from the fact, which we have already encountered,[1] that a different wage rate in terms of output entails different relative values of commodities, capital goods and labour time, so that there is no simple unit of value in which to reckon.

We therefore cannot embark upon comparisons between our golden-age economies without discussing what the concepts entering into the comparisons are to mean.

OUTPUT PER UNIT OF LABOUR

In reality output per man is a very difficult concept to define exactly, for in any actual comparison both the composition of output and the characteristics of the men are never exactly the same in any two positions. The basic simplifying assumptions of our model rule out part of the difficulty. We assume that in all our economies men are alike, each particular commodity is the same wherever and whenever it occurs, and the proportions of commodities making up the flow of output of consumer goods are always and everywhere the same.

Even these drastic simplifications do not dispose of the problem, for output also contains net additions to the stocks of capital goods, and these are different in physical characteristics when the techniques in use are different.

In the conditions of a golden age it is possible to demarcate net investment precisely within each economy. Where there is no technical progress going on this can be done in physical terms. Goods of all kinds (including work-in-progress) in existence at the beginning of a year are subtracted, item by

[1] See above, p. 88.

item, from those in existence at the end. The difference is
the increment of physical capital.[1]

Where technical progress is going on, physical net investment has no precise meaning, for each item of the stock of
capital as it wears out is replaced by a physically different item
of equipment. But since (in a golden age) the rate of profit
is constant and future quasi-rents are believed to be known,
the value of capital in terms of commodities has an unambiguous
meaning; worn-out capital goods are replaced by new types
of the same value, and the excess of the value of all capital
goods (that is, all goods owned by entrepreneurs, including
unsold stocks) at the end of a period over the value of those
in existence at the beginning, is the net investment of that
period.

The value of a year's output of a given labour force is
the value of sales of commodities *plus* the value of net investment. For some purposes it is useful to divide the whole
labour force in the same proportion as the value of output is
divided between commodities and net investment.[2] We can
then compare output per man of commodities as between two
economies using different degrees of mechanisation.[3]

We cannot say anything in general terms about output
per man in terms of capital goods, for different quantities of
labour in different economies are producing physically different
outputs. When, in two economies, the real-wage rates (and
therefore rates of profit) are equal we can compare the value
of output per man of net investment, but its physical composition is different. When, in two economies, the technique is

---

[1] This calculation cannot be made exactly in any conditions except
those of a golden age, for even if there are goods in existence at the beginning
and end of a year of the same physical specifications, the age composition
of items making up the stock of equipment is different when the ratio of
accumulation to the stock of capital is in course of changing.

[2] This is quite a different conception from the division between the
sectors of the economy, for the investment sector is producing replacements
of equipment, and the labour so occupied is contributing to the value of the
output of commodities, not to the value of net investment.

[3] In Alaph and Beth equal quantities of labour are employed and the
output of commodities is equal. In Alaph net investment is 20 per cent
of the value of output and in Beth 10 per cent. Then in Alaph 80 men
produce the same output of commodities as is produced in Beth by 90. In
Beth output per man of commodities is $\frac{8}{9}$ of that in Alaph.

the same, physical output per man of capital goods is the same; but the value of a given machine in terms of commodities is different. When both techniques and real-wage rates are different there is no common unit in which to measure output per man in the production of capital goods.

Thus an over-all comparison of output per man can properly be made only between economies in each of which there is zero net investment. Then, in each, the whole labour force of both sectors is occupied in producing and maintaining a flow of output of commodities, and output per man is a definite and measurable concept (under our simplifying assumptions). In any other situation, a comparison of physical outputs per man is subject to an index-number ambiguity similar to the ambiguity in the notion of a quantity of commodities made up of different proportions of particular consumption goods.[1]

THE QUANTITY OF CAPITAL

The evaluation of a stock of capital goods is the most perplexing point in the whole of the analysis which we have undertaken. Indeed, in reality it is insoluble in principle, for the composition of output, the characteristics of men employed and techniques in use are all different in any two positions, and in any one position the stock of capital goods in existence is not that which is appropriate to the conditions obtaining in that position, but is made up of fossils representing the phases of development through which the economy has been passing. The historic cost of existing equipment is out of gear with its value based on expected future earnings, and that value is clouded by the uncertainty that hangs over the future. Only the roughest kind of measurement can be made in actual cases.

Under the protection of our basic simplifying assumptions and in the imagined conditions of a golden age, there is no difficulty in measuring the stock of capital within any one economy. In each golden-age economy the physical stock of capital per man employed is governed by the technique of production and the rate of accumulation. The technique

[1] Cf. above, p. 27.

determines the specifications of capital goods required for each element in output; the rate of accumulation determines the division of the stock of equipment between the two sectors of the economy and the age-composition of the stock of capital goods of each kind. (The more rapid is the rate of accumulation the larger are the younger generations of machines of any given type compared to the older, and therefore the lower the average age of equipment.) The value of the stock of capital is then determined by the rate of profit ruling in the given golden-age conditions.

But even then it is by no means obvious how stocks of capital should be compared which belong to golden-age economies in which the rates of profit, or the techniques of production, or both, are different.

Four ways suggest themselves of measuring capital: (1) in terms of physical quantities of capital goods; (2) in terms of physical productive capacity; (3) in terms of the value of a stock of capital goods reckoned in commodities (or in money of given purchasing power over commodities); and (4) in terms of the labour time required to produce the capital goods. Each method of measurement raises its own problems of definition.

(1) *Physical Capital.* A measure in terms of physical capital goods has very limited application. When different techniques are in use, the who's who of capital goods in each economy may have few or no recognisable items in common, and even those items that they may have in common (say the railway system, or a particular kind of machine) have a different economic significance in a different setting.

For some purposes a very rough indicator of the degree of mechanisation, say in terms of horse-power per head, may be useful. But it is obviously extremely crude, and it is liable to be misleading, for a technique which uses very little horse-power may require a large amount of capital in work-in-progress just because its productive processes, including transport, are very slow.

Even when two economies are using the same technique because their respective wage rates lie in a single range (say, both are within the Beta range of wage rates) so that the same types of capital goods are in use in each economy in either sector considered separately, yet since the rate of accumulation is different in the two economies, the ratio of the sectors to each other is different, and the total stock of equipment in each economy is made up of different proportions of types appropriate to each sector. There is therefore an ambiguity about the conception of the two quantities of equipment which reflects the index-number ambiguity in the quantities of output.

Moreover, the age-composition of the stock of machines of each type is different in the two economies (the average age being younger in the economy where accumulation is going on faster). The only case in which an exact comparison between physical stocks of capital is possible is that in which the stocks are identical item by item and the two differ only in the number of complete sets of items in each.

(2) *Productive Capacity.* A comparison in terms of productive capacity is subject to some of the same difficulties. A stock of capital goods of balanced age composition, including the machine-making machines required to keep the stock intact, has a definite productive capacity in terms of commodities, in the sense that there is a definite rate of output that can be maintained in perpetuity with the appropriate amount of employment. On this basis we can compare the productivity of Alpha, Beta and Gamma technique, taking a balanced stock of capital of each type of an equal productive capacity. The superiority of a more mechanised technique then shows itself in the smaller amount of labour required to maintain the given rate of output.

This comparison has an exact meaning only for economies in a state of zero net investment. When, as is generally the case, accumulation is going on at different rates in economies using different techniques, the composition of output (which includes increments of capital goods) is different in each, and the comparison is subject to the same index-number ambiguity that we encountered above.

(3) *Value of Capital in Terms of Commodities.* The value of capital may be regarded from three points of view, as the selling price of a productive unit as a going concern, as the future profit expected from it discounted back to the present

at the appropriate notional interest rate, or as the costs incurred in building it up, accumulated up to the present at the appropriate notional interest rate, allowing for the profit that it has yielded already. (These represent value from the point of view of entrepreneurs. The value of a stock of capital regarded as the means of producing either wealth or welfare for the inhabitants of the economy considered as a whole is another story, and raises philosophical difficulties still more fundamental than those with which we are now concerned.)

In the conditions of a golden age with a uniform rate of profit ruling throughout an economy, which has obtained for a long past and is expected to obtain for a long future, these three ways of looking at the value of capital all yield the same result. Thus in each economy the value of capital has a definite meaning.

We can compare the value of capital per man employed in two golden-age economies in a straightforward manner. This comparison has a real meaning. It shows how much accumulation has taken place up to date in each economy (relatively to labour available). For some purposes this is significant and important as a measure of the wealth of an economy. But it does not tell us how the economies compare in respect to productive capacity, for, with different wage rates, stocks of capital of equal value in terms of commodities have different contents in terms of equipment. This is seen most clearly when we compare economies with different wage rates and the same technique of production (say, two economies in which the wage rates lie within the Beta range). Since the technique in use is the same in the two economies, examples of any given item of equipment can be found in each, but machines of the same specification and the same age had different costs and promise to yield different quantities of future quasi-rent when the wage rate for the labour which has produced them, and will operate them, is different.

Nor can we say that the difference is simply proportional to the wage rate, for different rates of profit are ruling in the economies in which the machines exist, and the notional interest that enters into their cost is therefore different. It might happen by a fluke that the lower interest rate in one economy was just compensated (in the case of a particular type of machine) by the higher wage rate that goes with it, so that the value of the two machines was equal, but it would be misleading to say that their costs were alike, or that they represented the same quantity of investment, for labour time and notional interest are not made of the same stuff and we cannot add them up as a quantity of cost, any more than we can add apples and strawberries as a quantity of fruit.

(4) *Capital in Terms of Labour Time.* We can divide the value in terms of commodities of the stock of capital in any economy by the wage per man-hour in terms of commodities ruling in that economy and so obtain the quantity of capital in terms of labour time. This is in some ways the most significant way of measuring capital, for the essence of the productive process is the expenditure of labour time, and labour time expended at one date can be carried forward to a later date by using it to produce physical objects (or to store up knowledge) which will make future labour more productive, so that capital goods in existence to-day can be regarded as an embodiment of past labour time to be used up in the future. But even when we look at capital goods in this way we cannot escape from the basic problem. The past labour time which produced to-day's capital goods was itself operating upon pre-existing capital goods or natural resources. (When Adam delved he already had a spade, and when Eve plucked fruit there was already a full-grown tree to bear it.) At any moment when work is being done to-day's labour is being added to the product of past labour, which in its own day was added to the product of still earlier labour. Under the capitalist rules of the game this shows itself in the element of interest in the cost of to-day's capital goods, but the reality that underlies it does not depend upon any particular man-made rules. It is deeply rooted in the technical nature of production.

Once again the issue is clearly seen if we compare two exactly similar machines drawn from two economies using the same technique but with different real-wage rates. We cancel out the difference in wage rates and express each machine as a quantity of man-hours of labour. Since the technique of production is the same in the two economies the man-hours that went into producing each machine were spread out in the same time pattern. In the economy with the higher wage rate the rate of profit is (and has long been) lower. The notional interest rate used in accumulating past labour-cost up to the present is therefore lower. The machine has a lower cost reckoned in terms of labour time, though the number of man-hours expended in making each machine was the same.

This difference between the machines is significant. It is not a mere arithmetical illusion due to the way the calculation is made. In the economy with a lower rate of profit capital is less scarce relatively to labour (because of some difference in the past history of the two economies) and the machine produced in that environment represents a smaller value of investment in a real sense, for the capital goods which were used in producing it were in a real sense less valuable in terms of labour time.

(5) *The Quantity of Capital.* The problem of measuring capital is a problem about words. The capital is whatever it is, no matter what we call it. The reason for taking so much trouble about how we describe it is to save ourselves from being tricked by our own terminology into thinking that different things are alike because they are called by the same name. Since no one way of measuring capital provides a simple quantity which reflects all the relevant differences between different stocks of capital goods we have to use several measures together.

By *physical capital* we mean a who's who of goods fully specified in every respect. By *productive capacity* we mean an outfit of capital goods that can be used by the appropriate quantity of labour to produce a flow of output specified in physical character and in its future time-pattern. By *employment offered* we mean the amount of labour that is required to man an outfit of capital goods for its normal capacity rate of output at a particular moment.

The value of a stock of goods in terms of commodities we shall call *capital* simpliciter, for this corresponds most closely to the meaning of capital from the point of view of an individual entrepreneur.

The ratio of capital reckoned in terms of labour time to

the amount of labour currently employed when it is working at normal capacity we call the *real-capital ratio*, for this corresponds most closely to the conception of capital as a technical factor of production. It is important to observe that though both elements in this ratio are expressed as quantities of labour time they are not in *pari materia*; one consists of past labour time, compounded at interest, embodied in a stock of capital goods, the other is a flow per unit of time of current labour.

In an economy enjoying the conditions of a golden age, productive capacity is increasing through time in proportion to the rate of increase in employment (the growth of the labour force with the growth of population allowing for reductions in working time per family) *plus* the rate of increase in output per man. Capital (measured in value in terms of commodities) per unit of output remains constant through time; capital (measured in the same way) per unit of labour employed rises with the real-wage rate; and the real-capital ratio (the ratio of capital in terms of labour time to current employment of labour) is constant. These conditions obtain within each golden-age economy, and provide the basis for the comparison between economies with different wage rates or at different positions of the mechanisation frontier.

CHAPTER 12

THE TECHNICAL FRONTIER IN A GOLDEN AGE

ARMED with these concepts, we may now explore the characteristics of the mechanisation frontier. Since the argument is concerned with the technique chosen in a given state of knowledge we will postulate that there is no technical progress going on. Let us suppose that we can draw up a continuous series of economies, each enjoying a golden age appropriate to its own circumstances, each at a different position of the frontier, or with a different wage rate, but with a common body of technical knowledge. A different position of the frontier implies a different rate of profit and therefore a different rate of accumulation, but we are not interested in this aspect of the matter for the moment, and we will simply assume that in each economy in the series the rate of growth of population is just sufficient to accommodate the rate of accumulation that is going on.

To simplify exposition we will suppose that the labour forces in all economies at the moment when the comparison is made are exactly alike in every respect, and that the price level of commodities is the same. Differences in real-wage rates are then reflected in differences in money-wage rates.

THE COMPARISONS

The series of economies fall into groups corresponding to the ranges of wage rates. There is a group of economies in which the Gamma-Beta wage rate rules (with a different mixture of Beta and Gamma capital goods in each economy), a group where wages fall within the Beta range, a group at the

Beta-Alpha wage rate and so forth. From the series we select some typical specimens. Alaph is an economy in which the wage rate lies within the Alpha range. Alaph-Beth and Beth-Alaph are two economies where the Beta-Alpha wage rate rules, the first having a predominance of Alpha equipment and the second a predominance of Beta equipment. Upper and Lower Beth are two economies where wages are within the Beta range, the first having a higher wage rate than the second, and Gimmel one where wages are in the Gamma range.

Wage Rates Equal, Techniques Different. We first compare Alaph-Beth with Beth-Alaph, two economies in which the Beta-Alpha wage rate obtains.

The annual output of commodities is the same in the two economies, for the wage rate is the same, and we have assumed for convenience that we are comparing economies in which the total labour forces are alike. Since the physical composition of the stocks of capital is different we cannot be certain of being able to divide the two economies into consumption and investment sectors in a comparable way (the division is useful only when the ratio of work-in-progress to equipment is constant),[1] but we can compare their rates of net investment in an unambiguous manner. The higher degree of mechanisation in Alaph-Beth means that a smaller number of workers are required to produce the given output of commodities, while maintaining the stock of capital goods, and a larger number of workers are therefore occupied with net investment. The value of net investment is higher in Alaph-Beth, therefore the total value of output is higher.

Since the rate of profit and the rate of real wages are the same in the two economies there is no difficulty in comparing the value of their stocks of capital. The value of capital per man (in money of a given purchasing power over commodities) is higher in Alaph-Beth in the same proportion as profit per man.[2] Capital in terms of labour time is proportionate to capital in terms of value, and the real-capital ratio is higher in Alaph-Beth in the same proportion as capital per man.

[1] Cf. above, p. 74.
[2] The situation is that shown with a wage rate of 1·1 in the numerical illustration (p. 107 above, note).

The ratio of net investment to the value of the stock of capital (which is the same thing on our assumptions as the rate of profit) is the same in both economies and productive capacity is increasing at the same proportional rate in each. (According to our assumptions, therefore, the rate of increase of population must be the same in each.) The greater value of net investment per annum in Alaph-Beth reflects the greater cost of capital per unit of output with the more mechanised technique.

There must have been some difference in the past history of the two economies which accounts for their different degrees of mechanisation. At the point when we are making the comparison each is enjoying a golden age appropriate to its own circumstances. The essential differences between them now is that the total value of output (commodities plus net investment) is higher in Alaph-Beth, and that the whole difference in output accrues to profits. The position of the workers is the same in both economies. The entrepreneurs in Alaph-Beth have the advantage of possessing a larger value of capital goods and of acquiring a larger value of annual increment of capital goods. The whole benefit of the higher level of mechanisation has gone to the entrepreneurs. Or, looking at the same thing in another way : the number of workers required to provide real wages for the whole labour force is less in Alaph-Beth than in Beth-Alaph, and the entrepreneurs can therefore employ more labour for themselves — that is, in accumulating capital goods.

Techniques Alike, Wages Different. We now compare Upper and Lower Beth, where only Beta technique is in use, at two different levels of wages. (We have already examined some aspects of this comparison under the assumption that only one technique is known.) [1] Since the same technique is in use in each economy we can divide them into sectors in a comparable way. Output per head in each sector considered separately is the same in both economies, but the ratios of the sectors are different since there is a higher rate of accumulation in terms of physical capital in Lower Beth (where the wage rate is lower and the rate of profit higher). To satisfy the

[1] See p. 77.

conditions of a golden age (without technical progress) employ-ment must be increasing at a correspondingly faster rate in Lower Beth. Profit per man employed in the consumption sector is greater in Lower Beth and consequently a larger number of men can be employed in the investment sector.

The two stocks of capital goods are made up of similar items, but in Lower Beth a larger part consists of equipment for the investment sector and the average age of equipment is younger.[1] In short, a larger proportion both of labour and capital is required in Lower Beth to provide for the more rapid rate of increase in population, and a correspondingly smaller part is available to provide for current consumption.

A comparison of the value of the stocks of capital in each sector in terms of labour time can be made.[2] Since the rate of profit is lower in Upper Beth the cost in terms of labour time of plant of a given specification is less, and the real-capital ratio is therefore lower in each sector considered separately.

It follows that we cannot say in general that the value of capital in Upper Beth is greater, for the lower interest cost may outweigh the greater cost of labour time in terms of commodities.[3]

It appears, then, that in spite of the fact that the stocks of capital in Upper and Lower Beth are made up of physically similar capital goods, while in Beth-Alaph and Alaph-Beth they were different, yet the comparison of capital considered as quantities of value is simpler and more straightforward between the latter than between the former. A difference in the wage rate is more far-reaching in its significance than a difference in the mixture of techniques at a given wage rate.

Technique and Wages both Different. Now let us make a comparison between Gimmel and Alaph, where both the wage rate and the position of the technical frontier are different.

---

[1] With technical progress going on this would mean that a larger proportion of plant is of the latest design.

[2] We cannot make any generalisation about the total stock, for capital per head (in physical terms) is likely to be different in the two sectors of each economy, and the ratio of the sectors to each other is different in the two economies.

[3] See above, p. 120.

We choose a pair standing in a normal relation to each other,[1] so that the wage rate is lower in Gimmel, where Gamma technique is in use.

The difference between Gimmel and Alaph can be regarded as made up to two components, those which arise from a different degree of mechanisation, such as we found between Beth-Alaph and Alaph-Beth; and those which arise from a difference in wage rates, such as we found between Lower and Upper Beth.

The output of commodities is greater in Alaph and the wage rate is higher, but we cannot generalise about the ratio of investment to consumption for the two sets of influences tell against each other. The higher wage rate tends to make the ratio of consumption to investment larger in Alaph (as in the case of Upper compared to Lower Beth); but the higher output per head due to the higher degree of mechanisation tends to make it smaller (as in the case of Alaph-Beth compared to Beth-Alaph).

The ratio of net investment to the stock of capital in terms of productive capacity is higher in Gimmel, where the rate of profit is higher, but we cannot generalise about the annual value of net investment. The higher degree of mechanisation in Alaph means that a unit of productive capacity requires a larger investment of labour time, and a unit of labour time costs more in terms of commodities, so that although the proportionate rate of increase of productive capacity in Alaph is smaller, the value of investment per annum may be greater.

Nor can we make any generalisation about the share of wages and profits in the value of output. The real-capital ratio tends to be higher in Alaph (as in Alaph-Beth compared to Beth-Alaph) because of the greater mechanisation of Alpha technique; but against this (as in Upper compared to Lower Beth) we have to set the effect of a lower notional interest rate, which reduces the cost of a given investment in terms of labour-time expended.

If the real-capital ratio is, on balance, higher in Alaph, *a fortiori* the value of capital is higher (because of the higher

[1] Cf. above, p. 109.

cost of labour time in terms of commodities). If the real-capital ratio is *sufficiently* lower in Alaph, the value of capital may be lower. This, however, can be regarded as a somewhat cranky case, for in general we should not expect the effect of a lower notional interest rate on the cost of capital goods to be great enough to outweigh both the influence of a higher degree of mechanisation and the influence of the higher wage rate.[1]

Let us suppose, therefore, that in the case that we have chosen the value of capital is considerably greater in Alaph than in Gimmel. We still cannot say in which economy the share of labour, relatively to the share of profits, in the value of output is greater, for while the value of capital is less in Gimmel, the rate of profit on capital is higher, so that the share of capital in the value of output may be either greater or less than in Alaph.[2]

These comparisons bring out in another way the dual nature of capital which we encountered when we tried to define a quantity of capital. From one point of view the stock of capital in the economy consists of concrete capital goods whose usefulness depends upon the productive capacity which they provide; from another point of view it consists of purchasing power at the disposal of the capitalists, and its profitability depends mainly upon the quantity of labour that it will command. The intricacy of the argument is partly verbal; it arises from the number of separate but interconnected meanings that have been crammed into the one word, 'capital', and it is necessarily somewhat laborious to sort them out.

WAGES AND MECHANISATION

A higher degree of mechanisation is associated with a higher level of wages. But it would not be true, in any simple sense, to say that the higher wage is a consequence of the higher productivity. If we imagine that Gamma were the most advanced technique known (Beta and Alpha do not

---

[1] See above, p. 120.
[2] This is sometimes expressed by saying that the 'elasticity of substitution between labour and capital' may be greater or less than unity.

exist), and that Gimmel had sunk into the state of zero net investment where all output is consumed by the workers, the wage rate there might be higher (in that condition) than the actual wage rate in Alaph. If so, we cannot say that the feasibility of the high-productivity Alpha technique is a cause of high wages.

On the other hand, it is true to say that the higher actual wage rate in Alaph is the proximate cause of the higher productivity, for it is higher wages which make a more rather than a less mechanised technique preferable from the entrepreneurs' point of view. It might be possible to have higher wages without higher productivity (provided that there was a lower rate of accumulation), but it would not be possible (under competitive conditions) to have higher productivity without higher wages.

Comparisons such as we have been making do not bring to light the basic difference between the situations existing in different economies. They show the relation between the wage level and the degree of mechanisation, but they do not account for wages being different in different economies. A difference in the wage level must be rooted in some difference in the underlying characteristics of economies or in their past history.

A relatively low wage rate and degree of mechanisation accompany a relatively high ratio of net investment to value of capital. A low wage (and consequent low degree of mechanisation) may be caused by a high rate of accumulation, in the sense that entrepreneurs are particularly eager and active. In a golden age the conditions must be such as to permit the high rate of accumulation to continue, but it may be that the activity of the entrepreneurs is itself generating these conditions by making it possible for the economy to support a rapid rate of growth of population [1] (or if we admit technical

---

[1] If we relax the assumption that an economy is completely isolated and already completely dominated by capitalism, we may allow also for the fact that a high rate of accumulation causes a rapid rate of increase in employment, by attracting immigrants or drawing workers away from a non-capitalist peasant population that exists side by side with the capitalist economy and provides it with recruits when employment is offered by the entrepreneurs.

progress, by keeping up a rapid rate of innovations under pressure of the competition between entrepreneurs each to expand his own business).

On the other hand, population may be increasing, so to say, for reasons of its own (or technical progress may be due to independent scientific discoveries). The causation then works the other way : there is a tendency for conditions of surplus labour to develop which is being prevented from actually producing unemployment because it keeps wages low and therefore permits the entrepreneurs to accumulate rapidly.

Finally, relatively low wages may be due to exceptionally high profit margins resulting from monopolistic price policy.[1] (To maintain the conditions of a golden age it is necessary that the entrepreneurs in a monopolistic economy should be taking advantage of the possibility of rapid accumulation which their high margins create for them ; if they do not, the age is far from golden and the economy sinks into stagnation.[2])

In every case where wages are lower the degree of mechanisation tends to be lower (with a given spectrum of technical possibilities). A low degree of mechanisation is a symptom of the underlying cause of low real wages, not a cause of low wages in itself.

[1] See above, p. 77.   [2] See above, p. 92.

CHAPTER 13

PRODUCTIVITY AND THE REAL-CAPITAL RATIO

WE must now consider how the comparisons are affected when our economies are at different phases of technical development, as well as at different positions of the mechanisation frontier.

The analysis is somewhat complicated. Within any one economy, in a golden age, the real-capital ratio and the rate of profit remain constant through time, but as between one economy and another differences in the real-capital ratio may be due either to a different position of the mechanisation frontier or to a different bias in technical knowledge as between labour and capital.

THE CRITERION OF NEUTRALITY

A different phase of technical knowledge is shown in a different spectrum of possible techniques. One phase of knowledge is superior to another, at a given real-capital ratio, if output per man is greater at that real-capital ratio. (One spectrum may be superior to another at high ratios and inferior at lower ratios. Then if each economy has developed technique along the lines suited to its own situation — the one with relative scarcity of labour having developed more capital-using methods of production, and the one with relative scarcity of capital having developed less capital-using methods — we cannot say in general which one is superior to the other.[1])

There is no direct way of comparing the degree of mechanisation of techniques taken from spectra representing different

[1] This is a question of very great importance for the so-called under-developed economies. They would do better by developing efficient methods of using man-power than by imitating capital-using techniques evolved in 'advanced' economies which enjoy conditions of scarcity of labour.

states of knowledge, but we can identify a technique by the wage level and rate of profit obtaining in the situation when it is preferred. On each spectrum a lower rate of profit is associated with a higher degree of mechanisation (ruling out perverse cases).[1] There is a Beta-plus technique which is chosen (in one phase of development) when the rate of profit is the same as that at which Beta technique is preferred in an inferior phase; and Gamma-plus and Alpha-plus techniques corresponding to Gamma and Alpha.[2] The improvements and discoveries which have brought the superior spectrum into existence consist partly in making it possible to reduce the amount of labour required to operate capital goods of a given productive capacity, and partly in reducing the amount of labour required to produce and maintain a given amount of productive capacity. (When improvements in one respect are made at the expense of inferiority in the other, as when labour per unit of output is saved by a more costly investment in capital goods per man employed, it is best to regard what has happened as an improvement within the old spectrum of techniques rather than as the introduction of a superior spectrum.)

A neutral relationship between the two spectra means that, with the superior technique, labour per unit of output and capital in terms of labour time per unit of output are reduced in the same proportion over the whole range of techniques, so that the real-capital ratio is the same with Beta-plus as with Beta technique, the same with Alpha-plus as with Alpha and with Gamma-plus as with Gamma.

When the superiority is biased in the capital-saving direction (labour required to produce and maintain an outfit of capital goods of given productive capacity is reduced in a greater proportion than labour required to operate it) the real-capital ratio represented by Beta-plus technique is less than that represented by Beta, and so forth. Contrariwise, with a capital-using bias, Beta-plus technique represents a higher real-capital ratio.

[1] See above, p. 109.
[2] If there is an appreciable gap between techniques and the width of the gap is different in the two spectra, it is necessary to use a more complicated notation with intermediate terms for the spectrum with the finer gradations of techniques.

PRODUCTIVITY AND RELATIVE SHARES

We now have three balls to keep in the air — the degree of superiority of one spectrum of techniques over the other, at the relevant real-capital ratios; the bias in the relation between spectra; and the point on its own spectrum at which each economy is operating.

Neutral Superiority with Equal Rates of Profit. The simplest case (which corresponds to two phases of development within a single golden age) is that in which the real-capital ratio and the rate of profit are both equal in two economies. One is operating Beta technique and the other Beta-plus technique, and the relationship between the two is neutral, so that Beta and Beta-plus require the same real-capital ratio.

Real wages in the superior economy are then greater than in the inferior one in the same ratio as output per man. Capital per man (measured in terms of product) is greater in the same proportion, and the relative shares of wages and profits in the value of output are equal in the two economies.

Superiority Neutral, Rates of Profit Different. The relations between the spectra may be neutral, while each economy is in a different position on its own spectrum. When the rate of profit in the superior economy is lower, it is operating with Alpha-plus technique, while the inferior economy is operating with Beta. Wages are then higher in the superior economy in a greater ratio than output per head at the Beta degree of mechanisation. The real-capital ratio is the same as that which would have been required in the inferior economy for Alpha technique. As we have seen, this is not necessarily a higher real-capital ratio than that required for Beta technique, because of the influence of a lower rate of profit on the cost of capital goods (a lower notional interest rate entering into their cost in terms of labour time). Nor can we say in general which economy yields the larger relative share of wages, for wages per man are higher in the superior economy, but labour per unit of output is less.

When the superior economy has the higher rate of profit it is operating a Gamma-plus technique, at the real-capital ratio that would have been required in the inferior economy

with Gamma technique.   Again it is impossible to generalise
about the real-capital ratio (comparing Beta with Gamma-plus
technique), or about the relative shares.

Biased Superiority, Rates of Profit Equal. The rates of
profit may be the same in two economies, so that the superior
one is operating Beta-plus technique, and the inferior one
Beta, while the real-capital ratios are different, owing to a
biased relation between the two spectra of techniques. Where
the bias is capital-saving, Beta-plus requires a lower real-capital
ratio. The wage rate is then higher, in the superior economy,
in a greater ratio than output per head, and the share of wages
in the value of output is greater. The workers are better off,
both because they are in a superior economy and because the
technique in operation requires less capital per unit of output.
Conversely, when Beta-plus requires a higher real-capital ratio,
the share of labour in the value of output is less.

The permutations and combinations of these comparisons
cover all possible technical relationships between economies,
but it is only as between pairs with the same rate of profit that
we can say, in general, how the comparative productivities in two
economies affect the relative shares of labour and capital in the
value of output.

INTERPRETATION

In spite of the extreme abstraction of our assumptions our
analysis supplies some pointers to the comparison of productivity in actual economies, provided that differences between
them are sufficiently marked to stand out from the haze of
index-number ambiguities which surround the measurement
of output, labour, wages and profits in actual situations.

When we find two economies with widely different levels
of productivity and real wages the high-productivity economy
may correspond (in our scheme of analysis) to Alaph using
Alpha technique while the low-productivity economy corresponds to Gimmel using Gamma technique; or the high
productivity economy may correspond to Gimmel using
Gamma-plus technique. The difference, that is to say, may
be due either to a higher degree of mechanisation or to technical superiority. The situation is not easy to diagnose.

According to our analysis the distinguishing feature of Gimmel is that it has a higher rate of profit, but the rate of profit which is relevant to the choice of technique is the expected return on investment, and of all data this is the hardest to find.[1] We might be able to compare the real-capital ratios in the two economies in a rough way, say by taking the book value of capital goods deflated by the cost of labour in terms of commodities,[2] but such a measure is very crude, and even if it were reasonably satisfactory it would be subject to the objection that a high real-capital ratio is partly a reflection of a high rate of profit, rather than the consequence of a low rate, because of the element of interest in the cost of capital goods.[3]

Nevertheless a marked difference in the real-capital ratio should be possible to detect, and a higher real-capital ratio is likely to mean a higher degree of mechanisation.[4] Therefore we may venture to identify the economy where this ratio is higher as Alaph, and that where it is lower as Gimmel.

Cheap Labour and Low Wages. When Alaph is the high-productivity country the level of wages is lower in Gimmel. From the entrepreneur's point of view Gimmel is a 'cheap labour country' in an obvious sense. The lower level of wages may be due to having more monopolistic entrepreneurs (or weaker trade unions), to a smaller inheritance of capital from the past (which in turn may be due to stagnation resulting from low wages), to a capital-using bias in technique, to a rapid growth of population, which has been absorbing accumulation without permitting capital per head to rise; or it may be that Gimmel has started late, and is carrying out a rapid rate of accumulation which will soon carry it past the position that Alaph now holds.

Whatever the reasons that make labour cheap, the low level of real wages is associated with a low level of productivity. We cannot hope to be able to apply our analysis with such nicety as to say whether the technique in use in Gimmel is properly to be called Gamma (that is, the technique that

[1] See below, p. 192.
[2] This differs from the real-wage rate when workers do not consume an average sample of all commodities.   [3] Cf. above, p. 121.
[4] We have not yet brought differences in natural resources into our analysis. These of course may be of a predominant importance in reality.

would have been used in Alaph if the Gimmel rate of profit were ruling there) or Gamma-minus (a technique belonging to a lower phase of development of knowledge), but we can give the distinction an operative meaning as follows: If missionaries from Alaph (the high-productivity economy) visit Gimmel and offer its inhabitants advice on how to improve their lot, it would be pertinent to ask to what extent the difference between the two economies is due to a scarcity of capital in Gimmel which can be remedied only by a long process of accumulation (with low real wages while it goes on) [1] and to what extent it is due to lack of knowledge which could be imparted by educating a handful of Gimmel technicians.

Cheap Labour with High Wages. Now let us suppose that it is Gimmel which is the high-productivity country. The real-capital ratio is appreciably lower there than in Alaph, but the level of technical knowledge is higher, or rather there is a better application of technical knowledge (roughly speaking, Gamma-plus technique is in use, though we cannot hope to identify it exactly) so that output per man and the level of wages are considerably higher than in Alaph. Because of the high cost of labour in terms of commodities the value of capital per man is likely to be higher in Gimmel than in Alaph; productive capacity per head is higher in Gimmel (any rough measure of physical capital, such as horse-power per man employed, will show Gimmel to have more physical capital per head). All the same, Gimmel is the 'cheap labour country', for wages there, in relation to output per man, are low enough to make a lower degree of mechanisation profitable. The wages cost in terms of commodities, from the point of view of entrepreneurs, of a unit of output is less in Gimmel, though the cost of an hour of labour is greater, and we can infer that the rate of profit on investment there is higher, though we cannot hope to measure it directly.[2]

The existence of a situation in which Gimmel (where the scarcity of labour is less) has the higher wage rate is not incompatible with the view that it is scarcity of labour which is the

---

[1] Or an import of capital (see below, p. 370).
[2] Cf. T. Balogh, 'The Dollar Crisis Revisited', *Oxford Economic Papers*, p. 284 (September 1954).

main cause of high wages.   The basic difference between the
two economies is that accumulation is being maintained at a
faster rate relatively to the growth of population in Gimmel
than in Alaph, so that the entrepreneurs are continually tending
to create conditions of scarcity of labour, but at the same time
they are continually fending it off by making innovations that
raise output per man.   The very fact that technical progress
is rapid tends to keep capital scarce by shortening the profitable life of plant, and there may also be a capital-using bias
in the innovations made, so that a larger amount of accumulation is absorbed per unit of employment offered in Gimmel
than in Alaph.   But these are minor points.   The main point
is that the high rate of accumulation is prevented from creating
a scarcity of labour because the effective amount of labour
provided by a given number of workers is being increased
sufficiently, by improvements in technique, to keep up with
the increase in productive capacity.   In Alaph the entrepreneurs
are walking to stay where they are, and in Gimmel they are
running to stay where they are.

This interpretation of our analysis must be made with all
due regard to the abstract nature of our assumptions, but at
least it serves to suggest some questions which seem likely to
repay investigation.

CHAPTER 14

ACCUMULATION WITHOUT INVENTIONS

So far we have been comparing positions of the mechanisation frontier at each of which the economy concerned was enjoying the conditions of a golden age. In each economy the rate of profit remains constant through time, and expectations about future profits are being continuously fulfilled, and therefore renewed, as time goes by. A change in the position of the mechanisation frontier in one economy is quite another story. It is an event taking place in time. It involves a change in the rate of profit and a revision of expectations. This introduces many complications into the argument and to isolate the essential point we will temporarily make some further simplifying assumptions.

SPECIAL ASSUMPTIONS

(1) The labour force is constant.

(2) There is no technical progress, and the spectrum of known techniques is fully understood and blue-printed.

(3) Entrepreneurs expect prices and wage rates in the future to continue to be what they are to-day, even if they have recently changed.

(4) The length of life of individual capital goods is short so that an individual entrepreneur can readily change his stock of capital goods from one form to another, without loss of value, by refraining from renewing items that have ceased to be profitable and investing accrued amortisation funds in items which he expects to be profitable.

(5) There is perfect mobility of labour between occupations.

(6) There is a large gap between techniques, so that the

amount of investment required to raise the labour force by one step (from Gamma to Beta or from Beta to Alpha technique) absorbs the accumulation of many years.

(7) There is a clear-cut distinction between the sectors of the economy, which does not vary with the technique in use (there are specific capital-good industries which adapt themselves to provide equipment for various techniques as required, including equipment for themselves). To start operating a new piece of equipment entails investment in work-in-progress, and, for commodities, this has to be built up by workers in the consumption sector, but total physical investment is governed by the output of equipment, for to operate each type of equipment requires a specific amount of work-in-progress.

These assumptions are designed to make it possible to analyse the transition from one technique to another as though it took place without any disturbance to tranquillity. The argument, for this reason, is somewhat fanciful, but setting it out in this way enables us to see the workings of the mechanism, which are hard to follow in the hurly-burly of short-period disequilibrium in which it actually operates.

THE PROCESS OF TRANSITION

Raising the Real-capital Ratio. Let us suppose that when our story opens the real-wage rate has been constant for some time at just a shade above the Gamma-Beta level, so that Gamma and Beta techniques are almost exactly equally profitable, with a very slight preference for Beta. A process of transition from one technique to the other is under way, and the existing stock of capital goods is made up of both types. The current output of new capital goods is also made up of both types, for the investment sector has neither the capacity nor the man-power to produce all the Beta equipment required for the transition in the twinkling of an eye, and meanwhile the stock of capital is being maintained partly by replacements of Gamma capital goods, which require less labour to produce per unit of employment offered and for which specialised equipment is already in existence (the slight preference of entrepreneurs for Beta equipment is offset by longer delays on delivery, so that the demand for plant of each type is adjusted to the supply forthcoming). By analogy with our former argument we may call this phase of development the Gamma-Beta period.

The rate of accumulation which is going on is just sufficient to offer a constant amount of employment, with a very small margin of unemployment, when capital goods are working at normal capacity. (If it were not so, a surplus or scarcity of labour would have developed and the wage rate would have been driven below or above the Gamma-Beta level.) With constant employment and a constant wage rate the demand for commodities is constant. Now, every time a Beta outfit of capital goods is substituted for a worn-out Gamma outfit, output per head in the consumption sector rises. But the market for commodities is constant, so that an increase in output per head entails a release of labour from the consumption sector.[1] The labour released from the consumption sector is taken on by the investment sector, and the proportion of Beta to Gamma type capital goods in gross investment is increased (the delay on delivery of Beta equipment is reduced as more labour becomes available to produce it). The rate of release of labour from the consumption sector is therefore increased, and the whole process gradually speeds up as it goes on.

Each month the number of Beta outfits of capital goods in operation is larger than it was the month before, and each month the total of quasi-rents is larger than the month before. The amount of employment in the investment sector is greater, the value of gross investment is greater, and the number of Beta outfits produced is greater. Thus the *increment* of employment in the investment sector, of quasi-rent and of output

---

[1] When the higher degree of mechanisation consists in a longer length of life of equipment (cf. above, p. 102, note), the saving of labour is in replacement, and will not be felt for a certain time after the new equipment has been installed. Meanwhile there is no release of labour when a given output is produced by a more mechanised technique ; there may even be a temporary increase in demand for labour, for it may happen that a new Alpha plant requires more labour to man it than a Beta plant of the same capacity which it replaces.

of Beta capital goods is greater each month than the month before.

The value of the total stock of capital goods, the annual replacement cost of capital goods wearing out, and total annual net profit, increase in step with each other, and the rate of profit on capital remains constant.

The situation resembles a golden age, so long as it lasts. We may call it a *quasi-golden age*. But it contains within itself a contradiction which will bring it to an end. After a time the whole output of consumption goods will be produced with Beta technique, and no further labour will be released from operating Gamma plant. If, after that stage has been reached, a further increment were made to the stock of capital goods (which are now all of Beta type) there would be no hands to man them and no market for their product.

A Rise in Real Wages. A new chapter in our story now opens. At the moment when the last Gamma plant has disappeared, the rate of output of capital goods (all of Beta type) has reached a high level. But now old Beta plant is being replaced by new, which requires no less labour to man it. Any increase in the number of plants creates a condition of scarcity of labour. To man up the last batch of capital goods produced, entrepreneurs are scraping up the remnants of the reserve of unemployed labour (which we assumed to be very small) and bidding up money-wage rates in the attempt to recruit more hands. At the same time, no new orders for Beta equipment are being placed; the prospect of a further increase in the rate of output in the investment sector has disappeared, and investment in expanding capacity to produce Beta capital goods (which was going on all the time that the rate of output of Beta equipment was rising) comes to an end. The high rate of output of Beta capital goods at the end of the Gamma-Beta period has turned out to be a maximum, and from now on it will shrink.

There has now been a release of labour from the investment sector. Consequently the wages bill of the investment sector has risen less than in proportion to the rise in money-wage rates induced by the competition for labour, and therefore the total of money quasi-rents in the consumption sector has also

risen in a smaller proportion than the wage rate. Prices must
have risen less than in proportion to wages costs, the real
wage has risen and there is an additional demand for consumption goods. The last batch of capital goods to be
installed in the consumption-good industries has thus been
provided with man-power released from the investment sector
and with a market by increased consumption paid for out of
wages.

This is the situation which we have already discussed under
the assumption that there is only one possible technique,[1] but
we may now examine it in more detail.

The real-wage rate is gradually rising, as employment in
the investment sector falls and output of consumption goods
increases. (We may suppose that the money-wage rate rose in a
single bound when scarcity of labour first emerged, and that
thereafter the prices of commodities gradually fall as productive
capacity in the consumption sector increases.)

Let us call an early date in the period of rising real wages
the Lower Beta period and a later date the Upper Beta period.

We may compare the situation in the Lower and Upper
Beta periods in various respects.

Wages and the Value of Capital. In the Upper period
quasi-rent per man employed in the consumption sector is
lower by the amount by which the wage per man is higher.
Relying upon the assumptions that the present rate of profit
is always expected to be maintained, and that the life of individual items in the stock of capital is very short, we suppose
that a uniform rate of profit is established throughout the
system (entrepreneurs have switched productive capacity from
the investment to the consumption sector fast enough to check
any tendency for relative rates of profit to get out of line).
The prices of capital goods (notional or actual) *i* are therefore
adjusted to their costs (including a due allowance for interest
at a rate equal to the new rate of profit on the capital required
to produce them).[3] In principle, the cost of an outfit of
capital goods of a given specification and age composition
may (as we saw when we compared Lower and Upper Beth) [4]

---

[1] See p. 81.   [2] See above, p. 104.
[3] Cf. above, p. 121.   [4] See p. 126.

be greater or less (in terms of commodities) at Upper than at Lower Beta, according as the effect of the higher real-wage rate is less or more than offset by the effect of the lower notional interest rate. But since the length of life of individual capital goods is short the influence of a change in the rate of interest cannot be very great, and we may take it that the cost of a particular set of capital goods (in terms of commodities) is higher than that of its opposite number in the Lower Beta phase almost in proportion to the rise in the real-wage rate that has taken place since that date. Looking at the matter from the point of view of the value of capital : annual profit on a comparable outfit of capital goods has fallen by an amount equal to the fall in its quasi-rent (the rise in the wages bill for labour employed to operate it) *plus* the rise in its amortisation charge (which is nearly proportionate to the rise in the wage rate) ; to arrive at the value of capital this profit must be discounted at a rate of interest equal to the rate of profit. The rate of profit has fallen more than in proportion to the annual profit to an extent depending on the rise in the cost of capital goods. Therefore the value of the capital has risen by the same amount as its cost.[1]

Though we have assumed the length of life of individual capital goods short, it is not negligible.[2] An individual item of equipment lives through a period of time during which a small rise in wages takes place. It will be replaced at a higher level of wages than that at which it was originally produced. An entrepreneur who is maintaining a given physical stock of capital experiences a rise in its value in terms of commodities, but this does not make him richer, for its reproduction cost has risen above its historic cost to a corresponding extent ;

[1] The assumption that the effect of interest on cost is small is in no way essential to the argument. When the effect of the rate of interest is so great that the cost of comparable capital goods is unchanged, the rate of profit has fallen in the same proportion as profit per annum. When the effect of the rate of interest is greater than this, the cost of capital goods is reduced and the rate of profit has fallen in a smaller proportion than profit per annum.

[2] We are treating as negligible the effect of a *change* in the rate of interest. This is a second order effect. Cf. D. G. Champernowne, 'The Production Function and the Theory of Capital', *Review of Economic Studies*, vol. xxi (2), No. 55 (1953–4)

or, looking at the same thing in another way : the value of his capital has risen in terms of commodities, but the purchasing power of commodities over capital goods has fallen proportionately. Amortisation quotas based on historic cost are always too small to replace worn-out equipment, and to maintain a physically constant stock of capital goods requires net investment of finance.

The Diminuendo of Accumulation. The amount of labour employed in the investment sector is smaller in the Upper than in the Lower Beta phase, and the composition of its output has changed. The output of the investment sector now consists of a smaller proportion of capital goods required to produce capital goods, and a larger proportion of capital goods to produce commodities. The rhythm of development of the process of transition depends upon the relation of the amount of labour required to man an outfit of capital goods to the amount of labour required to produce the equipment required to produce it. Each batch of productive capacity added to the consumption good industries draws away labour from the investment sector. The rate at which productive capacity in the investment sector must shrink is dictated by the rate at which labour is being lost. A shrinkage of productive capacity means that a certain amount of labour is released from making replacements for investment-sector equipment that is reaching the end of its life. If the amount of labour released in this way were to exceed the amount required by the consumption sector, in one month, the excess would be used to increase the output of capital goods for the consumption sector, and next month the loss of labour to the consumption sector would be greater; and vice versa if labour released fell short of labour required. Thus there is a definite time pattern of shrinkage of the investment sector and increase of productive capacity of the consumption sector which ensures continuous full employment of the labour force. The rate of rise of real wages is determined by the rate of growth of productive capacity in the consumption sector.

Sooner or later the wage rate rises to the point where Alpha technique becomes preferable to Beta, and the Beta-Alpha period dawns.

A.C.—F

A Shift of the Frontier.   When wages reach the Beta-Alpha level orders for Alpha equipment are placed, and within the investment sector a switch takes place to the production of capital goods required to produce Alpha capital goods.   The loss of labour to the consumption sector gradually falls and comes to an end.   The rate of net investment sinks to a minimum.   As soon as some Alpha equipment has been installed in the consumption sector a return flow sets in, the rate of investment begins to increase again, and a quasi-golden age establishes itself with real wages steady at the Beta-Alpha level.

The economy has moved, so to say, one step on the way to bliss.[1]   The wage rate is higher (and the rate of profit lower) than during the Gamma-Beta period, and it will rise again when the Beta-Alpha period comes to an end.

The Amount of Accumulation.   The total accumulation required to raise the whole labour force from Gamma to Alpha technique (from the beginning of the Gamma-Beta period to the end of the Beta-Alpha period) is equal to the difference in the value of capital per head with Gamma technique at the Gamma-Beta wage rate and with Alpha technique at the Beta-Alpha wage rate.   This may be regarded as made up of two components, the difference in the real-capital ratio at the beginning and end of the whole period, and difference in the wage rate.

The difference in the real-capital ratio, in turn, is made up of the excess of capital measured in terms of man-hours per man employed with Beta technique over that with Gamma technique, at the Gamma-Beta rate of profit, *plus* the excess for Alpha over Beta, *minus* (when the effect of interest is not negligible) the reduction in the cost of capital per head in terms of man-hours due to the fall in the rate of profit that takes place over the Beta period (the reduction in the cost of Beta capital goods due to a lower notional rate of interest).

Broadly speaking, the greater the rise in the real-wage rate that takes place over the Beta period (the gap between the Gamma-Beta and Alpha-Beta wage rates) the larger the amount of accumulation required to bring about a given increase in the degree of mechanisation.   The more accumulation is

---

[1] See above, p. 83.

absorbed in raising wages the smaller the rise in mechanisation due to a given amount of accumulation,[1] or the more is absorbed in raising the degree of mechanisation the less will the wage rate rise for a given amount of accumulation.[2]

The Perverse Case.[3]   Where there is a perverse relation in the spectrum of techniques so that Gamma (instead of Alpha) becomes preferable to Beta when the wage rate rises, the degree of mechanisation begins to be reduced when the wage rate reaches the Beta-Gamma level. Labour is released from the investment sector as it switches over from producing Beta to producing Gamma capital goods (which require less labour to produce per unit of employment offered) and absorbed by the consumption sector, where Gamma technique requires more labour per unit of output. When the investment sector is producing nothing but Gamma capital goods, scarcity of labour sets in in that sector and the attempt to check the out-flow of labour to the consumption sector drives up money wages. This only makes the production of commodities all the more profitable and the consumption sector refuses to part with labour. Unless the system explodes in a hyper-inflation, the consumption sector must win in the competition for labour, so that net investment shrinks and the real-wage rate rises. This rise in real wages continues gradually until a switch back to Beta technique becomes profitable (assuming that Delta technique is not preferable to Beta at wages above the Beta-Gamma level). There must be a 'normal' Gamma-Beta wage rate, above the 'perverse' Beta-Gamma rate, for

---

[1] Cf. Wicksell, *Value Capital and Rent*, p. 137.

[2] Our numerical illustration (p. 107) was set up on different special assumptions from those which we are now making, but the numbers will serve. For a complete transition from Gamma to Alpha technique the value of capital per head rises 4·4 times ; the real-capital ratio rises 4 times. The wage rate rises 10 per cent and annual profit 100 per cent. The share of wages in product falls from approximately 0·9 to approximately 0·84. The real-capital ratio is doubled in the Gamma-Beta period, and doubled again in the Beta-Alpha period. The value of capital per head rises 10 per cent over the Beta period. The numbers have been chosen for clarity and have no significance. They happen to show a very large rise in the real-capital ratio yielding a small percentage increase in output per head and it is for this reason that there is a dramatic fall in the rate of profit (from 20 to 9 per cent) accompanying a 10 per cent rise in the wage rate.

[3] This paragraph is recommended only to readers who take a perverse pleasure in analytical puzzles.

the reason that Gamma technique is preferred to Beta at a high wage rate is that the cost of its capital goods are peculiarly sensitive to changes in the notional interest rate;[1] as the rate of profit falls the weight of the influence on cost of the notional interest corresponding to it declines, so that at some point it must give way to the influence of the wage rate. On a spectrum of techniques containing a perversity, therefore, there is a low 'normal' Gamma-Beta wage rate, a high 'perverse' Beta-Gamma rate and a still higher 'normal' Gamma-Beta rate. The perverse case, where it occurs, can only be an excursion from the main line of development.

THE MEANING OF THE SPECIAL ASSUMPTIONS

(1) When population is increasing, the rate of accumulation that will generate conditions of scarcity of labour and so shift the mechanisation frontier is correspondingly greater. With a rapid rate of growth of population the contrary condition, of a tendency to a surplus of labour, is more likely to develop.

(2) The relation of technical progress to the analysis is discussed below.

(3) It is somewhat contradictory to postulate conditions of tranquillity when unforeseen changes in the rate of profit are taking place. On the other hand, if we suppose that entrepreneurs foresaw the rise in wages that would take place during the Beta period, we must suppose that they began to make the switch to Alpha technique before the wage rate has actually reached the Beta-Alpha level. But if they do so, the rate of rise of wages is slowed down. To have correct foresight each must foresee what the others are going to do as a consequence of the foresight which they also enjoy. The assumption of correct foresight, therefore, is highly fanciful.[2] It is more natural to assume that the entrepreneurs have some degree

[1] This implies long-lived plant. To fulfil our special assumptions, therefore, the rate of accumulation must be extremely slow, so that the length of life of capital goods is short relatively to the time taken to change the composition of the stock of capital.

[2] Cf. above, p. 66.

of foresight but that there is considerable uncertainty about the future.

When future prospects are uncertain, the meaning of the rate of profit on investment becomes hazy; the meaning of realised profits is ambiguous, for they may be reckoned on historic cost or on reproduction cost, and the relation between the two is shifting as the situation develops. The whole analysis then becomes blurred, though it can still be applied in a broad and rough way.

(4) Where the length of life of plant is long relatively to the pace at which changes are going on, it is impossible for equilibrium in relative rates of profit to be preserved during the transition. For instance, when the output of Beta capital goods begins to shrink below the maximum reached at the end of the Gamma-Beta period, plant specialised to their production becomes permanently redundant, and its owners suffer a capital loss.[1]

When we cannot assume a uniform rate of profit on all kinds of capital we cannot say in general terms what happens to the prices of newly produced capital goods. When there is unused capacity in shipyards, what governs the price of ships?[2] The answer depends upon the intensity of competition and the price policies pursued in the shipbuilding industry. We shall return to this question later. Meanwhile we must observe that it introduces another patch of haziness into the analysis, for it means that the relation between the rate of investment in physical terms and in terms of value is highly variable.

(5) It is obvious enough that without the assumption of perfect mobility of labour between the sectors the whole analysis would be much more complicated. In particular, it would be impossible to generalise about the time pattern of the processes going on in the three periods of the transition from Gamma to Alpha technique, for this depends upon a movement of labour to and fro between the sectors.

(6) When the amount of accumulation required to increase the degree of mechanisation by one step is small, or the rate of accumulation is rapid in relation to the size of a step, so

---

[1] Cf. above, p. 82, note.   [2] See below, p. 189.

that the time taken by one phase of the transition is short in relation to the length of life of capital goods, items dating from an earlier period and belonging to a lower technique will still be in use, earning some quasi-rent (though less than was expected when they were constructed) while the transition to higher techniques is going on.   Then Delta, Gamma and Beta techniques are being operated when the first Alpha capital is installed.   This makes it impossible to generalise in a simple way about output, profits and the division of the labour force between the sectors in each period.   Moreover the phases of the transition overlap and interfere with each other.   Some Delta plant may be finally rendered unprofitable by a rise of wages during the Beta period.   It is then replaced by Beta plant, releasing labour (for Delta requires more labour per unit of output) and checking the rise in the wage rate.   The analysis then becomes extremely intricate.   However, the main mechanism that the analysis displays is still at work.   The contrary pulls of accumulation creating scarcity of labour and mechanisation relieving it are operating against each other in the manner shown, though no longer alternating in time.   The special assumptions were made in order to see the operation in detail in slow motion.   Once the principle is clear we can speed up the picture to make it look more lifelike.

(7) The possibility of under-capacity working removes the rigidity of the relation between work-in-progress and equipment, so that the physical amount of investment required to build up productive capacity ceases to be unambiguously determined by the technique in operation.   This adds to the general haziness of the value of investment.

INTERPRETATION

It is impossible to make any application of the foregoing analysis as it stands.   The adaptation of the stock of capital to a shift of the mechanisation frontier (however small) must take a considerable time, and during that time inventions and discoveries are made.   Moreover the very process of adaptation involves the acquisition of fresh know how, and discoveries may be made in the course of adapting technique to a change in the level of wages which it would have been profitable to introduce at the old level if it had been thought of. The spectrum of techniques retains its form for long periods only in stagnant economies where accumulation is very sluggish. We should not expect to find in reality an economy in which the ratio of capital to labour is rising appreciably in a constant state of technical knowledge, and it is only in such a case that the foregoing analysis applies.

The analysis has been set out with so much elaboration not to provide a model for actual economies but in order to guard against a confusion of thought into which it is only too easy to fall. The proposition that an increase in mechanisation is associated with a fall in the rate of profit and rise in real wages is liable to be confused with the doctrine that increasing mechanisation causes profits to fall and wages to rise.[1] Our argument brings out the fact that it is accumulation as such which tends to raise wages, while mechanisation checks the fall in the rate of profit that would occur if accumulation continued in the absence of scope for mechanisation.

This distinction is of the utmost importance, and becomes all the more significant (as we shall see in a moment) when technical progress is brought into the picture.

Our analysis is significant also in another way. A failure of accumulation to be maintained in actual economies is often attributed to a 'lack of investment opportunities' but, in a technical sense, there is never a lack of investment opportunities till bliss has been reached.[2] There is always a use for more capital so long as it is possible to raise the degree of mechanisation. And even if inventiveness had completely dried up, and the highest known technique was already being exploited, further accumulation could be absorbed by rising real wages until the rate of profit fell to zero.

The conception which underlies 'the failure of investment opportunities' is rather that the capitalist rules of the game create a resistance to a rise in the ratio of capital to labour when it entails a fall in the rate of profit. When, say Beth has been enjoying a golden age with a certain rate of profit at

---

[1] By lowering the 'marginal productivity of capital' and raising that of labour (see below, p. 310).   [2] See above, p. 83.

the Beta real-capital ratio, and then finds itself in a situation (in the absence of technical progress) where the rate of growth of population has slowed down, it ought, to maintain harmony, to continue accumulating and raise the economy to the Alpha degree of mechanisation.   But it is much easier from the entrepreneurs' point of view to continue along the line of one golden age than to go over the corner into another that lies, so to say, above it.   To make the transition requires accumulation to be maintained in face of a falling rate of profit on investment, and requires the development of techniques of a higher degree of mechanisation than any yet exploited.   If the entrepreneurs in Beth, in the situation that we have imagined, cannot supplement the labour force by calling in immigrants (and do not make technical improvements) they are very likely to fail to maintain the rate of accumulation. They jib, so to speak, at the fall in the rate of profit which a rise in the ratio of capital to labour would entail.[1]   They cannot thus succeed in maintaining the rate of profit, for each, by reducing his rate of investment, narrows the market for the rest, and the only consequence of refusing to accept a fall in profits due to a rise in wages is to precipitate a fall due to a slackening of demand.[2]   For each, in that situation, the 'failure of investment opportunities' becomes real enough, for in stagnant conditions it is impossible to see outlets for investment that promise to be profitable to the individual who undertakes them.   But if all together pushed ahead, each would find opportunities in raising mechanisation ; and, though the rate of profit would be lower than it had been in the preceding golden age, the total annual profit obtainable would be higher than in the stagnant condition induced by their own inertia.

It is true that, at some stage on the way to bliss in the absence of technical progress, total annual profit, as well as the rate of profit, must begin to vanish.   Then sooner or later the rules of the capitalist game became unplayable, and the economy is presented with a choice between sinking into permanent stagnation and adopting a different set of rules.

[1] The influence of monetary policy is discussed below, p. 238.
[2] We are assuming no consumption out of profits. An alternative way out of the impasse is for rentiers to increase the ratio of consumption to investment.

CHAPTER 15

A SURPLUS OF LABOUR

To examine the other side of the medal (a surplus of labour leading to a falling degree of mechanisation) we reimpose the special assumptions, except that we now assume that in the economy concerned the supply of labour available for employment has recently begun to increase. This situation is not exactly symmetrical with the former one, for now labour and capital are both increasing, while formerly only capital was increasing.

THE PROCESS OF TRANSITION

A Falling Real-capital Ratio.—When the story begins all labour is employed with Alpha equipment and the rate of output of the investment sector (all of Alpha capital goods) is that which, in our former story, was established at the end of the Beta-Alpha period. Now the labour force is increasing and new Alpha equipment can be manned without difficulty. If the rate at which labour is becoming available just matched the rate at which employment offered was rising, the economy would settle into a golden age at the Alpha real-capital ratio with the Beta-Alpha rate of profit. We will suppose that the increase in the labour force is somewhat greater than this, and that the real-wage rate has dropped a little below the Beta-Alpha level. Beta technique is therefore slightly preferable to Alpha. An Alpha-Beta period has just begun. An outfit of Beta equipment offers more employment than an Alpha outfit of the same value. As the output of the investment sector is gradually switched from Alpha to Beta equipment, the annual increment of employment offered rises, and the consumption sector recruits the labour newly becoming available *plus* a gradually increasing number released from the investment sector. As in our former story there is one time-pattern for the transition which is compatible with quasi-golden-age conditions at a constant rate of profit.

A Breathing Space. When all labour is equipped for Beta technique the annual rise in the increment of employment offered comes to an end. If the increment of employment offered (determined by the rate of output of Beta equipment which has now been reached), when it is thus temporarily stabilised, happens to coincide with the rate at which labour is forthcoming, the economy moves into a golden age with the Beta real-capital ratio at the Beta-Alpha rate of profit. (There was no such possibility in the former case, for with a constant labour force and constant technical knowledge there is no golden-age position short of bliss.)

A Fall in Real Wages. If the rate of growth of the labour force is greater than this, a surplus of unemployed labour gradually appears, and sooner or later the weak bargaining position of workers leads to a fall in money-wage rates (consumption per head has already fallen, for the employed workers are supporting their unemployed relations). The economy, as we have seen,[1] is now in danger of falling into stagnation, for, if outlay on investment is reduced in proportion to the cost of capital goods, employment in the investment sector remains constant at the level reached at the end of the Alpha-Beta period, the rate of profit fails to rise, and the real-wage rate falls as the result of the stickiness of prices.

Let us suppose that this danger is avoided because entrepreneurs keep up money outlay on investment, when the money-wage rate falls, sufficiently to increase employment in the investment sector. Again it is possible for a golden age to set in ; this time at the Beta real-capital ratio with the Lower Beta rate of profit. Assuming that the growth of the labour force is larger than can be accommodated in such a position, the wage rate continues to fall ; the back flow of labour to the investment sector goes on, and the annual increment of unemployment gradually falls as the increment of employment offered gradually catches up upon the increment of labour becoming available.

[1] See p. 79.

So far as the value of capital is concerned, the situation is symmetrical with that in the Beta period which we have already examined. Each item of capital is replaced at less than its historic cost. There has been a book-keeping fall in capital values [1] accompanied by a rise in the purchasing power of capital goods over commodities.

When the real-wage rate falls to the Gamma-Beta level, a switch to Gamma technique begins. The annual increment of employment offered jumps to a higher level and the whole story is repeated at a lower wage rate.

Wages and Employment. The increase in employment which comes about as the transition from Alpha to Gamma technique runs its course cannot be said, in any simple sense, to be due to the fact that Gamma technique requires more labour per unit of output than Alpha, for (as we have already seen) the adjustment of employment offered to the available supply of labour can come about just as well if there is only one technique known, provided that falling money wages induce an increase in employment in the investment sector. And if investment in physical terms did not increase, the rate of profit would not rise when money wages fell and the de-mechanisation of technique would not take place even though Gamma methods were well known. Rather the possibility of using less mechanised techniques may be said to limit the fall in real wages required to cause surplus labour to be absorbed into employment. Just as a rise in the degree of mechanisation limits the fall in the rate of profit which a scarcity of labour would otherwise cause, so a reduction in the degree of mechanisation limits the fall in real wages that a surplus of labour would otherwise cause.

At the same time, the existence of a wide spectrum of techniques reinforces the mechanism (which, however, remains very imperfect) by which accumulation adjusts itself to the available supply of labour, and makes it easier for the economy to find a harmonious course of development than it would be if technical possibilities (at any given phase of knowledge) were narrowly limited.

[1] Assuming, as before, that the effect of rise in the notional interest rate is weak relatively to the effect of the fall in real wages.

INTERPRETATION

The story of an economy in which technique is demechanised under the influence of falling real wages seems even more artificial than the story of the degree of mechanisation rising in a given state of knowledge. The artificiality lies precisely in the concept of a given state of knowledge. In reality techniques are not fully blue-printed before they are about to be used. The spectrum of techniques is a real phenomenon, but a very amorphous one. The possibility of using less or more mechanised techniques than those actually being operated is known only in a vague and general way. When a new technique is to be applied it requires adaptation and a period of 'teething troubles' quite as much when it is introduced in response to a change in costs as when it follows from a new discovery.

Now, an economy where there is a growing surplus of labour is, in general, one where accumulation is sluggish and entrepreneurs lacking in vigour. They are likely to be just as sluggish in devising labour-using techniques as they have been in accumulating capital, and the very same characteristics that make capital scarce prevent the resulting real-capital ratio from being exploited to the best advantage. Thus surplus labour is more likely to be left in quasi-permanent unemployment than to be absorbed by a demechanisation of technique.

A surplus of labour may be created suddenly, by massive immigration. In that case investment may go for a time into lower techniques than were used by the old inhabitants. But if the economy is vigorous the impetus to accumulation given by the new supply of labour may soon carry it forward, so that within a few years the former real-capital ratio is restored or surpassed.

Massive destruction of capital goods in war creates surplus labour, but it is usually not worth while to devise special techniques to employ it, and entrepreneurs aim rather to restore the formerly orthodox methods of production. (The famous suggestion for running the Ruhr railways in 1945 by teams of bicyclists was not taken seriously.)

For these reasons the phenomenon of a demechanisation of technique, taking place through time, is not likely to be common, though the phenomenon of the degree of mechanisation being prevented from rising by abundance of labour is present, in greater or less degree, in any economy that has not reached bliss, that is, in all economies ever known.

COLONIAL INVESTMENT

It is interesting to consider an economy in which one investment sector supplies two distinct consumption sectors. Entrepreneurs from a country in which industry is highly developed undertake investment in another part of the world where there is abundant surplus labour available at low real wages.

It does not follow, as we have seen,[1] that labour is dearer in the home country, but let us suppose that the discrepancy in wages is greater than in efficiency, so that the low-wage country provides cheap labour for operating machines, though it is incapable of producing them. The entrepreneurs import machinery from the home country. According to our analysis they should find it profitable to use a less mechanised technique abroad than at home.[2] But the difference in profitability would have to be large to make it worth while to devise a special technique (all the more so if there are economies of scale in the production of machines which would be lost by increasing the number of types produced). It is much less troublesome to use the same methods in both countries so far as mechanised production is concerned. On the other hand, investment on the spot, say in road-building and local transport, may be carried out with an extremely low real-capital ratio.

DISGUISED UNEMPLOYMENT

When there is persistent unemployment in a stagnant economy the redundant workers may take to employing

---

[1] See p. 137.

[2] In our numerical illustration (p. 107, note) the rate of profit on Gamma technique is 20 per cent at the wage rate of 1 and zero at 1·1, while on Alpha it is 15 per cent at 1 and 9 per cent at 1·1. If wages for labour operating machines are 1 while the cost of machines is governed by a wage of 1·1, the profit on Gamma would be 18 per cent and on Alpha 13·6 per cent.

themselves with tiny quantities of capital (say as shoe-blacks and pedlars) or by selling their services direct to consumers (as domestic servants, porters, odd-jobmen, etc.). This kind of occupation is usually described as disguised unemployment. From a formal point of view it may be regarded as an extreme kind of demechanisation of technique. The possibility of making a living in this way sets a bottom to the fall in real wages and so to the level of technique in regular capitalist industry. When free land is available, this bottom limit is set at a relatively high level,[1] while emigration may reverse the whole position, turning redundancy of labour into scarcity.

[1] Cf. E. Rothbarth, 'Causes of the Superior Efficiency of U.S.A. Industry as compared with British Industry', *Economic Journal* (September 1946).

ACCUMULATION AND TECHNICAL PROGRESS

CHAPTER 16

ACCUMULATION WITH NEUTRAL TECHNICAL PROGRESS

WE may now examine technical progress in slow motion in the same manner as we have examined shifts in the mechanisation frontier. We adopt the same special assumption as before, except that now neutral inventions are being made. They come forward just so frequently, relatively to the rate at which accumulation is going on, as to permit a steady rate of accumulation with capital goods appropriate to no more than two phases of development co-existing at any time (there are only two players in the game of leap-frog).[1]

The argument covers the same ground as that of Chapter 9 in more detail and with the added complications introduced by the existence of a spectrum of techniques.

NEUTRAL INNOVATIONS

When our story opens, the rate of profit has long been constant, and is expected to remain so. At this particular moment, nearly all labour is employed with one technique, Beta, which has recently superseded Beta-minus; but the most progressive firms have meanwhile developed a superior technique, Beta-plus, and a small part of the labour force is engaged in filling a pipe-line in the investment sector with capital goods appropriate to Beta-plus. The relation of Beta-plus to Beta technique is neutral: that is to say output per head is raised by it in the investment sector (in terms of productive capacity) in the same ratio as in the consumption sector. As Beta-plus equipment begins to be installed in the consumption

---

[1] Cf. above, p. 86.

sector in place of worn-out Beta equipment, the output of commodities rises, and their prices fall relatively to money wages (either prices fall with costs under the influence of competition, or, prices being sticky, the money-wage rate is rising),[1] so that there is sufficient market to absorb them. Meanwhile the rate of output of Beta-plus equipment is increasing from month to month as the new productive methods spread through the investment sector. The rhythm of the process of transition speeds up as it goes on. Each month the amount of labour required to produce a rate of output equal to that of last month is a little less than it was last month, and the labour so released is available to man equipment which has accrued since last month. The characteristic of neutral innovations is that the labour time required, in the investment sector, to produce equipment offering a given amount of employment, in either sector (allowing for the concomitant build-up of work-in-progress), remains constant. The division of the labour force between the sectors remains constant. Output per man, the wage per man and the value of capital per man all rise in the same proportion while the ratio of Beta-plus to Beta capital goods in the total stock gradually rises, and the rate of profit remains constant.

If there were no further innovations, output from the investment sector would begin to fall to replacement level when the transition to Beta-plus technique had been completed. But, meanwhile, the progressive firms are developing Beta-double-plus technique. As the pipe-line of partially completed Beta-plus capital goods begins to empty, a new pipe-line of Beta-double-plus capital goods is being filled, and so the level of employment in the investment sector remains steady; the continuous rise in output per head goes on without a break, at a constant rate of profit. In short, the economy is in a golden age.

A CHANGE IN THE RATE OF ACCUMULATION

Now suppose that a round of innovations is made at an unexpectedly early date so that Beta-plus technique has come

[1] See above, p. 94.

into being before the transition from Beta-minus to Beta was nearing completion. There is then a spurt of demand for capital goods in excess of what can be provided by the existing labour force in the investment sector. (Alternatively we may suppose that the original impulse to increase investment came from an urge to accumulate more rapidly, and that the invention of a new technique was a response to the scarcity of labour that was threatening to develop.)

There is now an excess demand for labour in the investment sector, and the economy is in danger of plunging into inflation. But as soon as some Beta-plus plant is ready to be installed in the consumption sector, it takes the place of worn-out Beta-minus plant (which, if this sudden speeding up of progress had not occurred would have been replaced by Beta plant). Output per head in the consumption sector now begins to rise at a faster pace than it did formerly (taking two steps to one) and the scarcity of labour is relieved by a release of workers from the consumption sector, who become available to the investment sector. The desire for a more rapid rate of accumulation can thus be satisfied (at least to some extent) and it carries with it a more rapid rate of rise of productivity with the more rapid diffusion of the new technique.

But now there is a further complication. With a higher ratio of employment in the investment sector, profit per man in the consumption sector has jumped to a higher level (total quasi-rent in the consumption sector is equal to the now larger wages bill of the investment sector), and with the new level of costs a less mechanised technique, Gamma-plus, becomes preferable to Beta-plus. New investment and replacements of old Beta and Beta-minus plant now begin to be devoted to Gamma-plus capital goods.

But Gamma-plus technique requires more labour per unit of productive capacity than Beta-plus. The drainage of labour from the consumption into the investment sector is therefore staunched, and if entrepreneurs are now satisfied with the rate of accumulation that is going on, and keep up the now hotter pace of innovations, the economy (after some wobbles while the inappropriate Beta-plus capital goods that were installed during the flurry of readjustments are digested) settles into a new golden age, at a lower level of mechanisation and with a higher rate of profit.

Conversely, a slowing down of the rate of accumulation (and of the diffusion of new techniques) causes a switch-over towards Alpha-plus technique. In this case the transition is characterised by a period of slack demand, and a danger of falling into stagnation, instead of a danger of inflation.[1]

THE SPECIAL ASSUMPTIONS

When the slow-motion picture of a golden age is speeded up so that the pace of innovations is more rapid relatively to the length of life of plant, capital goods belonging to earlier phases survive several rounds of progress (some Beta-double-minus plant is still in existence when Beta-double-plus is first installed). As we have seen, the speed of diffusion of a single round of innovations accelerates as the investment sector becomes adapted to producing the appropriate capital goods. Now, provided that the new inventions come forward at an even pace through time, and provided that the length of life and the gestation period of capital goods (including the build-up of work-in-progress) is unchanged on the average, the peak phases of output of each successive type of outfit of capital goods occur at regular intervals of time, so that when, say, Beta-plus is at its maximum, the number of Beta-double-minus plants due for replacement is also at its maximum (the legacy of an earlier maximum rate of output of Beta-double-minus capital goods) and the excess of output of the new plant over retirement of the old (in terms of productive capacity) is in conformity with the rate of net investment required by the golden-age conditions.

If the gestation periods of successive types of capital goods or their length of life vary, a perfect golden age is not possible, and investment proceeds in a series of erratic wobbles.

The removal of the special assumptions introduces all the complications and ambiguities referred to above, and in the case which we are now considering a further complication as well.

[1] Cf. p. 90.

When the length of life of plant is long relatively to the pace at which the stock of capital is being adapted to new techniques, then, if innovations are expected, obsolescence is foreseen.[1] This reduces profit per unit of capital invested (because a larger part of annual quasi-rent is required for amortisation) and tends to keep the degree of mechanisation lower than it would otherwise be.

Unforeseen obsolescence causes capital losses to particular entrepreneurs and tends to speed up investment, whenever it occurs, by creating an unexpected demand for premature replacements.

AN INVENTION AS A SHOCK

A great basic discovery, such as a new form of power, dislocates expectations and causes widespread losses and widespread opportunities for profitable investment. It completely breaks the connection (which at best is tenuous in an uncertain world) between future expected profits on investment and the realised rate of profit of the recent past.

From a formal point of view it may be regarded as an example of the stimulus to accumulation given by an unforeseen speeding-up of technical progress, but it is better to treat it as a special kind of shock to tranquillity, which has repercussions (favourable and unfavourable) throughout the economy, and which renders its past development largely irrelevant to its future course.

[1] See above, p. 90.

CHAPTER 17

ACCUMULATION WITH BIASED PROGRESS

WE must now consider the effect of a capital-saving or capital-using bias in technical progress. When technical progress is neutral a rate of accumulation which is such as to keep the rate of profit constant at the same time keeps the real-capital ratio and the share of wages in the value of output constant. Productive capacity and the value of capital increase at the same rate. With biased progress the rate of profit and the real-capital ratio cannot both remain constant, and the relation of the value of capital to productive capacity is altered. The manner in which the system develops depends upon how accumulation reacts to the change in technical possibilities.

CAPITAL-SAVING BIAS WITH A CONSTANT RATE OF PROFIT

Let us suppose that a bout of discoveries with a capital-saving bias has been made (that is, the spectrum of techniques has changed in such a way as to reduce capital in terms of labour time per unit of output more than current labour per unit of output, over the relevant range of degrees of mechanisation), and examine the situation when they have been digested into the stock of capital goods. The situation then depends upon how much accumulation has occurred while the new technical knowledge was being digested. We will proceed by assuming provisionally that accumulation has been just sufficient to keep the rate of profit unchanged, and later inquiring whether it is plausible to suppose that this should occur.

The rate of profit being constant, the economy has moved from Beta-minus to Beta technique. Since the innovations

that have been made have a capital-saving bias, the value of
capital per unit of output is lower when Beta technique is in
operation than it was with Beta-minus technique.   Consequently, with a constant rate of profit, the share of profits in
the value of output is less, and the share of wages greater.
The real-wage rate has risen in a greater proportion than output
per man in terms of commodities.

If the next and subsequent bouts of innovations are neutral
(so that the real-capital ratio for Beta-plus and Beta-double-
plus is at the reduced Beta level) and accumulation continues
to be such as to keep the rate of profit constant, the economy
moves into a new golden age, and there has been a once-for-all
fall in the real-capital ratio.

If the next bout of innovations is capital-saving compared
to the last (so that Beta-plus has a lower real-capital ratio than
Beta) and the rate of profit continues constant, the economy
is in a kind of quasi-golden age, with a continually falling
real-capital ratio and rising share of wages in the value of output.

ACCUMULATION AND CAPITAL-SAVING INNOVATIONS

Is it plausible to suppose that accumulation is such as to
keep the rate of profit constant when capital-saving innovations occur ?   Let us look at the matter from the point of view
of an unambitious entrepreneur who is content with his
position and is not expanding his business.   When the time
comes for him to replace worn-out Beta-minus equipment he
finds that he can acquire plant of the same productive capacity
at a smaller cost (in terms of money of given purchasing power
over commodities).   If his conception of keeping his business
at the same level is that his productive capacity should be
maintained, he can now operate with less capital (the amortisation fund based on the historic cost of the Beta-minus plant
is more than is necessary to reproduce his productive capacity).
But if he thinks rather in terms of the value of capital he will
now install Beta plant of the same value as his old Beta-minus
plant, and consequently increase his productive capacity.

The second attitude of mind seems the more natural one.

Assuming that most entrepreneurs, presented with the opportunity of expanding capacity without any new investment of finance, are pleased to embrace it, the rate of accumulation in the economy as a whole is greater (with a capital-saving bias in progress) than that required to keep the rate of profit constant. The consequent growth of capacity causes conditions of scarcity of labour to develop, drives up real wages so much as to reduce the rate of profit, and so makes it preferable to raise the degree of mechanisation (Alpha capital goods replace Beta-minus).

This situation is similar to that which arises when technical progress is neutral but the rate of accumulation faster than that appropriate to the golden-age conditions. Capital-saving innovations, in a sense, reduce the need for capital relatively to labour, and have the same effect as an increase in the supply of capital brought about by rapid accumulation.

In this case, if the next and subsequent bouts of innovations are neutral, and accumulation henceforth goes on at a rate just sufficient to keep the new, lower, rate of profit constant (the next technique installed is Alpha-plus) so that a new golden age supervenes, there has been a once-for-all rise in the degree of mechanisation.

If the bias persists, the economy is chronically subject to scarcity of labour, and the rate of profit falls as time goes by.

On this view, capital-saving innovations tend to raise real wages, relatively to output per man, but they do not necessarily raise the share of labour in the value of output, for the value of capital per man may be raised (a movement from Beta-minus to Beta reduces the real-capital ratio, but a movement to Alpha may raise it) so that, in spite of the fall in the rate of profit, it is possible for the share of profit in the value of output to be raised.

CAPITAL-USING BIAS WITH A CONSTANT RATE OF PROFIT

When a bout of innovations with a capital-using bias takes place and accumulation is such as to keep the rate of profit constant, the real-capital ratio rises and the share of wages in the value of output falls.

As before, the economy may thereafter experience neutral progress, and move into a golden age after a once-for-all rise in the real-capital ratio, or, if the bias continues, it may enjoy a quasi-golden age with a constant rate of profit, a continually rising real-capital ratio and falling share of wages in the value of output.

ACCUMULATION AND CAPITAL-USING INNOVATIONS

The individual entrepreneur who wants to keep up the rate of growth of capacity must, in face of capital-using inventions, make an additional investment of finance when his old plant requires to be renewed, for his old value of capital is not sufficient to provide the former growth of capacity with the technique that is now giving his rivals a competitive advantage.

If he, and many like him, fail to make the necessary investment, accumulation is insufficient to keep the rate of profit constant. It may even be insufficient to maintain the pre-existing productive capacity, for, if the capital-using bias is pronounced, it requires a large investment (in excess of accrued amortisation funds) merely to replace old Beta-minus plant with Beta plant of equal capacity. If this absorbs more than all the accumulation that entrepreneurs are willing to undertake (or if the attempt to undertake it drives the economy into inflation) total capacity is reduced. The output of commodities falls and the real-wage rate is actually lower than before.

With a higher rate of profit, a lower degree of mechanisation becomes profitable, so that the economy moves from Beta-minus to Gamma technique. The innovations have increased the need for capital relatively to labour, and the failure of accumulation to respond reduces the demand for labour. But since Gamma technique requires more labour per unit of output than Beta the decline in mechanisation softens the effect of the fall in demand for labour, and brakes the reduction in wages (or rise in surplus of labour) that would occur if the degree of mechanisation were not reduced.

With a capital-using bias, however, it is the hypothesis of a constant rate of profit (or an approximation to it) that is the more plausible. When the capitalist rules of the game are being played with vigour and success, most entrepreneurs are continually trying to expand their businesses, and new men are always ready to jump into any gap in the market caused by a decline in output of old firms, so that when the amount of investment required to maintain the growth of productive capacity (in a form that can hold its own in competition) rises above accrued amortisation, the additional finance will be found somehow or other, and productive capacity will continue to expand.

If this view is correct, there is an asymmetry in the response of the economy to the two types of bias, a capital-saving bias tending to lower the rate of profit and a capital-using bias to raise the real-capital ratio.

THE PROCESS OF TRANSITION

Biased innovations introduce considerable complication into the analysis of the transition from one technique to another, and we will not set it out in slow motion. The broad lines are as follows :

Capital-saving Innovations with an Increasing Degree of Mechanisation. When Beta technique is capital-saving relatively to Beta-minus, there is a release of labour from the investment to the consumption sector, for output per head (in terms of productive capacity) is rising faster in the investment sector (as an output of new Beta capital goods begin to replace Beta-minus ones) than in the consumption sector.[1] This is checked, and may after a time be reversed, by the adoption of Alpha technique.

Capital-using Innovations with a Constant Degree of Mechanisation. When Beta technique is capital-using relatively to Beta-minus, output per head rises faster in the consumption sector. Labour is released from the consumption sector and absorbed into the investment sector. When a single bout of capital-using innovations is followed by a neutral bout the investment sector remains at its enlarged size. When subsequent innovations are also capital-using the investment sector continues to grow relatively to the consumption sector.

[1] Cf. above, p. 98.

TYPES OF BIAS

A capital-saving bias in technical progress may be due to equipment being designed in such a way as to require less labour time per unit of productive capacity relatively to the labour time required to operate it. Thus inventions which dispense with the need for heavy investment in equipment (say, wireless instead of cables) are capital-saving.

Conversely there is a capital-using bias in techniques which require a greater investment (in terms of labour time) per unit of employment offered.

Innovations which are capital-using at the point where they are introduced may be neutral or capital-saving for the economy as a whole; the mechanisation of the production of capital goods reduces the real-capital ratio in the industries using them. For instance, the mechanisation of building, though capital-using from the point of view of the building industry, would be highly capital-saving from the point of view of the economy as a whole.

A different kind of capital-saving bias is introduced by improvements which consist in speeding up the processes of production or in reducing the length of time that elapses between completing a batch of output and receiving the proceeds from selling it, for this reduces the amount of capital (at a given wage rate) embodied in work-in-progress in the pipe-lines of production and marketing.

An increase in the durability of plant, say by the discovery of hard steel (assuming that physical life was not already longer than expected earning life), means that a given investment of labour time provides more capital in the sense of future productive capacity, so that it represents an increase of productivity in the investment sector. It reduces the amount of labour required to keep a given stock of capital goods in being, and reduces correspondingly the annual amortisation quota with which an item of plant is charged. At the same time it increases the value of capital (at a given wage rate) per unit of current employment. This type of improvement therefore belongs to the capital-using category.

An *expectation* of an increased rate of technical progress

shortens the expected earning life of plant, and requires a heavier amortisation quota (to allow for obsolescence) and a higher ratio of labour employed in maintaining a stock of capital goods to labour employed in operating it. In itself, therefore, it is a disimprovement, comparable to steel growing more brittle owing to a change in the climate.[1] It requires an increase in capital per unit of output without any saving in labour per unit of output.

A special kind of change in the real-capital ratio comes about as an automatic consequence of changes in working hours. A shorter working day entails an increase in capital equipment per man-hour, and the adoption of a shift system reduces it. A shift system is sometimes introduced in order to make it possible to take advantage of some highly capital-using discovery which with single-shift working would have been uncompetitive with other techniques.

There is no reason to expect technical progress to be exactly neutral in any one economy, but equally there is no reason to expect a systematic bias one way or the other. Capital-using innovations raise the cost of machines in terms of commodities and give entrepreneurs an extra motive to find ways to cheapen them. Capital-saving innovations tend to produce scarcity of labour in the consumption sector and give entrepreneurs an extra motive to increase productivity. Each type of bias tends to get itself compensated by the other.

It is true that there may have been a systematic bias in the capital-using direction for technological reasons, since (at least until very recent times) it has proved easier to devise robots to carry out the operations of mass production of consumer goods than it is to devise robots to make robots. But, against this, there is an important tendency towards a bias in the other direction due to improvements which consist in speeding up the processes of production. The development of transport, and the reorganisation of marketing which accompanies it, have played a role in technical progress which is of the utmost historical importance and is by no means yet at an end. This kind of economy of capital is therefore a strong counterweight

[1] Cf. above, p. 90.

to any bias there may be in technology in a capital-using direction.

It seems, then, unlikely that there should be a permanent bias in the direction of technical progress, but at the same time it is possible that a bias should persist, in one direction or the other, for a considerable period, phases of one bias, perhaps, alternating with phases of the other.

TECHNOCRACY

According to the argument set out above, there is an asymmetry between the reactions of the economy to capital-saving and capital-using biases in technical progress. Capital-saving innovations are accompanied by more accumulation than is necessary to keep the rate of profit constant, scarcity of labour and a rising degree of mechanisation. Capital-using innovations stimulate accumulation so as to raise the real-capital ratio, and may do so sufficiently to leave the rate of profit more or less constant.

In a phase of capital-saving innovations, a quasi-golden age with a constant rate of profit and falling real-capital ratio is a logical possibility, but, on this view, would never be realised. On the other hand, in a phase of capital-using innovations, a quasi-golden age with a constant rate of profit and a rising real-capital ratio is not excluded.[1]

The vision of a rising real-capital ratio is the technocrat's nightmare. While it goes on, consumption is rising, if at all, very slowly, and the proportion of labour employed on replacements and new investment is continually rising as techniques requiring more and more capital in terms of labour time per unit of employment come into use. This is quite different from the under-consumption nightmare (where real wages remain constant while more or less neutral technical progress goes on, and the economy falls into stagnation from a failure of demand) for it does not lead to unemployment (except through

---

[1] The type of quasi-golden age represented by the Beta-Alpha period, when the real-capital ratio is rising with a constant rate of profit, may be regarded as a special case of this ; the distinguishing feature of it is that the real-wage rate is also constant.

a failure of mobility of labour, or a failure of finance to be available to implement the high level of investment required to maintain the quasi-golden age). But it would lead, at best, to very slowly rising wages, and a rapidly falling ratio of consumption to investment. Moreover, it would be highly unstable, for if at any stage the bias in innovations failed to be maintained, the rate of investment would abruptly fall and a violent slump would set in. In short, while capital-using innovations are favourable to the interests of entrepreneurs (by making capital scarce relatively to labour) an excessive indulgence in them creates conditions in which the capitalist rules of the game become unplayable.

CHAPTER 18

SYNOPSIS OF THE THEORY OF ACCUMULATION IN THE LONG RUN

(1) THE rate of technical progress and the rate of increase of the labour force (allowing for any change in working hours per family) govern the rate of growth of output of an economy that can be permanently maintained at a constant rate of profit. The potential growth ratio (increase per annum of output as a percentage of annual output) is approximately equal to the percentage rate of growth of employment *plus* the percentage rate of growth of output per head.[1]

(2) When the potential growth ratio is being realised the economy is in a golden age (Chapter 9).

(3) The conditions of a golden age require the growth ratio to be steady (Chapters 8 and 9).

(4) The conditions of a golden age require technical progress to be neutral, so that the real-capital ratio remains constant at a constant rate of profit (Chapters 9 and 16).

(5) A quasi-golden age with a constant rate of profit and changing real-capital ratio is logically conceivable, but with a falling real-capital ratio (a demechanisation of technique or a persistent capital-saving bias in progress) it is unlikely to be realised (Chapters 15 and 17). With a rising real-capital ratio (a rising degree of mechanisation or a persistent capital-using bias in progress) it may be realised for a time but is unlikely to last for long (Chapters 14 and 17).

(6) The conditions of a golden age require that the proportion of annual replacements to the stock of capital is constant.

---

[1] More accurately, if a is the proportionate rate of growth of the labour force and l the proportionate rate of growth of output per head, the growth ratio is $(1+a)(1+b) - 1$. Thus, if $a=2\%$ and $b=3\%$, the growth ratio is 5.06%.

This entails that the age composition of the stock of capital goods is appropriate to the growth ratio (Chapters 9 and 16).

(7) The conditions of a golden age require that a constant proportional rate of net investment yields a constant rate of growth of the stock of capital in use. This entails that the gestation period of capital goods is constant on the average (Chapters 9 and 16).

(8) In a golden age the percentage rate of growth per annum of productive capacity is equal to the growth ratio, the absolute rate of growth per annum in productive capacity varying, from one golden age to another, in the same proportion as productive capacity per man employed.

To any given productive capacity per head there corresponds a value of capital per head (in terms of commodities). The proportionate rate of growth per annum of the value of capital is equal to the growth ratio, a higher absolute rate per annum of growth of capital (annual net investment) corresponding to a proportionately higher value of capital in existence at any moment (Chapter 12).

(9) A higher growth ratio is likely to be associated with a lower degree of mechanisation (Chapters 12 and 13).

(10) A higher degree of mechanisation may be associated with a larger or smaller value of capital per unit of output (because of the opposite influences of higher wages and lower notional interest on the cost of capital goods) (Chapters 11 and 12).

(11) A static state is a special case of a golden age with zero growth ratio (labour force and technique constant). On the assumption of no consumption out of profits, the rate of profit is then zero and wages absorb the whole of net output. This is the condition of economic bliss (Chapters 8 and 14).

(12) The growth ratio represents the highest rate of accumulation of capital that can be permanently sustained at a constant rate of profit (Chapter 9).

(13) An economy which is accumulating at a lower rate is experiencing a growth of unemployment (which may be partly or wholly absorbed by a reduction of hours worked per family) (Chapters 8, 9 and 15).

(14) After lagging behind the growth ratio for a time the rate of accumulation may accelerate towards it, or, where there is still a reserve of unemployed labour, rise above it for a time, thereby reducing the amount of unemployment (Chapter 8).

(15) Even in the absence of a reserve of unemployed labour capital may accumulate for a time at a faster rate than the growth ratio, thereby raising the degree of mechanisation. The economy is then experiencing a falling rate of profit over the long run, and the rate of accumulation is decelerating towards the growth ratio. In the special case of zero growth ratio the economy is then approaching bliss (Chapter 8). At certain stages in the process the rate of profit may remain constant in conditions of a quasi-golden age, with an accelerating rate of accumulation (Chapter 14).

(16) A once-for-all change in the growth ratio makes a new golden age possible. To attain the new golden age appropriate to an increased growth ratio requires a rise in the proportion of productive capacity in the investment sector. Consumption for a time must be lower than it would have been if the old golden age had continued, to permit the more rapid rate of accumulation now appropriate to get under way. Conversely, adjustment to a fallen growth ratio entails a period either of unemployment or of increased consumption (Chapters 8, 9 and 15).

(17) A phase of biased technical progress followed by neutrality creates a situation in which it is possible, after passing through a period of transition, to attain a new golden age with different characteristics. If the growth ratio of the new golden age is the same as of the old one, the rate of profit is the same, but the real-capital ratio is different (Chapter 17).

(18) Frequent and erratic changes in the growth ratio or in the bias of technical progress destroy the conditions for a golden age by making tranquillity impossible (as, indeed, it normally is in reality) (Chapter 9).

(19) The absence of tranquillity makes it impossible to define precisely the meaning of a quantity of capital (Chapter 11).

(20) Even when the growth ratio remains stable without any disturbances there is a worm in the bud. As the total stock of capital rises competition is apt to be blunted and the urge to accumulate slackens, so that the economy is liable to fall out of a golden age into a state of stagnation (Chapters 8 and 9).

BOOK III
THE SHORT PERIOD

Chapter 19

PRICES AND PROFITS

In the tranquil conditions of a golden age productive capacity, actual output and effective demand all expand together. When the conditions of a golden age are not being maintained demand may expand faster than capacity (as, for instance, when there is an unforeseen speeding up of technical progress, leading to an investment boom) or may drop below it (as, for instance, when an increase in monopoly lowers real wages without a corresponding increase in the rate of accumulation). We must now examine these situations in more detail.

LONG AND SHORT PERIODS

At any particular moment there is a particular amount of productive capacity in existence, represented by a who's who of capital goods appropriate to a particular technique (or a particular mixture of techniques), and a particular distribution of available labour between different lines of production. The stock of capital goods is in course of changing in quantity or being transmogrified in form, but in a short period of time it does not alter very much. The *short period*, in the analytical sense, is not any definite period of time, but a convenient theoretical abstraction meaning a period within which changes in the stock of capital equipment can be neglected. Within a short period the rate of output can alter, for it is possible to utilise given equipment more or less by employing more or less labour to operate it. The range of output that is technically possible, in a given short-period situation, is anything from zero to the maximum that can be squeezed out of existing resources. The range of technically possible rates of consumption is anything from zero to the maximum rate of output of commodities that is possible without replacements, *plus* the consumption of pre-existing stocks of finished commodities. Within these technical limits, the short-period swings of output and consumption are governed by the movements of effective demand.

Everything that happens in an economy happens in a short-period situation, and every decision that is taken is taken in a short-period situation, for an event occurs or a decision is taken at a particular time, and at any moment the physical stock of capital is what it is; but what happens has a long-period as well as a short-period aspect. Long-period changes are going on in short-period situations. Changes in output, employment and prices, taking place with a given stock of capital, are short-period changes; while changes in the stock of capital, the labour force and the techniques of production are long-period changes. Similarly we can distinguish short- and long-period decisions of entrepreneurs. Short-period decisions affect the utilisation of given equipment (as, for instance, when a sudden spurt of demand leads to an increase of sales and output is speeded up to replace stocks), long-period decisions affect the stock of productive capacity (for instance, through the replacement of worn-out or obsolete plant). Investment has a short- and long-period aspect. In its short-period aspect it governs the level of employment and the relations of prices to wages, for these are influenced by entrepreneurs' outlay on the investment sector of the economy during the period when capital goods are being produced but are not yet ready for use. In its long-period aspect it governs the rate of accumulation or decumulation of capital and the technique of production.

A given short-period situation contains within itself a tendency to long-period change. For instance, when employment in the investment sector remains steady from week to week the short-period situation is unchanging (assuming that other conditions also remain constant), but if the output of the investment sector exceeds replacements of plant being scrapped, the stock of capital goods is increasing and a new short-period situation is coming into existence. At a later date the stock of productive capacity is larger and if it happens that, in the short-period situation then obtaining, the level of employment and the rate of real wages are the same as in the earlier one (so that the demand for commodities has not risen), the utilisation of equipment has fallen (there is more capital competing for the same markets) and the level of profit is lower. This in turn leads to a fresh short-period situation, as entrepreneurs alter their price and investment policies to meet the conditions that have now emerged.

In a golden age the rate of net investment is rising in accordance with the growth ratio appropriate to the given golden-age conditions; therefore demand is increasing in step with capacity so that the short-period situation is continuously adapting itself smoothly to the long-period changes that are taking place. Similarly, in a quasi-golden age, when the real-capital ratio is in course of changing with a constant rate of profit, the short-period situation is changing smoothly from week to week as the ratio of employment in the two sectors of the economy alters. But these are imaginary situations; they constitute an analytical device, not a description of reality. In reality to-day is a break in time. Yesterday lies in the past, and has ceased to be relevant to what happens to-day, except in so far as experience of it colours expectations about what will happen next. To-morrow lies in the future and cannot be known. The short-period situation in existence to-day is like a geological fault; past and future developments are out of alignment. Only in the imagined conditions of a golden age do the strata run horizontally from yesterday to to-morrow without a break at to-day.

COMPETITION

There is a long- and a short-period aspect of competition and monopoly. From the long-period point of view competitive conditions mean that it is easy for new sellers to enter a market, so that when the prospect of profit is above the average in a particular line of production investment is deflected into it, or when costs are reduced by innovations, imitators quickly copy the new methods and bring prices into line with the new level of costs.

In its short-period aspect, competition means that no individual seller can raise the price of a particular commodity without losing the bulk of his customers to rival suppliers, and that if he were to lower his price he would have a very large increase in sales, at the expense of his rivals.

When a market is highly competitive in this short-period sense, and the number of independent sellers is large, no one individually has much influence upon the price of the commodity concerned, and each regards the price as being given by the market. His concern is to get his costs as low as possible so as to enjoy the most profit that he can at that price.

Where there are a few sellers (oligopolists) serving a particular market, acting independently of each other, each one has an influence on price, but he has to take into account the effect of his price policy upon that of the others. If he alone were to raise his price, they would be likely to win customers from him, but if he were to lower it, they would be likely to defend their share of the market by following him down. Competition then takes the form mainly of sales pressure.

An outright monopolist has considerable freedom in fixing prices, but has to keep up sales pressure to deflect demand from other commodities to his own.

The two aspects of competition are not necessarily found together. There may be a high degree of competition between sellers already in a particular market, although the rate of profit that each makes on the reproduction cost of his capital goods is considerably above the rate of profit that can be expected on the general run of investments, while outsiders know that any attempt to break into the market would involve a long and expensive battle (in terms of cut prices or heavy selling costs) with the insiders already entrenched behind the goodwill that each has built up in the market concerned. Conversely, a monopolist may be in a strong position to control prices in his market in a particular short-period situation, but not to defend it from new competition as time goes by. On the whole, however, the two aspects of competition are likely to be associated, for to a large extent they spring from common causes.

COSTS OF PRODUCTION

The costs of production of the output being produced in a given short-period situation may be divided into the following categories. (As usual, the categories are not very precise, and border-line cases have to be dealt with according to convenience on common-sense lines.) [1]

Prime costs are involved by production of a particular batch of goods, and would not be incurred if that batch were not produced. They consist principally of wages (for if less output were produced workers could be dismissed or put on short time, so that the wages bill would be reduced); materials, power and transport bought by one firm from another (which need not be purchased if output were less); and user-cost, that is the extra wear and tear of plant due to running it rather than resting it (this may be negative, for in some cases plant deteriorates more through being idle, or requires expenditure on care and maintenance when it is not being used). *Overhead costs* are the general expenses involved in maintaining a business as a going concern, which do not vary with the rate of output from given productive capacity.

These are actual costs. There is also the notional cost represented by *amortisation charges* — the sums required to provide for replacement of plant, calculated on the basis of its expected earning life. The loss of earning power of plant due to the passage of time (including expected obsolescence) is often hard to distinguish from user-cost, and when output is running within the normal capacity of plant it is better to throw user-cost in with amortisation rather than to treat it as an element in prime cost. It becomes important as an element in prime cost when plant is being over-driven to speed up output, so that its physical life is shortened (or extra costs incurred for repairs) compared to what it would be when worked at its designed capacity.[2]

Designed capacity is not a very precise concept, particularly when plant for some preparatory process contributes to the

[1] Cf. above, p. viii.
[2] Cf. Keynes, *General Theory*, p. 66, and P. Wiles, 'Empirical Research and the Marginal Analysis', *Economic Journal* (June 1954).

output of a variety of commodities; and it depends upon the length of the normal working day (the length of a shift, and the number of shifts worked). However, for the purposes of our present analysis it is sufficient to say that plant is being worked at the limit of normal capacity when any increase in the weekly rate of output would involve a rise in prime cost per unit of product (whether because output per unit of labour falls when more product is squeezed from given capacity, because user-cost rises when plant is run faster or without normal pauses for overhauling, or because overtime rates of wages have to be paid for longer hours of work).

When output is running beyond normal capacity, in this sense, short-period *marginal cost* exceeds average prime cost per unit of product, that is, the difference in prime costs per week, due to a unit increase in the week's output, exceeds prime cost per unit of output.[1]

When technical conditions are such that prime cost per unit rises continuously, from very low rates of output (say because there is a variety of plant of different ages and states of efficiency, so that each increase in the rate of output is made by calling into use machines that entail a higher running cost per unit of output) there is no definite normal capacity output, and over- and under-capacity working are matters of degree. We shall simplify exposition by ruling out cases of this kind, and assuming that there is, in any given situation, a fairly well-marked point for each outfit of capital goods at which prime cost begins to increase with output, so that, at that rate of output, marginal cost rises sharply above average prime cost. This simplification suits factory production fairly well. It is inappropriate for technical reasons to extractive industries (agriculture and mining) which, in the main, provide raw materials for manufacture.[2] We shall postpone consideration of them till we have discussed land as a factor of production.

---

[1] A week's output of 100 costs 1 per unit. An output of 110 costs 1·1 per unit. Then marginal cost, due to the additional output of 10 units is 21, or 2·1 per unit.

[2] It is also difficult to apply with precision to services such as urban transport or electricity supply which are subject to variations in demand over the day and the week. Capacity output must then be regarded as the peak load that can be carried.

The excess of total receipts over costs is profit.[1]   There may be a hierarchy of levels of profit for firms of different types operating similar equipment.   Thus progressive firms may always earn higher profits than imitators,[2] or firms with a monopolistic position in the markets that they serve may enjoy a permanently higher level of profit than those subject to strong competitive pressure.   Entrepreneurs with limited finance may be content with lower profits than those who can operate large concerns.[3]   Provided that the mixture of firms of various types remains constant through time, we may ignore this complication and speak of the expected level of profit meaning the appropriate complex of individual expected levels, the stock of capital goods being given.

NORMAL PRICES

The *normal price* for any type of commodity consists of prime cost *plus* a gross margin calculated to cover a due share of overhead cost, amortisation and profit at the ruling rate on the capital invested, when plant is being worked at normal capacity.   When a variety of products are produced from the same plant we have to think in terms of normal receipts for the mixed bag of output, the allocation of the gross margin between them depending upon the degree of competition in the various markets supplied.[4]

Since the concept of normal price involves both the earning life of plant and the expected rate of profit on investment, it has an unambiguous meaning only in conditions of perfect tranquillity.[5]   There is, however, a rather vague but very important conception, which we may call the *subjective-normal* price, which is such that the gross margin entering into it is calculated to yield a profit that the entrepreneurs concerned

[1] The consideration of interest charges for finance borrowed from outside the firm will be postponed until we have introduced rentiers into our simplified model.   Meanwhile entrepreneurs may be assumed to lend to each other (see below, p. 229), but interest is treated simply as part of profit.

[2] See above, p. 86.   [3] See above, p. 110.

[4] See Eli W. Clemens, 'Price Discrimination and the Multiple-Product Firm', *Review of Economic Studies*, vol. xix (1), 48 (1951–2).

[5] Cf. above, p. 103.

have come to regard as attainable (on the basis of past experience) with the productive capacity in existence in the given short-period situation.[1]

Where fluctuations in output are expected and regarded as normal, the subjective-normal price may be calculated upon the basis of an average or standard rate of output, rather than capacity.

Selling at subjective-normal prices is by no means the same thing as earning the profits on the basis of which the prices are calculated, for profit depends upon the volume of sales as well as on the margin per unit sold. The 'normality' of normal prices does not consist in the fact that they *will* yield the expected profit, or that they *tend* to do so, but that they *would* yield it if normal output were sold at those prices over the lifetime of plant.

The relation of actual to subjective-normal prices depends upon the relation of demand to capacity. We may examine three distinct types of situations, according as equipment is being worked at, over, or under capacity.

PRICES AT CAPACITY

When things happen to be working out so that the plant in existence in a particular short-period situation is being worked just comfortably within capacity, and sales are taking place at subjective-normal prices based on that rate of output, the expected level of profit is being earned for the time being.

In this situation no entrepreneur is anxious to increase his sales for the moment (though all may be confidently looking forward to increasing both productive capacity and output in the near future). To increase output with existing capacity would entail a rise in marginal cost, and to increase sales would require either a cut in prices or more aggressive sales pressure to lure customers away from competitors. The amount of

---

[1] This gives rise to the so-called 'full-cost theory of prices', for entrepreneurs, when asked by economists how they fix prices, are apt to reply by describing how they calculate subjective-normal prices. See R. L. Hall and C. J. Hitch, 'Price Theory and Business Behaviour', *Oxford Papers* (May 1939), and R. F. Kahn, 'Oxford Studies in the Price Mechanism', *Economic Journal* (March 1952).

sales pressure that each is keeping up is *ex hypothesi* sufficient to permit him to sell his designed capacity output, and further efforts would only reduce his profits.

On the other hand, no one wants to raise his price (or relax his sales pressure) so that output would fall below capacity (those who enjoy monopolistic positions are already exploiting them as they think fit, and have adjusted their capacity to their designed rate of sales).

If this short-period situation exists in the setting of a golden age, it will be reproduced in the short-period situation that is coming into being, with a larger stock of productive capacity. When the conditions for a golden age are not fulfilled, there is some contradiction in the situation that prevents it from perpetuating itself (say, the rate of investment now going on is greater or less than corresponds to the growth ratio of the economy, so that conditions of scarcity or surplus of labour will soon emerge and lead to a change in the rate of profit). Meanwhile subjective-normal prices are yielding the expected profit and the disturbances towards which the system is heading are not yet apparent.

A SELLER'S MARKET

When the short-period situation is such that the demand for goods at subjective-normal prices exceeds capacity output entrepreneurs find themselves in a *seller's market*. The short-period situation then in existence will continue until either demand slackens or productive capacity is increased.

The typical reaction to this situation is as follows : Selling at subjective-normal prices, entrepreneurs find themselves able to dispose of more than normal capacity output without any extra sales pressure. In the first instance output expands up to the point at which the marginal cost (including an estimate of user-cost) of an extra batch of output is equal to the proceeds from selling it. To go beyond this point at the old price would mean to incur an addition to costs greater than the addition to proceeds, and so to reduce profits below what they would be at a smaller output. If the increase in output which comes about in this way is not sufficient to meet the excess demand, a rise in price occurs, for now each seller, protected by the high marginal cost of the others, can raise his own price without fear of losing customers to his rivals. With higher prices it is worth while to incur higher marginal costs, so that the rise in prices is accompanied by some further increase in the rate of output. A position of short-period equilibrium is established at a price at which demand just absorbs the rate of output for which marginal cost is equal to the price.

This standard pattern of reaction may be modified in a number of ways. Firms which are in a strong monopolistic position, or which have an open or tacit agreement ·about price policy, may prefer to keep output within capacity, and raise prices sufficiently to cut back demand accordingly. On the other hand, where goodwill is important they may prefer to keep price at the subjective-normal level, even in face of a large excess demand, and either to meet the demand, incurring marginal costs in excess of price (thus making a lower total profit than could be got in the short-period situation, while building up useful market connections for the future), to ration customers or (in the case of durable goods) to book orders and delay delivery dates. On the whole, it seems that monopolists are generally more anxious to increase sales than to squeeze the last drop of profit out of a favourable short-period situation, while in highly competitive markets the individual seller has no means of attaching customers to himself, and so has no future gain from moderating present prices to offset the sacrifice of present profit. For this reason, paradoxical as it may seem, prices often rise more in face of a rise in demand relatively to capacity in highly competitive markets than in those where monopolistic price policies are being pursued.

In any case, whether price rises or not, profits are higher (for the time being) than those on which the subjective-normal price is calculated, because total receipts have risen at least in proportion to sales, while a large part of cost (including amortisation quotas) remains constant.

A BUYER'S MARKET

When total demand is insufficient to absorb capacity output at subjective-normal prices, the entrepreneurs are in a *buyer's market*, and it is impossible for them all to be earning the expected level of profit. In this situation it is not possible to pick out any one typical course of events, for the development in each market depends upon the degree of short-period competition obtaining in it, and upon the policy pursued by the entrepreneurs concerned. Where there is unmitigated competition (in the short-period sense), prices are driven down towards prime costs, for so long as there is any quasi-rent to be got each seller would prefer to cut prices and expand his sales. Where considerations of goodwill come in (including connections with suppliers of raw materials and with banks supplying finance) prices may even fall below prime cost. For this very reason, unmitigated competition is not usual. Each seller is restrained from cutting prices by the knowledge that if anyone starts, all will suffer losses. Thus prices may remain rather precariously at the subjective-normal level, merely because no one seller will incur the odium of being the first to cut.[1] When this feeling is not sufficiently strong to prevent price-cutting, a period of losses may lead to the formation of rings, sellers agreeing to keep up prices and to share the market on the basis of some kind of quota system. A prolonged buyer's market usually produces a crop of monopolistic agreements, many of which become permanent. Where monopoly already exists, prices are unlikely to be cut, and may even be raised, the monopolist finding that what demand there still is for his products is coming from customers so firmly attached that a rise of price will make a less than proportional fall in purchases. (Such a rise in price in face of a fall in demand is often explained, to make it sound reasonable, by the need to recover overhead costs from a smaller output.)

Where there is an oligopoly of sellers of more or less equal standing, they are likely to behave much as though they had a price agreement, but where the balance of power between them is unstable the one who is in the strongest position (because of lower costs or greater financial reserves) may take the opportunity to break some of his rivals, by price-cutting or sales pressure, so as to obtain a more nearly monopolistic position for the future.

[1] See Marshall, *Principles* (7th ed.), p. 375.

Since entrepreneurs buy from each other (materials, power, etc.), the price policy pursued by one group affects prime costs for others, and this in turn affects their prices, so that the policy pursued by any one group ramifies through the economy in a highly complex manner.

All this makes it impossible to generalise about behaviour in a buyer's market, and each such situation has its own history. The important point, for our present argument, is that whatever happens to prices, profits are running below the level which would be realised if capacity output were being sold at subjective-normal prices.

NORMAL AND AVERAGE PRICES

The average of prices over a run of years may exceed or fall short of subjective-normal prices, according as periods of seller's or buyer's markets have predominated in the period.

Even when prices have not departed much from the subjective-normal level that obtained at the beginning of any stretch of time, profits may exceed or fall short of the level on the basis of which the subjective-normal prices were conceived. Then experience gradually modifies the views of entrepreneurs about what level of profit is obtainable, or what the average utilisation of plant is likely to be over its lifetime, and so reacts upon subjective-normal prices for the future. Thus when we descend from the clear air of a golden age, where normal prices always rule, into the fogs of historical time, our analysis cannot but be blurred and imprecise.

THE RATE OF PROFIT

The rate of profit on capital, in a short period situation, is an even more foggy notion than the level of profits earned by given equipment, for to express profits as a rate we must know the value of capital.

For entrepreneurs operating in an economy (as opposed to economists observing it) the concept of capital as a quantity of value comes up in a number of different contexts but has no precise meaning in any.

Investment decisions have to be taken in the light of guesses about an uncertain future. An entrepreneur contemplating a scheme of investment knows what sum of money must be spent on capital goods (even this is not quite precisely known, for, if the gestation period of plant is long, costs may change while it is being built) and he knows what that sum of money is worth in terms of commodities at present prices and labour at current wage rates. He does not know (but guesses) what the amount and the time pattern of the earnings of the capital goods will be. The value, as opposed to the initial cost, of the capital goods is a vague idea, and the same situation appears differently to individuals of different temperament. An optimist tells himself that the value of the capital will turn out to be greater than its cost, for he wants to invest and must persuade himself that he is being prudent in doing so.[1] A pessimist can find reasons for inaction just as persuasive in the very same data.

The present value of an outfit of capital goods operating as a going concern comes into question rather rarely, say when one business is buying up another. For each such bargain the market is very narrow and every potential buyer has his own particular situation to consider, so that the price which emerges has little general meaning. The present value of the placements representing property in a going concern (shares) depends upon three sets of considerations : what its earnings are expected to be, and the degree of uncertainty surrounding expectations about them ; what the policy of the directors of the company is going to be *vis-à-vis* shareholders ; and what the views of the placement market are likely to be in the future about the value of the shares. Thus the value of the concern in the placement market is very loosely connected with the value of the capital goods that it is operating.

The valuation of capital for balance-sheet purposes represents neither the actual historic cost of the capital goods nor an estimate of their future earning power, but a mixture of the two (which varies from one business to another according to the formulae that each adopts), depending upon the rate at which the value of equipment is written down

[1] Cf. Keynes, *General Theory*, p. 162.

out of amortisation and the manner in which stocks are valued.

When an entrepreneur is giving evidence before a Royal Commission or arguing with tax inspectors, the value of capital comes up in still another way. He may have an interest in showing that the rate of profit realised over the recent past was very low, or that if it was high, it was abnormal because of some peculiar feature about the years under discussion. There is ample room for argument, without any actual deception, as to the value of the capital represented by the concern. The historic cost of the capital goods generally differs from current reproduction cost, for prices and wage rates are rarely perfectly stable over a run of years. Current reproduction cost is not at all a precise notion. There is no such thing as the present cost of reproducing plant ten years old. Technical or relative-price changes during the life of the plant mean that it is no longer the most appropriate, and that, if it were due to be replaced, it would be replaced by something different. All this provides room for argument as to what is the *true* value of the capital.

When the entrepreneur both wants to satisfy the tax inspector that his profits have been very low and to give the impression on the placement market that his future dividends will be high, he is in an awkward situation and often hops from one basis of calculation to another in a somewhat confusing manner.

In reality, to find the expected rate of return which governs investment decisions is like the famous difficulty of looking in a dark room for a black cat that probably is not there, and to give a true account of realised returns is like the famous difficulty of the chameleon on a plaid rug.

This does not mean that all our elaborate analysis of golden ages and quasi-golden ages has been a waste of time, for the long-period influences which we have been considering are working themselves out through the fog of uncertainty in which short-period situations develop, though they cannot be seen with any great precision.

CHAPTER 20

WAGES AND PRICES

THE real-wage rate obtaining in any short-period situation emerges from the total operation of the economy and is not controlled by any conscious decisions, but the money-wage rate is the subject of particular bargains between entrepreneurs and workers and is fixed consciously. In our simple model with all labour alike we assume a rapid diffusion of a change in money-wages taking place at any one point through the system as a whole, so that in effect a single scale of wages (for normal hours and overtime) is in force at any moment. The effect of a change in the money-wage rate upon prices, real wages, profits and employment depends upon the situation in which it is made and upon the state of competition and the price policy of entrepreneurs.

AT CAPACITY

Rising Money Wages with Competition. We first consider the situation when output is running just about at capacity, subjective-normal prices prevail, and the situation is expected to reproduce itself, in the manner of a golden age. There is only a small reserve of unemployed labour. Trade unions are exerting a constant pressure to raise money wages, and from time to time they succeed, so that over the long run an upward drift in the money-wage rate is going on.

A rise in the money-wage rate raises both prime cost and the reproduction cost of capital goods. It therefore raises subjective-normal prices. In competitive conditions the natural reaction for each entrepreneur is to raise the prices of his products correspondingly, for each knows that others are suffering the same rise in costs, and since all were working near capacity none is much afraid of his competitors expanding sales at his expense. If each in the first instance raises his prices by the amount by which his subjective-normal prices have risen, those who buy materials, etc., from others find that these elements in prime costs have risen, as well as wages, and raise their own prices accordingly. Thus, if all act in the same way there is a general rise of prices in proportion to the rise in the wage rate. The reproduction cost of each item of physical capital, including work-in-progress, is now higher than its historic cost. Assuming that the requisite additional finance is obtainable without a rise in the rate of interest [1] there is no reason why the level of physical gross investment should alter, for with prices raised in proportion to money-wages the real demand for commodities is unchanged, and production can continue at the same level as before at the new, higher, subjective-normal prices. The situation then remains just as it was in real terms, and the only difference is that there has been a uniform fall in the purchasing power of a nominal unit of money. [2]

Rising Money Wages with Monopoly. A group of oligopolists may have been intimidating each other into keeping prices lower than any one individually would like to make them. A rise in costs may break the tension and lead to a rise in prices more than in proportion to the rise in costs. Similarly a monopolist may be in a situation where he feels that he could make a better profit at a higher price, but is afraid of sacrificing goodwill if he raises his price in cold blood. A rise in costs gives him a colourable excuse, and as no one knows exactly how much his costs have risen, he can now raise his price more than proportionately.

A rise in prices in a greater proportion than wages reduces real consumption, and output therefore falls below capacity.

On the other hand the oligopolists may still be in a cat-and-mouse equilibrium, [3] none wishing to be the first to raise prices for fear the rest will not do so; and the monopolist may be pursuing a long-range policy and prefer (within reason) to swallow a fall in his gross margin. In such a case, prices rise

---

[1] See below, p. 238.

[2] The existence of rentiers complicates the situation (see below, p. 268).

[3] See E. A. G. Robinson, *Monopoly*, p. 24.

less than in proportion to money wages, the real demand for commodities is increased, and a seller's market develops.

Falling Money Wages. Now let us suppose that in the initial situation although plant is working at capacity there is a large reserve of unemployed labour (the accumulation of capital has been failing to keep up, over the recent past, with the growth ratio of the economy). The trade unions are weak, and the level of wages is drifting downwards. So far as commodities are concerned the analysis is symmetrical with the above. If an uneasy equilibrium is upset, and prices fall more than in proportion to wages, the real demand for commodities expands. If prices are sticky, it tends to contract.

But in the investment sector there is likely to be an asymmetry similar to that which we found with biased technical progress. There has been a fall in the reproduction cost of capital goods below their historic cost; this is true, to some extent at least, whatever happens to prices of goods sold by one entrepreneur to another, for each entrepreneur undertakes part of his gross investment directly (if only the element in cost of work-in-progress represented by wages). General prospects are quite satisfactory from the entrepreneur's point of view and the finance released by the fall in reproduction cost of capital goods is likely to be invested over and above whatever net investment was going on before wages fell.

If so, employment in the investment sector rises, and a seller's market develops. While it lasts prices are lower (if at all) in a smaller proportion than wages, and the real-wage rate is reduced. The total consumption of the workers is increased or reduced according as the effect of increased employment more or less than offsets any rise there may have been in gross margins as a result of the monopolistic stickiness of prices. (This is the mechanism by which the existence of a surplus of labour may cause a spurt in accumulation.[1])

A SELLER'S MARKET

When a seller's market develops, with a rise in prices, and low unemployment, the trade unions have a double reason for

[1] Cf. above, p. 80.

pressing for higher money wages ; their bargaining position is strong, and real-wage rates have recently fallen. Even if labour is unorganised money wages may be raised by entrepreneurs eager to recruit more hands. If prices rise in proportion to money wages (on top of having risen, relatively to money wages, with the rise in activity) real wages are no higher, and the upward pressure persists. The economy is then in the foothills of the inflation barrier.[1] If monopolists are keeping prices steady, real wages rise with money wages, and this adds fuel to the fire of the seller's market.

When a seller's market develops in an environment of surplus labour, long-run unemployment (open or disguised) is likely to keep the tendency for rising wages in check.

A BUYER'S MARKET

The unemployment that occurs in a buyer's market is of quite a different nature from a surplus of labour relatively to capacity. A surplus of labour (or technological unemployment)[2] means that the stock of capital goods in existence offers employment, at capacity, to less than all available labour. In a buyer's market employment has fallen below capacity. From a long-period point of view there may be no surplus, or even a scarcity of labour. The unemployment is due to the failure of demand, not to a lack of capital equipment for labour to operate.

The unemployment in a buyer's market is even more likely to bring wages down than unemployment due to a surplus of labour, for it is accompanied by abnormally low prices, and low profits or actual losses are being made. On the other hand, it is much less likely to bring relief through stimulating investment, for there is already idle capacity, and the prospect of future profit is coloured by present gloom.

It is difficult to generalise about the effect on prices of a fall in wages in a buyer's market. On the one hand prices are likely to be already below the subjective-normal level, and entrepreneurs see no sense in cutting them further because subjective-normal prices have come down. On the other hand,

---

[1] See above, p. 48.   [2] See above, p. 95.

the feeling that if anyone is going to cut prices it is best to be the first to do so, is likely to prevail at least in some markets. In so far as prices fall with wages the situation is unaffected in real terms. In so far as they remain sticky, it is worsened by a further decline in real demand.[1]

THE ADJUSTMENT OF CAPACITY TO AVAILABLE LABOUR

In golden-age conditions capacity is continually adjusted to available labour because any chance emergence of surplus labour tends to speed up accumulation. The mechanism operates through falling money-wage rates, which make the reproduction cost of capital goods less than their historic cost and so induce some extra investment.

This mechanism is much impaired by short-period fluctuations in demand. A surplus of labour is unlikely to cause a fall in money wages in a seller's market (though it may prevent a rise) for a seller's market means that the demand for labour has recently risen. In a buyer's market when short-period unemployment is superimposed upon a surplus of labour, wages are likely to fall. In this situation, however, the stimulus to investment is unlikely to operate.

A downward drift in money wages due to a long-run surplus of labour takes the form of falls in wages during periods of buyer's markets, not offset by rises during seller's markets. The impact of a fall in wages is therefore felt at times when it does least good as a stimulus to investment, and the mechanism which tends to adjust capacity to available labour is much weaker when the economy is subject to fluctuations in demand than it would be in golden-age conditions.

This strongly reinforces the conclusion that a deficiency of demand for labour relatively to supply is much less likely to be self-correcting than a deficiency of supply relatively to demand.[2]

[1] See above, p. 79.
[2] A further consideration to the same effect is found in the operation of the monetary system (see below, p. 239).

CHAPTER 21

FLUCTUATIONS IN THE RATE OF INVESTMENT

THE accumulation of capital over the long run takes place as the result of decisions to invest made in a succession of short-period situations, for every day the sun rises upon an economy which has, that day, a particular who's who of capital goods in existence, and a particular state of expectations based upon past experience and the diagnosis of current trends. In the short period of a seller's market current experience indicates that more productive capacity could be profitably used, and this is likely to cause decisions to invest in replacements and extensions of plant. A high level of employment in the investment sector means high quasi-rents in the consumption sector.[1] Thus, high profits cause profits to be high. Contrariwise, in a buyer's market there is excess capacity, and investment is discouraged. Low profits cause profits to be low.

This double interaction between investment and profits is the most troublesome feature of the capitalist rules of the game, both from the point of view of entrepreneurs who have to play it and of economists who have to describe it.

A BOOM

In the course of our examination of accumulation over the long run we have encountered a number of situations in which investment is speeded up, for instance when new inventions are causing innovations to be made at an unexpectedly rapid rate. Let us consider how the economy reacts to this situation. An increase in employment in the investment sector

[1] This conclusion, we shall find, is not contradicted by the introduction of rentiers into the model.

198

has caused an increase in demand relatively to capacity in the consumption sector. This leads to the development of a seller's market; or if there was a buyer's market in the preceding short-period situation, it is now less intense.

In the situation of a seller's market that is expected to last, entrepreneurs already in business are anxious to expand productive capacity so as to be able to enjoy a higher rate of sales without incurring high marginal costs. Those who are beginning their careers find the moment favourable to enter a market without fear of defensive price-cutting from insiders (whose capacity is already fully occupied). The prospect of a seller's market continuing for some time therefore promotes net investment. Even if sad experience has taught entrepreneurs that a seller's market never does last, yet competition impels them to carry out investment, for, in the succeeding reaction that the canny ones expect, those who have installed new plant (with all the latest improvements) will have lower costs than those who have not, and will be in a better position to stand up to the pressure of a buyer's market in the future. Thus even the canny entrepreneurs are impelled to invest, though they may regret the necessity.[1]

If a buyer's market prevailed in the first instance, it has now grown less intense, and replacements begin to be made to maintain capacity that would have been allowed to go out of existence if the rise in demand had not occurred.

In either case, the initial increase in investment leads to a further increase. Every increase in investment outlay by one group of entrepreneurs improves the situation for others, so that, up to some limit, each increase in the rate of investment promotes a further increase.

An upper limit of the rate of investment may be reached because the demand for capital goods ceases to expand. The process of diffusion of investment decisions from one group to another takes time, and meanwhile the stock of productive capacity is increasing. After a certain time has gone by (from the beginning of the upward movement) it may happen that, between one month and the last, the proportionate increment

---

[1] See A. J. Youngson, 'Investment Decisions, Trade Cycle, and Trend', *Oxford Economic Papers* (September 1954).

of employment in the investment sector is not greater than the proportionate increment of productive capacity that has come into service (allowing for the build up of work-in-progress that follows the installation of new plant). Then the intensification of the seller's market ceases, and after another month has gone by (with more capacity in operation) it will begin to slacken.

On the other hand, the limit to the expansion of demand for capital goods may fail to come into operation before a limit to the possible rate of output is reached.

The upper limit to the possible rate of investment with a given labour force is set by the inflation barrier.[1] But under the normal operations of the economy (as opposed to war-time, rearmament, etc.) this limit is not usually reached (though the economy may penetrate some way into the foot-hills) for another barrier lies in front of it, set by the capacity of plant in the industries specialised to the production of plant. When the limit of capacity is reached in the basic capital-good industries (iron and steel, ship-building, etc.)[2] employment in the investment sector cannot increase any further for the time being. The investment industries themselves are experiencing a seller's market, and part of the investment which is going on is in their own capacity (though as we shall see in a moment they expand less readily under the influence of a seller's market than do those in the consumption sector). When an enlargement of their capacity is ready for use, it is possible for a further increase in the rate of investment to take place. But when that stage is reached, the seller's market in the investment sector has weakened or disappeared, and investment in plant to produce plant slackens.

Thus it is impossible (except by a most unlikely fluke) for

---

[1] This may operate to check investment through the monetary system (see below, p. 238).

[2] An important part of the investment sector consists of the building industry, and building by traditional methods does not require much plant, but it requires a labour force of skilled craftsmen. This takes us outside the assumptions of our simplified model in which all labour is alike. The supply of craftsmen represents a bottle-neck limiting the physical rate of investment similar in some respects to plant such as shipyards. Trade unions build up resistance to recruitment in a passing boom, and, from the entrepreneurs' point of view, recruitment requires a period of training which is comparable to investment in plant with a long gestation period.

the economy to settle smoothly into the higher rate of investment corresponding to the new situation. The process of adapting itself to a given rise in the rate of investment involves a still higher rate of investment, which cannot be maintained.

There is a maximum level of employment in the investment sector which is reached at some stage. Up to that point it has been expanding, steadily or in a series of rushes. Beyond that point it ceases to expand and investment for a time runs at its maximum level.

The economy then remains poised for a time in short-period equilibrium with investment at its maximum rate. But capacity in the consumption sector is continually increasing as new plant comes into service. The seller's market, therefore, first ceases to intensify and then slackens. Consequently new orders for capital goods fail to keep up with the rate at which old orders are being fulfilled, and employment in the investment sector falls below its maximum. Then demand for commodities falls, and surplus capacity emerges.

The essential character of a boom (as opposed to golden-age accumulation) is that it is based upon a contradiction. Investment is going on under the influence of the seller's market which investment itself creates. Over and above the investment due to whatever cause started the boom (say, an unforeseen invention), there is some extra investment due only to the high level of demand (relatively to capacity) induced by the investment. It would be possible for the seller's market to continue only if the rate of investment (and therefore demand for commodities) continued to expand from month to month in proportion to the increase in capacity that is taking place, and since the increase of the rate of investment cannot continue indefinitely while the rise in capacity goes on continuously as more and more equipment emerges from gestation, the seller's market cannot continue. Investment due to a seller's market is sawing off the bough that it is sitting on by bringing the seller's market to an end.

Each boom has its own history, depending upon the initiating cause of the boom, the preceding situation, and the extent and character of the long-period changes (such as growth of population and technical progress) that take place during the period of time that the boom lasts, but we may discuss some general characteristics of a typical boom.

THE COURSE OF INVESTMENT

Plant. A boom such as we are considering may be initiated by decisions to invest in an extension of equipment. Some schemes are started, and employment upon them continues over their gestation period. Meanwhile the development of the boom causes fresh schemes to be started; and there is a further increase in employment in the investment sector. When the capacity bottle-necks are reached, delivery dates are lengthened, and the investment projects form a queue awaiting their turn to be begun. While the boom is at its height, the industries specialised to the production of plant are working down the queue, starting operations on fresh projects as each batch is completed. It is for this reason that a high-level short-period equilibrium can persist for a considerable time. If the bottle-necks are widened (by the completion of schemes of investment in plant to produce plant) while the queue is still in being, the rate of investment rises, there is a further increase in employment and a new higher high-level equilibrium is reached. Investment of this type, however, often has a long gestation period, so that the new capacity may not be ready for use before the boom is over.

The boom passes its peak when new projects cease to be added to the queue at a faster rate than earlier ones are being completed; the down-turn occurs when the queue has been absorbed and commencements on new schemes cease to keep up with completions of earlier ones.

Stocks. The initial increase in employment leads within a week to increased purchases of commodities (as workers spend their wages) and in the first instance this leads to a fall in the stocks of finished goods. At a later stage these stocks are replaced, and there is, moreover, an increase of stocks to raise them to the level appropriate to the higher rate at which sales are taking place. This means additional employment. When the stocks have caught up with requirements, employment falls to the level appropriate to current sales, and for this very reason current sales relapse to a lower level. The period of production for commodities produced with existing capacity is short relatively to the gestation period of plant. Therefore there is likely to be a series of ripples in employment due to accumulation and decumulation of stocks superimposed upon a wave of investment in equipment.

Work-in-progress. As soon as the initial fall of stocks has occurred, production begins on goods to replace them. For most commodities the period of production is considerably longer than a week (during which work is done in advance of payment) so that a further decline in stocks takes place as more wages are being spent, until commodities begin to emerge from the pipe-lines of production to replace those being sold to the newly employed workers. These stocks also have to be replaced later, and this further contributes to the wobbles in investment.

As soon as the first batch of equipment (additional to that in existence when the boom began) is ready for use, employ-ment in operating it begins, and, again, it takes more than a week to fill the pipe-line of work-in-progress. Provided that employment on the production of plant has not already fallen off, this raises the total of employment, and consequently the demand for commodities, still further.

The combination of these three types of investment pro-duces complicated time-patterns in the movements of employ-ment, and each boom has its own detailed pattern according to the prevailing technical and market conditions, while conforming to type in its broad lines.

THE CONCERTINA EFFECT

The level of real-wage rates (though not total consumption of the workers) tends to be reduced by a boom. It might therefore be argued that the investment that takes place in a boom is devoted to less-mechanised techniques than are appro-priate to the average level of real wages over the long run, while any replacements that are made in a slump are appropriate to a higher level of mechanisation.[1] It seems rather doubtful,

[1] See N. Kaldor, 'Professor Hayek and the Concertina Effect', *Economica* (November 1942).

however, whether this influence is likely to operate; employment is higher in the boom and lower in the slump, and it seems likely that the ease or difficulty of recruiting labour is a more important influence on the choice of technique than the level of real wages. The shift of the mechanisation frontier is to be regarded as a long-period phenomenon. It comes into play through the relative scarcity or surplus of labour from boom to boom, rather than in response to the changes in the real-wage rate that take place during a short-period increase in employment.

PRICES AND EMPLOYMENT

The course of commodity prices over a boom is complicated by the tendency for money-wage rates to rise while it is going on. Let us first consider the behaviour of prices on the assumption of a constant money-wage rate. The movement lies between two extremes: constant output of commodities and constant prices of commodities.

To illustrate the first extreme let us postulate that the capacity of the consumption sector is quite rigid, so that there is a definite rate per week of output of commodities which cannot be exceeded, and which was already being produced before the boom began; and that employment in the investment sector reaches its maximum during the gestation period of the first batch of capital goods that have been ordered, so that the seller's market comes to an abrupt end as soon as they are ready for use. Then the output of consumption goods, and consequently the total of real wages, remains constant throughout the boom. Employment in the consumption sector does not increase, and prices rise and the real-wage rate per man-hour falls in proportion to the rise in total employment, which takes place only in the investment sector.[1]

At the opposite extreme, suppose that there was initially ample unused capacity in the consumption sector. The prices of commodities, before the boom began, were being held, by tacit or open agreement between entrepreneurs in each market,

---

[1] Say, in the initial position 20 per cent of labour was employed in the investment sector, and employment there increases by 25 per cent. Then total employment increases (and the real-wage rate falls) by 5 per cent.

at the ruling subjective-normal level, and are not raised when demand expands.   Then the real-wage rate remains constant throughout the boom, and the total of real wages increases in proportion to the increase in employment.   Since quasi-rent per man employed in the consumption sector is constant, the total increase in employment is proportional to the increase in the investment sector.[1]

The *employment multiplier* is the ratio of the total increase in employment to the increase in the investment sector (comparing the initial position with that reached when the investment sector is working at the maximum rate reached during the boom).   In the first extreme case the multiplier is equal to 1. In the second it is equal to $1/q$ where q is the ratio of quasi-rent to the value of output per man (the gross margin per man) in the consumption sector.[2]

Neither extreme case is likely to obtain in any actual situation.   Prices (relatively to money wages) normally rise with an increase in the ratio of demand to capacity so that as the boom runs up to the point of high-level equilibrium there is some fall in real wages per man-hour accompanied by an increase in total real wages.   At the same time there is a fall in output per head as more labour is squeezing extra product from a given capacity.   The multiplier is somewhere between the possible extreme values.[3]

When the maximum level of employment in the investment sector has been reached, and the economy is poised at a high-level equilibrium, capacity in the consumption sector is

[1] In the initial position 80 per cent of labour was employed in the consumption sector and 20 per cent in the investment sector.   An increase of 25 per cent in the investment sector requires an increase of 25 per cent in the consumption sector, so that employment rises in the ratio of 80 plus 20 to 100 plus 25.

[2] This depends upon the assumption of no consumption out of profits. The same principle applies when that assumption is relaxed (see below, p. 266).

[3] In the initial position with 80 teams of men employed in the consumption sector and 20 in the investment sector, the real wage was 1 per team and 100 units of commodities were being produced.   At the high-level equilibrium 25 teams are employed in the investment sector and the real wage is, say, 95.   It requires, say, an addition of 5 teams to the consumption sector (before its capacity has increased appreciably) to produce an extra 4·5 units of output.   The employment multiplier is then equal to 2.   Total employment rises to 110 teams, and output of commodities to 104·5.

gradually rising. During this period the intensity of the seller's market begins to slacken somewhat, supplies catch up on demand, and while employment in the investment sector remains constant, the output of commodities rises and prices fall somewhat. The real-wage rate therefore rises. During this phase, therefore, there may be some further increase in employment, but output per head has also risen in the consumption sector as the labour force is deployed more economically with the new capacity, so that the increase in employment (if any) is less than in proportion to the rise in output. Prosperity, from the entrepreneur's point of view, is coming to an end, for a constant total of quasi-rent (equal to the wages bill of the investment sector) is being shared by a growing amount of capacity in the consumption sector. As capacity continues to increase the seller's market disappears, and when, in consequence, employment in the investment sector begins to fall, the boom is over.

The movement of money-wage rates and monopolistic price policy play across this underlying pattern. Money-wage rates are likely to rise during the course of the upswing and during the period of high-level employment. If, at each point, prices are higher than they would otherwise have been in proportion to the rise in wages it makes no difference to the course of events in real terms.[1] If prices are sticky, consumption is higher at each stage, and at the height of the boom the seller's market is prolonged as new capacity is met by rising demand. This cannot maintain the boom indefinitely. Monopolists will not allow their gross margins to be eroded by rising wages beyond a certain point, so that the increase in real demand is limited, and after a time the growth of capacity catches up upon it, and the seller's market comes to an end.

THE REACTION

The end of the seller's market leads to a fall in the rate of investment, and the fall in the rate of investment causes a buyer's market to develop, which further discourages investment and further intensifies the buyer's market. The economy

[1] But monetary factors may come into play to check the incipient inflation (see below, p. 238).

passes through a slump (a period of contracting output) and falls into a depression (a period of contracted output).

The limit to the run-down in output in a slump is less definite than the limit to expansion in a boom. Employment in a boom reaches a maximum when (or soon after) the investment sector has run into a bottle-neck of physical capacity, but there is no technical limit to the possible fall in employment. When employment in production of equipment falls there is no immediate effect upon productive capacity, and for a time output continues to emerge from the pipe-line of work-in-progress at the same rate as before. Since sales have fallen, stocks for a time accumulate. These are seen to be redundant to the shrunken level of demand and the pipe-line of work-in-progress is therefore not refilled as fast as it is emptying. There is no technical limit to this process, short of the complete cessation of production.

The limit to the run-down comes from demand. If prices were held constant as output declines (or cut only in proportion to money wages) so that the real wage per man-hour of employment was constant, then every decrease in employment would be followed by a decrease in sales and consequently by a further decline in employment.[1] But at some stage in the process prices begin to fall (relatively to wages) as a result of competition or of the deliberate policy of monopolistic sellers, so that the real-wage rate rises, and sales per unit of employment rise. A low-level equilibrium is reached at the point where the rise in consumption per man employed offsets the fall in the number of men employed.[2] The volume of sales of commodities then ceases to fall, and consequently the amount of employment ceases to fall.[3]

[1] This conclusion will be modified when we introduce rentiers into the model.

[2] As before, when 80 teams of men are employed in the consumption sector and 20 in the investment sector; the wage is 1 per team. A fall in employment in the investment sector to 15 teams accompanied by a rise in the real wage to 1·05 and a rise in output per team in the consumption sector from 1·25 to 1·26 units of commodities would lead to a fall in employment in the consumption sector to 75. Total employment is then 90, and the output of commodities 94·5.

[3] Other buffers to the fall in output, for instance rentier consumption and unemployment pay, will be considered later (see below, p. 267).

Any further fall in prices (relatively to money wages), after this point has been reached, brings about an increase in sales of commodities, and the economy bounces up to a somewhat higher low-level equilibrium. An increase in monopolistic price agreements introduced as a defence against falling margins prevents such a rebound, and keeps the economy at the low-level equilibrium that it has reached. An increase in margins reduces real wages and pushes the economy down to a still lower equilibrium. Each downward movement is accompanied by an accumulation followed by a decumulation of stocks, causing corresponding wobbles in employment.

Meanwhile, surplus capacity is gradually shrinking, as old plant becomes unserviceable and is not replaced.[1] Sooner or later, to maintain even the low-level rate of output requires investment in plant, the buyer's market grows less intense and a revival begins.[2]

When the initial disturbance was a fall in the rate of investment (due, say, to a retardation of technical progress) the story begins at this stage. Disinvestment[3] in the depression goes on until a seller's market develops and a period of high investment sets in.

Thus whenever the long-run trend of accumulation goes round a corner, the short-run course of investment swings too far, and the path appropriate to the new situation can be found only through a violent oscillation, often followed by a series of further wobbles.

THE TRADE CYCLE

A boom or a slump may occur as the result of some long-period cause, such as a speeding-up or retardation of technical progress. They may also occur when all the long-run conditions for a golden age obtain.

---

[1] Cf. R. F. Harrod, 'Notes on Trade Cycle Theory', *Economic Journal*, p. 267 (June 1951).

[2] It is not necessary that there should be an over-all net disinvestment, as some entrepreneurs continue to carry out investment during the depression, and their investment may be sufficient to outweigh the disinvestment of the rest.

[3] Or at least the cessation of investment in some lines.

For each individual entrepreneur the future is uncertain even when the economy as a whole is developing smoothly, and the actions of each entrepreneur affect the situation for the rest. For this reason there is an inherent instability, under the capitalist rules of the game, which generates fluctuations, so to say, from within the economy, quite apart from any change in external circumstances.

The typical entrepreneur, as soon as he finds his existing capacity operating at what seems to him a reasonable rate of profit, wants to operate more capacity. Unless investment just hits off the golden-age rate, at which demand grows with capacity (or unless it is effectively controlled), it will always be oscillating, for whenever it happens to rise it generates a seller's market, and so stimulates a further rise.

Every time a seller's market develops, investment over-shoots and a period of low investment follows. The very fact that there has been a boom causes a subsequent slump. Every time a buyer's market develops, disinvestment goes too far and a period of high investment follows. The very fact that there has been a depression causes a revival.

Accumulation then takes the form of a more or less regular cyclical succession of four phases of development — a phase when the rate of investment is increasing; a high-level equi-librium with a high steady rate of investment, and capacity gradually increasing relatively to output; a phase of declining investment (whether gradual or an abrupt drop); and a phase of a precarious low-level equilibrium with capacity gradually shrinking relatively to output.

Normally prices rise relatively to money wages during the boom, so that the share of quasi-rent in the value of sales is higher during the boom than on the average over the long run. This means that the employment multiplier is considerably less than the ratio of total employment to employment in the investment sector on the average over the long run; [1] and the investment sector experiences greater proportional fluctuations

---

[1] In our numerical illustrations employment is divided between the two sectors at the middle position between minimum and maximum employ-ment in the ratio 80 to 20, and at the maximum, 85 to 25. The ratio of total employment, on the average, to investment employment is 5 and the multiplier 2.

than the economy as a whole. The average rate of output (good years with bad) is a smaller proportion of total capacity in the investment sector than in industry as a whole. Then total capacity is larger than it would be if the same long-run rate of accumulation were made steadily in the manner of a golden age.

Entrepreneurs who specialise in the production of equipment, being accustomed to greater fluctuations in demand, expand their own capacity in a seller's market less readily than others, so that the proportion of investment-sector investment, at the height of the boom, is less than the ratio of investment-sector capacity to total capacity.

The typical course of the cycle then may be conceived as follows : starting from a low-level equilibrium, when prices and employment have been stable for a little while, some renewals of plant are taking place, but not enough to maintain the existing stock.[1] As capacity shrinks, the buyer's market gradually grows less intense. Those plants which remain in operation gradually find sales increasing as rivals give up the struggle to survive, and sooner or later some entrepreneurs find themselves in a situation in which they can expect to make a profit on more plant than they have. Orders for equipment are placed, and employment in the investment sector increases. Consequently demand for commodities expands, more entrepreneurs find their capacity inadequate and the upswing of investment continues. As we have seen, a boom may come to an end before investment has reached the maximum physically possible, or it may be strong enough to reach capacity in some bottle-necks in the investment sector. When it does so, some investment in the investment sector is likely to be going on, so that after a little while the bottle-necks are widened but investment in the capacity to produce equipment, as we have seen, bears a smaller ratio to pre-existing capacity than does investment in general; so that the widening of the bottle-necks is not sufficient to permit investment to continue expanding as fast as the stock of capacity is growing. The

---

[1] Or, if total output continues to expand somewhat, not enough to keep the stock of capital expanding in proportion to output. See above, p. 208, note 3.

growth of capacity in the consumption sector therefore overtakes the expansion of demand, the seller's market comes to an end and a downswing carries the economy to a low-level equilibrium.

INTERPRETATION

The course of development since the capitalist rules of the game began to be played has been marked by a strong rhythm which gives rise to the view that there has been a definite trade cycle of the type described above, with a period of eight or ten years from high point to high point. According to this view, it just so happens that the four phases of a cycle take this time to run through, and it is easy to give plausible-seeming values to the time-lags involved — the period of diffusion of decisions to invest on the upswing, and of the fall in the rate of investment on the downswing, the duration of the high-level equilibrium before sufficient additional capacity has accumulated to kill the seller's market, and the duration of the period of shrinking capacity which leads to a revival — though it is by no means easy to demonstrate that the assumed values are in fact correct.

The alternative view is that each boom is started by some particular event, such as a major technical discovery. Once a boom has begun to develop it attracts into its stream any events favourable to investment that occur while it is going on, so that booms differ from each other in strength according to the force of the various elements (such as the amount of new technical knowledge awaiting exploitation) which contribute to each. The condition of a seller's market induced by the boom causes an over-shoot in the expansion of capacity, for however great the investment opportunities opened up while the boom goes on, the extra investment induced by the seller's market itself cannot last. A slump then follows, and depression continues, with minor fluctuations, until a fresh event occurs.

The crucial difference between these two views concerns the recovery from a depression. According to the first, recovery comes, so to say, from within the system, because the shrinkage of capacity relatively to demand recreates a situation

favourable to investment. According to the second the internal
power of recovery of the system is too weak to overcome the
shock of a slump and the apparent regularity of the cycle is
accidental, being merely due to the fact that, so far, something
always has turned up to cause a revival after a depression has
been going on for a few years at most.

Perhaps the question will never be satisfactorily answered.
The champions of each view can interpret the incomplete
historical data each way with equal plausibility, and it seems
unlikely that the future will provide a crucial experiment to
settle the dispute, for nowadays peoples and governmênts have
become conscious of the problem of instability, and deliberate
action is likely to be taken to check a slump or cure a depression
long before there has been time for interested observers to see
whether a revival would occur if the system were left to follow
its natural rhythm.

CHAPTER 22

CYCLES AND TRENDS

THE instability of the economy makes the maintenance of a golden age impossible. When all other conditions are satisfied tranquillity is still disturbed by fluctuations generated from within. Accumulation periodically lags behind the growth ratio of the economy and then leaps to catch up. Each overshoot brings a reaction, and another lag, to be followed by another leap. Even when accumulation goes on steadily over the long run it is not steady from year to year, but occurs in bursts.

The very fact that accumulation takes place unsteadily reduces the growth ratio below what it would be in golden-age conditions, for uncertainty weakens the urge to invest and consequently slows down technical progress. The trend which emerges *ex post* from the operation of the trade cycle is not the same thing as the growth ratio of a golden age, but is an imperfect reflection of it.

Nevertheless accumulation is still possible if entrepreneurs pursue it with vigour, and our analysis of accumulation keeping step with, surpassing or falling short of the potential growth ratio of the economy holds good when it is translated into terms of cylical fluctuations.

CYCLICAL ACCUMULATION

When accumulation is going on over the long run the end of a boom sees a larger stock of capital than has ever been in existence before. The first point to be considered is what prevents disinvestment in the subsequent depression from reducing it again to no more than was formerly in existence.

The essential condition is that monopoly (in the short-period sense) should not have increased compared to the last depression. With a given degree of competition, prices tend to be lower, relatively to money wages, the greater the amount of idle capacity. If the output of commodities ran down, in this slump, to the same absolute level as in the last, there would be more idle capacity in the consumption sector, and a higher level of real wages. Therefore output does not run down so far, and the low-level equilibrium is reached at a higher rate of output. In short, competition ensures that some of the additional capacity that has come into existence since the last slump is utilised during the depression. Therefore the shrinkage of capacity that occurs as plant wears out without being replaced does not go so far, and part of the increment of plant survives the depression. A revival starts at a higher level of output.

The second condition required for positive accumulation over the long run is that the total net investment made during the following boom shall be greater than in the last. The upswing must be strong enough to carry investment into the bottle-necks in the industries producing plant. If the bottle-necks in the investment sector were widened during the last boom the rate of investment is now higher than ever before. If the bottle-necks have not been widened since the beginning of the last boom, this boom will go on longer than the last. The rate of output of new productive plant reaches a maximum at the same level as before (in bottle-necks of the same capacity) and since the stock of capital has been growing, the amount of new plant representing replacements is larger than during the last boom, net investment per annum is less and a longer time passes before excess capacity appears. If this occurs in a succession of booms the seller's market in the investment sector grows more intense from boom to boom, and (unless monopoly in the long-period sense has increased) the bottle-necks will be widened. Thus, just as in an imaginary golden age, the fact that accumulation has been going on in the past creates conditions favourable for it to be maintained.

When the labour force has grown since the last upswing occurred, and output per head has risen because during the course of the last boom, the new capital goods produced embodied the latest improvements (and so did whatever

replacements were made during the last depression), there is
labour available for a higher rate of output in the next boom.
A growth in the labour force does not directly cause accumulation,[1] but makes long-run accumulation possible without a
fall in the long-run rate of profit.

THE RATE OF ACCUMULATION

When the bottle-necks are sharply distinct, then if each
upswing is strong enough to run into the bottle-necks and each
boom lasts for the same length of time, the long-run rate of
accumulation is governed by the rate at which the bottle-
necks are widened. With neutral technical progress, the realised
growth ratio of the system is equal to the proportionate
net increase in the productive capacity of the bottle-neck industries made over each cycle, divided by the number of years
from peak to peak.[2]

With a capital-saving bias in innovations, if our assumption
of asymmetry is correct,[3] successive booms would leave capacity
in the consumption sector expanded in a greater proportion
than in the investment sector; with a capital-using bias,
the investment sector would grow faster than at the realised
growth ratio of the economy, while the consumption sector
grew at a slower rate.

The conception of a perfectly regular cycle is self-contra-
dictory, for if the cycle were predictable investment in the
boom would be curtailed and replacements in the depression
maintained, so that the cycle would flatten out. The above
stylised scheme indicates the underlying pattern of the relation
between the cycle and the trend of accumulation, which is
overlaid by variations in intensity and timing, and deflected
by unpredictable events, so that uncertainty is kept alive.

The uneven load on the industries producing long-lived
capital goods means that their productive capacity is greater
than would be required for the same long-run rate of accumulation if it were carried out continuously. In a golden age

---

[1] But see below, p. 262.

[2] Cf. N. Kaldor, 'The Relation of Economic Growth to Cyclical
Fluctuations', *Economic Journal* (March 1954).

[3] See Chapter 17.

with the same productive capacity in the investment sector (and the same labour force) the rate of accumulation would be more rapid (being maintained constantly at the boom rate), and to accommodate the accumulation there would have to be a more rapid rate of technical progress, or a higher degree of mechanisation would have been established. In a golden age with the same long-run rate of accumulation there would be a higher ratio of capacity in the consumption sector to capacity in the investment sector, and consequently a higher level of real wages.

Given productive capacity, the average of consumption, good years with bad, would be higher in a golden age, for the deficiency of output over periods of under-capacity working is generally much greater than the excess of output (due to overtime working, etc.) that is realised for short spells at the height of booms.

A SCARCITY OF LABOUR

Though instability is unfavourable to investment, yet accumulation may exceed for a stretch of time the long-run rate at which labour is becoming available. Accumulation over the long run in excess of the potential growth ratio of the economy shows itself in a scarcity of labour during booms. During a depression a scarcity of labour (relatively to capacity) is disguised by short-period unemployment (with idle capacity), but during a boom high short-period demand for labour is superimposed upon long-run scarcity. Then during a boom the diffusion of technical improvements is speeded up, for, with a general scarcity of man-power combined with a seller's market, entrepreneurs are anxious to get plant which yields the maximum output per head, and for the same reason they are more than usually anxious to seek out new inventions. The boom is prolonged by replacements of plant rendered obsolete by new discoveries.

At the same time the degree of mechanisation may be increased, for it seems worth while to increase output per head (in the prevailing condition of high demand and difficulty of finding labour) even at the expense of a high cost of investment per unit of employment.

In the special case of no technical progress, increasing mechanisation is the only means available to increase output per head, and investment in each boom is devoted to a more mechanised technique than in the last.

STAGNATION

As we have seen, the maintenance of accumulation over the long run requires that competition in the short-period sense remains effective. Monopoly may have increased in one depression compared to the last slump, either because the last depression led to the formation of price rings which have become permanent or because of a secular tendency for monopoly to grow as each round of the competitive struggle leaves fewer victors in possession of each market. Weaker competition means that a larger amount of surplus capacity is compatible with a given real-wage rate. The run-down in one slump may then go as far or further than in the last, even though capacity has been increased in the intervening boom. Then (in the absence of fresh events favourable to investment) the revival does not occur until capacity has shrunk as far or further than it did in the last depression. Over the long run capacity is stationary or declining.

The maintenance of accumulation depends upon the vigour with which entrepreneurs pursue it as well as upon the persistence of competition. If the urge to accumulate has grown weaker during a depression, the emergence of a seller's market, when the revival comes, brings a smaller upswing than it did last time. The high-level equilibrium is reached before investment runs into the old bottle-necks. Consequently replacements in the investment sector fail to keep pace with the scrapping of worn-out capacity, and the bottle-necks gradually contract.

Zero accumulation over the long run, in such a case, would be a fluke. It may just so happen that investment in each boom is exactly sufficient to restore the capacity worn out in each slump, while unemployment (from boom to boom or depression to depression) grows gradually greater, as the labour force increases or output per head rises, but there is no mechanism in the system to keep net investment over the long run just at zero. Indeed, zero net investment has no very precise meaning, for as we have seen,[1] a constant stock of capital can be exactly defined only when the physical specification of each type of capital good, and the age composition of the stock of capital goods, remains unchanged over the long run.

Thus when stagnation has set in there is no reason to expect the stock of productive capacity to be stationary. A mild degree of stagnation permits of some positive accumulation, though not enough to keep up with the potential growth ratio of the economy. A more severe degree means a progressive decline, each depression leaving the total stock of capital (according to any rough reasonable measure) smaller than the last.

In stagnant conditions demechanisation of technique may be going on, for the surplus of labour unemployed even at the height of a boom is tending to grow greater as time goes by. Falling money-wage rates meet sticky prices, and real wages fall by more in each boom and rise by less in each slump than in the last, so that the plant scrapped in each slump is likely to be replaced in the succeeding boom by plant for a less mechanised technique.

THE STATIC STATE

The imaginary condition in which the labour force is constant, all possible inventions have already been made, and the highest feasible degree of mechanisation has already been reached, represents potential economic bliss. This (like a potential golden age) may be marred by the inherent instability of the economy.

An upper limit to capacity in the investment sector is brought into being by the inflation barrier. The inflation barrier sets a limit to the ratio of employment in the investment sector to employment in the consumption sector.[2] In

---

[1] See p. 119.
[2] The operation of the inflation barrier through the monetary mechanism is discussed below, p. 238.

conditions of potential bliss, the absolute amount of employment represented by this ratio does not change through time,
and there is no point in having capacity which would not be
used even in a boom. Thus capacity in the investment sector
must be conceived to have become stationary. There is zero
net investment in the investment sector (gross investment in
each boom just making good the disinvestment of each slump),
the bottle-necks are never widened and a zero growth ratio
cannot be exceeded.

There is no similar mechanism to prevent decumulation
over the long run. The inherent instability of the economy
may not only mar the condition of bliss, but also cause the
economy to slip below potential bliss, disinvestment during
depressions being more than is made good during booms.

THE APPROACH TO BLISS

When the growth ratio of the economy is zero but mechanisation has not yet reached its limit, accumulation involves,
as we have seen, a gradual fall in the ratio of employment in
the investment sector to employment in the consumption
sector until net investment comes to an end.[1] With fluctuating investment this would show itself by the total investment
made in each boom being less than in the last, while consumption in each depression was greater than in the last.
From boom to boom, capacity in the consumption sector
would grow, while capacity in the investment sector fell.
Total employment (comparing boom to boom and depression
to depression) would be constant over the long run, rising in
the consumption sector and falling in the investment sector,
total real wages rising and total profits falling.

This is a logical possibility, which is most unlikely to be
realised under the capitalist rules of the game. A falling rate
of profit over the long run, combined with cyclical fluctuations,
is likely to mean losses during depressions, which both undermine the urge to accumulate and promote defensive mono-
polies. An economy heading towards bliss is never likely to
be able unaided to pass the slough of stagnation to arrive there.

[1] See above, p. 81.

EMPLOYMENT AND UNEMPLOYMENT

To see the movements of employment over successive cycles it is convenient to consider technical progress and population increase separately. First, suppose that the same techniques are in use all the time. A higher level of output in one depression than in the last then entails a higher level of employment. The population has increased since the last depression. The amount of unemployment may therefore also be greater. (Population growth is slow relatively to the swings of employment that take place over the cycle, so that the difference in unemployment between one depression and the next is in any case small relatively to the difference in employment between depression and boom.) When long-run accumulation is going on, the succeeding boom (provided that it is strong enough to go all the way) finds the bottle-necks in the investment sector somewhat wider than in the last boom, and total employment rises to a higher level. Consequently the total real-wage bill, and the output of commodities, is higher in each boom than in the last. In stagnant conditions employment rises little, or falls, from boom to boom, while unemployment increases with the growth of population.

Now let us suppose that the investment made during a boom embodies improvements due to technical progress, but that the labour force is constant.

With long-run accumulation going on, the output of commodities is greater in one depression than the last, but the amount of employment may be less. In each boom output per head in the consumption sector is higher than in the last boom (for the improved capacity created in the last boom is now in use) and (on the assumption that competition is not weaker) the real wage per man is higher. Thus if employment in the investment sector reaches the same level as in the last boom, the total real-wage bill and the output of commodities is higher.

In stagnant conditions, total output rises from boom to boom in a smaller proportion than output per head and (unless working hours are being sufficiently reduced) there is long-run growth in technological unemployment.

The effects of population growth and technical progress are superimposed on each other. When accumulation is going on at a sufficient rate to keep unemployment in each boom at a low level, there is a rise in output over the long run (comparing peak to peak and trough to trough in successive cycles) compounded of more employment and more output per man. In stagnation, output rises little or even falls, from peak to peak, while there is a growth of unemployment over the long run compounded of the effects of increasing population and reduced employment per unit of output.

Given the fluctuations in employment in the investment sector, unemployment in the consumption sector during depressions is less (the employment multiplier is smaller) the more rapidly real wages rise as the utilisation of plant falls, both because the run-down in the slump is smaller and because the amount of shrinkage of capacity required to produce a reaction is less (so that, with a given age composition of capital goods, the depression lasts a shorter time).[1]

When slumps are shallow and depressions short, the unemployment that they cause can be endured; and when there is in any case a long-period surplus of labour the extra misery of a slump is lost in the general swamp. But when unemployment is low during booms and heavy and prolonged during depressions, the totally irrational suffering that it causes (which is something over and above the low level of consumption that goes with it) becomes painfully obvious, and leads to far-reaching political reactions.

[1] Cf. N. Kaldor, *op. cit.*

BOOK IV
FINANCE

CHAPTER 23

MONEY AND FINANCE

WE must now examine the influence of the monetary system upon accumulation. Our model economy has evolved (we will suppose) beyond the stage of paying the weekly wage bill in nails.[1] Certain highly respected banks have long been established which cater for the monetary needs of the system.[2]

The banks have to observe certain rules of the game. In reality these have been evolved in a complicated legal system full of anomalies and fossils from the past, and are regulated by public institutions such as the Bank of England or the Federal Reserve System. To make our analysis both as general and as simple as possible we will assume that our banks behave in the proper manner without specifying any particular form of discipline.

In reality the forms of borrowing, and therefore the types of titles to wealth represented by the obligations of debtors, are infinitely various, but we can exhibit all the main features of the capitalist financial system while making use of a few sharply distinct types. We shall assume that titles to wealth consist only of notes, bonds and bank deposits, and that there are only three kinds of borrowing — borrowing by entrepreneurs from the banks against bills ; borrowing by entrepreneurs from each other (we have not yet introduced rentiers into the model) against bonds, which may be purchased at second hand by the banks ; and borrowing by the banks from entrepreneurs against deposits.

We shall introduce these forms of borrowing successively, beginning with notes issued against bills. In order to keep a

---

[1] Cf. above, p. 27.
[2] In reality also banks may take some part in entrepreneurship, but we will assume that there is a strict separation of functions.

clear distinction between money as a medium of exchange and money as a placement we still assume that all transactions involving money payments are carried out against notes, and that notes are never held for any purpose except as balances for convenience in carrying out transactions.

THE NOTE CIRCULATION

Notes bearing the name of a respected bank are acceptable to retailers and other entrepreneurs and so provide a medium for paying wages. The notes now circulating came into existence as the results of loans from the banks to entrepreneurs, who pay out wages in advance of receiving the proceeds of selling the goods which the workers produce. For the moment we are assuming that the only form of borrowing is by discounting bills (long-term bonds will be introduced later). A bill represents an undertaking to pay a certain sum at a specified date (say in six months' time) which is sold to-day for a sum in notes less, by the discount, than that for which the bill is drawn.

The basic reason why the entrepreneurs have to pay interest to the banks (in the form of discounts) against the circulating medium is that their own I O U's would not be acceptable as a means of payment, while the notes of respected banks are. (The determination and the influence of the rate of discount will be discussed later.)

The size of the stock of notes required for the economy as a whole depends on the value of the weekly wages bill, the extent of specialisation amongst entrepreneurs (which governs the number of transactions between them involving payments in notes) and the average delay between receipts and disbursements, which governs the speed at which notes travel through the pipe-lines of circulation.

Entrepreneurs can to some extent economise requirements, and so save interest, by timing disbursements to fit with receipts or by handling transactions with other entrepreneurs by book entries. Thus there is some tendency for the note circulation (given the total value of transactions per annum) to be lower the higher the discount rate. But this effect is likely to be slight for any moderate range of levels of the discount rate, because habits of payments cannot readily be altered, and, unless the rate is very high, it is not worth while to bother about economising balances.

When an entrepreneur requires, for making payments in the near future, more notes than have come to hand from recent receipts, he can discount a bill ; and when he finds himself with more than he needs, he reduces his outstanding bills (in order to save the interest) by paying off, with notes, those that are falling due and not renewing them. The notes then return to the banks. Thus the quantity of notes outstanding is continuously being adjusted to the requirements of the circulation. When employment is increasing (or money-wage rates rising) the entrepreneurs are paying out every week more than they received from last week's sales, so that the entrepreneurs, taken as a whole, are continually increasing their indebtedness to the banks, and the circulation increases as required. When the wages bill is declining, bills are retired and the circulation is shrinking.

THE BANKS

A stock of notes is just as necessary for the conduct of industry as an outfit of productive equipment but it would be very far fetched to regard the bankers as belonging to the category of manufacturers of capital goods. It is best to treat them as a group of capitalists *sui generis*, and to look at the interchange between them taken as a whole and the entrepreneurs taken as a whole as a special class of transactions.

Subject to the requirements of monetary policy (to be discussed later) the banks, within reason, can make the discount rate what they please. Competition between them for business may drive it down to a level which just covers their expenses, or they may have an understanding amongst themselves that holds it at a level which enables them to earn profits comfortably. (They cannot, however, keep it permanently so high as to drive the entrepreneurs to escape from dependence upon them and devise other means of settling transactions.)

The capital assets of a banker consist primarily in his reputation; he also requires a certain quantity of reserves of the notes of others to make his own acceptable,[1] and office buildings of an impressive appearance. We will suppose that all bank profits are reinvested in banking concerns (the bankers vying with each other in the splendour of their offices) so that bank capital and industrial capital are two water-tight compartments.[2]

To the entrepreneurs, bills are debts to be set against the assets acquired by investing the sums borrowed, and the interest payments represented by discounts are a deduction from profits. To the bankers this interest is not profit, but gross proceeds. With it they pay their running expenses, and the balance (their profits) they invest in equipping offices. (It is a strict rule of the banking game not to make any payments with newly issued notes, for otherwise the bankers could carry out an indefinite amount of investment, which would disorganise the rest of the economy.) The whole of the gross proceeds of the banking business (that is, the interest paid by entrepreneurs) returns to industry as quasi-rent arising from the expenditure of the bankers, as investment or via the expenditure of their employees. Thus the entrepreneurs' total profits, over any period, are equal to their own net investment *plus* the expenditure of the bankers. Since the latter is equal to the interest paid to the banks, profits net of interest are equal to net investment. The addition to the wealth commanded by the entrepreneurs made in any period is the increment in the stock of capital goods (the net investment of the period) *plus* the addition to the stock of notes in circulation [3]

---

[1] In reality the constitution of reserves and the rules regulating them are the means by which Central Banks keep control over the monetary system.

[2] This assumption can be relaxed when we introduce rentiers into the model, see below, p. 249.

[3] This is not quite accurate. On an average day workers are in possession of notes equal to about half a week's wages bill (somewhat less or somewhat more according to whether they spend more or less on the earlier than the later days of the week). Thus the addition, over, say, a year, to the stock of notes owned by entrepreneurs taken as a whole is equal to the addition made over the year to the stock of notes in circulation *minus* approximately half the difference between a week's wages bill at the beginning and at the end of the year. Against this, however, there is a corresponding addition to the entrepreneurs' stock of capital goods over and above what they have

and *minus* the net addition to outstanding bills. Since the last two are equal, the addition to property for entrepreneurs, taken as a whole, is the addition to the stock of capital goods.[1]

THE BOND MARKET

There may also be lending and borrowing between entrepreneurs.[2] This arises, first, because some entrepreneurs are more active and energetic than others, and like to invest in excess of their own profits, and second, because many schemes of investment have, for technical reasons, to be carried out in large bursts. Thus an entrepreneur who is building and equipping a new factory spends in a year many times a year's profit. And periodical renewals of large units of equipment have to be made by expending the amortisation fund that has been accumulated out of quasi-rent over many years past. When a large scheme of investment has recently been completed, the entrepreneur requires a period of digestion to organise his now extended scale of operations, and refrains for some time from further investment. And when an item of equipment has just been installed, its amortisation fund begins to be built up, to be expended some years hence. Thus, in any one year, some entrepreneurs are carrying out investment in excess of the year's profit, and find themselves at the end with an addition to their indebtedness ; while others invest less, and find themselves at the end of the year with a smaller outstanding debt or an addition to property over and above their capital goods. Let us call those whose debt has increased the *excess-investors* of the year, and those whose net debt has fallen the *savers* of the year. The excess-investment

---

paid for. The workers are paid at the end of the week, and consequently advance a week's worth of work-in-progress to their employers. At the end of a year when the wage bill has been increasing, the workers, taken as a whole, have added to their advance to entrepreneurs taken as a whole roughly half the difference between a week's work at the end and at the beginning of the year. They have no property in the work-in-progress thus financed, and it is an addition to the capital of the entrepreneurs which just about balances the addition to notes not owned by the entrepreneurs.

[1] Cf. above, p. 45.

[2] In real life this is generally mediated through rentiers, but the main principles at work can be exhibited in our model without rentiers.

of the one group is equal to the saving of the other group, for it is precisely the excess of the outlay of the first group over their profits which generates the quasi-rents in excess of outlay for the others. Both excess investment and saving are gross. The one includes outlay on replacements of equipment and the other the accumulation of amortisation funds.

We will suppose that excess-investors in the past have been accustomed to borrow against bonds which have been taken up by savers. For simplicity we will suppose that there is only one kind of bond, carrying a fixed interest, and that they have no redemption date, but can be bought in and retired at any time at their market price. The nominal interest on a bond reflects the terms of borrowing at the time when it was issued. There is a second-hand market in bonds, in which their prices become adjusted to the nominal interest that they carry, thus bringing their yields into line with each other. The yield of a bond at any moment reflects both the general level of interest rates and the particular credit of the particular concerns (those most respected and reliable enjoying the lowest yields). We may select the very best concerns, about whose ability to honour their obligations there is the least possible doubt, as a marker, and call the yield of their bonds *the* bond rate of interest. Others have higher yields in varying degrees. The relative yields fan out in times of insecurity and lie close together in periods of general prosperity when profits are easy to earn and fears of default are far from everyone's thoughts.

The outstanding stock of bonds at any moment does not bear any particular necessary relationship to the value of the stock of capital goods in existence. It largely depends on the historical accident of how great the dispersion between the operations of savers and excess-investors has been over the past, and how far one-time excess-investors have since become savers and retired their own bonds instead of acquiring those of others.

Nor is the issue of new bonds over any one year closely related to the excess-investment of that year. Part of a year's excess-investment is financed by discounting bills with the banks, and part by selling out bonds acquired by the entrepreneurs concerned in a previous period of saving.

For each entrepreneur the rate that he has to promise on new issues depends upon his credit; and the amount that he can borrow, at any moment, depends upon the ratio of the interest he is already pledged to pay to what are believed likely to be his earnings. Since each takes an optimistic view of his own prospects (and need not worry about his own honesty) he reckons the cost (in interest forgone) of financing his own excess-investment by parting with any bonds that he may hold (the fruit of past saving) at less than the interest he would have to pay on new borrowing. Excess-investors, therefore, generally use up reserves before issuing new bonds. There is a continual circulation of second-hand bonds between excess-investors and savers; and the issue of new bonds over any period represents the excess of the excess-investment of that period over the utilisation of reserves built up by past saving. The total of bonds offered for sale, however (after cancelling in and out transactions in the second-hand market), over any one year, is equal to the amount required to provide placements for the year's saving. The excess-investment has been financed by selling bonds (newly created or taken out of holdings acquired by saving in the past) and by discounting bills. Savings, which accrue in the first instance as an excess of receipts of notes over outlays, are used to buy bonds and to pay off bills.[1] Thus, over any period of time, the purchase of bonds by savers *plus* the increase in the note circulation is equal to the sale of bonds by excess-investors *plus* the excess of bills drawn over bills redeemed. The borrowing of the excess-investors releases paper for the savers to acquire at the same rate as their expenditure generates the quasi-rents to be saved.

LIQUIDITY PREFERENCE

The holdings of bonds, at any moment, represent savings of the recent or remote past which are not being used, for the time being, to finance excess-investment. If the prices of bonds were perfectly stable the interest on them would be

---

[1] A third alternative, making deposits with the banks, is introduced below, p. 233.

a pure gain and the competition of savers with idle funds to place would ensure that the bond rate was no higher than the bill rate fixed by the banks. But bond prices are liable to vary (under the influence of the interactions between expected profits and monetary policy, which we shall discuss in a moment, and under the influence of beliefs about what those interactions are likely to be). An entrepreneur who is intending to use past savings to finance excess investment in the near future is therefore unwilling to hold bonds unless the interest on them reckoned from to-day till the time when he expects to sell them is sufficient to compensate for any fall in their price that is likely to occur meanwhile. This reluctance to hold bonds tends to keep their yield some way above the bill rate (except at moments when there happens to be reason to think their prices much more likely to rise than to fall in the near future).

Since the yield of bonds in the second-hand market is normally above the bill rate, interest offered on newly issued bonds must also be higher. How is it that excess-investors are willing to incur greater expense for borrowing on bonds than by discounting bills ?

The choice between bills and bonds as a means of financing excess-investment depends partly upon technical considerations. An entrepreneur does not like to borrow on short term to invest in long-lived equipment for there is always a risk that the cost of renewing loans may rise (or finance become unobtainable at any price) before the initial cost of the equipment has been paid off by accumulating an amortisation fund from its quasi-rents ; whereas capital embodied in work-in-progress turns itself over at about the same rate as bills fall due to be renewed, so that in case of need the capital can be disinvested (by refraining from refilling the pipe-line as it empties) and the loan paid off. There is an overlap between types of excess-investment suitable to finance by bills and suitable to finance by bonds, so that the choice between the two is influenced by the relative costs of the two forms of borrowing. When the bond rate is high, bills are preferred. The amount of bonds sold in any week by excess-investors then falls short of the increment of demand for bonds represented by the week's savings, and bond prices rise. The overlap is limited, however, and even if it were not, the banks are not willing to permit an indefinite amount of discounting, for fear of defaults ; [1] so that, although the divergence between the rates is kept within limits by substitution between bills and bonds, it cannot be wiped out. When they have discounted bills up to the desired or permitted extent, would-be excess-investors must be prepared to incur the higher rate earned by bonds in the form of additional interest payments, or reduced interest receipts, according to whether the excess-investment is financed by new issues or sales of bonds out of reserves.

BANK DEPOSITS

The reluctance of savers to hold placements whose capital value is liable to fall, and the consequent high yield of bonds, creates an opportunity for another kind of banking business (besides the provision of the medium of exchange) which we must now bring into the picture. As well as issuing notes, the banks borrow from savers by accepting deposits.[2] They are repayable at short notice, and owing to the good reputation of the banks they are not subject to any risk.

The banks offer interest on deposits, for if they did not, a saver with notes to dispose of might be tempted to undercut them by discounting bills for colleagues in whom he had sufficient confidence. The superior convenience and security of dealing with banks makes the savers willing to accept a low rate of interest on deposits, and the banks (to prevent competition amongst themselves from destroying the profitability of the business) fix it at a conventional level somewhat less than the bill rate. Under these arrangements a saver who is unwilling to take up bonds, and does not have outstanding bills of his own to retire, can make a deposit, losing the difference of interest between the deposit rate and the bond rate,

[1] They are also restrained by the rules imposed upon them by the monetary authorities.

[2] Historically deposit banking preceded note issuing. It was part of the process of evolution from commodities (gold) to placements as a medium of exchange (cf. above, p. 31).

but securing himself against the risk of a loss of capital. The
saver, in effect, is allowed a share in the earnings of the banking
business which he could otherwise get for himself by amassing
a hoard of notes and lending them at short term. At the same
time the banks are enjoying an opportunity for earning profits
by creating a kind of placement which is desired by savers
because it is more liquid than bonds.

In order to take advantage of this opportunity the banks
enlarge the scope of their lending by buying bonds,[1] receiving
the difference between the bond rate and the deposit rate as
earnings on the business.[2]

The banks have no direct control over the amount of note
circulation [3] (beyond the minor extent to which the speed of
circulation is affected by the level of interest rates).[4] If they
issue more notes than are required for use as a medium of
exchange, the excess returns to them as deposits or in cancel-
lation of bills. But they can influence the amount of deposits.
On any day, by buying bonds they can raise the bond price
level, and, with a lower yield, bonds become less attractive as
a medium for holding wealth relatively to deposits. A purchase of bonds by the banks from the second-hand market
raises their price to whatever extent is required to induce the
sellers to make deposits with the proceeds of the sales. Or,
over any period, when the banks buy bonds being sold by
excess-investors, there are so many the less for the savers
of the period to buy, and their prices go to the level at which
the savers are induced to make deposits instead of buying
bonds.

The effect upon bond prices of a given volume of purchases by the banks at any moment depends upon the prevailing

---

[1] In reality banks are chary of holding undated bonds in any quantity,
for fear of loss of capital, but we gain simplicity without losing any essential
point by continuing to assume that there is only one kind of bond.

[2] Both transactions by cheque and hoarding of notes are excluded, in
order to keep a clear view of the distinction between money as a medium
of exchange and money as a placement. In reality the distinction is blurred
by these phenomena.

[3] The interest rates have an effect upon the rate of accumulation and
therefore upon the volume of transactions, so that indirectly the banks can
influence the amount of the note circulation through their influence upon
the interest rates.   [4] Cf. above, p. 226.

state of opinion in the second-hand bond market. When bond prices rise, in a given state of expectations, some placement owners become bears, expecting a fall, or all of them become somewhat bearish. They are consequently willing to sell bonds to the banks and make deposits instead (intending to buy bonds again later when their prices have relapsed). The rising tendency of bond prices is damped by bearish sales. When owners of bonds are very strongly convinced about what their price will be in the near future they are ready to sell an indefinite amount as soon as their price rises at all above the expected level, and a very large increase in deposits is accompanied by a very small fall in the bond rate. When their ideas about future prices are vague and uncertain, many expect any rise that occurs to be as likely as not to be maintained, or even to go further, and a small purchase by the banks produces a big effect.

Conversely, if a bearish change in opinion occurs, for any reason, the banks can counteract it by buying bonds and giving the bears the deposits which they require, or when a bullish movement sets in they can damp it by selling bonds to the bulls.

When bears are selling bonds they are hoping for a profit (when they buy bonds again) which exceeds the difference between the bond rate and the deposit rate (or the bill rate, which they can save by using the proceeds of sales of bonds to cancel bills) over the bear period. Thus a purchase of bonds by the banks has a bigger effect if it is accompanied by a reduction in the discount and deposit rates. A reduction in the discount rate also has a direct effect on bond prices by influencing opinion, if it is taken to be the signal for a change in the banks' policy.

In this respect it is easier for the banks to operate on the other tack, for there is a limit to the extent to which the discount rate can be lowered, whereas it can be raised without limit. They can always find a level high enough to induce the holders of bonds to start selling, whereas when bearishness is rife, even a nominal discount rate may not be low enough to induce the holders of deposits to start buying.

THE FUNCTION OF THE BANKS

The operation of the banks may be summarised as follows :
Their liabilities (apart from their own capital) consist of notes
and deposits. Their assets (apart from their own capital) consist of debts arising from direct loans (bills discounted) [1] and
second-hand loans (holdings of bonds). Their liabilities in
the form of notes provide a convenient medium of exchange [2]
while deposits provide a kind of placement which some owners
of funds prefer to bonds. They thus facilitate the supply of
finance to excess-investors partly by lending and partly by
taking bonds out of the market and so making savers more
willing to hold what remain. If there were no banks, finance
would be harder to come by, less convenient media of exchange
would have to be used, and the yield that bonds would have to
offer to get themselves held would be higher.

At any moment the outstanding amount of notes outside
the banks is the difference between notes issued in the past
and those returned as deposits or repayment of loans. Since
notes yield no interest to their holders, while a return of notes
to a bank means receiving interest payments (on a deposit) or
a saving of interest payments (on a debt) the outstanding amount
of notes cannot exceed the amount that is required for convenience in circulation. The amount of deposits, however, can
be varied, for the sale or purchase of bonds by the banks varies
their prices and so makes deposits less or more attractive, as
an alternative to holding bonds, to owners of uninvested funds.
The larger the amount of bonds held by the banks, the smaller
the amount available to be held by placement-owners and
therefore (in any given state of market opinion) the higher
their price and the lower their yield.

The yield of bonds in the placement market determines
the terms on which new bonds can be sold. Thus by fixing the rate for direct loans (the discount rate) and operating
upon the market for bonds, the banks can determine (within
limits) the rates of interest at which finance can be obtained
by excess-investors.

---

[1] Which, in our simplified scheme, stand also for advances.
[2] In reality this function is also fulfilled by deposits.

CHAPTER 24

THE RATES OF INTEREST

FOR what purpose do the banks use their powers to influence the interest rates? In reality policy is imposed upon them by monetary authorities, but we are conducting the argument on the assumption that they are operating according to certain rules without specifying the manner in which they are compelled to do so.[1]

MONETARY POLICY

When the entrepreneurs are keen and eager to accumulate, they may be attempting to carry out investment on such a scale as to push the economy up to the inflation barrier. In particular, this may occur when a strong boom is superimposed upon a long-period scarcity of labour.

The barrier is not an abrupt precipice but rather a mountain range approached through undulating foothills. A rate of accumulation involving both a high demand for labour and a high rate of profit sets up a tendency for money-wage rates to rise faster than productivity, so that prices rise and the pressure to raise money wages is increased. If this process goes on slowly, with occasional interruptions and relapses, it does not undermine the conventional belief in the stability of the purchasing power of money [2] which is a necessity (or at least an important convenience) for the smooth operation of the economy. But if it speeds up too far it threatens to disrupt the monetary system. The most important rule of

---

[1] We are also omitting the extremely important aspects of monetary policy that arise from the fact that monetary authorities are national and are largely concerned with international transactions (see below, p. 283).

[2] Cf. above, p. 25.

banking policy is to prevent this from happening. When they consider it necessary to check an inflationary tendency the bankers must raise the discount rate, and sell bonds.

The owners of bonds are aware that the rise in interest rates is likely to be temporary and bull purchases prevent the price of bonds from falling very far. But even a moderate rise in the bond rate retards investment if it is not expected to last. Entrepreneurs will postpone borrowing, and this may involve postponing outlay on investment. Moreover, as an alternative to investment, funds can be used to buy bonds and hold them till their price rises again. This yields a return which exceeds the interest over the period for which the bonds are held by the rise in their price, and it is this yield, or rather what this yield is expected to be, that must be compared to expected profit in order to see whether it is more advantageous to commit funds to investment immediately or to use them temporarily for holding bonds. Thus, quite a moderate level of interest rates may check investment if a future fall in interest rates is expected.[1]

It takes some time to curtail investment plans once embarked upon ; the rise in wages and prices may continue after the interest rates have been raised ; the bankers, not aware that they have already gone far enough in discouraging investment for the near future, may push them up still further. Investment, in a little while, falls off sharply, and unemployment checks the rise in wages. Now the bankers must lower their rates again (according to the rules) but after this dislocation of plans investment takes some time to recover.

It is through the operation of this mechanism that the inflation barrier sets a limit upon the rate of accumulation. By the same token, too high a level of interest rates causes loss and waste by discouraging accumulation. Thus the ideal rules of banking policy are that the interest rates should be neither so low as to stimulate accumulation up to the inflationary level nor so high as to stop it short of that level by more than the minimum margin required for safety.

---

[1] In these conditions it pays to borrow on short term in order to buy bonds, so that the short-term rate of interest is driven above the long-term rate.

The rules can at best be very imperfectly followed. The banks have learned by trial and error to keep more or less within the lines laid down, but circumstances are constantly changing. In particular, in a boom the rate of investment is at its highest when it is just about to fall. The banks cannot know the future. They become aware of what has happened only when the rate of accumulation has fallen, and the entrepreneurs are then in a nervous state, and cannot readily be induced to start up again by a reduction in interest rates; particularly as, in this situation, credit is impaired, and the yields of bonds fan out,[1] so that for most entrepreneurs finance has become dearer rather than cheaper.

From time to time they allow an inflationary movement to develop too far, but on the whole the rules are both more imperative[2] and (as we have seen) easier to implement in respect to checking inflation than in respect to stimulating accumulation, so that a tendency to suffer from excessive interest rates has been a more prevalent weakness of capitalist economies than inflation due to over-rapid accumulation. (Inflation brought about by political events is another matter.)

AN AUTOMATIC SYSTEM

Instead of aiming to keep the rates of interest between certain limits, the banks may operate under a system of rules which are intended to absolve them from the need to pursue any conscious policy.

They agree to fix the total of notes in existence at some figure in excess of the active circulation, and each to maintain a reserve of notes equal to his deposits.[3] To prevent ruinous competition, they fix the deposit rate at a nominal figure. They then leave the other interest rates to find their own level.

---

[1] See above, p. 230.

[2] This is largely because monetary systems are national, and a great part of their functions is directed towards the external relations of the currency concerned (the exchange rate). This aspect of the matter cannot be exhibited in our model of unified capitalist economy (see below, p. 382).

[3] This is unlike any actual monetary system, but it produces the same effect as a policy imposed by the authorities of keeping the total quantity of money constant.

The amount of deposits in existence is determined as follows : The agreed total of notes, *minus* the active circulation, constitutes the reserves. When any banker finds his reserve of notes in excess of deposits, he buys bonds, and when he finds it lower, he sells. The price of bonds is thus continually adjusted so that the placement owners are induced to hold a total of deposits that absorbs the excess of the agreed total of notes over the active circulation. This operates in the direction required by the rules of monetary policy but not necessarily to the right extent.

When an inflationary rise in the wages bill is going on, the discount rate is driven up sharply by an increase in demand for notes. As we have seen, a rise in the interest rate on bonds that is not expected to last will not go very far. There is no reason why the rise in bond yields that is sufficient to reduce deposits to the extent required by the fall in bank reserves (due to notes being drawn into circulation) should be the same as that required to reduce investment, cause unemployment and check the rise in wage rates. It may be too great, but equally it may be too slight.

It is true that if inflation continues unchecked, the progressive rise in demand for notes in active circulation is bound to drive the discount rate very high. But then it becomes worth while to economise on balances — money circulates more rapidly — and, in the extreme, entrepreneurs may create media of exchange for themselves, paying their workers in vouchers on their products and settling transactions amongst themselves by note of hand, so that the existence of an absolute limit to the note issue is no guarantee that the interest rates will rise high enough to kill the inflation.

On the other tack, a situation in which the rate of investment has fallen is very likely to be accompanied by an atmosphere of uncertainty which increases the preference for liquid placements. A rise in deposits then sucks notes into the banks, and may do so to a greater extent than corresponds to the automatic fall in the active circulation brought about by a decline in employment. The bill rate is then driven up, just when it ought to be lowered.

Given time, unemployment will lead to falling wage rates.

In principle, any rate of accumulation can be accommodated by any volume of notes, provided that money-wage rates are adjusted accordingly, but the process of squeezing the money value of output down to fit an inadequate stock of notes is excessively disagreeable both for entrepreneurs and for workers, and the loss of production while it is going on is a pure waste.

In short, the automatic scheme is a very poor substitute for intelligent policy, and there is no way of absolving the bankers from the responsibility for managing the monetary system in sympathy with the requirements of the economy.

A minor objection to the conception of an automatic system is that, when banking policy is conceived in terms of the note issue, it fosters an exaggerated belief in the importance of the quantity of money. Two opposite kinds of fanatics then flourish. One group holds that inflation is caused by 'using the printing press' and maintains that the note issue should never be increased — come rain or fine. The other group (applying the same argument in a different context) hold that unemployment can always be cured by 'using a fountain pen', though this opinion is usually mixed up with the more cogent argument that if notes were continually printed and given to workers to spend — creating a kind of excess-consumption similar to excess-investment — there would always be enough demand to keep output up to capacity.

INTEREST AND PROFIT

Over the long run the ratio of total annual interest payments to total annual profits depends upon the amount of outstanding debt (which is the sediment, so to speak, of past excess-investment financed by bonds) relatively to the stock of capital, and upon the levels of the rates of interest when debts now outstanding were incurred relatively to the current level of profits.

The relationship of the level of rates of interest at any moment to the level of the prospective profits on investment depends partly upon the objective riskiness of investment and partly on the optimism of entrepreneurs. When profits are

easy to make and entrepreneurs full of confidence, the ratio of
the level of interest to the level of profit is high, for if the
excess of profit over interest on new borrowing were large
(in those conditions) investment would run up to the inflation
darrier, and the rates of interest would have to be raised.   In
the extreme, in ideal conditions of perfect tranquillity, the
rates of interest (which, as we have seen, would then be equal
to each other) [1] would be equal to the rate of profit.

In reality risk is ever present, and interest rates may be
much below the profit actually being realised on the reproduction cost of existing capital goods without causing a risk
of inflation.   The level of interest rates is therefore not closely
tethered to the level of profits and enjoys, so to say, a life of
its own.

Its course, over any period, depends upon the interaction
of the expected level of profits on new investment with monetary
policy.   The ease with which monetary policy can be put into
effect depends, as we have seen, very much upon beliefs about
what the rate of interest will be, which in turn depends upon
beliefs about what the monetary policy will be, and about how
easily it will be put into effect.

Generally speaking, the wider and less predictable are
fluctuations in the level of interest rates, the higher, on the
average, the level will tend to be, for it is uncertainty about
future interest rates which gives rise to reluctance to hold
bonds and keeps up their yield.

In so far as high interest rates are discouraging to investment they tend to retard accumulation, and the slower is
the rate of accumulation the lower is the level of profits [2]
and the more discouraging any given level of interest rate
becomes.

Thus we must add to the list of causes of stagnation to
which capitalist economies are subject, stagnation due to a
chronic tendency for interest rates to rule too high, relatively
to the rate of profit, to permit accumulation to go on.[3]

---

[1] See above, p. 232.
[2] This proposition will have to be modified, but not reversed, when we
introduce consumption out of profits.
[3] This is one of the main contentions of Keynes's *General Theory*.

FINANCE AND ACCUMULATION

We must also bring monetary influences into the account of the concentric circles of limits to the long-run rate of accumulation set out above.[1]

Within the limit set by the technical surplus lies the inflation barrier, which operates through the mechanism of the interest rates. Within this may lie a limit due to over-cautious or clumsily operated banking policy, which keeps investment (on the average over a run of years) lower than is necessary to avoid inflation. Within this, the limit set by the energy of entrepreneurs involves a complex of technical, human and financial influences.

The return to be obtained on a scheme of investment lies in the future and cannot be known. Each entrepreneur has to judge his own situation, and judgment depends upon individual temperament and social convention. The bolder each is, the better all will flourish, and the more cautious and conservative each is, the harder will profits be for all to come by. The level of profit is a case of thinking makes it so, but no one alone can think himself into profits. The habits and traditions on which they all act collectively are therefore of fundamental importance for each.

The level of interest rates affects investment decisions, for the profit expected from an investment must exceed the yield of placements or the cost of borrowing to make it worth while. In general, the margin by which uncertain expected profit has to exceed certain interest cost in order to make investment attractive is so large that any reasonable difference in the level of interest rates cannot affect the calculation very much. But expected changes in interest, as we have seen, may have an appreciable influence in retarding or speeding up the pace at which investment plans are being carried into effect.

Granted that an entrepreneur is willing and anxious to undertake excess-investment, his power to do so depends on the credit that he commands.

The banks will hold only a certain number of bills drawn by any one entrepreneur lest he draws more than he can

[1] See p. 83 above.

redeem. And bonds outstanding cannot be more than a certain proportion of an entrepreneur's liabilities, for the more interest he is already pledged to pay, relatively to his earning power, the greater the risk of default on further borrowings. Over a long run, with luck and good management, a concern can go on growing indefinitely, alternating periods of excess-investment with periods of saving, or carrying on continuously a rate of excess-investment moderate in relation to its investment out of profits, but at any moment its borrowing power is more or less strictly limited. For entrepreneurs as a whole (established concerns and potential newcomers) there is a more or less definite limit to total borrowing power, depending upon the distribution of property and outstanding debt amongst them, and upon the strictness of the banks' standards of credit-worthiness and the state of mind of potential holders of bonds.

At any moment there are usually a number of entrepreneurs whose concerns have been savers in the past, who have reserves of bonds, or a low ratio of debt to assets, so that they have ample borrowing power, but who do not feel inclined just now to embark upon excess-investment, while others have their heads full of schemes, but cannot carry them out for lack of borrowing power.

The rate of investment (given the general state of expectations and the level of interest rates) thus very much depends upon the relation between the distribution of borrowing power amongst entrepreneurs and the distribution of lethargy or optimism amongst them. And the distribution of borrowing power depends partly upon legal rules and technical conditions in the capital market and partly upon the subjective attitude of potential lenders. Psychological factors come in on both sides of the account, and there is no way (even for the purpose of our model) of reducing the complexities of the inducement to invest to a simple formula. We must be content with the conclusion that, over the long run, the rate of accumulation is likely to be whatever it is likely to be.

BOOK V
THE RENTIER

CHAPTER 25

CONSUMPTION OF PROFITS

So far we have abstracted from consumption out of profits and the existence of rentier income. This exclusion was made purely for the sake of exposition. Having established the main lines of the analysis without rentiers, we must now introduce them into the model. The political and social importance of consumption out of incomes derived from property is very far reaching, but so far as the analysis of accumulation is concerned we shall find that it complicates the argument without requiring any substantial change.

RENTIER INCOME AND EXPENDITURE

We use the term *rentier* in an extended sense, to represent capitalists in their aspect as owners of wealth, as opposed to their aspect as entrepreneurs. We include in the incomes of rentiers dividends as well as payments of interest and we include the sums handed over to their households by entrepreneurs who own their own businesses.

The distinctions between interest, dividends and personal profits are important in some contexts, but, if we adhere to our conception of the entrepreneur who identifies himself with his business as a thing in itself rather than as a means to acquire wealth and enjoy consumption, the differences appear less in real content than they are in legal form. Dividends and personal profits are an out-payment from the firm, similar to interest. An obligation to pay interest is a contractual agreement, while the amount of dividends and personal profits paid out is at the discretion of the entrepreneur; but neither the obligation nor the discretion is absolute in practice. When profits are so low that the payment of interest would lead to bankruptcy, creditors often find it preferable to compromise and keep alive a goose that they hope will lay again in the future, so that, to some extent, interest payments fluctuate with earnings. On the other hand, dividends fluctuate less than earnings, for entrepreneurs are reluctant to reduce dividends, for fear of impairing their credit and making future borrowing difficult, and they are reluctant to increase them, because they prefer reserves under their own control. Thus interest to some extent behaves like dividends, and to an important extent dividends behave like interest. A similar argument applies to personal profits.

Rentiers' outlay, in any period, is not closely tied to their receipts in that period, for they own wealth and command borrowing power (titles to wealth can be pledged against loans, such as bank overdrafts). They are free to spend more than their receipts whenever they please. Normally, over the long run, they are spending less than their receipts ; they are saving and increasing their wealth.[1] Consequently the out-payments made by entrepreneurs, in a normal year, exceed their receipts, and their indebtedness (including shares) has increased, over the year, by an amount equal to the saving made during the year by the rentiers.[2] The more thrifty are the rentiers (the smaller the ratio of their expenditure to their receipts) the greater is the proportion, over the long run, of the external obligations of firms to the value of capital.

---

[1] A large part of rentier saving consists of saving up to spend later — after marriage, for education of children, in old age, etc. The expenditure in excess of receipts of families using up their past savings is financed by selling out placements (individually or through insurance companies), and this absorbs a part of the current saving that is going on. For the purposes of our present analysis it is the net saving of the rentiers taken as a whole that is relevant.

In any one week some workers also are saving while others are drawing on past saving, for funeral expenses, etc. We have simplified our analysis by ignoring this phenomenon, assuming wages fully spent from week to week.

In so far as some working-class families make net savings over a life-time they become *pro tanto* rentier families. Some rentier families are always in process of dissipating their fortunes and entering the ranks of the working class. This turn-over between classes is of great social importance, and in economies where it is common it colours the whole psychological and political atmosphere. We have excluded all this from our model for the sake of simplicity, but from a purely analytical (as opposed to a political) point of view its inclusion would not make much difference to the argument.

[2] Cf. numerical illustration, p. 45 above, note.

From the rentier's own point of view the distinction between saving and spending for consumption is very vague. Consumption occurs after purchase, and takes a certain time. The purchase of long-lived consumption goods is a kind of investment, and some consumption goods (houses, works of art, etc.) are partly an alternative to placements as a form of holding wealth. They may be bought out of past savings, or out of loans to be repaid from future saving. There is an important difference, however, between consumer's investment and entrepreneur's investment. The typical entrepreneur's investment is intended to be permanent and, if all goes according to plan, will renew itself out of its own earnings. The typical consumer's investment merely means that consumption can go on for some time at a higher level than before it was made without any fresh expenditure. The durability of consumption goods is important in making consumption more stable than expenditure (a fall in purchases of durable goods from a high level to replacement level leaves consumption unchanged) but over the long run the maintenance of a given level of consumption requires the maintenance of expenditure, whereas the maintenance of a given stock of productive capacity does not require net investment.

From the point of view of entrepreneurs, taken as a whole, the distinction between consumer's outlay and consumer's saving is quite sharp. Outlay means receipts of money by the entrepreneurs, while saving by consumers means an excess of money outlay by entrepreneurs over their receipts and an increase in their net indebtedness.

In this respect incomes earned by financial operations — bank loans, underwriters' commission, etc. — are on all fours with rentier income. They differ in so far as they are payments for performing services which may be of great importance to the functioning of the economy, as opposed to merely owning wealth; but from the point of view of entrepreneurs they represent outlays in excess of the wages bill, and expenditures made from them, whether for personal consumption or for investment in bank premises, calculating machines, etc., represent receipts in excess of the wages bill. For the general discussion of accumulation, therefore, it is convenient to include

financial incomes with rentier incomes, and to include investments made by financiers in the products of industry in
expenditure for consumption. Investment of finance in finance
(bank reserves, etc.) is washed out on both sides of the
account.

Generally speaking, an average rentier income is considerably higher than an average worker's income, and the rentier's
consumption is made up of a different collection of commodities. From one point of view it would be desirable to elaborate
our model economy to allow for this fact, and to divide the
consumption sector into two parts, wage-good industries and
luxury industries. But to do so would complicate exposition
very much. We shall, therefore, compromise by adhering in
general to the simplification that consumption goods are always
purchased in the same proportions, while occasionally glancing
at the difference between the composition of workers' consumption and rentiers' consumption at points in the argument
where it is of particular importance. We continue to neglect
middle-class incomes made up of a mixture of earnings from
work and receipts from property, and professional salaries and
earnings.[1]

CONSUMPTION AND THRIFT

The relation of rentier expenditure to their receipts has an
important influence on the manner in which an economy
develops, both through its effect upon the relation of the demand for commodities to productive capacity, and through
its effect on the ratio of the outside indebtedness of firms to
the value of their capital.

How is the ratio of rentier expenditure to receipts likely
to behave over the long run? When the ratio of receipts to
wealth is constant (the level of interest rates and the dividend
yield of shares is constant), when the number of rentier families
is growing in proportion to the value of capital, so that wealth
per family remains constant, and when habits in respect to consumption do not change through time, the ratio of expenditure
to receipts remains constant.

[1] See p. 11.

How is it likely to behave when wealth per family is rising at a constant level of interest rates ?

When we examine the relation of expenditure to receipts of different families at a moment of time, it is generally found that, by and large, those with higher annual receipts have a higher proportion of saving to receipts, and from this it may be argued that it would be natural to expect a rise in income to be associated with a fall in the proportion of expenditure to income. On the other hand, it can be argued with equal plausibility that the object of saving is to increase wealth, and that the more wealth a family commands the less motive there is for saving.

Both these views are based on the conception of an individual, as so to speak, a hard lump of tastes and habits, impermeable to outside influences — a view of each human being existing on a psychological Crusoe's island, in which other people are part of the landscape, like the goats and the trees. But in reality consumption is very much a social affair, and everyone's habits are very much influenced by what everyone else is doing, so that when a whole community is growing richer together consumption tends to rise with wealth. This tendency, which probably exists to some extent in all societies, is reinforced under the capitalist rules of the game by the sales pressure of competitive entrepreneurs. Saving is something of a moral effort, even at a high standard of life, and good resolutions to behave in a thrifty manner are hard to keep when they are constantly assaulted by advertising and the temptation of new commodities. Moreover there is a kind of competition in consumption, induced by the desire to impress the Joneses, which makes each family strive to keep up at least an appearance of being as well off as those that they mix with, so that outlay by one induces outlay by others,[1] just as technical improvements by one entrepreneur induce improvements by his competitors. (Even in a social group where display is considered vulgar, it may be very expensive to be inconspicuous in a gentlemanly manner.)

[1] See J. Duesenberry, *Income, Saving and the Theory of Consumer Behaviour*. For another interpretation see F. Modigliani and R. Brumberg, 'Utility Analysis and the Consumption Function', *Post-Keynesian Economics* (ed. K. Kurihara).

It therefore does not seem unreasonable to expect the thriftiness of rentiers to be fairly constant through time (at a constant level of interest rates), with growing wealth, in a given society, though it may vary markedly from one society to another, according to the general pattern of habits of consumption that have been established.

THRIFT AND THE RATE OF INTEREST

The effect of differences in the ratio of receipts to wealth (differences in the level of interest rates and dividend yields) on the ratio of expenditure to receipts is not easy to disentangle. We may imagine a typical rentier family with the same annual receipts (of the same purchasing power over commodities) in two different situations; in one situation, Gamma, the rate of interest is, has long been and is expected to remain, higher than in the other, Alpha. In the Alpha situation the family commands more wealth (for annual receipts are the same and the yield per unit is less). They have less motive for saving for two reasons — the potential purchasing power they command is greater and the return per unit of additions to wealth is less than in the Gamma situation. On the other hand, if they have in mind a certain increase in future income that they wish to acquire they must save more, for each unit addition to wealth makes a smaller increase in future income when yields are lower. It is impossible to say *a priori* how they are likely to react, or, if different families react differently, which type is most likely to predominate.

Nor is the question easy to investigate by studying actual behaviour, for two situations with permanently different rates of interest must be separated either in space or in time (they belong to two different nations or to the same nation at different periods) and they are likely to differ in much else besides the level of interest rates. In particular, if real wages are higher in the Alpha situation an income of given purchasing power over commodities has a lower purchasing power over services, which affects the whole pattern of middle-class expenditure and habits of consumption.[1]

---

[1] Cf. above, p. 23.

For the same reason it is impossible to generalise about the effect on the ratio of expenditure to receipts of a long-run fall in the rate of profit accompanied by a corresponding fall in interest rates (such as would occur in an economy on the way to bliss). The question has to be left open.[1]

A permanent fall in the level of interest rates relatively to the rate of profit (such as may have occurred if the monetary authorities have been trying to counteract flagging investment by keeping interest rates low) has reduced the rentiers' share in profits (assuming that dividends have not been raised correspondingly), and this is likely to have a more important effect in reducing the proportion of consumption to profits than any effect there may be of lower interest in increasing the ratio of consumption to rentier income.[2]

A fall in the level of interest rates which is not expected to last is on the whole likely to stimulate rentier expenditure. On the one hand the prices of long-dated bonds and of shares have risen, so that the command over purchasing power of rentiers as a whole has been raised, and on the other hand placements for the moment are unattractive (for *ex hypothesi* their prices are expected to fall in the fairly near future) and rentiers may prefer to buy durable goods (especially houses) rather than to hold wealth in a liquid form. This phenomenon reinforces the effect of changes in interest rates as a means of stimulating or retarding activity, but since changes of this kind occur in particular short-period situations when there is in any case some disturbance going on which may be swamping the influence of changes in interest rates, it is not possible to make any hard and fast generalisations about their effects.

[1] See Marshall, *Principles* (7th ed.), p. 533, and J. de V. Graaf, 'Mr. Harrod on Hump Saving', *Economica* (February 1950). The effect of changes in rentier thriftiness on the proportion of profits consumed is not likely to be of great quantitative importance. If 60 per cent of profit is handed over to rentiers as interest, dividends and personal income of entrepreneurs, and initially 90 per cent of rentier income is consumed, then halving the saving ratio would increase the proportion of profits consumed from 54 to 57 per cent.

[2] A reduction in the rentier share of profit from 60 to 50 per cent, while 10 per cent of rentier income is saved, reduces the proportion of profits consumed from 54 to 45 per cent. If at the same time the saving ratio was halved, the proportion of profits consumed would be reduced from 54 to 47½ per cent.

An expectation of rising prices over the long run is equivalent, from the rentiers' point of view, to the rate of interest being lower than its nominal level (for the purchasing power of future money is expected to be less than that of present money) and combines the effect (whatever that may be) upon saving habits of low interest with a tendency to set up a preference for shares and durable goods over money and bonds as vehicles for holding wealth.[1]

A fall or rise in prices which is expected to be reversed in the near future may have a very strong effect in stimulating or retarding rentier expenditure.

SOCIAL SECURITY

So far we have assumed that the only source of worker's expenditure was current wages, and that unemployed workers were supported out of the earnings of friends and relations. In reality, even at their harshest, the capitalist rules of the game were always somewhat softened by charity from rentiers to workers (humanitarian impulses mingling with enlightened self-interest) and in modern times the support of unemployed workers has been systematised through social insurance. This, as we shall see, requires an important modification of our analysis, both of accumulation over the long run and of the trade cycle. We shall not burden our simplified model with the apparatus of a state, but we will assume that rentiers have arranged to pay some kind of allowance to unemployed workers, and that these payments do not affect their own expenditure (when unemployment is high, they save less than they would otherwise have done from given receipts). ,

For simplicity we continue to assume that the workers do not save, so that their expenditure is always equal, from week to week, to the wages bill plus allowances.[2]

---

[1] For this reason an expectation of rising prices tends to make the bond rate of interest higher than it would otherwise be (see below, p. 279).

[2] See above, p. 248, note.

CHAPTER 26

CONSUMPTION AND ACCUMULATION
IN THE LONG RUN

THE most important modification to be made in our analysis, to allow for rentier consumption, is that profits are equal to net investment *plus* rentier expenditure (net of any second-hand purchases by one rentier from another).

Since profits exceed net investment it is not the case that the rate of profit on capital, in tranquil conditions, is equal to the growth ratio of the economy. In general it is considerably greater.[1] In any given situation total real wages are equal to the output of consumption goods *minus* purchases by rentiers. The excess of receipts in the consumption sector over the wages bill is equal to the wages bill of the investment sector *plus* the outlay of rentiers. The capitalists (combining their aspect as entrepreneurs and as rentiers) employ a certain number of workers to maintain and expand the stock of capital goods, a certain number of workers to provide for consumption, and whatever further number of workers is required to provide for the consumption of these workers and their own.[2] The prices of consumption goods exceed their wages costs to a sufficient extent to permit of capitalists' consumption, as well as investment.

Consumption out of profits eats into the resources available

---

[1] For instance when the following annual ratios obtain :

	Value of Capital	Net Income	Wages	Net Profits	Net Investment
Year 1	400	100	40	60	12
Year 2	412	103	41·2	61·8	12·36

the growth ratio is 3 per cent per annum and the rate of profit 15 per cent. Consumption out of profit is 48 per cent of total income and 80 per cent of net profit.   [2] Cf. above, p. 75.

for investment. Yet at the same time a reduction in con-sumption might be unfavourable to accumulation. There is double-sided relation between entrepreneurs and rentiers. Just as each entrepreneur individually gains by paying his workers less, but suffers through a loss of markets from others paying their workers less, so each entrepreneur would like his wife and his shareholders to be content with little, so that he can use the bulk of his profits for investment (or for reserves to finance future investment) while he gains from the expenditure of other wives and other shareholders, which makes the market for commodities buoyant.

PRIMITIVE STAGNATION

The aspect of consumption as the enemy of accumulation is seen in its clearest form in the extreme case in which the whole technical surplus (the excess of output over necessary minimum wages) is being consumed. Consider an economy in which real wages are at a low level, which has come to be regarded as providing bare subsistence, with techniques of production in use at the lowest possible level of mechanisation. (It is hard to visualise such an economy with free land, and we may depart from our assumptions for a moment to admit property in land, which for present purposes may be regarded simply as a fixed stock of indestructible capital goods yielding profits in the form of rent.) The distinction between entrepreneurs and rentiers has not yet arisen, and the annual consumption by owners of property is equal to the whole excess of annual net output over wages. Individual families may be saving, but others are spending in excess of income, selling property at second hand to savers ; there may be a considerable amount of consumers' investment, say in creating temples and palaces.

This represents the primitive state of stagnation which commonly prevails in pre-capitalist economies. It is very far from the state of economic bliss, for if any net investment were to take place, technical progress and increasing mechanisation would begin to raise productivity.

What prevents accumulation from beginning ? In this

kind of situation there is generally a considerable amount of disguised unemployment, so that it would be physically possible to increase output. Any owner of wealth commands purchasing power equal to many years income, so that there is no lack of potential finance. What is lacking, primarily, is the *idea* of accumulation and a class of entrepreneurs to play according to the capitalist rules. So long as these are lacking, thrift is powerless to set accumulation going. If the spendthrift families reformed their ways and began to live within their incomes while those which were saving spent no more than before, the only consequence would be an increase in unemployment.[1]

But when there are entrepreneurs anxious to carry out investment, the consumption of profits frustrates them. When entrepreneurs appear, in such an economy, and set investment going, the demand for commodities rises, for the workers taken out of disguised unemployment, who were formerly consuming the equivalent of their own product, now spend their wages on the products of the rest. It will be some time before an appreciable increase in output of commodities can occur, and meanwhile, if rentiers maintain their customary standard of consumption, there is no room for increased consumption by workers. Prices rise relatively to money wages, but since real wages were already at the minimum, inflation sets in.[2] Thus the consumption of the owners of property sets a barrier to accumulation.

It is necessary, to start the game, that there should be thrifty rentiers as well as active entrepreneurs.

In a less extreme case, where there is some room for the real-wage rate to fall, entrepreneurs could begin to accumulate. Profits would then emerge, and rentier consumption would increase. The issue, as between the workers and the rentiers, is a straightforward case of 'the more there is of mine, the less there is of yours'. The workers' consumption, in the initial stages, falls by an amount equal to net investment plus the additional consumption of rentiers. If the rentiers grow thrifty and reduce consumption, the fall in workers' consumption is so much the less, and if rentier consumption fall

---

[1] Cf. below, p. 272, note.   [2] Cf. above, p. 48.

by the equivalent of the whole net investment, real wages remain constant.

In a situation of this kind the different composition of workers' and rentiers' consumption is of great importance, and we must relax our assumption that commodities are always purchased in the same proportions in order to glance at it. In so far as the reduction of rentiers' outlay consists in building fewer or less splendid cathedrals, the workers released are available for industrial investment. In so far as rentiers employ a smaller retinue of servants, again labour is released for investment. (The training of an industrial labour force may be included under the head of technical progress which automatically begins as the entrepreneurs learn the know how that goes with the investment that they are carrying out.) In so far as rentiers give up purchasing luxury products which are in any case outside the sphere of workers' consumption there are losses and unemployment in the luxury trades, so that a part of the thrift of the rentiers runs to waste and fails to contribute to accumulation immediately. As time goes by the appropriate redeployment of the labour force and productive capacity is gradually made, so that the thrift gradually becomes useful for accumulation, after a period when it has caused great misery.

RENTIER CONSUMPTION IN A GOLDEN AGE

Now let us consider rentier consumption in an economy where accumulation has long been under way.

One of the basic characteristics of a golden age is that the demand for commodities (and therefore their output) increases through time at the growth ratio of the economy. With neutral technical progress, the share of profits in the value of output remains constant. For golden-age conditions it is necessary that the proportion of profits devoted to expenditure on consumption goods should remain constant. So far in our discussion of golden ages we have assumed it to be constant at zero.

To maintain a constant proportion of rentier consumption to profits it is necessary, first, that the share of profits distributed to rentiers should be constant, and second, that the proportion of rentier receipts saved should be constant (or that changes in the one should be offset by opposite changes in the other). The sum of annual rentier saving *plus* the internal saving of firms (undistributed net profit) is equal to the annual rate of investment, so that when these two conditions are satisfied the ratio of indebtedness of entrepreneurs to the value of capital remains constant, and the demand for commodities (expenditure of rentiers *plus* the wages bill) expands with productive capacity ; then no disturbance is introduced to upset the golden-age conditions.

The first condition, a constant proportion of profits distributed, is satisfied when the rate of interest is constant, the proportion of entrepreneurs borrowing on fixed interest terms is constant and the proportion of profit, net of interest, distributed as dividends is constant. (It is also possible that the condition should be satisfied by compensating changes in these elements, for instance, a falling ratio of interest to profits just offset by a rising proportion of dividends.)

The second condition, that the proportion of saving to rentier receipts is constant, is fulfilled when the standard of consumption rises progressively with wealth (in the manner discussed above).[1]

Provided that these conditions are satisfied the whole of our analysis of golden ages holds good, but it is important to remember that when we remove the assumption of no consumption out of profits it ceases to be true that the rate of profit on capital is equal to the growth ratio of the economy. We could set out a fresh series of comparisons of golden-age economies all with the same rate of profit (and therefore at the same position of the mechanisation frontier) and different growth ratios, the ratio of consumption to investment being higher, and therefore the growth ratio lower, the less thrifty the rentiers. Or we could set out a comparison of economies all with the same growth ratio, the rate of profit being higher (and the degree of mechanisation lower) the less thrifty the rentiers. This is merely an elaboration of our former analysis. Our former comparisons may be regarded as a selection from

[1] See p. 251.

this more general scheme of the cases of a hundred per cent thriftiness.

The conception of stagnation due to increasing monopoly is somewhat weakened by consumption out of profits, but not reversed. An increase in gross margins means an increase in quasi-rent per man employed, and an increase in rentier consumption per man employed. But only part of profit is distributed to rentiers, and of their share a part is saved. Thus a rise in quasi-rent per man raises rentier consumption per man employed by less than it reduces the real wage per man. Demand, therefore, rises by less than the value of output per man employed, and surplus capacity emerges as the result of a rise in gross margins.

RISING THRIFTINESS

The Socialist under-consumption thesis is that stagnation sets in because the share of wages in the value of output tends to fall as output increases.

There is also what we may call a Liberal under-consumption thesis [1] based on the view that the proportion of saving to income tends to rise with income, quite apart from a change in distribution between wages and profits. When the number of rentier families is rising in proportion to total rentier wealth, and the distribution of wealth between them remains constant, the conditions of a golden age merely require that their consumption habits should be unchanging. But if wealth per family is growing through time, or becoming more concentrated, a constant ratio of consumption to income means a continuously rising level of expenditure per family. On the view that wants are satiable, so that the moral effort of saving grows less as the standard of life rises, a rising ratio of saving to income is to be expected, and this entails a falling ratio of consumption to investment, which brings stagnation in its train.

When thriftiness is rising through time, each round of increase in productive capacity meets an increase in demand insufficient to keep it in use at the former rate of profit. In

[1] This is one strand of thought in the *General Theory*, which has been elaborated by many writers, especially R. F. Harrod and Alvin Hansen.

so far as prices fall as surplus capacity emerges, the real-wage rate is raised, and the amount of surplus capacity is consequently less, but the rate of profit per unit of output has fallen. If prices are held constant, profit per unit of output has not altered, but output per unit of capacity has fallen all the more. In either case, the inducement to invest in still more capacity is weakened and stagnation sets in.

If a failure of demand to expand with productive capacity were foreseen by entrepreneurs (each considering his own market) investment would be discouraged in advance, and the fall in profits would come about all the sooner.

The entrepreneurs could find no escape by reducing investment. The remedy is to increase it, so that, with a rise in employment, workers' consumption makes up the deficit in rentier consumption. But from the point of view of each entrepreneur individually, prospects in such a situation would be bad and an increase in investment would appear imprudent.

Thus, increasing thriftiness would frustrate itself. Some rentiers might succeed in increasing their wealth, but for rentiers as a whole income would fall. Accumulation would be retarded and unemployment increased.

If rentier thriftiness could be curbed by low interest rates monetary policy could prevent this situation from arising. The favourite Liberal prescription is to stimulate consumption (and to counteract the discouraging effect on investment of poor prospects of profit) by reducing interest rates. This, however, is admitted to be a weak remedy, both because of the problematical effect of low interest on rentier saving [1] and because it may be impossible for the monetary authorities to get the level of interest rates to fall fast enough to do much good.

According to the Liberal thesis, therefore, there is an inherent contradiction in the conditions for a golden age (or any approximation to a golden age with cyclical accumulation yielding a steady long-run trend) with rising wealth per head, and it is the inevitable destiny of prosperous economies to drown themselves in cream.

All this, however, is based on an *a priori* view of consumers' behaviour, and so far as the evidence goes it seems as though

[1] See above, p. 252.

emulation and salesmanship succeed pretty well in keeping thriftiness within bounds (even at constant interest rates), so that, as long as entrepreneurs do their part in accumulating productive capacity, rentiers can be induced to do their part in consuming the product.[1] From a long-run point of view the Liberal thesis of under-consumption as a menace to prosperity does not seem to have been vindicated.

CONSUMPTION AND UNEMPLOYMENT

Now let us consider the situation of rentiers in an economy which has fallen into stagnation because of an inadequate urge to accumulate.

A long-period surplus of labour is likely to cause a downward drift of money-wage rates and (unless monopoly is growing) of money prices. Since there is a considerable time lag between a fall in profits in money terms and the consequent fall in rentier receipts of interest on bonds, and since, so long as annual receipts tend to be maintained and the rate of interest is constant, the value of placements tends to be maintained, while bank deposits are fixed in money terms, the total of rentier wealth falls more slowly than the money value of the capital to which it corresponds. Thus both annual receipts of rentiers and their wealth in money terms fall more slowly than the purchasing power of money rises. Consequently rentier consumption tends to rise as money wages fall.

Moreover, if unemployment allowances are additional to rentier consumption, the mere existence of unemployed workers generates demand for consumption goods.

In these ways the emergence of surplus labour tends to stimulate consumption, and so, by raising demand relatively to capacity, helps to keep accumulation going.[2]

Moreover, a low level of money wages relatively to average rentier income fosters the employment of domestic servants and helps unemployment to disguise itself in jobbing work of

---

[1] Cf. Duesenberry, *op. cit.*

[2] But as we shall see (p. 278) the existence of rentier incomes means that falling money-wage rates have a highly adverse effect on the supply of finance.

all kinds, so that the existence of rentiers greatly enhances the process of demechanisation which contributes to absorb surplus labour.[1]   Indeed, rentiers have a much more comfortable life in a stagnant economy (provided that profits are not being so much squeezed as to provoke defaults) than in a highly progressive one.

All this helps to mitigate the evils of stagnation, but it cannot be more than a mitigation, for if the cure was so successful as to remove the surplus of labour, the downward tendency of wages which helps to mitigate it would cease to operate, and it is falling wages, not low wages, that brings relief through raising rentier purchasing power.

[1] See p. 158.

CHAPTER 27

RENTIERS AND THE TRADE CYCLE

THE existence of rentier incomes complicates the analysis of short-run fluctuations in activity, without affecting the main lines of our former argument.

THE BOOM

When the rate of investment first begins to increase during the revival from a depression rentier receipts may still be falling, as the backwash from an earlier period of low profits, but after a time they begin to rise. Their rise in money terms is less than in proportion to the rise in profits, partly because of interest payments fixed in terms of money, and partly because many entrepreneurs try to keep dividends stable, so that they retain in the business a larger proportion of profits when profits are high. Against this, the second-hand value of placements is likely to be rising (a bull movement on the Stock Exchange follows improved prospects of profit) so that in so far as rentiers regard capital appreciation as part of spendable income, their spending power in money terms may increase as much or more than in proportion to profits.

In general, it seems that the former influence is more powerful than the latter. Moreover, rentiers may regard boom dividends as exceptional and prudently refrain from spending them. Thus the addition to rentier spending that takes place as profits rise bears a smaller ratio to the addition to profits than does total spending to total profits.

We discussed the movement of output and employment in the consumption sector in terms of two extreme cases. At one extreme the output of commodities remains constant and the boom shows itself entirely in a rise in prices. In that case, the real purchasing power of rentier receipts rises by less than their money value, and may even fall below what it was in the preceding depression. The output of commodities available for rentiers and consumption-sector workers taken as a whole falls by the amount by which consumption of investment-sector workers (formerly unemployed) rises. In so far as rentiers allow their purchases in real terms to fall, the real-wage rate per man falls by so much the less. If rentiers maintain their purchases in real terms (making up for the difference between the rise in prices and the rise in their money receipts by saving less) the whole increase in consumption of newly employed workers is at the expense of those formerly employed. Prices rise sufficiently to reduce the real-wage rate to whatever extent is required to allow the newly employed workers their share of consumption.

At the other extreme, where there is so much surplus capacity in the consumption sector that prices and output per head remain constant as investment increases, the expansion of output of commodities is limited only by the expansion of demand.

In this case, the existence of rentier incomes tends to damp the fluctuation in output. Rentier receipts increase with profits (after a time lag) and consumption increases with receipts, but, in general, it seems likely that a fairly constant proportion of rentier saving to income over the long run is maintained by raising the proportion of saving when income is higher than the average and allowing it to fall when income is lower, so that rentier's consumption rises less than in proportion to their receipts over the course of a boom.

The institution of unemployment allowances also damps the swings of output (and therefore of employment) in the consumption sector. The greater is the expenditure of unemployed workers the smaller is the increase in their consumption when they become employed.

These influences reduce the value of the multiplier, and would make the ratio of consumption to investment in the boom very much lower than its long-run average even if a rise of prices was not also operating to limit it.

The time pattern of the development of a boom is much complicated by the existence of rentier incomes. Profits are distributed after they have been earned, and in general rentier expenditure is likely to rise after rentier receipts (though expectations of higher receipts combined with present capital gains may cause expenditure to rise in advance) so that the expenditure out of profits generated by investment occurs some months later. The multiplier operates, so to say, in two layers. Increased employment in the investment sector causes an increase in expenditure out of wages within the week, but the corresponding expenditure out of profits follows later. Thus, when the rate of investment is changing from month to month, the wages component in the multiplier is reflecting current investment and the rentier component is reflecting investment of some months earlier. This destroys the simplicity of the notion of a position of short-period equilibrium corresponding to a given rate of investment. A definite high-level equilibrium with investment at its maximum rate may never be attained, for investment may have begun to fall before consumption has caught up with the peak of investment, so that the multiplier is never operating on both layers at once.

All this adds to the variety of patterns which booms go through, but taking it by and large it does not affect the main mechanism of the cycle which we have already discussed. Rentier expenditure increases (with a time lag) when investment increases and so helps to generate the conditions of a seller's market that make investment increase further. When investment has run into bottle-necks and cannot increase any further, consumption may go on increasing for some time, as the backwash of the high profits of the recent past, and this delays the emergence of a buyer's market by providing demand to meet the increase in productive capacity that is taking place. When the time is reached at which rentier outlay is reflecting the maximum level of profits reached during the boom, it ceases to increase, but the increase in productive capacity goes on, as equipment emerges from the pipe-lines of production in the bottle-neck industries. The time lag in rentier expenditure can do no more than postpone the emergence of a buyer's market that brings the boom to an end.

THE SLUMP

The point at which the run-down into a slump is brought to a halt is very much affected by the existence of rentiers. Some rentier families find their real incomes higher after a slump than they were during the preceding boom, because money receipts (from fixed interest) are not reduced and prices have fallen. The expenditure in real terms of these families may be greater at the bottom of the slump than before the downswing began. Others find their money receipts reduced by more than prices have fallen (and the value of their placements may be reduced by a bear movement on the Stock Exchange) but they allow their savings to fall rather than cut their consumption. Rentiers' consumption is therefore at a higher proportion to investment, when the rate of investment has recently fallen, than it is on the long-run average, and this provides an important buffer to limit the depth of the slump.

Unemployment allowances also provide a buffer. The higher the ratio of expenditure by unemployed workers to the wage of employed workers, the less demand falls as unemployment increases.[1]

In our former analysis (with no consumption out of profits) the only stopper to the run-down in a slump was provided by a fall in prices and rise in real-wage rates, so that if prices were held constant there would be no limit to the extent of the slump. Rentier expenditure and unemployment allowances provide stoppers which would operate to some extent even if prices were constant. On the other hand, the very fact that rentier expenditure tends to be maintained (and unemployment pay to increase) as investment falls, brakes the fall in prices, so that the operation of these buffers is partly a substitute for the buffer provided by rising real wages, as well as being partly a reinforcement of it.

The maintenance of consumption in face of falling incomes

---

[1] At one time capitalist opinion was hostile to 'the dole' as an infringement of the rigour of the rules of the game, but the experience of the great depression of the 'thirties has led them to regard it as a useful buffer to a decline in demand, as well as an insurance against political trouble.

is likely to be mainly in respect of perishable goods and of services, while demand for durable consumer goods falls sharply (outlay on food is maintained better than on clothes, and on clothes better than on motor-cars). A high proportion of durable goods in the pattern of consumption tends to increase instability. This effect is all the greater when hire purchase is common, so that part of current income is already pledged to paying for goods bought in the past.

In so far as rising wealth is associated over the long run with a rising proportion of outlay on durable goods, it makes the level of expenditure (though not of consumption) progressively more unstable in the short period as wealth increases.

DEPRESSION

The two-sided nature of the relation between rentiers and entrepreneurs complicates the development of a depression. On the one hand the maintenance of rentier income through fixed interest payments helps to keep up demand for consumption goods, but on the other hand they increase the financial difficulties of entrepreneurs. They help to soften the initial impact of a slump, but they may cause a subsequent further decline in rentier consumption as a result of defaults and bankruptcies. These react also upon gross investment, so that an initial slump may be followed by a period of further gradual decline, or a series of secondary slumps. In general, the longer is recovery delayed, the lower is the level to which activity falls.

The effect of falling money-wage rates during a depression is also double-edged. In so far as prices gradually fall after the initial run-down into a slump, rentier expenditure in real terms tends to rise (and if the rate of unemployment pay is fixed in money terms the consumption of the unemployed also gradually rises), but the increasing real burden of debt on the entrepreneurs may cause gross investment to fall still further.

This is important also in connection with the monetary system. A sharp fall in prices may ruin the banks, for their obligations (deposits) are fixed in terms of money while the placements they hold fall in value when profits in money terms fall, and debtors to whom they have made loans may default. Rumours about the solvency of banks cause depositors to run to withdraw, and if the banks close their doors large blocks of consumer purchasing power are immobilised (if not permanently lost), which causes a cataclysmic further fall in demand and in profits.[1]

This very much reinforces our former argument that at the time when a fall in money wages is most likely to occur (a depression) it is least likely to be of any use as a means of reducing unemployment.[2]

CYCLE AND TREND

Consumption out of profits plays an important part in the mechanism by which a long-run trend of accumulation emerges from the trade cycle. Each boom leaves behind it an increase in rentier wealth and consuming power due to the savings which took place while the boom was going on. Consequently the drop into each slump is checked at a higher level of demand for consumption goods, and provided that the depression is not so severe as to wipe out the additional rentier wealth through bankruptcies, each revival starts from a higher level of output than the last.

This is reinforced by the institution of unemployment pay. During a boom output per head is raised, as new investment goes into improved techniques, and population may be increasing, so that, in each depression, a given level of output is accompanied by a larger amount of unemployment, and a larger outlay of unemployment allowances. Therefore the amount of consumption accompanying a given level of investment is greater in each depression than in the last.[3]

These two effects reinforce each other, and check the decline in output of commodities at successively higher points from slump to slump. The amount of capacity that has to be destroyed during a slump before a seller's market reappears is

---

[1] See Keynes, *Essays in Persuasion*, p. 168.
[2] But see below, p. 270.
[3] Cf. R. C. O. Matthews, 'The Saving Function and the Problem of Trend and Cycle,' *Review of Economic Studies*, vol. xxii (2), No. 58 (1954–55).

then less than the addition to capacity made during the preceding boom, and accumulation over the long run is taking place.

CONSUMER'S INVESTMENT

As we have seen, the durability of consumer goods has a tendency to exaggerate the fluctuations in demand that accompany fluctuations in entrepreneur's investment. It may also generate fluctuations on its own. This is of particular importance in connection with houses — the largest and most durable type of consumer good. When for any reason the supply of houses has not kept up with demand, houses are a profitable investment for entrepreneurs (speculative builders) and they are also in demand from consumers who are anxious to buy them out of past savings (by selling out placements) or out of borrowing which must be repaid from future saving. The building industry runs into a bottle-neck [1] and the shortage of houses may persist for a considerable period. When the rate of new building exceeds the rate of collapse of old houses and the rate at which new demand is piling up, the scarcity of houses is being reduced and after some time rents begin to fall or lettings become more difficult, and new orders from consumers fail to keep pace with the completion of old ones. The rate of building then falls off.

A rise in employment in house-building has the same effect upon demand for commodities as an increase in entrepreneur's investment, and it may contribute to creating a seller's market for commodities in general and so inducing entrepreneur's investment. Thus a general boom may be set going by an increase in house-building, or a slump precipitated by a decline.

House-building for rentier families is likely to be stimulated by a general fall in money-wage rates which reduces the cost of a house relatively to rentier incomes. Building is also susceptible to a fall in the rate of interest. Cheaper terms for borrowing encourage consumer's investment, and a fall in the level of interest rates raises the value of existing houses relatively to the cost of building new ones. Where house-building

[1] See above, p. 200, note.

forms an important part of total output, therefore, there is some scope for falling wages and interest to stimulate employment. This may be important both in bringing revival from a depression and in mitigating stagnation.

Over the long run a given increase in total income accompanied by an increase in population probably produces, under strict capitalist rules, a smaller increase in demand for housing than the same increase in total income spread over fewer people, for though an increase in the number of bodies increases the need for housing, an increase in income per head increases the means to pay for it, and the second without the first is far more effective than the first without the second. On the other hand, when the strict rules have been modified by social conscience and political pressure, the provision of a certain standard of housing for workers may be partly charged to rentiers (through taxation) so that the mere existence of need to some extent generates effective demand.

When population is increasing and the standard of housing is being maintained, the rate of investment in building rises over the long run with the increase in available labour, just as investment in equipment rises when population is increasing and technique constant. A rise in the standard of housing creates a hump of investment (in slum clearance, etc.) which is somewhat similar to the hump of investment generated by a bout of capital-using innovations. In an advanced economy a growing dislike for squalor may be helpful in fending off stagnation by stimulating investment in housing and other amenities when entrepreneurs' accumulation is beginning to flag.

RENTIER CONSUMPTION AND REAL WAGES

Given the rate of investment, the level of real wages is lower the greater is the rentiers' consumption; or, given the rate of real wages, the greater is rentiers' consumption the smaller is the rate of investment that can be carried out without depressing the wage rate. On the other hand, in any given situation an increase in rentier expenditure increases the demand for commodities, so that (unless absolutely full employment already prevails) it increases employment. The effect upon the total of real wages depends upon the elasticity of supply of commodities. If there was a buyer's market before an increase in the rate of rentier spending occurred, prices rise very little, if at all, and the fall in the rate of real wages per man is less than in proportion to the increase in employment, so that the total of real wages rises. When an increase in rentier spending takes place in a seller's market, it depresses the real-wage rate (by causing prices to rise relatively to money wages) more than it increases employment.

This double relation between rentier consumption and wages causes a good deal of confusion, and raises the question whether thriftiness on the part of rentiers is favourable or unfavourable to the interest of the workers. The essential point, however, is quite simple. When a high level of employment is in any case being maintained by investment, extra consumption by rentiers is harmful to the workers in the short run (by lowering real wages), and if it goes so far as to cause a danger of inflation which is checked by curtailing investment, it is harmful in the future also, because it retards accumulation. When the rate of investment is low and depression prevails, extra consumption by rentiers is favourable to the workers in the short run, for it increases employment immediately ; and in the future, for by reducing the intensity of a buyer's market it helps to promote accumulation.

The same argument applies from a long-run point of view. In a buoyant economy, where productive capacity keeps up with available labour, the more thrifty are the rentiers the more rapid is the rate of accumulation and the long-run rise in real wages. In an economy which is sunk in stagnation, thriftiness of rentiers only makes matters worse.

Doctor Johnson was fond of arguing that the luxury of the rich was good for the poor.[1] This view held good in an economy where there was a plentiful reserve of labour in disguised unemployment in the countryside, and the energetic

---

[1] 'You cannot spend money in luxury without doing good to the poor. Nay, you do more good to them by spending it in luxury than by giving it ; for by spending it you make them exert industry, whereas by giving it you keep them idle.' Boswell's *Life of Dr. Johnson* (ed. Fitzgerald, pub. Allen and Unwin), vol. iii, p. 298 (see also p. 132).

entrepreneurs of the industrial revolution had not yet set accumulation going.

In modern times, during a depression or when the economy is threatened with stagnation through growing monopoly and a weakening impulse to accumulate, luxury expenditure, as a remedy for unemployment, is to be preferred to expenditure on armaments but is clearly less beneficial than investment in industrial productive capacity or social amenities.

CHAPTER 28

RENTIERS AND FINANCE

THE existence of a separate class of rentier incomes (apart from allowances to the households of entrepreneurs) implies that a substantial part of capital accumulation has been financed by borrowing, as opposed to reinvestment of profits. In general, our analysis of excess-investment and borrowing, liquidity preference and monetary policy is unaffected by the existence of rentiers. But there are certain respects in which the fact that a large part of wealth is outside the direct control of entrepreneurs (and that it is continually growing as rentiers save) has an influence upon accumulation through its effect upon the control over finance.

FORMS OF BORROWING

Of all the multifarious types of placements that exist in reality we choose only two representatives for inclusion in our simplified model economy — fixed-interest bonds and ordinary shares.[1] Besides borrowing in these forms entrepreneurs may borrow from banks, and besides holding these placements rentiers may make deposits with banks, the banks holding bonds as well as making loans. To retain the sharp distinction between money as a placement and money as a medium of exchange we continue to assume that cheques are not in use and that notes are not hoarded.

The amount of interest that entrepreneurs are obliged to pay in any year depends upon the terms on which they borrowed in the past and has no very definite relation to the present rate of interest or the present value of capital. However, we assume that bonds can be bought in at any time, so

[1] See above, p. 7, note.

that a permanent fall in the rate of interest means that entrepreneurs can re-borrow and use the proceeds to pay off bonds,
thus converting their debt to a cheaper form. And when the
replacement cost of capital goods falls below historic cost they
may use part of their redundant amortisation funds to redeem
bonds, so that by a gradual process outstanding debt is kept in
touch with the value of capital.

The whole capital of a firm legally belongs to the shareholders, but we assume that it is controlled by entrepreneurs
who are concerned with the firm as such, and who pay out, as
dividends, considerably less than net profit (though they may
pursue a dividend equalisation policy so as to relate dividends
to average profits over a long run rather than from year to
year). The amount of dividends paid is partly a phenomenon
of imperfect competition. Outside shareholders (as opposed
to insiders who really control a firm) [1] prefer dividends to a
legal title to ownership in undistributed profits (abstracting
from taxation, which in reality distorts their preferences) and
it is necessary for one entrepreneur to be about as generous
to his shareholders as others or he will fail to get takers when
he wants to make a new issue, or may even provoke a revolt of
existing shareholders. Similar considerations apply to the
entrepreneurs' wives. We assume that some kind of tradition
has been established that permits entrepreneurs to retain a
considerable proportion of profits undistributed, and that the
proportion is kept more or less constant by a tension between
the competition for outside shareholders and the entrepreneurs'
preference for self-financed investment.

THRIFT AND THE SUPPLY OF FINANCE

Cancelling out transactions between rentiers in second-hand
property and loans between entrepreneurs, we can consider
transactions between entrepreneurs as a whole and rentiers as
a whole. The rentiers receive interest and dividends from
entrepreneurs and make payments to them for consumption
goods. Over any period, say a year, the excess of rentier
receipts over their expenditure (that is, their saving) is the

[1] See above, p. 8.

same thing as the excess of entrepreneurs' outlay over their receipts (the excess of gross investment over quasi-rent retained as amortisation and undistributed profits), assuming that workers neither save nor dis-save, and including social security allowances in rentier expenditure. Thus, over the year the increment of rentier wealth is equal to the increment of entrepreneurs' debt.

It is necessary to guard against the confusion of thinking of rentier thriftiness as providing finance for investment.[1] In so far as thrift assists investment it does so by leaving more room within the inflation barrier — refraining from consumption, so to say, releases man-power for investment. It does not help by providing finance. So far as finance is concerned, rentier expenditure, by generating profits, provides it in a more direct way than saving, which obliges entrepreneurs to borrow if they want to maintain future investment.

When the ratio of rentier saving to net investment, in any period, exceeds the pre-existing ratio of debt to value of capital, that ratio is rising, for the proportionate increment of debt (equal to rentier saving) is greater than the proportionate increment of value of capital (net investment). The borrowing power of entrepreneurs, taken as a whole, is then growing less, for, in the typical case, the share of profit already pledged to interest has risen from one year to another, or the margin of earnings over dividends at the former level has fallen, so that the security offered to lenders or new shareholders has grown less good. Contrariwise, if the ratio of rentier saving to net investment is less than the ratio of obligations to value of capital, borrowing power is growing progressively greater.

To maintain a steady rate of accumulation over the long run it is necessary that the ratio of rentier saving to profits should not be rising. (This, as we have seen, is also necessary because of the relation of demand to productive capacity.)[2]

---

[1] This confusion came to the surface in connection with the Savings Campaign during the war. The public had the impression that savings were needed 'to pay for the war'. A respected government has no difficulty in finding means of payment, and with a well-disciplined monetary system it can make the rate of interest at which it borrows pretty much what it pleases. The purpose of the Savings Campaign was to induce the public to refrain from consumption and so relieve the inflationary pressure of demand on limited supplies of civilian goods.   [2] See p. 260.

LIQUIDITY PREFERENCE AND FINANCE

It is also necessary that the willingness of rentiers to lend to entrepreneurs should not be falling. As we have seen, uncertainty about the future course of the rate of interest gives rise to a desire to hold wealth in a liquid form.[1] On the whole, the liquidity preference of rentiers is probably less than that of entrepreneurs. An entrepreneur when he is holding uninvested funds (amortisation and reserves) is generally expecting to use them in the fairly near future, for replacements of capital, for dividend payments or for new schemes of investment, and the integrity of the principal when it comes to be expended is more important than interest to be earned meanwhile. Many rentiers, on the other hand, expect never to need to spend their capital, and are primarily concerned with the income it yields. They are highly sensitive to lack of security (fear of default) and it requires high yields to tempt them to hold securities of doubtful borrowers, but they are not so sensitive to lack of liquidity (fear of loss of capital value due to a general rise in interest rates).[2] All the same, they do feel some liquidity preference, and like to hold a part of their wealth in bank deposits. Every increment of rentier wealth (due to saving) therefore leads to a smaller increment of demand for securities, and to keep the yield of bonds constant the banks must allow the total of bank deposits to increase with the total of wealth. By doing so they provide the rentiers with the liquid placements that they require, and lend to entrepreneurs (directly or by taking up second-hand bonds), the difference between rentier savings and rentier lending.

If they failed to do so there would be a long-run tendency for the bond rate of interest to rise, which would make new borrowing more expensive to entrepreneurs and so discourage accumulation.

The willingness of rentiers to hold securities at any particular moment depends very much upon the state of opinion. In this respect the behaviour of the financial system is apt to

[1] See p. 30 and p. 231.
[2] See R. F. Kahn, 'Some Notes on Liquidity Preference', *Manchester School* (September 1954).

be unhelpful to stability, for the very same causes that make
entrepreneurs dubious about future profits make rentiers
dubious about the value of placements, so that the interest
rates rise and borrowing becomes harder just when stability
requires investment to be given every possible encouragement,
and borrowing is easiest just when investment is least in need
of stimulus.

PRICES AND FINANCE

The existence of rentier income much enhances the importance of movements of the general level of prices. Payments
to rentiers are related to past profits, so that over any period
when profits in money terms are rising, the rentiers' share in
currents profits is abnormally low, and contrariwise when
profits are falling. A general proportionate rise or fall in money
wages and prices leaves total profit in real terms unchanged
but reduces or raises the share of rentiers (except in so far as
there is an over- or under-distribution of profits due to illusory
gains or losses on inventories).[1] So far as consumption is
concerned, as we have seen, this is likely to mean that a rise
in wages tends to reduce employment and a fall to increase it.
But now we must consider its effect on employment through
its effect on finance. A period of rising wages and prices is
a period of high net profits, and since net profits have risen
(after a rise in wages has occurred) more than in proportion
to wages, they have risen more than in proportion to the cost
of capital goods; finance is therefore easier to come by — a
smaller amount of new outside borrowing is required for a
given gross investment in real terms. Contrariwise with falling
prices. It seems, then, that (under competitive conditions,
when prices fall with costs) a fall in money wages is actually
undesirable from the point of view of entrepreneurs taken as a
whole, for it increases the real value of the sums that they have
to pay to rentiers. This is one of the most curious of the
paradoxes that arise under the capitalist rules of the game. In
the opposition of class interests, the capitalists regarded as
active entrepreneurs are to some extent on the same side as

[1] See above, p. 43.

the workers, against the capitalists regarded as passive owners of wealth.

This phenomenon helps to weaken or even reverse the tendency for falling money wages to stimulate investment, and so further impairs the mechanism by which surplus labour tends to get itself employed.

On the other hand, a reduction in money-wage rates may tend to make finance easier when the banking system is pursuing any sort of automatic policy under which a fall in demand for money in active circulation tends to bring down the interest rates.

Finally, an *expectation* of falling prices makes fixed interest bonds attractive to rentiers (as opposed to shares and real property), while it makes enterpreneurs prefer short-term borrowing from the banks, so that the demand for bonds is high relatively to the quantity on offer, and the bond rate of interest tends to be lower than when prices are expected to be rising.[1]

Lower interest rates have some effect (though probably a weak one)[2] in encouraging investment, and in this way falling money-wage rates have some influence favourable to investment to set against the unfavourable effect of the rising real value of the rentier's claims on the entrepreneurs and the discouraging prospect of falling prices.

These phenomena are concerned with the process of falling wages; when wages have been for some time at one level, no matter whether high or low by any absolute standard, the value of debts has become adjusted to the value of capital, and the absolute level of wages and prices affects nothing except the names (number of pounds sterling) by which values are called.

---

[1] Keynes denies this (*General Theory*, p. 142) but his argument is extremely obscure.   [2] See above, p. 243.

BOOK VI
LAND

CHAPTER 29

LAND AND LABOUR

FROM an historical point of view we have been putting the cart before the horse in discussing capital without mentioning land. Land is of the greatest importance as a factor of production, and the development of a technical surplus of food is the first requisite for accumulation. Moreover, as we saw with the robins, property in the right to exploit territory is the archetypal form of property. The whole structure of a society is affected by the rules of the game in respect to land tenure and inheritance. Industrial societies have carried on the rules appropriate to agriculture. (This often produces anomalous results, such as great wealth being accorded to the owners and the descendants of owners of patches of the earth's surface under which minerals have been found or over which cities have been built.) The habits and traditions of landowners, whether aristocrats, peasants or frontiersmen, have impregnated industrial societies and coloured their development. An analysis of the role of land, even in a highly simplified model economy, would require a volume to itself. Here we shall do no more than indicate some aspects of the subject which are germane to our central theme.

MARGINAL PRODUCTS

It is impossible to imagine an economy without some regulation of the right to use land (even Adam Smith's hunters of beavers and deer must have had their customary beats [1]), but where land is plentiful (as we have so far assumed in our model) and everyone can operate as much as he chooses, the technique of production adopted is such that nothing could be

[1] *Wealth of Nations*, chapter vi.

added to the output of a given amount of labour by taking more land into use.[1]

The usual state of affairs, however, is that land is scarce relatively to available labour, so that techniques are such that output per man is greater or less when labour per acre is less or greater. This is usually expressed by saying that the marginal product of labour falls and of land rises as the ratio of labour to land is increased.

As we shall see, a combination of the analysis of the real-capital ratio and the hierarchy of degrees of mechanisation with an analysis of differences in the ratio of land to labour is somewhat complicated. We will begin by eliminating the hierarchy of techniques, so as to be able to concentrate on the ratio of land to labour.

We assume that physical capital per acre is very rigidly fixed by technical conditions.[2] Just so much seed per acre is always used ; such-and-such ditches were long ago dug and are now kept clear ; and so forth. Land is all alike, and the period of production (the length of the crop cycle) is given by nature (the procession of the seasons). Further, the unit of labour is a man-year, so that we need not worry about the time-pattern of work over the year (a worker may be more busy or more idle in some weeks than others, but he cannot be stood off by an employer in slack seasons, so that the time-pattern of wage payments is uniform over a year ; while for a peasant employing himself labour-time is reckoned simply as twenty-four hours a day over the year, irrespective of how long he sleeps).

We can then specify the marginal product of labour : it is

[1] In some cases techniques may be used such that a larger total output could be got by a given labour force from a smaller space (the marginal product of land is negative). Rights in land are desired for their own sake as well as for the sake of product, and if the rules of the game require the owner of land to keep up an appearance of cultivating it, while the supply of labour is limited, he may use labour over a greater space than that which would yield the maximum product. Further, empty land may reduce the productivity of neighbouring cultivation, by breeding weeds, rabbits, tigers, etc., so that some expense is required merely to keep the marginal product of land at zero.

[2] This may be expressed by saying that the marginal product of any particular kind of capital good falls abruptly to zero when its quantity per acre is raised about a certain amount.

the addition to total output due to employing an additional man-year of labour on a given space.[1] The average product per man falls as more men are employed on a given space, and the marginal product of labour, when $n+1$ men are employed, is the average product of $n+1$ men *minus n* times the difference between the average product of n and that of $n+1$ men (the number n being sufficiently great to make the difference between the marginal produce of $n+1$ and $n-1$ inappreciable). Similarly we can specify the marginal product of land as the addition to total output when an additional acre is cultivated by a given labour force. It is the average product per acre when $n+1$ acres are cultivated, *minus n* times the difference between product per acre when n acres are cultivated (slightly more intensively), and the product per acre when $n+1$ are cultivated (slightly less intensively).[2]

It is useful to observe that, in the assumed conditions, the total product is equal to the sum of the marginal product of each factor multiplied by the amount of that factor.[3] This can be seen as follows: imagine that the economy loses a small area of land. Output is reduced by the marginal product of land multiplied by the area lost, and this loss is equal to the product of the land *minus* the addition to product of the remaining land due to the labour displaced from the lost land being deployed upon it. This addition (due to the slight increase in intensity of cultivation of the remaining land) is equal to the marginal product of labour multiplied by the number of men displaced. It follows that if land and labour were both lost, in such a way as to keep the proportion between them constant, the loss of product would be equal to the marginal product of land multiplied by the area lost *plus* the marginal product of labour multiplied by the number of men

[1] In the course of the year the man produces whatever capital goods he needs. The shepherd cuts a crook out of the hedge. See D. H. Robertson, 'Wage Grumbles', *Economic Fragments*, p. 46.

[2] The marginal product of land multiplied by the area occupied by a given labour force (which is equal to the difference between the average and marginal product of labour multiplied by the number of men employed) is sometimes called the 'true economic rent' of that area of land. But we shall be using rent in its everyday sense as the hire price of land.

[3] This is an application of Euler's Theorem. See Wicksell, *Lectures*, vol. i, p. 127.

lost. Assuming that product per man (or per acre) is independent of total output (there are no economies or diseconomies of scale for output as a whole), the whole product can be accounted for in this way.[1]

When the total area of land (with its appropriate capital goods) available to the economy is given, and is scarce in the sense that it has a positive marginal product, an increase in the total labour force can increase output (when the land is all alike) only by more intense cultivation (closer weeding, etc.). When land varies in quality (each individual acre having its own capital goods), if a given labour force is deployed over it in such a way as to get the maximum product from the whole area, there is likely to be a greater concentration of man-power on better land. With a larger labour force the area as a whole is cultivated more intensively, and this may involve labour being deployed upon some low-grade land which with a smaller labour force would be left vacant.

Assuming no economies of scale (due to greater specialisation of labour and land at a larger total output), the output per head of a larger labour force is less than of a smaller labour force; the marginal product of labour to the whole economy is less than average product (because average product falls as the number of heads rises), and there is a certain size of the labour force at which marginal product is zero.

This is the basis of the famous Law of Diminishing Returns from Land.

Given technical conditions, the division of the total product between workers and owners of property depends, first of all, upon how the relations between them are organised, and secondly, upon the over-all ratio of labour to land.

We will first discuss a primitive agricultural economy where simple traditional techniques are in use, and capital goods play a minor role, so that the technical conditions can be regarded as approximating to the above assumptions, and we will discuss the effect of changes in population in a given space under various sets of rules of the game in respect to property.

[1] See below, p. 304.

FREEHOLDERS

Free peasants who own the land they cultivate and· enjoy the whole product of their work are rentiers, entrepreneurs and workers all in one. The over-all factor ratio in such an economy is determined by demography (the relation of population to land). The distribution of income between families may be very unequal, depending on how much land per head each happens to own. Some, who own more land than they can cultivate without making its marginal product very low, may rent a part of it to others who dispose of more labour than can be deployed on their own holdings without making the marginal product of labour very low. There is then some tendency to equalise the marginal product of labour throughout the economy. But there is no tendency to equalise income per head. On the contrary, those who have a level of income (derived from their own work on their own land and possibly also from rents of land hired out) which permits of saving, may acquire land from those who are driven to consume more than their product by poverty or fecklessness. The distribution of the product of a holding of land between its owners is carried out according to whatever intra-family rules of the game are in force.

In such an economy an increase in population in a given space reduces land per head and therefore output per head. Average income per head exceeds the marginal product of labour, and (with a dense population) the marginal product of labour may well be zero or even negative (splitting up holdings between more workers reduces total product).

Here the distinction between wages and profits has no meaning. There may, however, be interest. Some families may consume less than they produce in any one year, while others borrow to consume more, pledging land as security. The major part of any investment in capital goods that occurs (say, breeding livestock) is made out of the product of the land where it takes place, and has little effect upon the demand for loans. The rate of interest, therefore, has very little connection with technical conditions, and its level varies from year to year according to the accidental relationship of the demand for loans (coming from distressed families) to the supply made available by families whose product happens to exceed what they want to consume and invest on their own land.[1]

LANDLORDS AND PEASANTS

Where land is owned by a special group of families (whose titles date from past history and are established under the current rules of the game) they can obtain rent by hiring it to producers. We will suppose that work is provided by peasant families who own what little capital goods there are (ploughs, livestock, etc.) and finance their own consumption out of the carry-over from harvest to harvest. When the landlords' traditions forbid them to compete against each other for tenants, they can make the level of rents what they think right, and if they are ruthlessly exploiting their powers they fix them at a level which just permits the tenants to live.[2] They then enjoy the whole technical surplus of production. An increase in population reduces the surplus per man, but it increases the total of rents, up to the point where an additional man-year of work adds no more to total output than the man must eat in order to live (the marginal product of labour is equal to the subsistence minimum).[3] Growth of population can then go no further, and rents are at the technically possible maximum. A decline in population reduces total rents without altering the peasants' income per head.

[1] There is no logical reason why the rate of interest should be positive rather than negative. If there is a preponderance of wealthy families, whose product exceeds what they want to consume or can conveniently invest or store on their own ground, but who want to carry consuming power into the future, there would be a premium on future over present goods, and negative interest.

In fact, however, in societies of this type, it is usual for the custom of lavish consumption at weddings and funerals to generate a sufficient demand for loans to keep the rate of interest positive, indeed, exorbitant.

[2] We assume that rents are paid in kind out of product. Another system is that rent is paid for part of the land by working on another part without wages. The same principle applies here. The peasants are left just enough labour time to keep themselves alive.

[3] In practice, of course, this is a very vague notion — a man may be less or more alive — but here we are concerned only to illustrate the broad principle and it can be seen more clearly by making the case sharper than it is in nature.

When landlords compete for tenants and tenants for land the level of rents is settled by supply and demand. At any moment a peasant finds himself faced by a certain level of rents in terms of product. If he believes that the addition to product that his family could get from cultivating more land exceeds the rent, he wants to increase his holding. If he finds that he could save more rent by reducing his holding than he would lose in product by having less land to cultivate, he reduces it. (He adjusts the marginal product of land for his family to the rent per acre.) An excess of demand for land drives up rents till no one wants more, or a deficiency of demand causes rents to drop till all the land is taken up. The level of rents (given technical conditions) then depends upon the amount of labour.

An increase in population drives up rents, reduces the size of holdings, reduces average product per head, and reduces the excess per family of product over rent. When income per head is reduced to subsistence level the peasants are no better off than under the landlords' monopoly, and the landlords no worse off because they are competing.

A decline in population would reduce total rents and raise the peasants' income per head. Thus at any population size less than that at which the marginal product of labour is equal to subsistence, total rents are higher under monopoly, but, when the population has reached that size, competitive demand for land establishes the same level of rents as would obtain under monopoly. (This is an example of the principle which we found in our short-period analysis, that in a seller's market monopoly is unnecessary to support prices.) [1]

FINANCE

The peasant in the above economy (fanciful as it sounds) is a capitalist entrepreneur hiring land from a rentier and employing himself as a worker, for he is financing his own production. His income is not a wage, but corresponds to wages

[1] The analogy is not accidental, for the fixed supply of equipment in a short period is similar to the permanently fixed supply of land (this is the origin of the term quasi-rent — gross profits being regarded as a rent due to the scarcity of equipment).

plus profits on capital. This becomes obvious if we suppose that he owns no reserves of food and is obliged to borrow from a bania to keep his family alive from harvest to harvest. When rents are at the maximum the peasants' income per head cannot be any lower, for it is then at the subsistence minimum, but if banias are taking a levy from the peasants, fewer can live at any given level of rents. Population is kept in check, and the level of rents therefore kept down sufficiently to provide a margin for the payment of interest. Over all, product *minus* rent is equal to wages *plus* interest payments (the marginal product of labour is equal to subsistence *plus* interest payments per head).[1] The level of the rate of interest depends upon the amount of funds at the disposal of the banias,[2] for it settles at the point where there are enough peasants in existence to provide a use for all the funds available. Thus an increase in funds leads to a fall in the interest rate, an increase in population at constant income per head and a rise in rents.

When the peasants supply their own finance and are independent of the banias, an element of interest (or rather profit) is concealed in what appears to them as income from work. But when the population is so large that rent absorbs the whole technical surplus, this notional interest in the peasants' income has fallen to a zero rate.

RENT AND WAGES

Now let us consider the case where landlords finance production by employing the peasants at weekly wages paid in kind. The landlord is then an entrepreneur paying rent to himself as a rentier out of his profits.[3]

[1] As we have seen, the marginal products multiplied by amounts of the factors account for the whole product. Finance is not a factor of production in this sense, and has no marginal product of its own, though, in the assumed conditions, it is necessary in order to keep the labour force in existence (see below, p. 307).

[2] Nominal interest is kept in these conditions, at fantastic levels. But this is mainly a device to keep the peasants permanently in debt. The actual payments exacted cannot exceed the margin between subsistence and rent.

[3] The interposition of farmers complicates the argument without altering its essence. Farmers supply most of the management and part of the work and part of the finance. Their income is an amalgam of profits and notional wages.

Under competition, given the population, the level of wages depends upon the amount of funds (in the form of carry-over from harvest to harvest) that the landlords dispose of. We will postulate that no accumulation or decumulation is now going on, so that the total of available funds in real terms remains constant through time, and, to keep the argument simple, we ignore capital goods such as seed corn or implements supplied by landlords. When the marginal product per man on a given estate exceeds the wage per man, it is worth while to employ more labour on that piece of land, but the total number of men available is fixed. When demand for labour exceeds the supply, competition between landlords to get their land cultivated tends to drive up the wage rate. Every rise in wages means a larger outlay of finance, for a given labour force, in the form of payments in advance of the harvest;[1] or when supply of labour exceeds demand, wages fall and a given finance fund offers more employment. Thus the level of real wages settles at the point at which the total available finance (in real terms) is just sufficient to employ the total labour force.[2] (This is merely a repetition in a simpler form of our analysis of capital and wages.)

Given the level of wages, the total surplus is total annual product *minus* the year's wages bill. How is this surplus divided between owners of land and owners of finance? A landlord whose funds are large relatively to the size of his estate cannot profitably use all the labour he is able to employ on his own ground. He is willing to hire land provided that the rent does not exceed the addition to the total product of his labour force due to deploying it on more space. Rent, we will suppose, is paid in arrears so that it does not have to be financed by the tenant. A landlord in the reverse situation is willing to borrow finance, so as to be able to employ more labour on his estate than his own funds permit, provided that wages

---

[1] The same principle applies where there is continuous cropping, but a rise in the wage rate there involves an investment in work-in-progress of roughly half the increase in the wages bill for the period of production, while with an annual harvest the increase in the carry-over must be equal to the increase in the annual wage bill.

[2] The 'wages-fund doctrine' is often considered to be a fallacy, but in this form it seems to be unexceptionable.

plus interest per man employed do not exceed the addition to
product that can be got from his estate.　Thus the play of
supply and demand for land and funds establishes a position
in which the level of rents is equal to the marginal product of
land with the given labour force, while the marginal product of
labour is equal to wages *plus* interest per man employed.　(This
is similar to the position in which banias provide finance.)

The total of interest is equal to total surplus *minus* rent
(notional rent and interest being attributed to land and funds
employed by their owners), and the rate of interest on finance
is the ratio of the total interest payments (in real terms) so
determined to the finance fund (in real terms).

An increase in the finance fund (such as could be made by
landlords saving part of the surplus) would lower the rate of
interest and raise the rate of wages ; but it would not affect
rents, for with a given labour force and given methods of production the marginal product of land is technically determined
and is not affected by the rate of wages.

An increase in population lowers the rate of wages (thus
permitting a given fund of finance to employ more labour)
and increases total product, while reducing average product
per man.　Assuming that the time-pattern of wage payments
over the year is invariable (and neglecting interest over the
period of build up of work-in-progress) [1] so that finance per
man bears a fixed ratio to wages per man-year, the wage rate
falls in proportion to the increase in the number of workers,
and the total wages bill is constant.　Total surplus has therefore
increased.　(This, again, is merely a repetition of our former
argument in a simpler setting.)　The share of this increase
taken by rent depends on technical conditions, for the rise in
the level of rents is governed by the rise in the marginal product
of land due to the increase in population.　If the rise in intensity
of cultivation raises the marginal product of land sufficiently,
rents rise by more than the total surplus, so that interest is
squeezed, and the rate of interest falls. [2]

---

[1] Cf. above, p. 104.

[2] Under the stringent assumptions that permit us to define the marginal
product of labour, it is possible to specify the conditions in which this
occurs.　If the marginal product of labour, when there is an increase in
employment on a given space, falls in the same proportion as employment

In so far as individual landowners are also owners of finance this is a matter of little concern, but when the two types of property belong to distinct groups there is a conflict of interest between them.

As before, when wages are reduced to subsistence level population can increase no further, the total surplus is at the technically possible maximum, and its division between rent and interest is governed by the ratio of the marginal product of labour to that of land.

In this case (as in that where banias provided finance) the population at the maximum is smaller than when peasants financed themselves, for in that case the limit is reached when the marginal product of labour is equal to the subsistence level, while in this case population must be small enough to permit the marginal product of labour to exceed the wage, which is equal to subsistence level, by the amount of interest per man employed.

The reason for this apparent anomaly is that the peasants prefer to receive a zero interest on their property rather than to be dead.

DIFFERENTIAL RENT

So far we have ignored differences in the fertility of different parts of the available space. Where some land is more fertile than others its owner receives a higher income. This is obvious enough in the case of the free peasants. Where monopolistic landlords are holding tenants down to the subsistence minimum they are exacting larger rents for more fertile land. Where rents are settled by supply and demand the peasants bid more for better land; their income per head is more or less equal wherever they work and differences in

---

increases, the total interest is constant, for wages per man have fallen in the same proportion, and therefore interest per man has fallen in the same proportion. Since the wages bill and total interest are constant, total rents rise by the whole increase in the product. (This condition is sometimes expressed by saying that the *elasticity of substitution* between land and labour is equal to unity.) If the marginal product of labour falls in a greater proportion than employment increases (the elasticity of substitution is less than unity), total interest falls, and rents rise by more than the increase in product. Since the capital, *ex hypothesi*, is constant in terms of product, the rate of interest on capital is proportional to the total interest.

yield are reflected in differences in rent. Similarly capitalist
tenants bid more for land that yields a larger surplus. Given
the total population, the extensive margin of cultivation is
established where the marginal product of land is zero — that
is, where it would add nothing to total product to take labour
from better land and deploy it more widely. When population
increases new peasants will take over worse land (provided
that the total product there exceeds what their marginal product
would be if they crowded onto the better land), so that the
margin is extended, while rents on the intra-marginal land
rise. The same principle applies when labour is employed for
wages. When population is of the size at which peasants'
income (where they do not pay interest) would be at the subsistence minimum, the extensive margin is established on land
where the total yield is equal to subsistence for the workers
employed on it. This is the famous phenomenon of No Rent
Land.[1]

In any given position, when some land is yielding zero
rent per acre, the rent of the rest appears as though it were
due to its superior fertility. But it is important to observe
that, with a given population, superior fertility of the whole
area does not mean a higher level of rents. Compare two
economies with the same population and the same technical
conditions, occupying territory of the same area, one of which,
Alaph, is more fertile than the other, Beth. Land in Alaph
has not a higher marginal productivity per acre. Rather the
reverse. With heavier crops the area that given labour can
handle is likely to be smaller. If so, at a given level of rents
per acre, demand for space is less in Alaph than in Beth, and
for all the land to be used under competition, rents must be
lower.[2] (The expression 'marginal productivity' has a rather
misleading sound. The marginal productivity of land is not
high because its product per acre is high, but because land
is scarce relatively to the labour force.)

On the other hand, peasant incomes (with a given population) are higher in Alaph than in Beth, and if population in
each rises to the point where income is reduced to subsistence

---

[1] That is, land which yields no technical surplus.
[2] And may be nil.

level, Alaph has a larger population and is likely to yield a larger total rent. Land in Alaph originally was, in a sense, less scarce than in Beth, and it has now made itself equally scarce by breeding more people.

INTERPRETATION

In all this we have been reading back into a primitive economy the principles that become clear only when capitalism is developed. It cannot be taken literally as an account of any actual historical situation, for each society has its own rules of the game, and the principle of maximising profits by equating marginal product to price and establishing price by free competition is quite alien to a society of landlords and peasants. Even when landlords are capitalist employers their view of life is often quite different from that of industrial entrepreneurs. However, the argument is useful in enabling us to see how these principles would work out in the simplest possible setting.

CONSUMPTION OF THE SURPLUS

We have assumed that no accumulation is going on, under the landlord regime, and that it does not occur to anyone to try to increase output by investing in capital goods or improving methods of production. The landlords consume the whole of their share of the product (which is equal to the whole technical surplus when wages or peasant incomes are at the subsistence minimum). Apart from consumers' investment in palaces and temples, they do so mainly by employing servants, soldiers, priests and artists.

For this reason the results would be disappointing if the workers or peasants rose up and dispossessed the landlords. If cultivable land has been used for parks and hunting-grounds the peasants gain by seizing it : but the greater part of the landlords' wealth would simply evaporate. Even if the peasants chased off all the mouths that the landlords have been feeding, they would be better off only by the food — the services that have contributed to the landlords' comfort are of on value when the landlords disappear.

The situation is different when an industrial sector of the economy is already in existence and the landlords use their share of the surplus to export food and raw materials to towns and to buy luxury products from them or to display themselves at court. When the workers dispossess the landlords this export surplus comes into their control and they can use it to import goods from the towns.

Such a revolution may cause a serious problem for the industrial sector. While the landlords were in existence the peasants were obliged to work hard and eat little. When they are free they may prefer to work less and eat more rather than to maintain the same export surplus and import from the towns, for their habits of consumption are simple and their own traditional crafts provide most of their needs. The improvement in their terms of trade (rise in the price of food and raw materials in terms of manufactures) which follows a reduction in exports causes serious distress in the towns and it may only reduce exports further, for the better the terms of trade the less product need the peasants sell to get what manufactures they need from the towns.

The industrial sector can solve the problem to a certain extent by infecting the peasants with new desires and by breaking them of the habit of handicraft production by offering them cheap manufactures, but this process is limited [1] and the peasants have the whip hand, for they are trading necessaries against dispensable goods.

The basis of industry is the agricultural surplus, and the institution of rent squeezing agricultural wages or peasant incomes to the minimum is a brutal but effective way of providing it and making it available to the industrial sector of the economy.

IMPROVING LANDLORDS

These considerations apply to an economy in which the surplus is wholly devoted to consumption. The situation

---

[1] Cf. the German peasant during the food scarcity in 1945 : 'Now that I have got a carpet for the pigsty I cannot think of anything more that I want to buy'.

develops very differently when landlords take on some of the characteristics of entrepreneurs and devote a part of the technical surplus to experiments and improvements in agricultural production or to setting up manufactures. When they do so, the economy may break out of a state of primitive stagnation, and the process of accumulation and technical progress be set going.

FRONTIERSMEN

When new lands are settled by immigrants from the industrial sector who take possession of the ground that they cultivate, they become free peasants — rentiers, entrepreneurs and workers in one. The agricultural surplus is then exported to industry without the intermediacy of rent. With plenty of space available, average product per family is high, and their own consumption takes a relatively small bite out of it. New settlers lack the traditional crafts of an old peasantry, and have a high demand for imported manufactures (including implements) and (after a period of initial pioneering hardships) develop the habits of a high standard of consumption.

Moreover, their notions were formed in a society dominated by money transactions and they produce primarily for sale rather than for consumption. This solves the problem of feeding the towns, but it has a serious drawback. The settlers are dominated by business morality, and think of capital in terms of purchasing power rather than in kind. They have no scruple, therefore, in extracting value from the soil by mining its fertility, and if they can leave capital in terms of money to their children they think no harm in leaving deserts to posterity in general.

While the process of mining is going on the agricultural surplus is all the greater, the terms of trade are favourable to manufactures, and the development of industry is promoted; thus natural resources are, so to say, transmogrified into industrial capital goods. From a long-run point of view the menace of this procedure to future welfare is obvious enough, but under the capitalist rules of the game it is no one's business to be concerned with it.

CHAPTER 30

FACTOR RATIOS AND TECHNIQUES

WHEN we have to take account of a variety of possible techniques the meaning of the marginal productivity of land and labour is not obvious, and we must spend some time in seeking it out before going any further.

To keep the problem to its bare essence, let us consider land as mere space, and regard all investments made in improving the soil, laying out roads, etc., as part of the capital goods required by the technique of production in use.[1] When the area of land that entrepreneurs (and consumers) would like to use if it were free exceeds the area available to the economy, land commands a price, and (except where the entrepreneur or consumer who wants it happens to be the owner) it is hired by the payment of an annual rent, the general level of rents depending upon the relation of demand to the available supply. We have to consider what governs this demand.

THE JIGSAW PUZZLE

We set out on our quest by examining an economy in conditions of perfect tranquillity, with given technical knowledge, where a uniform rate of profit obtains throughout the system, and the rate of profit has long been constant. (This is not intended to correspond to any actual historical situation; it is merely a device for sorting out our ideas.) To satisfy these conditions, in a given space, the population must have long been constant, and no accumulation can be going on,

---

[1] Much of the investment in land has a very long short-period life compared to machinery, so that unless perfect tranquillity has prevailed for a very long past, the outfit of capital goods in existence at any monent is out of line with prospective profitability (cf. above, p. 181).

298

for, if the ratio of labour to land were changing or investment taking place, it is only in fluke conditions that the rate of profit would remain constant. We assume, therefore, that the whole current output is being consumed, and that the stock of capital goods is continuously being maintained physically intact. This does not entail a zero rate of profit ; profits are being distributed to rentiers who consume them, and rent incomes (as well as wages) are also consumed.

Output is composed of a variety of commodities and (as usual) we assume that they are required in fixed proportions. Each particular commodity has a certain limited range of land-labour ratios at which it can be produced. Whatever the level of rents, the quantity of wheat in the composite unit of consumption goods requires more land per head than the corresponding quantity of nylon stockings. But, for each taken separately, considerable variation is possible, and at a higher level of rents relatively to wages each squeezes itself into less space.

Each entrepreneur, in the tranquil economy, is faced by a set of prices for all kinds of capital goods, a level of rents for land, a rate of wages and a notional interest rate equal to the ruling rate of profit. He is conceived to organise production so as to minimise the cost of a given flow of output in the ruling conditions. If continuous variations are possible, then when cost is at a minimum, a small increase or decrease in the ratio of land to labour currently employed leaves it unchanged. Even a small difference in this ratio involves a different technique of production, with its appropriate capital goods, and the blue prints for two techniques yielding an equal rate of profit may be utterly different, even when the difference in the ratio of land to labour is very small. Moreover, some ratios may be markedly more convenient than others when it comes to designing capital goods to fit them, so that there are likely to be discontinuities in the possible ratios of land to labour for each type of output. Given the conditions for each commodity separately, the composition of output dictates the pattern of pairs of techniques for producing the whole annual flow of commodities.

On top of this is the now familiar fact that at certain wage levels, at which two degrees of mechanisation are equally profitable, there are two ratios of capital to output, in a given situation, which yield the same rate of profit — an Alpha technique with a lower rate of output per unit of capital than obtains with Beta technique, but with correspondingly more quasi-rent per unit of output, or, alternatively, a Gamma technique of which the converse is true.

Thus there may be as many as four techniques which yield the same rate of profit — a Beta-R technique involving a higher cost of rent and a lower cost of wages per unit of output, a Beta-W technique involving a higher cost of wages and lower cost of rent, and a similar pair of either Alpha or Gamma techniques.

When tranquillity prevails with, say, the Beta-Alpha rate of profit ruling, we may divide all eligible techniques, first into Beta and Alpha classes ; those in the Beta class being distinguished by the characteristic that if the rate of profit were a little lower than it is, they would not be eligible, while those in the Alpha class would not be eligible at a somewhat higher rate of profit. Then we divide all eligible techniques into R and W classes ; those in the R class require a ratio of land to labour higher than the over-all ratio for the economy as a whole, and those in the W class require a higher ratio of labour to land. We now have four classes — Alpha-R and Alpha-W and Beta-R and Beta-W. All these techniques compete with each other when the cost (including profit on capital invested) of a given output is the same with each.

If we compare a Beta-R technique with an Alpha-W technique producing the same rate of output at the same cost per unit of output, land per unit of output is greater with the Beta-R technique, and labour and capital per unit of output are both less. Comparing Beta-R with Alpha-R, capital per unit of output is less with the Beta-R technique ; and either labour or land per unit of output, or both must be greater. Comparing Beta-R with Beta-W, land per unit of output is greater and labour per unit of output less with the Beta-R technique ; capital per unit of output may be either greater or less.

To simplify the picture, let us suppose that our tranquil

economy sank into static conditions (with zero accumulation)
after completing the installation of capital goods appropriate
to the Beta degree of mechanisation and before beginning on
the Alpha degree of mechanisation.   A small rise in the rate
of profit would cause a switch to Gamma techniques, or a
small fall a switch to Alpha, but at the ruling rate of profit
Beta alone holds the field.   There are then only two classes
of techniques to choose from, Beta-R employing more land
per unit of capital and Beta-W employing more labour per
unit of capital.   Whether the differences in these ratios are
large or small depends upon the make-up of the composite
commodity and the technical possibilities embodied in the
engineering characteristics of the capital goods required for
each technique, but whether large or small, the excess of the
rent bill for a given output per annum in the one case is equal
to the excess of the wages bill in the other (allowing appropriately for interest over a year if rents are paid at longer
intervals than wages) *plus* or *minus* profit at the ruling rate on
any difference in capital per unit of output that there may be.

Now, in the economy as a whole, the ratio of land to
labour is given, and (with full employment) all the demands
of all the entrepreneurs for land and labour must add up to
the available supplies.   If too many entrepreneurs had been
inclined to go in for Beta-R techniques there would have been
a small rise in the level of rents, so that others would have
been induced to go in for Beta-W.   The whole of the available
land and labour is employed in the postulated tranquil static
situation, the relative levels of rents and wages having settled
in such a way as to produce a fit between the over-all land-
labour ratio and the requirements of all the entrepreneurs.
There is a grand jigsaw puzzle of land and labour and techniques with all the pieces in place at the given rate of profit.[1]

MARGINAL RETURNS

For each individual entrepreneur when he has selected the
technique which maximises his rate of profit, the marginal

[1] Cf. Champernowne, 'The Production Function and the Theory of
Capital', *Review of Economic Studies*, vol. xxi (2), No. 55 (1953–4).

return on land, in terms of the additional sales value of output that he could obtain by employing another acre of land with a given value of capital and the appropriate employment of labour, is equal to the rent of land per acre (for if it had been greater, he would have acquired more land, and if it had been less, vacated some).　Similarly, the marginal return on labour employed for each entrepreneur is equated to the wage.　The marginal return on capital to the individual entrepreneur is the same thing as the rate of profit, for if he had more capital he would have more profit, in the proportion of the general ruling rate of profit.　(We are assuming no economies or diseconomies of scale to the individual business, and we are assuming that when one market is failing to yield the ruling rate of profit, the entrepreneur can switch production to another.)

MARGINAL PRODUCTS

This tells us nothing about the marginal products of land and labour to the economy as a whole.　At different over-all ratios of land and labour all the techniques and prices would be different and so would the rates of wages and levels of rent. Nor does it tell us anything about the marginal product of capital goods to the economy as a whole, for if there were, in some sense, less or more capital goods, with the same land and labour, they would be of quite different physical specifications, and again, prices and the level of rents and wages would be different.

We have already compared economies with the same body of technical knowledge and different ratios of labour to capital (in various senses).[1]　There is not much that can usefully be said about the comparison of economies with different ratios of land to labour.　For if the economies co-exist in time, they are occupying areas of land that differ not only in extent but also in kind (different facilities for different types of crops, a different convenience in the situation of rivers, etc.).　The composition of output is different, and the tastes and habits and the very character of the populations are different, for they have been moulded by a different environment and a

[1] Chapter 12.

different history. If the same area of land is compared at
different points of time with different populations, again tastes
and habits and characters are different, and even if these are
near-enough unchanged to make the comparison reasonable,
technical knowledge must have altered between the two dates,
if only in the process of adapting a given corpus of technology
to the circumstances of a different ratio of land to labour. Any
actual comparison, then, is so clouded by index-number ambiguities as to be excessively vague, and the assumptions required
to rule out ambiguities would deprive the comparisons of any
interest even as an exercise in pure analysis.

However, we can turn the flank of the problem in the
following manner. In the given tranquil and static situation,
with the Beta degree of mechanisation prevailing, compare the
products of two equal quantities of labour, each producing
a representative sample of total output, one working Beta-R
techniques (with more land per head) and the other Beta-W
techniques (with less land per head).[1] Two equal quantities
of labour are then operating on two different areas of land.
The value of output, where more land is in use with the same
amount of labour, is larger. Measuring the extra output in
terms of units of the composite commodity and the extra land
in acres, we may call the ratio between them the *Beta marginal
product of land* at the given over-all land-labour ratio. It
represents the additional product which the given labour force
could produce at the Beta degree of mechanisation (with the
appropriate capital goods) if one more acre were available.
The value of the additional product (at normal prices) of a
given number of men is equal to the excess of rents plus
profits in the Beta-R output compared to the Beta-W output
(for the wages bills for the two are equal) and this is equal to
the value of the Beta marginal product of land multiplied by
the additional area of land required by the Beta-R techniques.

Similarly, we may calculate the Beta marginal product of
labour, as a quantity of product per additional man, by taking
equal areas of land, one, where Beta-W techniques are in use,

---

[1] Where there are a variety of techniques in each category (using super-
average proportions of one factor) the sample must be chosen so as to
represent them in due proportion.

being operated by more labour than the other. The extra product is equal to the excess of wages *plus* profits in the Beta-W output, the rent bills for the two samples being equal.

As in the simple case that we assumed in the last chapter, the total quantity of output per annum, in the static Beta economy, is equal to the marginal product of land multiplied by the area of land in use *plus* the marginal product of labour multiplied by the number of men employed. This can be seen in the same manner as before : Imagine that a small number of men disappear, the jigsaw puzzle being rearranged accordingly. In the new static position that prevails after the reorganisation it will be found that a certain number of men have been switched from Beta-W to Beta-R techniques, making use of the land vacated by those that have disappeared. The loss of output, therefore, is the Beta marginal product of labour multiplied by the number of men who have been lost. Then remove a small quantity of land ; when static conditions have been restored the loss of output is the Beta marginal product of land multiplied by the area lost.[1] Assuming that there are no economies or diseconomies of scale to the system as a whole (output per head depends only on the factor ratio and not on the total of employment),[2] we can imagine the whole output being eroded piecemeal in this manner, so that the whole output can be accounted for as the sum of marginal products of each factor multiplied by the amount of the factor in use.

We now repeat the foregoing analysis for an economy in a tranquil static state with the Alpha degree of mechanisation, and, again, for an economy with the Gamma degree of mechanisation and so on. Thus, over the relevant part of the spectrum of techniques, we can find the marginal products of land and labour, at the existing ratio between them, for each

---

[1] Each change must be small, for if the land-labour ratio were altered by more than can be accommodated by switching the remaining factors between R and W techniques, the wage rate and level of rents would alter, and a fresh situation with different techniques would emerge.

[2] Where there are economies or diseconomies it is still true that the marginal products multiplied by the quantities of factors account for the whole product in any one position, but the marginal products themselves would vary with the scale of total output.

degree of mechanisation. Then we can specify what may be called the *potential marginal products* of land, and of labour, at the given ratio, as a list of these marginal products.

At very low levels of mechanisation the marginal product of land may be zero ; capital goods are then the bottle-neck, and it would be of no use to have more land with given labour unless there were more capital goods to go with it (say, ploughs and seed). Also at very high degrees of mechanisation the marginal product of land may be zero. The capital goods in use have then raised output per acre beyond what a given labour force can handle, and with a given population some land would be redundant.

THE RATIO OF LABOUR TO LAND

There is a corresponding schedule of potential marginal products at each over-all ratio of land to labour in the economy.

A small increase in the labour force (at, say, the Beta degree of mechanisation) can be accommodated by substituting Beta-W for Beta-R techniques without any change in relative rents and wages, just as a small amount of accumulation can be accommodated by substituting Alpha for Beta equipment without any change in the rate of profit. But as soon as all labour is employed in Beta-W farms and factories a further increase in employment entails a change in rents, wages and profits. A new set of choices of quite different sets of techniques then presents itself, and the lists of potential marginal products at different degrees of mechanisation are completely redrawn.

In general, we should expect the potential marginal product of labour to be lower and of land higher at high labour-land ratios, but this is by no means an invariable rule. Alpha techniques, for instance, may be much more favourable than Gamma techniques to a high land-labour ratio, so that the lists of potential marginal products may cross and recross each other as the ratio of land to labour alters. But in any given state of knowledge there is a limit to the extent to which more labour can be used to dispense with land in producing a given output, whatever form capital goods may take. At very high

ratios of labour to land the marginal product of labour is zero
at all levels of mechanisation. Land is then the bottle-neck
and (with the given technical knowledge) there is no way of
increasing output by increasing labour per acre.

THE SCHEME OF ANALYSIS

We set out on the quest for marginal products by examining
the jigsaw puzzle of techniques in a tranquil static state, and
we found that there was a separate picture for each degree of
mechanisation and for each over-all ratio of land to labour,
when total output consists of commodities. There is a corresponding three-dimensional jigsaw puzzle for each ratio of
investment to consumption.

And the whole complex alters through time as technical
knowledge changes.

In principle, we could repeat the whole of our formal
analysis in terms of this scheme. Thus, as an economy moves
through time with capital accumulation and technical progress
going on and the ratio of land to labour altering, it is moving
from, say, Beta-W_1R_1 towards Alpha-plus-R_2 or Gamma-
plus-W_2, with concomitant changes in rents, wages and the
rate of profit, and in the rate of accumulation. To set this out
would clearly be a most formidable task, and when it was
done we should have to superimpose upon it all the short-
period complications (greater than ever now that we have to
bring into the picture long-lived investments sunk in the
earth) and then smudge it over with the uncertainties of an
untranquil world.

We shall not embark upon this undertaking, but rather
pick out one or two problems to illustrate the manner in which
the analysis might be developed.

A DIGRESSION

ACCORDING to this way of looking at things there is nothing that can be called the 'marginal product of capital'. At each ratio of land to labour in the economy as a whole the difference between the appropriate Beta-R and Beta-W techniques (whatever difference in the outfit of capital goods it entails) is simply the manner in which the Beta marginal productivities of land and labour are brought into effect.[1]

THE MARGINAL PRODUCT OF INVESTMENT

Although we cannot specify a marginal product of 'capital' independently of the products of land and labour we can specify what may be called the *marginal product of investment*. Let us suppose that the whole economy (with given land and labour) has been raised from the Beta to the Alpha degree of mechanisation, and that tranquillity has been re-established in a new, Alpha, static position. Total product is now greater. This additional product may be called the Beta-Alpha marginal product of investment in the given state of knowledge. We cannot call this the marginal product of 'capital' for we cannot say how the quantity of capital, in any sense, has altered merely from the technical data. Now the specifications of all capital goods are different, the level of wages and rents have altered, consequently the costs of capital goods of a given specification at a given notional interest rate have altered, and the rate of profit is lower (for with given knowledge a higher degree of mechanisation only becomes eligible from the point of view of individual entrepreneurs at a lower rate of profit) so that the appropriate notional rate of interest has also

[1] Cf. A. Lerner, 'On the Marginal Product of Capital and the Marginal Efficiency of Investment,' *Journal of Political Economy*, vol. lxi, No. 1 (February 1953).

changed.[1] There is no way of saying how much 'capital' the investment represents, though if we knew the whole history, including, in particular, the levels of wages that have prevailed, we could say how much accumulation had been necessary to make it, and how much finance has been invested.

A change in technical knowledge alters the marginal product of investment at various degrees of mechanisation, at the same time as it redraws the lists of potential marginal products of the factors of production.

When available supplies of factors increase (say there is an increase in population) some investment is generally required to make it possible for them to produce. But if the necessary equipment is partly or wholly supplied by a de-mechanisation of technique or a shortening of the period of production [2] the meaning of the marginal product of investment becomes highly sophisticated.

We can eliminate this complication in a case (such as we discussed in Chapter 29) where for a given amount of land there is only one conceivable outfit of capital goods — so and so much seed and so many ploughs — and the time pattern of production is dictated by the seasons. In such a case the factor ratio can change without any change in the who's who of capital goods in existence. One more man-year of work can be applied to the given stock of physical resources. There is then a single marginal product of labour at each factor ratio instead of a list of potential products. Even this involves an investment of a man-year of work made up of man-hours spread out in a certain way from seed-time to harvest. The marginal product of this investment is identically the same thing as the marginal product of labour.

THE COST OF INVESTMENT

The cost of an investment to an entrepreneur is the cost of the finance required to make it. Can we attach any

---

[1] As we have seen, there is a certain Beta-Alpha range over which the rate of profit remains constant as Alpha technique is progressively substituted for Beta, and over this range the marginal product of investment is equal to the rate of profit.

[2] This is negative waiting, see below, p. 309.

meaning to the cost of investment to the economy ? During the period that an investment was made in raising an economy from a static Beta position to an Alpha position (assuming full employment of a given labour force throughout the whole story) the level of consumption must have been lower than in the initial static Beta position, more labour and land being employed for a time in the investment sector, and less in the consumption sector. This may have come about either by a lower real-wage rate or by saving by rentiers and landowners (or by a mixture of the two). After the transition, in the Alpha static position, the level of consumption is higher, and either wages or rentier incomes, or both, are higher than in the Beta static position. In a certain sense the consumption forgone during the period of transition may be regarded as the cost to the economy of making it, but this concept has very little meaning, since in human terms the cost to workers of having to accept lower real wages is a very different matter from the cost to rentiers of voluntarily refraining from expenditure on consumption, and the division of the cost between them does not depend upon the productivity of the investment but upon the thriftiness of the rentiers.

Where, in the absence of the investment, there would have been unemployment, the real cost to the workers is heavily negative — they are better off probably by more wages and certainly by less misery — while the real cost to the rentiers (if cost is the right word) consists in foregoing some potential consumption out of increased incomes and acquiring some wealth.

In certain cases we can detect something which may be called the *marginal product of waiting*. Suppose that the difference between Beta and Alpha technique consists only in having an annual instead of a biannual harvest, the employment of labour over a year being exactly the same in each case. (The annual harvest must be more than twice the biannual harvest, if the change is ever worth making.) The excess of annual output with a single harvest over that with a double harvest is the marginal product of waiting for six months.[1]

---

[1] The same line of argument applies to waiting for trees to grow or wine to mature. See Wicksell, *Lectures*, vol. i, p. 172.

The cost of waiting to an individual entrepreneur depends upon the level of wages and the notional interest rate. It is the same thing as the addition to the value of work-in-progress required for the Alpha compared to the Beta technique, and, in general, the cost of waiting is bound up with the cost of investment and can be separated from it only in very special cases. To workers there is no cost of waiting if wages remain constant during the process of transition, as would be the case if rentier consumption were reduced appropriately, but if rentiers consume at their usual rate over the year, real wages must be lower until the transition has been completed. (With constant money wages, prices are raised during the period when a scarcity of commodities is created by the failure of one biannual harvest to come to market at the usual time.)

For an independent peasant who owns the land he works the cost of waiting is the postponement of one harvest. If he owns no stocks and commands no credit, while his whole product is only enough to keep him alive from biannual harvest to harvest, he cannot afford this cost, however great its marginal product might be.

FACTORS OF PRODUCTION

Looking at the matter in a philosophical light, the reason why there is no meaning to be attached to the marginal product of 'capital' is that, from a long-run point of view, labour and natural resources are the factors of production in the economy as a whole, while capital goods and the time pattern of production are the means by which the factors are deployed. From a short-run point of view the stock of capital goods in existence may be regarded as a who's who of factors of production, and land can be included in the who's who, for, from a short-run point of view, all are equally fixed in amount and the distinction between land and capital goods has no relevance. But there is no way of specifying the marginal product of a heterogeneous mass of objects (though each item has a marginal return to the entrepreneur employing it). From a short-period point of view it is more convenient to treat labour as the only factor of production, and to regard the stock of concrete capital goods as one element in the technical conditions that determine the productivity of a given quantity of labour.[1]

The reason why there is a meaning to the marginal product of investment is that by deploying the factors of production in a particular way for a certain time (embodying them in different capital goods or with a different time pattern from that formerly in use) their productivity in the future can be permanently raised. This productivity of investment is not something that can be added on to the products of the factors of production. It consists precisely in the additional productivity with which the factors are endowed by it.

In the economy of the robins, production can increase as a result of additional work without any prior investment. Every time the robin catches a grub he produces and consumes in a single act. His wife is accustomed to invest labour in consumers' capital goods — a nest — but she needs no finance, for she produces her own means of subsistence (catching grubs between fetching twigs) during the period of construction. The robins can deploy their labour on their territory without the intermediacy of capital. For humans, whose production and consumption are spread over time, capital (no matter who owns it) is a necessary condition for labour and natural resources to be productive. But it is not a factor of production independent of them.

THE RATE OF PROFIT

The reason why there is a rate of profit on capital is that, under the prevailing rules of the game, anyone who can command finance can employ factors of production in such a way as to produce a selling value of product that exceeds the wages and rent bill involved in employing them. The level of rents and wages and the rate of profit are not determined by the marginal products of land, labour and investment. All three are determined together, in a complicated way, by the spectrum of technical possibilities, the supplies of land and labour available to the economy as a whole and the amount

[1] See Keynes, *General Theory*, p. 214.

of accumulation that has already taken place, and by the level of effective demand for commodities and the rate of investment.

In conditions of tranquillity the marginal return on investment to an individual, expressed as a ratio of future value of output to present finance, is equal to the rate of profit, for no entrepreneur (in tranquil conditions) maintains capital in one form if it could earn more profit by being invested in another, but, in a given state of knowledge with given supplies of factors, investment itself alters the relative values of commodities, capital goods and factors of production, so that the return to an individual in terms of value has no meaning for the economy as a whole.[1]

The relation of the rate of profit to the marginal product of investment is seen in its simplest form in the imagined state of bliss, where the highest technique known is already in operation throughout the economy and population is constant. The marginal product of investment is then zero. If there is no consumption out of profit (and no saving out of wages or rents) the rate of profit also is zero, and the wages and rent bill absorbs the whole annual output.

But if there is consumption out of profits (and no saving out of rent or wages) the rate of profit remains positive, for the prices of commodities (in relation to money wages and rents) are such that their total selling value exceeds their total costs by the amount of expenditure out of profits.[2] The total of real wages then falls short of total output by the amount of consumption of rentiers, that is, of purchases of commodities out of profit and rent incomes.

---

[1] Professor Champernowne has devised a unit for reckoning investment in terms of 'capital' (*loc. cit.*), but the definition hinges upon highly special assumptions similar to those that we made use of in Chapter 14.

[2] Cf. above, p. 255.

CHAPTER 31

LAND AND ACCUMULATION

WHEN capital is the dominant form of property and land has long been marketable it becomes more or less [1] completely merged in the general mass of rentier property. Entrepreneurs require the use of land in order to be able to employ labour to produce commodities and capital goods ; its owners obtain a share in the surplus of product over wages by hiring it to them in much the same way as any owner of wealth can obtain a share by lending finance to an entrepreneur who wants to operate more capital than he possesses himself. From the point of view of an individual owner of property, rent is merely one form of rentier income and from the point of view of an individual entrepreneur land is merely one kind of productive equipment, but for an economy developing in a given space the limited supply of land involves peculiarities which distinguish it from other forms of productive equipment.

As usual, the distinction is not clear cut. Many kinds of capital goods are inextricably involved in the soil itself (its fertility is partly the result of draining, manuring, etc.) and many kinds of equipment are so much dependent upon the space that they occupy (say, shipyards or the permanent way of a railway) that they cannot be much changed, and their supply is almost as completely limited as the sites on which they stand. Moreover, some capital goods have a long life, and the stock of them inherited from the past cannot be distinguished in any relevant way from the supply of natural resources. However, pursuing our policy of taking a high hand with border-line cases, we will continue to envisage, on

[1] The owner of an agricultural estate rented to small farmers often performs some of the functions of an entrepreneur. See J. R. Hicks, *Social Framework*, p. 93.

the one side, capital goods which have a limited life and are reproducible, and, on the other side, land which is of given area and permanently retains its identity. We shall avoid the complications associated with differential rent by assuming all land alike for all purposes.[1] (This is a simplification made for the sake of exposition and is not in any way essential to the argument.) We shall continue to rely on the assumption that the composition of the output of commodities remains rigid to defend us from the index-number fiend.[2]

ACCUMULATION AND TECHNICAL PROGRESS

We have found it convenient for purposes of analysis to give the spectrum of technical possibilities in existence at any phase of development a more precise character than it really has. In reality, when Beta techniques are in use the possible Alpha and Gamma techniques are not fully blue-printed and exist only as rather hazy hypotheses in the minds of entrepreneurs. A three-dimensional spectrum (in terms of degrees of mechanisation and land-labour ratios) can exist only in a very nebulous and scrappy state. And the mere process of adapting the stock of capital goods, in any sector of the economy, to a change in the factor ratio that has become appropriate there, involves acquiring experience (as well as losing old skills no longer needed) so that the distinction between changing the factor ratio and changing the corpus of technology is very hard to draw. Nevertheless it provides a useful framework for setting out the argument.

The relative marginal products of given quantities of land and labour may alter when technique moves within one spectrum (say from Beta to Alpha), and a different pair of potential marginal products becomes actual, just as much as

---

[1] Except for the point discussed below, p. 324.

[2] This is lacking in plausibility when total output increases with a given population, because the ratio of food to manufactures tends to fall as total consumption rises. The composition of output also varies with the distribution of consuming power between workers and rentiers. This necessarily reacts upon the demand for land, which is more important in food production than in any other line. We shall glance briefly at the complications which this entails in Chapter 34.

when technical knowledge is changing and the lists of potential marginal products are being redrawn.

Our former definition of neutral technical progress was that output per man-hour was raised by it (in each sector of the economy considered separately) in the same proportion at all degrees of mechanisation over the relevant range. The rate of profit then remained constant provided that real wages rose in the same proportion as output per head and accumulation was just sufficient to keep the real-capital ratio constant. The value of capital per unit of output was then constant. We must now elaborate the definition of neutrality. Neutral progress raises output per head in the same proportion at the relevant factor ratios over the relevant range of degrees of mechanisation — output per head is greater at Beta-plus-W than at Beta-W, at Beta-plus-R than at Beta-R, at Alpha-plus-W than at Alpha-W, etc., etc., all in the same proportion, so that the ratios of marginal products of land and labour remain unchanged (for the given over-all factor ratio) as technical progress goes on. When, furthermore, the ratio of the potential marginal product of land to the potential marginal product of labour is the same all along the relevant range of the spectrum of degrees of mechanisation (and remains so as technical progress goes on), we have a system which is neutral as between land and labour (at the given over-all factor ratio) whichever way we cut a slice through the three-dimensional jigsaw puzzle. This, obviously, is not a situation that is likely to exist, but it provides a convenient conceptual framework for discussion of the effect of accumulation with given supplies of land and labour in the economy.

NEUTRAL ACCUMULATION

When accumulation is going on in such a way as to keep the rate of profit constant (the system is moving from Beta to Beta-plus techniques) then, as we know, if the technical conditions are neutral from the point of view of capital, the value of capital per unit of output remains constant, and the proportionate share of profit in total income is constant. The share of wages and rents taken together is constant.

How does the share of each behave? In a tranquil static position each entrepreneur is in a situation where he could not increase the profit on a given value of capital invested by switching from an R to a W technique, using more labour so as to save rent, or by switching from a W to an R technique, using more land so as to save wages costs. In each line of production, therefore, the ratio of the marginal product of land (so much of the particular commodity per additional acre, when employment of labour is constant) to the marginal product of labour (expressed in terms of the same commodity) is equal to the ratio of the annual cost per acre and per man (allowing appropriately for interest when the intervals of payment are different), that is, to the ratio of rents to wages. Since this is true for each commodity and each type of capital good, and the composition of output is assumed constant, it is true of the whole output. The ratio of rents to wages is equal to the ratio of the marginal products of land and labour.[1]

When we assume neutrality throughout the jigsaw puzzle, so that the ratio of the marginal products is always the same, the ratio of the prices must be the same (when the jigsaw is all fitted together in tranquil conditions). Therefore as the economy moves from Beta to Beta-plus techniques with a constant rate of profit, the wage per man and rent per acre (in terms of commodities) rise equally, each rising in the same ratio as total output. The shares of land and labour in total output each remain constant, and the conditions of a golden age are satisfied.[2]

Looking at the matter from the point of view of the overall demand for land, the scarcity of land is being relieved by

---

[1] There is, of course, infinite complexity in the jigsaw puzzle when we admit differences in the suitability of different parts of the area available for different products.

[2] Suppose that over all (with the mixture of techniques in use) the value of capital (in terms of commodities) is equal to two years' output, and the rate of profit 20 per cent, then profit accounts for 0·4 of a unit of value of output, and rent and wages together for 0·6. Then if the ratio of the marginal products is 5 : 1, the wages bill accounts for 0·5 of the value of a unit of output and the rent bill for 0·1. Of a total net income of 100, profits receive 40, wages 50 and rents 10. With neutral accumulation, these shares remain constant as total income grows.

the rise in output per acre that the improved techniques make possible, but at the same time total output is expanding proportionally, so that the demand for land in terms of labour time remains constant, and the demand in terms of commodities rises with the real wage rate.

For a golden age to be realised, accumulation must be going on at a constant proportionate rate, and the ratio of consumption to income for each category of incomes must be constant. So long as the share of rent in total output remains constant (as it does in the assumed conditions of neutrality) and landowners maintain a constant ratio of expenditure to rents received, the existence of scarce land does not require any modification in the analysis of golden ages which we have already set out.

PRICES IN A GOLDEN AGE

In one respect the introduction of two forms of property yielding income (land and rentier capital) does complicate the analysis. The complication arises from the different rates of change of property and wage incomes in terms of money.

In a golden age when prices are constant, money-wage rates, as we have seen, rise in proportion to output per head. If money rents, in the first instance, are unchanged, when wages have risen, then all the entrepreneurs operating R techniques, are enjoying a higher rate of profit than those operating W techniques. The demand for land therefore rises (some entrepreneurs are trying to go over to techniques which economise labour per unit of output by using more land per man). Consequently money rents rise. The pressure of demand for land ceases to operate when money rents have risen in the same proportion as wages.

Since it is customary to hire land on long leases (for the entrepreneur must have security of tenure in order to build up physical capital and goodwill on a particular site) this process works very sluggishly, and when money-wage rates are in process of changing, the level of money rents is chronically out of alignment with the demand for land.

When money-wage rates and money rents remain constant,

prices (to satisfy the postulated conditions of a golden age)
fall in proportion to the rise in output, and the equal proportional rise in wages and rents in terms of commodities
comes about automatically. As the marginal products (*ex
hypothesi*) stand in the same relation to each other as before,
entrepreneurs have no reason to want to change the ratios in
which they are employing land and labour.

But when prices have fallen the real value of interest charges
on old loans has risen, while the prices of new capital goods
in terms of commodities are constant (for, technical progress
being neutral, the money cost per physical unit is falling in
the same ratio as the prices of commodities).

There is no behaviour of prices that maintains an automatic equilibrium all round. When money wages and rents
are constant and prices have fallen in proportion to the rise
in output that has occurred over the recent past, equilibrium
is maintained as between land and labour. But then interest
payments on old loans have risen in terms of commodities.
Interest receivers are getting a larger share of product than
their golden-age proportion and while the rate of profit on
investment is *ex hypothesi* constant, the return on old capital
goods has fallen (the real burden of debt on entrepreneurs
has risen). On the other hand, if prices are constant, the
ratio of interest payments to profits is unchanged and equilibrium in that respect is automatic, but as money rents have
not yet had time to be adjusted, landowners are getting too
small a share of the product to correspond to their golden-age
proportion and profits are swollen accordingly (the real burden
of rents on entrepreneurs has fallen). Thus, either way, a
perfectly perfect golden age is unattainable. (The asymmetry
arises because land retains its physical identity when its hire
price alters, whereas a quantity of finance given in terms of
money changes its purchasing power over physical capital
goods when prices alter.)

However, we are not here concerned with the torrents of
short-period fluctuations, but with the glacial progress of
accumulation over the long run, and we shall leave this phenomenon out of the story, assuming that the pace of adjustment
of rent by renegotiation of leases and of interest charges by

amortisation of debt is sufficiently rapid, relatively to the rate at which total output is expanding, to make the problem of trivial importance.

ACCUMULATION CAPITAL-BIASED, LAND-NEUTRAL

Let us now return to the analysis of accumulation with a three-dimensional jigsaw puzzle which is neutral every way as between land and labour.

If accumulation is going on in such a way as to keep the rate of profit constant, but technical progress is biased in respect to capital, the system is in a quasi-golden age. When the bias is capital-using the ratio of capital to output is rising (Beta-plus technique requires a larger real-capital ratio than Beta technique), and the share of profits in total income is rising. The share of wages and rents taken together is falling, and as the technical conditions are neutral as between land and labour, the share of each falls in the same proportion. Rent per acre and wages per man, in terms of commodities, rise in a smaller proportion than total output.

Conversely with a capital-saving bias in technical progress.

When accumulation is going on sufficiently rapidly to cause the rate of profit to fall, the degree of mechanisation is rising (the system is moving from Beta to Alpha-plus techniques). We have postulated that the ratio of marginal products of land and labour is the same at all relevant degrees of mechanisation. There is therefore no pressure to switch in the direction Beta-R to Alpha-plus-W or vice versa and wages and rents rise in the same ratio. We cannot now say anything in general about relative shares, for capital (in terms of value) per unit of output has risen while the rate of profit per unit of capital has fallen.

The converse, in every respect, applies when accumulation is falling behind the rate of technical progress,[1] the rate of profit rising and the system moving from Beta to Gamma-plus techniques.

---

[1] Allowing for its capital bias. A capital-using bias in technique requires a higher rate of accumulation to keep the rate of profit constant.

ACCUMULATION LAND-BIASED

When the jigsaw puzzle is not neutral the ratio of the marginal products may alter when the system moves from Beta techniques to Beta-plus, Alpha, Gamma, Alpha-plus or Gamma-plus techniques. For example, let us suppose that the rate of profit has recently fallen from the Gamma-Beta to the Beta-Alpha level. This means that wages and rents taken together have risen, so that Gamma-R and Gamma-W techniques are now less profitable than the Alpha and Beta techniques. Assuming for simplicity that the installation of Beta capital goods had been completed before the date that we are considering, new investment is now going into replacing old Beta by new Alpha capital goods. The Alpha marginal products of land and labour are different in relation to each other from the Beta marginal products. Let us suppose that the new ratio is more favourable to land than the old.[1] (We must allow in the calculation for any change that is taking place in the ratio of commodities to capital goods in total output as the transition from the Beta to the Alpha degree of mechanisation is being carried out.)[2] Then if, in the first instance, rents and wages remain in the same relation to each other (say both are constant in terms of money while prices have fallen) there is a strong competitive advantage in using techniques with a high ratio of land to labour, for now to produce a given output (with capital goods different from those hitherto in use) on one more acre of land means saving the wages bill of more men than before, while the level of rents is still that which was established when an acre saved fewer men. The demand for land has therefore risen, and rents are pushed up, while the jigsaw is in process of being reshuffled.[3]

[1] Suppose that the Beta ratio was 5 : 1 and the Alpha ratio 6 : 1. This means that a change from Beta-W to Beta-R technique meant saving the wage bill for five men by using an extra acre of land. Choosing Alpha-R instead of Alpha-W means saving the wage bill of six men while incurring an additional rent bill for one acre.

[2] See Chapter 14.

[3] To work out all the details of the transition would require an outfit of special assumptions on the lines of those used in Chapter 14, but considerably more elaborate.

Or, to take another example, suppose that, when Beta-plus techniques are first developed and are being diffused by competition, Beta-plus-W outfits of capital goods, employing labour in a higher ratio to land than exists in the economy as a whole, are found to be more profitable than any others. When new plants have been set up (or new methods introduced in agriculture) replacing a mixture of Beta-R and Beta-W capital goods, land has been released in a greater proportion than labour. To realise the expansion of total output that the new inventions have made possible, rents must fall relatively to wages,[1] and a sufficient element of Beta-plus-R techniques must be developed, to ensure full employment of land and labour.

In this way, as accumulation proceeds with a given labour force, the scarcity of land grows greater or less, according to the technical relations in the jigsaw puzzle, and the level of rents rises by or more or less than in proportion to total output.

With a sufficiently strong land-saving bias in the technical conditions the level of rents (in terms of commodities) may actually fall as accumulation proceeds. But it seems natural to suppose that, in general, output per acre is considerably more rigid than output per man — a man cannot produce much more stuff without more room to work in or cannot raise much more crops without more land to cultivate. If so, an increase in output must entail an increase in demand for land, and technical progress and capital accumulation have an inherently land-using bias.[2] (The meaning of neutral accumulation is that labour per acre remains constant when output per man rises.) To postulate an inherently land-using bias in accumulation is to restate the law of diminishing returns from land in a sophisticated form.

INTERPRETATION

Our three-dimensional jigsaw puzzle is too delicate a structure to be of much use for application to actual problems.

[1] They may have risen absolutely, for, over all, output per man-acre has risen, and the rate of profit is constant

[2] Also a growth in income increases demand for land as consumer's capital.

It would soon warp and crack when removed from the air-conditioned chamber constructed by our drastic simplifying assumptions. But the distinction between a land-saving and a land-using bias in accumulation is of great importance, especially in connection with agriculture, and we can apply our analysis to it in a rough and broad way.

Let us consider a case of very marked bias. Accumulation is running into increasing the stock of capital goods (say tractors) which raise output per man at a low labour-land ratio, while leaving output per acre more or less unchanged (machines can displace labour, but cannot raise the yield of a given area). With the new techniques (which may be Beta-plus, Alpha or Alpha-plus) the marginal product of labour, at the old labour-land ratio, has been sharply reduced compared to what it was in the former situation (with Beta techniques in use) while the marginal product of land is unchanged. A fall in wages relatively to rents may check the spread of the new techniques, or cause a less labour-saving technique to be introduced. But the marginal product of labour (at the old ratio) may well have become zero or even negative (too many men would clutter up space) and the old land-labour ratio, in this sector of the economy, would not remain what it was however low wages fell. Some men must be displaced.

Their fate depends upon what is happening in the rest of the economy. If the new techniques in agriculture are part of the response of the whole economy to a shortage of labour (due to rapid accumulation) the effect of releasing labour from agriculture is only to dampen a rising tendency of real wages, and the men displaced are being absorbed into industry. On the other hand, if there is no shortage of labour tending to develop, the displaced men are unemployed in the first instance. If investment is speeded up, and the real-wage rate falls, there is some relief, both through the absorption of labour into the investment sector and through a demechanisation of technique in the economy as a whole, but, as we have seen, there is no guarantee that a surplus of labour will get itself cured in this way, and long-period unemployment is the most likely outcome. It must be observed that the consequent decline in total consumption, leading to a reduction of output, may very well cause rents to fall, so that landowners gain no advantage from the excessive land-using bias in accumulation.

This situation is closely analogous to the case of capital-using innovations. As in that case, an accelerating rate of accumulation is necessary to keep the system running at full employment, and if accumulation fails to accelerate, the only result of the 'improvements' being made is an increase of misery all round.

This has an important moral for underdeveloped agricultural economies. It is of no use to mechanise agriculture (without raising output per acre) unless industry is ready to expand employment for the labour released from the land.

In the contrary case, where investment has been taking forms which raise output per acre without reducing labour per unit of output (say fertilisers have raised the yield of land without increasing the amount of crops that a man can handle) real wages have risen. Rent per unit of output must have fallen, but since total consumption has increased, the level of rents per acre may have changed in either direction.

Investments of this kind are highly desirable in backward economies, for by raising the level of real wages corresponding to a given level of investment they make it possible to raise the rate of investment without encountering the inflation barrier.

The scope for land-saving innovations in agriculture is, in principle, no less than for labour-saving innovations, but until recent times there has been a strong bias in a land-using direction. The capitalist rules of the game were developed in industry rather than in agriculture and engineers rather than botanists and biologists have been the leaders in technical progress. If the New World had not been opened up when it was, food would have been the bottle-neck for accumulation, and improving landlords would have been the architypical entrepreneurs. But so much natural wealth falling into the lap of the expanding capitalist economy fended off the need for land-saving innovations. Just as surplus labour makes technical progress lethargic in the labour-saving direction, so does surplus land make it lethargic in the land-saving direction.

It may turn out in the future that the law of diminishing returns from land in its sophisticated form (a land-using bias in accumulation) is not based on physical necessity but is rather the consequence of an historical accident.

RENT AND THE COST OF CAPITAL GOODS

The existence of rent introduces considerable complications into the relation between the prices of commodities and of capital goods. In general, an over-all change in the level of rents is likely to react differently upon the two sectors of the economy. Land regarded simply as space clearly plays a smaller part in the investment sector than in the consumption sector, which includes the production of food and of raw materials, such as cotton, required for the manufacture of consumption goods. On the other hand, special parts of the available area (sites suitable for shipyards, land containing particular minerals, etc.) are of the greatest importance for the investment sector.

On the whole it seems reasonable to assume that industries devoted to the production of capital equipment have their own requirements of land, which is specialised to their use, so that when consumption falls, or output per acre in the consumption sector rises more than consumption, the consequent fall in demand for land and fall in rents does not do the investment sector any good, nor does a rise in rents in the converse case do them any harm.

On this basis, we can apply the concept of neutral accumulation to the two sectors separately. Accumulation in the investment sector is neutral if an increase in its productive capacity (more or better machines to make machines) raises output per man (in terms of units of productive capacity for other industries) without increasing the demand for land in the investment sector.

There may be a very strong land-using bias in accumulation in the investment sector. A long-run [1] rise in the annual rate of output of ships sharply raises the marginal productivity of land on the banks of estuaries. A permanent rise in the

---

[1] We are here concerned, of course, with accumulation over the long run. Fluctuations in investment over the trade cycle cause big swings in output per acre in that sector.

rate of output of steel raises the marginal productivity of iron mines, etc. This need not complicate our analysis of accumulation. It means that output per head in terms of given types of capital goods tends to fall as the long-run rate of output rises. But in any case the specification of the machines is different (because the whole situation is different) when different rates of accumulation are going on, and we can subsume the effects of a fall in the marginal product of labour in the investment sector under the head of changes in the product itself. But it does very much complicate the philosophical problem of measuring a quantity of capital. A machine of given physical specifications would represent more labour-time if it was produced with difficulty in a period when a high rate of output was being squeezed from available land than if it had been produced by less labour operating more efficiently with more elbow room. (The problem is somewhat similar to the difficulty of evaluating capital in terms of man-hours at different notional interest rates.) [1]

This point is of some importance when geographically separate economies are being compared. Suppose that Alaph and Beth have similar labour forces operating identical techniques in their consumption sectors, while the investment sector in Alaph is far better provided with natural resources than that in Beth. In Beth the capital goods in existence represent more labour-time (say more work was required to produce the iron that has gone into them from lower-grade ores). The real-capital ratio (which is reckoned in terms of labour-time) in Beth is higher, and at a given real-wage rate the value of its stock of capital in terms of commodities greater. But clearly Beth is not a richer economy.

Here there is no way of escape from the index-number fiend, and all we can hope to do is to mollify him with sops of rough evaluations flavoured with common sense.

RENT AND EFFECTIVE DEMAND

Some recipients of rent, retaining the traditions of an aristocracy, may be more inclined to overspend their incomes

[1] See above, p. 121.

than to save. Others are ordinary rentiers who have placed some of their wealth in real estate instead of in paper securities.[1] Where the latter predominate we must assume that there is some saving out of rent. We continue to assume no saving out of wages, and we assume that only part of profits are distributed to rentiers. The ratio of consumption to income, therefore, is lower for rent than for wages, and higher for rent than for profits.

On this basis a rise in the share of rent in total income is similar, in its reaction upon effective demand, to an increase in the proportion of profits distributed to rentiers. It entails a larger amount of expenditure from incomes derived from property. The larger the share of rent, the lower the rate of real wages corresponding to a given rate of investment, and the larger the ratio of outside saving to profits.

When the situation is developing in such a way as to keep the proportionate share of profit in total income constant, while (owing to a land-using bias in accumulation) the share of rent is rising relatively to the share of wages, the real-wage rate corresponding to any given rate of investment is so much the less. Expenditure out of rent is, so to speak, a burden upon the workers without the consolation that what they forgo is adding, through accumulation, to the future wealth of the economy. At the same time the ratio of consumption to investment is somewhat less than it would have been if the relative shares of rent and wages had remained constant, since there is some additional saving out of additional rent.

Thus if the entrepreneurs are eager to invest and the economy is tending to run up against the inflation barrier, a rise in rent at the expense of wages sets a drag on accumulation by bringing the inflation barrier nearer at any given rate of investment, and it does so the more the *less* thrifty are the landowners. On the other hand, if the economy is sinking into stagnation, a rise in rent at the expense of wages enhances the tendency for long-run unemployment to develop

---

[1] Payments of rent for space are inextricably intermixed with payments for capital goods sunk in the soil, and part of rent is rather in the nature of gross profit — it covers an allowance for upkeep or amortisation of capital. The ambiguities which surround the concept of net profit (except in an imaginary world of perpetual tranquillity) also defeat any attempt to give precision to the concept of net rent.

and does so the more the *more* thrifty are the landowners.

When the situation is developing in such a way that the share of wages is more or less constant and rents are rising at the expense of profit, the ratio of consumption to investment is rising, and does so the more the less thrifty are the landlords.

In every case a rise in outside saving, at any given rate of investment, brings about a gradual increase in the ratio of debt to assets for the entrepreneurs taken as a whole, and so may impede investment by making finance harder to come by.

In these respects there is no difference between rent and other rentier incomes. But other rentier incomes are more or less closely related to the growth of the stock of capital, while land exists whether anyone is paid for owning it or not, so that an increase in rent incomes is a kind of levy upon the rest of the economy which is not related to any increase in production ; on the contrary, it arises from the limitation upon production set by the scarcity of land.

RENT AND MONOPOLY

We have been conducting our argument in terms of competitive factor markets in which the ratio of the marginal product of land to that of labour governs the ratio of their prices. In reality there is a considerable element of monopoly in the determination of rent. Each site is unique, and the rent that can be obtained for it depends very much upon the bargaining position of would-be tenants.

The monopoly element in rent is clearly seen in the difference between the price of the very same area of land when it is leased for agricultural purposes or for building. In a perfectly competitive market over-all supply and demand settle price and there can be no discrimination between particular buyers. But, in the land market, a buyer who expects a larger profit from its use can be made to pay more than one who expects a smaller profit — the landowner, in effect, receives part of the quasi-rent of the capital goods operating on his ground. This needs no overt collusion between landowners but rises spontaneously from the natural imperfection of the market.

In so far as rents are kept above the ideal competitive

level the burden falls in the first instance on profits, but expenditure out of rent incomes keeps prices, relatively to money wages, higher than they would be if rents were lower, so that entrepreneurs as a whole receive back (as receipts for the sale of commodities) a large part of what they pay in rent; the main burden therefore falls upon real wages.

LAND VALUES

Land has certain special characteristics in its aspect as rentier property.

When the level of rents is tending to rise, as accumulation goes on, while the rate of profit is more or less constant, the total capital value represented by a given space is increasing (a rising annual income capitalised at a constant rate of interest). This gives rise to the famous phenomenon of 'unearned increment' of wealth to landowners. The rise in the capital value of land is all the greater when the general level of profits, and with it the level of interest, is tending to fall.

Even with a constant level of rents and a constant rate of interest there is likely to be a secular rise in the total value of a given area of land. Since land is more versatile than most types of capital goods, its value is less dependent upon the fortunes of the particular firm utilising it at a particular moment and it therefore has an important advantage over other physical assets in offering security for loans (it can be mortgaged or sold and rented back, thus releasing finance for investment in new productive capacity). From the point of view of rentiers, land is primarily a placement, but it also offers attractions as consumer's capital. Because of these special advantages the demand for land tends to grow as wealth increases, even if the level of rents is constant. An increment of total wealth generates a demand for more land and, as the quantity is fixed, the price per unit must rise. From the point of view of an individual owner, a rise in the value of his holding of land is much the same as a rise in the value of well-chosen placements, but from the point of view of rentiers as a whole the rise in the total value of land is an increase in wealth that comes about without saving being necessary to acquire it.

CHAPTER 32

LAND, LABOUR AND ACCUMULATION

We have considered changes in the ratio of labour to land without accumulation, and accumulation with a constant ratio of labour to land. We must now consider both types of change together.

When population is increasing in a given space the law of diminishing returns in its unsophisticated form is operating and the share of rent in total income rises as time goes by (unless there is a sufficiently strong land-saving bias in accumulation). This sets a drag upon the rise in real wages that accompanies accumulation and technical progress; or, when accumulation is so sluggish relatively to the growth in the labour force that real wages are tending to fall, it helps to reduce them.

In the latter case the absolute level of rents is not necessarily raised by an increase in population. The fall in real wages may be so great as to reduce total consumption and, when it is, the fall in total output in the consumption sector may outweigh the rise in rent per unit of output.

LAND AND SURPLUS LABOUR

When accumulation is falling behind the growth of population and the rise of output per head due to technical progress, so that the demand for labour is not keeping pace with the growth of the available supply, redundant labour tends to silt up in the agricultural section of the economy. This happens partly because, owing to a differential birth-rate between town and country, the new workers first become available to agriculture, and are drawn off into industry only when the demand for labour there is expanding fast enough to absorb them;

and partly because it is easier to increase labour per unit of output by increasing the ratio of labour to land in agriculture than it is to bring about a demechanisation of technique in manufactures, so that workers offering themselves at lower wages can find work in the countryside when there is unemployment in the towns.

Moreover, if the situation is such that the demand for land has fallen (because of a decline in consumption due to low real wages) some inferior land may be left vacant, so that redundant workers have an opportunity to set themselves up as peasants. From an analytical point of view this is a kind of 'disguised unemployment',[1] though from a human point of view it is a particularly back-breaking kind of work.

The normal state of affairs, even in reasonably prosperous economies, is that demand for labour is less than the available supply except during short intervals at the height of booms. (Even then there is not necessarily full employment, when population is growing and technical progress going on, for capacity in the bottle-neck industries may not expand from boom to boom sufficiently to permit the absorption of the increase in the labour force that has become available meanwhile.) This reserve of labour is mainly attached to agriculture, and the level of wages in agriculture therefore tends to lag behind the level in industry. Consequently techniques are used which keep labour per unit of output high, and the low real wages appear on the surface to be a natural consequence of a low value of output per head, though, on a closer view, the causation is seen to run the other way.

CLOSING THE FRONTIER

So far we have considered economies in which land was available in excess of demand and economies in which land is scarce. We must also consider the transition from one situation to the other. Let us suppose that an economy has been expanding geographically, with population increasing and accumulation going on. Part of each year's investment has been devoted to breaking in new land, and (in competitive

[1] See above, p. 157.

conditions) these investments yield more or less the same rate
of profit as any other, but space commands no price. After
a time all the available space is occupied. When no vacant
space remains, a further increase in output increases product
per acre and reduces product per man. The marginal product
of labour has fallen below the average product and the marginal
product of land has risen above zero. Owners of land can now
charge rents. Of two entrepreneurs employing the same
amount of labour, the one who is occupying more space has a
larger product, and he is willing to pay rent equal to the value
of this extra product *minus* profit at the prevailing rate on any
additional capital required (assuming competitive conditions
all round).

To make the analysis as simple as possible we will imagine
that the economy has gone round a sharp corner — up to a
certain critical size of population and output there was no
rent, and just beyond it rent begins to be paid. Total real
income in the second position is very little larger than in the
first. In the second position entrepreneurs are paying rent.
A source of wealth has dropped into the lap of whoever happened to have acquired titles to land while the geographical
expansion of the economy was going on. The landowners
spend the bulk of their rents on consumption goods. The
entrepreneurs therefore are receiving back, in the sales value
of commodities, most of what they pay as rent. Prices, relatively to money wages, have risen accordingly, and the real
wage has fallen. Annual profits, in terms of commodities at
any given rate of investment, have been reduced only to the
extent of saving out of rent. Capital equipment, on the
whole, is much less affected than consumption goods by the
scarcity of land, so that the fall in real wages entails a fall in
the cost of equipment in terms of commodities. The rate of
profit on investment is therefore likely to have risen.

There is nothing in this to support the view that the ex-
haustion of the reserve of free land tends to cause stagnation.[1]
But there are some other aspects of the matter which may be
held to give it colour.

First, the change over from geographical expansion to

[1] See Alvin Hansen, *Full Recovery or Stagnation?*

accumulation in a given space involves changes in technique (as well as changes in the composition of output, which we have ruled out by our basic simplifying assumption) and it needs ingenuity and imagination to meet the new situation. The entrepreneurs may be disconcerted — all they had to do, until yesterday, was to plan for expansion of output at the long-established factor ratio ; now they must think again. If they fail to adapt themselves and merely wring their hands over the scarcity of land, investment falls off and stagnation sets in. The expansion which was taking place up till now proceeded cyclically, and the first slump after the economy has gone round the corner is particularly deep and prolonged, because the emergence from it requires a new kind of investment which no one yet understands how to make.

This argues, however, a rather feeble-minded class of entrepreneurs.

Second, while geographical expansion was going on, regular capitalist entrepreneurs may not have been the only ones to be making investment and expanding output. Let us suppose that the frontier was being opened up by settlers (of the type discussed above) [1] whose main investment was their own work. Total demand on capitalist industry was continually expanding beyond the bounds set by its own wages bill and distribution of profits, for the settlers were importing from it (each year more than the last) manufactured products in return for food and raw materials. This expanding demand required a corresponding expansion of the stock of equipment in the capitalist sector of the economy so that investment was continuously taking place to provide a growing capacity to produce goods for export.

In a self-contained capitalist economy, if the rate of investment happens to fall, demand for commodities falls, profits fall and investment is likely to fall all the more. When external demand for the products of a capitalist economy is growing as time goes by, a check to the rate of investment means that, after a little while, capacity will be found to have expanded less than demand. The terms of trade then turn in favour of capitalist industry (prices of manufactures rise in terms of

[1] See p. 297.

imported food and raw materials) and profits increase. The real wage in terms of home manufactures has fallen, so that the cost of labour to the capitalist entrepreneurs is reduced (though the real wage from the point of view of their workers may have risen as the result of a fall in the price of food) and the rate of profit on investment is raised. Consequently investment will be speeded up.

Thus the growing external demand gives buoyancy to investment and saves the capitalist economy from a tendency to fall into slumps,[1] or pulls it up out of a depression sooner than it would have emerged on its own. When the frontier population ceases to grow, the expansion of external demand comes to an end, and the capitalist economy is likely to find the first depression that sets in after this has occurred deeper and longer than those to which it was accustomed while the expansion was going on.

Third, the expanding economy may have been recruiting its population by immigration. If the closing of the frontier coincides with a cessation of immigration the rate of increase of population suddenly falls. There is still a great reserve of labour, from the entrepreneur's point of view, in the frontier population, but they cannot be absorbed into capitalist industry except at high real wages (for otherwise they prefer to stay where they are). Accumulation at the old rate can continue (in the absence of sufficient technical progress) only by raising the degree of mechanisation and depressing the rate of profit.

It is perfectly possible for an economy to change over from a more-or-less golden age based on population increase at a given state of technology to a more-or-less golden age based on technical progress. Indeed, the very fact that a tendency to develop scarcity of labour has set in may stimulate inventiveness so much that the second near-golden age has a more rapid rate of accumulation than the first. But the transition from one to the other sets great demands upon the entrepreneurs, and the economy may slip into stagnation in the crack between the two.

Finally, investment in opening up new land is not of the same nature as investment in capital goods. For reasons

[1] See also below, p. 371.

which we shall see in a moment it gives great buoyancy to expected profits. The disappearance of the lure to accumulation which it offers may so much weaken the urge to invest that stagnation sets in.

Once stagnation has set in it appears to be inevitable. The existence of surplus capacity is the greatest enemy of investment and the existence of surplus labour the greatest enemy of technical progress. With investment sluggish, profits are low and prospects discouraging. Monopolists, trying to defend their profits with high gross margins, are sawing off the bough they are sitting on by reducing real wages and limiting the demand for commodities. The absence of attractive prospects of profit discourages each entrepreneur from investing and so generating attractive prospects for others. But there is stagnation because there is stagnation, not because land has ceased to be free.

INVESTMENT IN LAND

Investment in opening up land (including mines, oilfields, etc.) is different in an important respect from investment in capital goods. The value of the resources obtained bears no relation to the cost of the investment. In spite of all the difficulties that we met with in evaluating capital goods, it is broadly true that the increment of value of equipment made by investment does not vary very much from the cost of the investment, so that over the long run the stock of capital corresponds more or less to the sum of all the net investments made; but, when natural resources are involved, a small investment may yield a huge increase in productive capacity. Moreover, one investment of this kind creates a situation highly favourable to further investment, as when railway-building brings a new territory into touch with a market, and opens up prospects of profit in developing its resources. For this reason the relation between growth of population and the available supply of land rarely follows a smooth course. At one time population is creeping up upon the available supply and land gradually growing more scarce. Then by some chance turn of history, or because the very scarcity of land has forced on development (transport, new crops), a huge area suddenly comes over the horizon of profitable exploitation and it is labour to exploit it which has become scarce. This interaction of the maps and the chaps [1] (together with the development of technique) is the chief subject-matter of economic history.

Political history also plays a part, in particular through the development of colonies. New supplies of labour and of land may become available together. Entrepreneurs of one race, by fair means or foul, obtain the right to exploit territory already inhabited by another, and, by fair means or foul, get the indigenous population to work for wages.

An ingenious variant was the importation of slaves and indentured labour into sparsely inhabited territory, thus bringing the surplus labour of one part of the world together with the surplus land in another.

Colonisation, in both forms, has been particularly important in enriching the industrial sector of capitalist economies with varieties of raw materials unobtainable in the territories where they grew up.[2]

To these large questions our formal analysis cannot make much contribution ; it is intended only to provide a framework within which they can be discussed in a coherent manner.

[1] 'Geography is about maps. Biography is about chaps', N. Clerihew Bentley.
[2] This is further discussed below, p. 369.

CHAPTER 33

INCREASING AND DIMINISHING
RETURNS

WE have already crossed the boundary of topics that can usefully be discussed in the framework of our simplifying assumptions, and the remaining chapters are intended only to sketch the links which connect our argument with certain topics that have been much elaborated in economic literature.

ECONOMIES OF SCALE

We have set out the foregoing analysis under the assumption that output per head is independent of the total scale of output. The long-run growth of output (as opposed to the upswing of a cyclical movement) is a slow process, and while it goes on the ratio of labour to land, the degree of mechanisation and the state of technology are all likely to be changing, and adapting themselves to changes in total output, so that it can never be possible to find out at all precisely what effects are due to the scale of the economy and what to other elements in its development. All the same, it is possible in a rough way to distinguish some connections between scale and productivity.

Scale of a Plant. The techniques adopted for producing a larger output from a single plant generally yield a larger output per head up to a certain size. This is due to the familiar economies of division of labour and of specialisation of equipment. These economies are the very basis of the capitalist rules of the game, for if entrepreneurs organising large groups of workers had not been able to undersell artisans, while offering their workers at least a living wage, the capitalist system could not have taken root.

For a small number of commodities these *internal economies* continue up to an enormous scale, but in most lines of production (at any given phase of technical development) the minimum efficient rate of output of a plant is found to be of moderate size.

In most lines of production there are unexhausted internal economies of scale even when the whole market for a commodity is a large multiple of the technically optimum rate of output of a plant. This occurs for three main reasons. First, in an uncertain world each entrepreneur wants to have a number of lines of production so that when one is not selling well he can fall back on another. Since many firms operate only one plant, this means that too great a variety of lines (looking at the matter from a purely technical point of view) is produced under one roof. Second, each entrepreneur can build up goodwill for a small rate of sales of each of a variety of commodities more easily than for a large rate for any one. The potential economies thus dammed up by risk and the imperfection of competition cannot be released by an over-all increase in the market, and are relevant to the question of economies of scale for output as a whole only in so far as the scale of the whole economy reacts upon the conditions of competition in particular markets.

A third influence damming up potential internal economies of scale is the cost of transport. Commodities which have to be sold as soon as produced because they are perishable, or which are bulky or fragile, so that transport costs are high in relation to the selling value of the objects in question, commodities which are tailor-made for the requirements of particular customers, those (such as gas) which have to be delivered to the customer's house by their own distribution network, and services which are performed direct to the buyer, all have a geographically limited market. The scale of operations of any one source of supply therefore largely depends upon the density of the market in their neighbourhood. So far as these particular commodities are concerned the potential economies could be released, at quite a small scale of total output, by concentrating the community in a smaller space, but when other factors (which we shall discuss in a moment) are keeping the economy spread out over space, so that a growth in its total size entails an increase of density at least in some parts of it, growth tends to improve productivity in respect to these types of commodities.

Scale of a Firm. A particular firm which operates a number of plants can attain technical economies by specialising between them (though even then the risk factor may cause the output of each to be diversified in order to ensure that each gets a certain share of whatever orders are going). This is a powerful influence tending to promote the growth of firms and so to reduce the number of competitors in each market, but potential economies of scale are continually being created and wiped out by technical change, so that the size even of the most successful firms is likely to be out of line with technical optima at any particular moment. Large firms have other advantages besides economies of scale : command over finance, bargaining power with suppliers, the ability to terrify potential competitors, and so forth. There may be, for these reasons, a tendency for firms to grow, in many lines, beyond the size at which technical economies are exhausted and to develop diseconomies of scale due to the bureaucratic hardening of the arteries that sets in in large organisations.[1] Once an economy has passed a very moderate total size there are probably few cases in which the whole market for a commodity is not sufficient to support one firm of the most efficient (as opposed to the most strategically powerful) size, though there are some spectacular exceptions, where the object produced (say a motor-car) is made up of many parts, which leave inexhaustible opportunities for specialisation. Apart from these cases, the advantage of a large over a small economy lies mainly in the possibility of having a greater number of firms and so being less a prey to monopoly.

Scale of an Industry. There are certain *external economies* which depend upon the scale of an industry made up of a large number of firms — the development of capital-equipment producers specialised to their requirements, facilities for training their operatives and technicians, etc. Some of these economies depend upon the localisation of the industry (they are enjoyed only by firms operating plants in centres where

[1] See E. A. G. Robinson, *The Structure of Competitive Industry.*

others are operating) and some depend on the scale of the industry in the economy as a whole and are enjoyed equally by scattered plants.[1]

Economies of this kind are released by a growth of the whole economy, but they are liable to be inextricably involved in accumulation and technical progress, and so to have a kind of ratchet effect — an industry of a certain size which had reached that size by shrinking from a larger scale would have a higher output per head than one which had just reached that size for the first time, so that the pure effects of scale cannot be disentangled from other influences.[2]

Economies of Uniformity. In all these cases what matters is the size of markets for particular commodities quite narrowly specified, and greater economies would be available in a small economy made up of consumers with standardised tastes than in a large economy composed of eccentrics.[3] (The conformist consumers get more for their money, though the eccentrics may have more fun.) One of the purposes of advertisement is to create uniformity of tastes (often by a somewhat blackmailing exploitation of the human fear of seeming odd) so as to gain economies of scale for particular suppliers.

Economies on the Overhead. The main economies of scale to output as a whole are not connected with any particular commodity.[4] They arise from the fact that there are certain services, such as the transport system, the banking system, etc., required by all industries, which cannot provide capacity for any service at all without providing capacity for a great deal. A railway line sufficient to carry one parcel of goods per month cannot help having the capacity to carry many tons per hour, at a marginal cost per ton very much less than the average cost including a return on the investment in the permanent way. Services of this kind, in relation to total output, are analogous to the overhead cost of a particular plant in relation to its own output.

The basic industries specialised on the production of

[1] See E. A. G. Robinson, *op. cit.* p. 142.
[2] See Marshall, *Principles*, Appendix H.
[3] See E. Rothbarth, *op. cit.* p. vii.
[4] See Allyn Young, ' Increasing Returns and Economic Progress ', *Economic Journal* (December 1928).

equipment (iron and steel, engineering) are in a somewhat similar position. In so far as they enjoy economies of scale, they depend much less upon the scale at which gross investment is going on in any particular industry than on its scale in industry as a whole.

With these types of economies the ratchet effect is very marked, and once the overhead investment has been made, a reduction in the scale of total output would cause losses on the investment but not a rise of current cost per unit of output.

Specialisation of Land. Far and away more important than any economies of scale in manufacture are the economies of scale arising from the occupation of a large territory.[1] Land in reality is by no means uniform in its suitability for different uses, and there are very great economies to be released by specialising different areas of land to different kinds of production.

A small isolated economy in a small space must get food, drink, textile fibres and building materials from its soil in the proportions in which it needs them, not in the proportions in which its territory is best suited to producing them. As it spreads geographically, and develops transport facilities, even if the new land is just like the old, it gains great economies by specialising production (some of the best pasture land was under wheat, because more wheat was needed than could be grown on the best wheat land — with a larger area and a larger market each type of land is put to its own best use). But the new land is never quite like the original area; it contains different minerals and different soils. The basic needs of the economy can now be met in new ways costing less labour.

Generally the advantages of specialisation of land are so imperative that they cause a wide geographical scatter of any given labour force (iron mines are at one corner of the map, river estuaries at another, vineyards at a third). When the total labour force is small this entails high transport costs, and dams up many potential economies in manufactures which are gradually released as the density of population increases.

---

[1] This is one of these points so obvious that it is generally overlooked, but it comes into its own to some extent under the heading of 'economies of international division of labour'.

OPTIMUM DENSITY

For all these reasons there is a tendency for output per head to grow with the scale of total output in a given space, and the law of diminishing returns from land in its simple form (an increase in labour per acre reducing output per head) or in its sophisticated form (a land-using bias in accumulation) begins to reduce output per head, on balance, only after a certain scale of output has been reached. This has led to the idea that it might be possible to specify the optimum size of population for any given space in terms of the size that maximises output per head, but such a notion is rather unsatisfactory for a number of reasons.

First, the optimum changes drastically with technical development and capital accumulation. In particular, the development of transport facilities is equivalent to an increase in density of population, so that a population which appears obviously below the optimum in one generation may cease to be so in the next without any growth having taken place.

Moreover, once the basic investments in the overhead (roads, railway lines, drainage, mine shafts, etc.) have been built up to cater for a large population, they do not disappear when population shrinks, so that there is a presumption, once these investments have been made, that, whatever the population may be, it is somewhat greater than the optimum size. (We shall return to this question in a moment.)

Second, if the notion is applied to particular parts of a whole economy (say to the area occupied by a nation) the optimum density depends upon the prevailing facilities for trade within the larger whole. In perfectly tranquil conditions with universal free-trade, a tiny population highly specialised on a narrow range of output is enjoying a share in the economies of scale of the whole world and has little if anything to gain by being larger. Cut off and obliged to produce everything for itself in small quantities, it would find important economies of scale released by a growth in its total output. Changing conditions for trade alter the optimum by sudden jumps, and it moves about much faster than population can alter.

Third, the notion of an optimum density in terms of output

per head ignores the question of distribution. A greater density of population may entail a higher output per head on account of economies in manufacture but a larger share of rent in total income, so that the workers are worse off, though the whole economy is richer.

Connected with this is the fact that relative prices of different commodities vary with the total scale of output in a given space. Once the main economies of specialisation of land have been realised, the remaining economies of growing density of population are likely to affect manufactures more than foodstuffs, so that the changes in prices that accompany a growth of scale are in the direction of raising food prices relatively to manufactures, and reducing the real income of those (the poorer part of the community) who devote the highest proportion of their consumption to food. (This type of consideration has hitherto been ruled out of our analysis by the assumption of a rigid composition of the composite commodity representing consumption goods.)

Moreover, land itself is an extremely important consumer's capital good, whether its services are consumed individually (private gardens), collectively with individual payment (golf courses, holiday resorts), collectively with collective payment (public parks, spacious layout of towns) or collectively without payment (wild country).

A great deal of the loss of real income per head in terms of land which accompanies an increase in density of population is masked by the rise in money values that accompanies it (higher rents, greater profits for holiday resorts, etc.) and another part never gets into the accounting system at all because it is a loss of an unpriced good.

Finally, the density of a population has the most profound effects upon the tastes and characters of the people concerned. There is not much sense to be made of a comparison between the real incomes of a Canadian trapper and a London barrow boy. The comparison makes sense only when small differences are considered in a given community. But it is only in respect to rather large differences that we can hope to disentangle the effect of scale from the differences in technique that are associated with it in actual situations, though not inherently dependent upon it.

There is another group of considerations which would completely undermine the optimum concept, even if it survived these objections. Differences in density come about through a process of change, which involves either migration or particular patterns of family life, and from a human point of view the consequences entailed by the process of change may be far more important than the consequences of a change that has taken place.

POPULATION AND INVESTMENT

Even if we hold that the concept of an optimum size of population is a will-o'-the-wisp, it is still possible to discuss the more limited question of how an increase in numbers, in any given situation, is likely to react upon income per head.

A Mature Economy. Consider first a capitalist economy which has long since laid the basis of the economic overhead (the transport system, industries specialised to the production of equipment, etc.) and where population is of a sufficient density to have realised the most important economies of scale in manufacture. If population is constant, all the accumulation that takes place runs into raising capital per head and improving the standard of housing. As accumulation goes on output per head is rising. In the absence of technical progress, the degree of mechanisation is being raised; the real wage rises as time goes by and the rate of profit falls.

If population is increasing, part of accumulation is required to maintain the real-capital ratio and the standard of housing (and if accumulation is less than proportionate to the growth of population there is actually a fall in the real-capital ratio or a growth of long-period unemployment).[1]

---

[1] If there is no technical progress and the rate of accumulation in each economy is initially equal to the rate of growth of population in the growing economy, then it continues to use Gamma technique, while the economy with a stationary population moves from Gamma to Beta and Alpha. If the rate of accumulation is somewhat higher, the first economy moves to Beta while the second is moving to Alpha. If technical progress is going on in each at the same rate, the first moves, say, to Gamma-plus while the second moves to Beta-plus. If technical progress is more rapid for the stationary population (because of greater pressure of scarcity of labour) the second economy moves to Gamma-double-plus while the first is moving to Gamma-plus.

There is a strong presumption, therefore, that, after some years have gone by, a representative worker's family will be better off if numbers have not increased than if they have.

In either case total output increases, and in respect to economies of scale from the overhead (transport, etc.) there is not likely to be much difference between the two situations. But where income per head has risen there is likely to be a greater variety of commodities consumed, and in the general run of manufacturing industry there may be more economies released by a given total increase in output when its composition is unchanged than when greater variety is being introduced. In this respect, therefore, the larger population has some advantage. But it is likely to be offset, from the point of view of a representative worker's family, by a rise in rents at the expense of wages and a loss of amenities in the form of free land.

Where the population is constant entrepreneurs may be spurred by scarcity of labour into speeding up technical progress. If so, the falling tendency of the rate of profit is counteracted or even reversed.

If they do not do so, and if they cannot bring themselves to continue to invest in face of a fall in the rate of profit, the economy sinks into stagnation.

The logical remedy, in that case, is to alter the rules of the game, for instance by collectively sponsored investment (both in industry and in housing) ; or to bring about a rise in the real incomes of the workers (say through taxation of profits and increased social services), so as to reduce the amount of investment required to maintain full employment.

Those who regard the rules of the game as sacrosanct, however, urge a rise in the birth-rate, on the ground that an increase in numbers would require investment that could be undertaken without a fall in the rate of profit.

From this it appears that there is a strong presumption that any increase in population, in a mature economy, sets a drag upon the rate of increase of output per head. Does the converse hold true — that a reduction in numbers raises output per head ?

When a decline in the size of families is due to some deep-seated psychological malaise or is the result of a loss of vitality,

it is a symptom of a sad state of affairs. When it is the result
of a reaction to a fall in infant mortality, somewhat over-
shooting the mark, it is a symptom of what most people
regard as a desirable state of affairs. Considerations at this
level are of more importance than economic consequences.
So far as the economic consequences are concerned, a decline
in numbers evidently raises output per head. Land per head
increases, and even if no new investment is taking place,
physical capital per head increases, for a great part of the
equipment built up for the larger population (the railway
system, ships, factory buildings) has a very long life ; the
investments made long ago in breaking in land are permanent ;
houses also have a long life, and as numbers shrink house-
room grows more plentiful relatively to people to be housed.

Output per acre and per unit of equipment falls, and rents
and quasi-rents fall. Real wages rise at the expense of profits
and entrepreneurs experience losses of capital values.

This makes the economy still more liable to fall into
stagnation than when numbers are merely failing to increase.
The age composition of a declining population (a smaller ratio
of children to grandparents), though not necessarily harmful
from a strictly economic point of view, has obvious dis-
advantages. Statisticians extrapolating the current trend for
a century predict race suicide. For these and other reasons a
decline in numbers gets a very bad press, and it is generally
presented to the public as a national disaster, though clearly
it is much more of a disaster for the landlords and the capitalists than for the workers in the nation concerned.

A Developing Economy. We now turn to a very different
scene. Consider an economy which has just begun to embark
upon making the basic investments and is operating under a
conscious plan instead of under the capitalist rules of the game.
Wages are held constant, and the whole surplus (after deducting
expenses of administration) is devoted to building up the overhead for industry and education and to laying out new towns
where families recruited from peasant agriculture will become
factory workers.

So long as the marginal product of labour exceeds the
wage, any increase in numbers increases the total amount of

investment. Of an increment of available workers, only a part
has to be set to provide for the consumption of the whole batch
of recruits, and the rest go to swelling the labour force engaged
on investment. While there is space available the marginal
product of labour can be prevented from falling (as total
employment increases) by devoting a relatively small part of
investment to breaking in new land and to labour-saving
equipment for agriculture, so that an increase in population
can go very far before it ceases to be true that total investment
increases with further increases in numbers.

If the total population is below the size that will be able
to realise the main economies of specialisation of land and
economies of scale in manufacture, when the basic investments
have been made, there is a gain from growth in numbers from
a very long-run point of view.

Even if the population is already large enough to provide
for what will ultimately prove, on any reasonable estimate, a
more than optimum density, there is still a middle-run gain
from increasing numbers. The basic investments take some
time to yield any fruit, and when the basic investments have
been made there is still a process of equipping consumer-good
industries to be gone through before a rise in consumption
becomes possible. The period of lean years, while investment
goes on at the maximum possible rate and consumption per
head remains constant, is shortened by an increase in the
amount of labour devoted to investment. An increase in
numbers brings nearer the day when the standard of life will
first begin to rise. At some later date the standard of life
will be lower than it would have been if numbers were less
(at that date) for capital per head grows more slowly the larger
the number of heads. But the middle-distance prospect of a
rise in the standard of life from its initial low level may be
of much greater importance than a far distant prospect of a
somewhat greater rise.

Over-population. Now consider an economy which has
been dwelling in primitive stagnation with a density of population so great that (with prevailing techniques) the marginal
product of labour in agriculture is round about zero. The
average peasant income is enough to support life at a miserable

level, while landlords and money-lenders are consuming the whole of rent and interest, or if they save, they amass gold, not productive capital. To break out of this situation it is necessary to get investment started. There is labour available, for peasant families can easily part with some of their members to industry and the consequent loss of output from agriculture is very small (if anything), for the marginal product of labour there was very low. But the families of the workers who have left are only too pleased to eat the whole of the dinner that they formerly had to share with those that have gone.

If landlords can be forced or induced to cut their consumption, a part of the technical surplus becomes available for investment, but it does not release much food, for even if the landlords were squeezed down to the peasants' standard there would not be much less eaten — the landlords' superior standard of life was mainly in services and luxuries.

The process of accumulation cannot be started on any appreciable scale without land-saving investments that raise the total output of food. The situation is not easy to master even with a constant population. If numbers are growing in any case or if each rise in consumption causes them to grow by reducing death rates, the benefit of land-saving investments is literally swallowed up and potential accumulation frustrated.

Malthusianism. The existence of economies in situations approximating more or less closely to these three types accounts for the very various views which are current nowadays on the population question, and the very wide differences in the esteem in which Malthus is held in different communities, quite apart from divergences in religion and ideology.

BOOK VII
RELATIVE PRICES

CHAPTER 34

SUPPLY AND DEMAND

FOR the individuals who make up an economy the details from which our simplified model has been abstracted are more important than the outline which it is designed to exhibit. An entrepreneur is interested in the fate of his own business, which may well run counter to the development of the industry of which it is a part, and the fate of the industry may well run counter to the development of the whole economy. The worker is interested in the level of wages (and general conditions) in his own line of production, and the differences between wages in one line and another may be much greater than any change in the general level of wages that takes place in his lifetime. His wife is interested in the purchasing power of his wage packet, not over a notional composite commodity, but over the particular things she wants to buy. The owner of property is interested in the value of his particular sites or placements, not in the general level of rents or the total stock of capital. The slow long-run movement of the whole economy is concealed by the agitation of its parts, and scarcely comes over the horizon of consciousness for the people who live in it.

The short-period movement of the whole economy does impinge upon individuals, though even there particular parts of the economy are differently affected; every boom has its own character, and a boom may consist in the development of new commodities or new methods of production that are ruining some entrepreneurs and depriving some workers of a market for their special skill, so that the investment which is generating prosperity in the economy as a whole is a disaster for them. Some entrepreneurs flourish better in a slump than in a boom, because they have specialised on cheap substitutes for goods which fewer families can afford when incomes have fallen. Workers who are secure in their jobs are better off when a rise in real wages accompanies a growth of short-period unemployment.

For these reasons the movements of demand and supply for particular commodities are more interesting to the inhabitants of an economy than those movements of output as a whole which have been the subject of our argument.

NORMAL PRICES

Let us return for a moment to an economy dwelling in a state of perfect tranquillity in the conditions of a golden age. The rate of profit is uniform throughout the economy, has long been constant and is not expected to change. All commodities and capital goods are selling at normal prices. All labour and all land is alike, and wages and rents are uniform. There are no unexhausted economies of scale.

How are the relative normal prices of particular commodities determined in these conditions ? As a first approximation, we may say that prices are inversely proportional to output per head (including in the heads an appropriate share of the labour force producing the capital goods required to maintain the flow of output of each commodity) so that prices are proportional to wages costs per unit of output. This is the basis of the famous Labour Theory of Value.

This is only a first approximation, for capital per head varies considerably from one line of production to another in a given state of technique, and the rate of profit on capital is everywhere the same. Thus the selling value of a year's output, relatively to the wages bill, varies from one line to another according to the annual profit required to provide the ruling rate of profit on the capital invested, commodities requiring more capital per head having a higher ratio of prices to wages cost. Similarly, land per head varies from one line of production to another, and prices must be such as to yield a uniform rent per acre.

The pattern of prices would be somewhat different at a different rate of profit. As we have seen, the rate of profit affects the real-capital ratio, because of the notional rate of interest that enters into the cost of capital goods, and this makes any simple generalisation about the effect of a difference in the rate of profit on relative prices impossible. Moreover, a different rate of profit entails a different degree of mechanisation, and some commodities yield themselves to mechanisation much more easily than others. It seems likely, however, that many commodities require a relatively high or low real-capital ratio over any reasonable range of rates of profit, so that, on the whole, the prices of commodities that require a more than average real-capital ratio in any one position would be lower relatively to prices in general if the rate of profit were lower, and those of commodities with a low real-capital ratio, relatively higher (the first group benefits, so to say, more than the second from a lower rate of profit).

Similarly, commodities with a high ratio of land to labour are more affected by a difference in the level of rents than those with a low ratio.

Further complications are introduced when we allow for differences in the aptitude of workers and of the various parts of the available territory for different lines of production, differences in the geographical distribution of the labour force, differences in the efficiency of entrepreneurs in different industries and differences in the economies of scale for different commodities. All these affect cost of production and influence the pattern of normal prices. Another group of complications flows from differences in different markets in monopoly and the imperfection of competition in its multifarious forms.

All these complications destroy the simplicity of the labour theory of value as an account of the determination of relative prices, but it remains valid as a rough generalisation, for differences in output per head are much greater, as between one line of production and another (say of motor-cars and drawing-pins), than the difference due to these various qualifications.

THE COMPOSITION OF DEMAND

We must now remove the assumption that has sheltered us all this time from index-number ambiguities and allow for differences in the composition of the output of commodities.

If we compare two tranquil economies with different rates of profit or different levels of rent we find two different patterns of consumption. There are three distinct groups of reasons for this. The first is that average income per head of all the inhabitants of the economy is, in general, different in the two cases, and this influences the pattern of consumption of a representative family. Generally speaking, wants stand in a hierarchy (though with considerable overlaps at each level) and an increment in a family's real income is not devoted to buying a little more of everything at the same level but to stepping down the hierarchy. The proportion of outlay on food is likely to fall where the total consumption rises; the proportion for house-room probably rises and so does the proportion for manufactures and entertainment. Of some commodities, *inferior goods*, the consumption declines not only relatively to the total, but absolutely, as the standard of life rises (bread and margarine give place to meat and butter).

The second group of influences on the pattern of consumption flows from the difference in the distribution of total income that is entailed by a difference in the rate of profit or the level of rents relatively to real wages.[1] Workers, landowners and rentiers have different patterns of consumption. The representative worker's family has a lower income than the representative rentier, and spends a higher proportion of it on food; the rentier family spends more on personal services; the habits of the various classes in respect to entertainment are different; and so forth. When we allow also for different patterns of distribution within the broad classes of income further complexities are introduced, and still more so when we allow for different tastes of particular families.

The third group of influences flows from the differences in the pattern of prices in the different situations. Consumer's habits are influenced in a number of ways by relative prices. In some cases commodities are in competition with

---

[1] In a fluke case where the elasticity of substitution between land and labour is equal to unity (see above, p. 293, note) and where profit per unit of output is constant (a greater value of capital per unit of output just balancing a lower rate of profit) the relative shares are not affected.

each other to satisfy the same basic wants, and consumers prefer the cheaper. Where the rent of land is higher and the rate of profit lower, natural wool is dearer relatively to artificial silk and smaller quantities of it are likely to be consumed. (Present tastes are often the result of price differences which existed in the past for reasons that have since disappeared — the English preference for mutton over veal was formed when mutton was a cheap by-product of English wool.) In other cases a smaller relative price for one commodity releases purchasing power for others lower in the hierarchy. Where bread is cheaper (relatively to wages) more milk is consumed. Where food in general is cheaper somewhat more is consumed but the main effect is an increase in consumption of housing and manufactures.

The pattern of consumption in turn reacts upon the pattern of normal prices. A larger proportion of consumption devoted to commodities with a high ratio of land to labour tends to make rents higher relatively to wages. A larger proportion of consumption devoted to commodities susceptible to economies of scale lowers their relative costs, and so forth.

The relations between demand and prices are subtle and complicated, and are interlinked by complex cross-connections. Where cars are cheaper, less shoe-leather is consumed, and, if no less meat is consumed, hides are likely to be cheaper.

A great part of economic literature is devoted to the subject of relative prices in conditions of tranquillity, and to the multifarious influence of different forms and degrees of monopoly and competition. The above remarks are not offered as a guide to the mazes of the theory of relative prices, but are intended merely to draw attention to the highly important details that have been excluded from our simple model.

In particular, we must observe first, that, as accumulation goes on, some outputs are constant or even declining. A golden age is not equally golden for all groups of entrepreneurs, and there is a considerable amount of uncertainty about the prospects of any particular investment even when conditions approximate to tranquillity for the economy as a whole.

Secondly, the increase in real wages which occurs, say, with rising output per head and a constant rate of profit, is not the same thing as a rise in the standard of life of the workers. A change in real wages in the sense of money wages divided by a working-class cost-of-living index may be widely different from a change in money wages divided by an index of prices of output as a whole. It is the latter which is important for the rate of profit and for accumulation. The real cost of labour to each employer is the cost in terms of his own product. From the point of view of the worker it is the price of his labour in terms of the commodities that he consumes that matters. The divergence between the two may be very great, especially when productivity is altering differently in manufactures and in agriculture. The weight of foodstuffs in the cost of living is considerably greater than its weight in output as a whole. The workers may be actually better off at a lower wage in terms of output as a whole if wages in terms of food have risen, or worse off at higher real wages in terms of output as a whole if wages in terms of food have fallen.

This consideration is of importance in connection with the inflation barrier, for the barrier operates through the demands of the workers (in a prosperous economy) for a certain standard of life, or through the necessity (in a miserable economy) of keeping them fed if work is to be done.

THE SIGNIFICANCE OF NORMAL PRICES

No actual economy dwells in tranquillity. And, even if, for a patch of time, something approaching tranquillity is experienced, the structure of the stock of capital and the distribution of the labour force, geographically and between occupations, is full of fossils of past phases of development which are out of line with current requirements, so that normal prices are never ruling for all commodities at once.

Nor can we say that normal prices represent a position towards which actual prices are *tending* to move; for the very process of moving to overtake a changed normal position involves investment (and may involve changing factor prices) which reacts upon the normal position itself. The significance of the concept of normal prices is rather to show what differences in the price of particular commodities, relatively to each other, are due to structural differences in the make-up of their costs (the real-capital ratio, labour per unit of output at capacity, etc.) as opposed to differences due to short-period fluctuations of demand relatively to supply.

BACKWARD AND PROGRESSIVE INDUSTRIES

As we have seen, the precise meaning of normal price is not unambiguously definable in an untranquil world, for normal price includes both amortisation and profit on invested capital, and the proper share of these items to be allocated to to-day's output depends upon what future quasi-rents will be. All the same, movements of relative costs are so marked, in some cases, that it is possible to detect their influence on movements of actual prices over the long run.

In any given phase of technology some lines of production lend themselves much more easily than others to innovations raising output per head, whether as the result of the application of new discoveries or as part of the process of raising the degree of mechanisation when accumulation is running ahead of the growth of the labour force. Relative prices tend to move over the long run more or less inversely with relative productivity, and the commodities for which output per head rises least become progressively more and more expensive as time goes by. When money-wage rates are constant, prices are falling for commodities where output per head is rising, while remaining more or less constant for those where it is not. When money-wage rates rise in the progressive industries, they are dragged up also in those where output per head is not rising (for otherwise, over the long run, their whole labour force would be drawn away from them) so that prices in the backward industries rise, while elsewhere they are constant or falling. In either case the relative prices of the commodities produced by the backward industries are rising as time goes by.

The leading example of this phenomenon in recent times has been house-building. The growing cost of dwelling space is a serious drag upon the rise in real wages which accompanies an over-all increase in output per head (for housing stands high in the hierarchy of wants) and may be so great as to make an apparent rise in wages a hollow mockery.[1]

The same phenomenon shows itself in a general tendency for services to grow more expensive relatively to goods as productivity increases. This has paradoxical consequences, for the proportion of property incomes spent on services (housemaids, bespoke tailors) is generally much greater than the proportion of wages, so that the purchasing power of the incomes of capitalists in their capacity as consumers tends to be undermined by the very success of their operations in their capacity as entrepreneurs.

BIASED CONSUMPTION

An increase in total output (which is not a simple quantity, but must be shown by a bracket of index numbers)[2] leads to a change in the composition of output, and the change may have a bias as between capital, land and labour which is similar in its effect to a bias in technical progress and accumulation.

This also is a subject of great complexity, and we will merely point out one or two important aspects of it.

First, in so far as a rise in the standard of life is generally accompanied by a fall in the proportion of food in total consumption there is a land-saving bias in accumulation. If accumulation is neutral from a technical point of view, so that output per acre is rising with total output, while the demand for commodities requiring a high land ratio expands less than in proportion to total output, there is a decline in demand for land and a relative fall in rents.

On the other hand, the demand for land as consumers' capital rises with the standard of life (less land under the plough and more gardens and football fields).

Second, the high place of housing in the hierarchy of wants gives a strong capital-using bias to consumption, all the more when house-building is a backward industry, so that

---

[1] It is partly for this reason that working-class housing is subsidised in a 'welfare state'.   [2] See above, p. 22.

the value of capital embodied in a given type of house (measured in terms of commodities in general) is itself rising as accumulation goes on.

Thirdly, the rise in the cost of services relatively to goods entails a capital-using bias in consumption. This applies not only to the substitution in well-to-do households of gadgets (produced by industries with a relatively high real-capital ratio) for domestic service (with a negligible real-capital ratio) but to such things as the substitution of more shoes for cobbling of old shoes, paper handkerchiefs for laundry work, cinemas for live acting, etc.

Fourthly, when accumulation and technical progress are cheapening durable consumer goods relatively to wages, or new types are being invented, there is likely to be a bias in consumption in their favour. When a new commodity involving a large lump of expenditure first comes over the horizon, it frequently absorbs more than the purchasing power released by the last round of technical progress, and eats into the market for commodities formerly being purchased (this is likely to be true no matter whether the new commodity is generally bought outright or on hire-purchase, that is, borrowed and paid for in arrears).[1] If, as seems probable, the industries producing commodities of this kind have a more than average real-capital ratio, this tendency constitutes a further capital-using bias in consumption.

The growth of demand for durable consumption goods, which has been so marked in recent times, is a source of instability in demand. Each time a new item becomes available a large number of families want to buy, and the demand is strong until everyone has made his first purchase. Demand then falls to replacement level. The sellers concerned try to overcome this by creating a psychological obsolescence of durable goods, placing even newer and more enticing models on the market.

The introduction of new types of commodities, whether

---

[1] It is not true if its purchase (by either method) is offset by a decline in saving. The influence of the selection of goods on offer upon thriftiness is another kind of complication that has to be introduced into a detailed account of accumulation.

durable or not, creates another kind of divergence between the standard of life and apparent real-wage rates. When new wants are created faster than the means to assuage them, subjective satisfaction is falling while physical consumption is increasing.

INERT AND VOLATILE PRICES

There is a general tendency for the prices of the products of agriculture and mining to fluctuate more strongly than those of manufactures with changes in demand.

There is normally unused capacity in industry (if only in the form of a possibility of overtime working) and the rate of output is limited (except sometimes at the height of a boom) by the difficulty of selling more, not the difficulty of producing it. Entrepreneurs generally prefer an increase of sales at subjective-normal prices to an increase in gross margins on the old rate of output, so that they respond to an increase in demand by increasing production. For most crops output cannot be expanded within a year, and for many much longer preparation is required. Moreover when land is all utilised, one crop can be expanded only at the expense of another, so that when demand has risen all round an all-round increase of output is impossible. In mining it is generally impossible to increase the rate of output quickly except at sharply rising marginal costs (working inferior seams, etc.). For these reasons the response of these *primary* industries to changes in demand is mainly in a change of prices rather than in the rate of output.

This tendency is reinforced by two further factors. First, monopoly is more prevalent in manufactures, and, as we have seen,[1] monopolistic prices generally fluctuate less than competitive prices with swings in demand. Second, a large part of agricultural output is produced by peasants and working farmers for whom the distinction between prime and overhead cost has no meaning — they cannot dismiss themselves to save wages when demand falls, and they cannot work much more when demand is favourable (indeed, their needs for cash may be very inelastic, so that they sell less at high than at low prices,

[1] See p. 188

enjoying more leisure or more consumption of their own produce). Where agriculture is in the hands of capitalist entrepreneurs the workers are often in a weak bargaining position (especially in colonial territories) so that the response to a fall in demand is a cut in wages rather than in output. In either case the incomes of primary producers fluctuate much more than wages in manufacturing industry.

Most manufactures depend upon raw materials that are the products of primary industries, but since the value added by manufacture changes, if at all, less than the prices of the raw materials, the final price of a commodity varies in a smaller proportion than the price of the raw materials entering into it. Thus the upswing and downswing of a trade cycle is usually accompanied by a marked rise and fall of the prices of raw materials relatively to manufactures; and, since this entails fluctuations in the relative price of food, it reinforces the tendency for real wages (looked at from the point of view of the standard of life of workers who are in employment) to rise in a slump and fall in a boom. At the same time it means that the rise in real wages which somewhat mitigates the suffering of a slump for industrial workers is largely at the expense of the incomes of peasants, agricultural workers and miners rather than at the expense of profits.

The output of agricultural products also fluctuates more than of manufactures because of the vagaries of the weather. A change in output relatively to demand causes sharp changes in prices, for demands are generally inelastic in response to price changes. A fall in the price of food is likely to increase consumption of things other than food, and a fall in price of raw materials, being reflected in a much less than proportionate fall in the price of the finished goods concerned, has a weak effect upon consumption even if the demand for the final product is quite elastic. The vagaries of prices are somewhat damped by the operation of dealers who amass or release stocks as prices fall or rise, but these operations are not generally sufficient to prevent the total income of primary producers from falling when their total production increases. It was for this reason that the farmer hanged himself on the expectation of plenty.

Technical change also causes strong fluctuations over the long run in primary relative to manufactured prices. A period when total output is increasing while technical progress lags in the primary industries, leads to a sharp rise in the relative price of raw materials and raises the share of primary producers in total income. A bout of important innovations in primary production, or the opening up of new territories, causing supply to increase relatively to demand, is often followed by a long period of reduced income for the producers concerned, for they have difficulty in moving out of their accustomed lines of production into others that are now more profitable.

Some are in the fortunate position of working in conditions of elastic supply — when their cash crop is yielding an attractive price they sell it, and when it is not they switch over to growing their own food. But in many cases land which has been specialised by planting to the cash crop cannot be switched without sacrificing the prospect of production in the future, when prices may have recovered; and in many cases the population of the area concerned has grown, on imported food, to a size which could not be supported from its territory even if the cash crop were completely abandoned.

One of the most dramatic paradoxes of the capitalist rules of the game is the spectacle of primary producers trying to cancel the effect of increased productivity by organising schemes to burn a proportion of their output and so keep the price of the remainder at a level which enables them to live.

THE JUGGERNAUT OF PROGRESS

Technical progress, accumulation and the changes in the pattern of consumption which accompany them, are continually destroying the demand for specialised factors of production. So far as capital is concerned this is an important source of riskiness. The uncertainty of the prospective earning life of capital goods keeps subjective-normal prices high, through high allowances for problematical obsolescence, and has a discouraging effect upon investment. The uneven incidence of realised obsolescence makes realised profits very uneven.

In some cases the feared loss of earning power does not occur, and capital goods continue to yield a return after their cost has been written off; in others it is so devastating that the investment in question would never have been made if it had been foreseen.

Specialised land may lose or gain value in a dramatic manner, but land generally retains some value at least as space, which is a highly versatile factor of production and can find new uses when old ones fail.

For specialised labour (the hand-loom weavers, the cinema musicians) a loss of market for their skill is a bitter misfortune (especially for those whom it strikes in middle age). They cannot usually build up obsolescence funds during their years of relatively good earnings, and the efforts that they make, after the blow has fallen, to protect themselves by restrictions on the use of new techniques are generally ineffective from their point of view, even when they are a considerable nuisance to entrepreneurs and consumers.

Progress in the economy as a whole tramples many groups of individuals into misery as it sweeps on its way. The cynical proverb: 'It is an ill wind that blows nobody good', takes on a melancholy tone when we turn it the other way round.

BOOK VIII
INTERNATIONAL TRADE

Chapter 35

EXTERNAL INVESTMENT

THERE are two distinct groups of reasons why international trade has always been the subject of a special compartment of economic theory.

The first is that for everyone some country is *my* country, and all problems may be looked at from the point of view of that country, treating the rest of the world as part of the economic environment, on the same footing as natural resources or the state of technique. The interests of the rest of the world come into the argument only to the extent that the behaviour of the rest of the world (say, by way of retaliation for some damage to its interests) reacts back upon the country being considered.

Problems of this kind do not depend upon the nature of the economic differentiation between nations (whether there is a single world monetary system or separate national systems, whether migration of labour is possible or not, etc.) but upon the focus of interest. If people had the same degree of patriotism for the county they live in as they have for the country, there would be books written about the problems of inter-county trade, studies of the manner in which a County Council could use its powers to foster the economic welfare of the inhabitants of the county, and sermons from inter-county-minded economists on the evils of using these powers so as to damage the rest of the world.

The second group of considerations does not concern the standpoint from which the argument is being viewed but arises from the very fact that the world is divided into nations. The relations between geographical areas each organised politically, each with its own patriotism and its own institutions, are different in important ways from the relations between regions under a single government. These features have to be taken into account when the world is viewed as a whole without favouring any section of it with particular attachment.

We shall not embark upon any discussion of the first group of problems (the interests of a single nation), but it is useful to show (though only in bare outline) how our analysis of accumulation connects with the second group (the characteristics of a world divided into nations).

TRADE BETWEEN THE CAPITALIST AND NON-CAPITALIST SECTOR

The capitalist economy (which for the moment we regard as a single whole, though composed of separate nations) exists in a non-capitalist environment. There are three main types of non-capitalist economies. The first exists where more or less empty lands have been settled by emigrants from the capitalist nations who trade with capitalist industry and rapidly become reabsorbed into the orbit of the capitalist economy. We have already glanced at this phenomenon in connection with the analysis of rent [1] and will not enlarge upon it further.

The second consists of lands inhabited by peoples at a simple level of culture and the third of highly complex ancient civilisations which somehow failed to develop the capitalist rules of the game, where the mass of the people are peasants living at a low standard of life dominated by a small wealthy class of landowners, merchants and money-lenders.

The relations of the capitalist sector with these nations consists partly in trade, and partly in development through investments made within their boundaries, which exploit their natural resources and recruit labour locally or import it from other non-capitalist areas. Both types of relations exist with each type of culture, but trade predominates with the ancient civilisations and exploitation on the spot with the simple peoples.

Let us first consider trade. The prime motive for trade with exotic countries is to obtain some speciality which cannot be produced at home, either because the natural resources are not available at home (metals, special crops) or because arts

[1] See p. 297.

unknown at home flourish in other economies (muslins, silk). The individual trader is not concerned with the balance of trade of the home country, but a one-way trade has to be paid for with some acceptable medium of exchange (say, gold) and sets up a drain on the reserves of the home country which is recognised as a national problem. For the trade to continue on a large scale it is necessary to find something to sell in exchange. Individual exporters can make a profit for themselves and, incidentally, staunch the drain of reserves, if they can succeed in doing so.

A static non-capitalist economy which is complete in itself may have no demand for imports from the capitalist sector of the world, and the problem then arises of creating wants amongst the producers of the exotic commodities so as to set a two-way trade going. This is done partly by underselling local handicrafts with cheap, mass-produced manufactures, partly by supplying to the wealthy class commodities formerly unknown to them (or attracting them to visit the capitalist countries and spend their fortunes there) and partly by changing the tastes of the whole population, teaching formerly naked people to demand cloth, formerly sober people to demand whisky and so forth. The most spectacular example of this process was infecting China with the opium habit in order to provide a counterpart for trade in tea.

The importance of this type of trade to the capitalist sector is primarily in giving access to exotic commodities, but it has a secondary effect in helping to maintain accumulation, for so long as the volume of exports (the counterpart to imports of exotic commodities) is increasing from year to year, investment in the industries producing them can continue to expand productive capacity when home demand is tending to fall, and so mitigates or reverses the fall.[1]

COLONIAL INVESTMENT

There are narrow limits to the extent to which it is possible to acquire exotic commodities by trade, for with a few exceptions (the specialities of the ancient civilisations) the products

[1] Cf. above, p. 207.

in which the capitalist sector is interested are not forthcoming in any large quantities unless capitalist entrepreneurs set about organising their production. The main way in which the natural resources of the non-capitalist sector are exploited is by investment on the spot — opening up mines, making plantations, etc.

The investment which goes into opening up these sources of supply partly consists in exportation of machinery and technicians from the capitalist sector. This is financed and organised in the same way as investment at home and from an economic point of view it is home investment, though geographically located overseas. But a large part of the investment must be made by employing local labour. (The navvies to build railways are local, or immigrants from other non-capitalist areas, while the steel rails and rolling-stock are imported. Jungles are cleared by local labour to make plantations, while implements and managers are imported, etc.) During the period of development outlay on local labour exceeds the value of the product, and during this period the capitalist sector is making foreign investment (exporting capital) in an economic as well as a geographical sense.

The sums spent locally (wages to local workers and expenditure out of salaries of foreign technicians and managers on local produce and services) increase local incomes and local expenditure. There is likely to be no saving out of local incomes except in the form of imports of precious metals. If so, the local investment outlay swells local incomes and expenditure up to the point where there are imports (of cheap cloth for the workers, motor-cars or foreign travel for the wealthy and gold for the savers) equal to the value of the investment. Thus that part of the investment which is not matched by movement of capital goods to the territory being developed is matched by a surplus of exports of commodities and gold [1] from the capitalist sector, and this export surplus is equivalent to investment from the point of view of the capitalist economy. It is matched partly by the profits of the firms engaged in the development, partly by retained profits

[1] The gold may itself be the product of other colonial investment which is already in production.

of firms who have been engaged in exporting commodities and gold or have benefited from the home demand generated by the investment, and partly by savings out of rentier incomes swollen by the profits that are made while the investment is going on.

Property in the new capital (including the natural resources brought into play by the development) accrues to the capitalist sector (apart from any payments to local landlords or governments for concessions) and is matched by the assets of the firms concerned and their indebtedness to rentiers from whom they have raised finance.

Investment of this kind may be a powerful influence fending off threatening stagnation in the capitalist sector.[1]

Once the development period is over and the new resources are in operation, the export of the product to the capitalist sector is balanced partly by payments out of the profits of the firms concerned as interest and dividends to rentiers in the capitalist sector, or by their retained profits, and by remittances out of the salaries of the managers, and partly by exports to the local population whose purchasing power has been increased directly by wages paid by the capitalist enterprises, or indirectly by local expenditure of these wages. (The income per head of the local population has not necessarily increased, for their numbers may have been swollen more than their total income.)

Local entrepreneurs may come into being under the influence of the foreigners, and local rentiers may begin to place their savings in business instead of gold, so that the economy is brought under the sway of the capitalist rules of the game, and after a time the local capitalists become nationalists and set up a movement to expropriate the foreigners.

[1] This is, essentially, the thesis of Rosa Luxemburg's *Accumulation of Capital*.

CHAPTER 36

INTERNATIONAL INVESTMENT

THERE may also be international investment within the capitalist sphere. If the capitalist sector were a single unified economy with free movement of labour over the whole area, free opportunities for entrepreneurs to organise investment wherever they please; and a unified capital market, so that rentiers of each nation buy and sell placements of all kinds without respects to their national origin; and if, furthermore, complete *laissez-faire* ruled — governments were completely passive in economic affairs — then the division of the capitalist world into nations would have no relevance to the process of accumulation. There would be a broad tendency to equalisation of the rate of profit and the level of wages throughout the capitalist world, and the analysis of a single economy which we have set out would be applicable with no more reservations and complications than are required for the discussion of accumulation within a country where different industries predominate in different geographical areas.

In so far as these conditions are not fulfilled there are special qualifications to be brought into the analysis.

In reality these conditions are fulfilled to some extent, but very imperfectly. Workers move more readily, as between industries and areas, within one country than over frontiers: and even when labour is immobile the level of wages in one industry has an influence on wages in others within a country (through setting up ideas of what is fair and what is possible) which is quite absent as between countries. Entrepreneurs find it easier to operate in an area whose language they understand and whose government is sympathetic to them. Rentiers have strong preferences (not necessarily in favour of their own country) as between placements of different national origin.

Governments are not passive, but operate on the conditions of trade deliberately through commercial policy (protective tariffs, etc.) or accidentally as a by-product of policies having other aims (embargoes on trade with potential enemies, etc.).

To separate out the effect of these various imperfections in the unity of the capitalist world we will draw sharper distinctions than exist in reality. We consider a world in which there is no international movement of labour at all, but there is complete *laissez-faire*, and complete freedom for entrepreneurs to make investments where they please, and at first we assume that there is a completely unified capital market. In these conditions the rate of profit and the level of interest rates are more or less uniform throughout the capitalist economy, but the level of real wages may vary to any extent as between one country and another.

We will assume that buyers and sellers have no particular national prejudices, and always prefer to buy a given type of product where it is cheapest and sell where it is dearest, but we will suppose that geography is so arranged that transport costs are less within national areas than between them, so that it requires an appreciable difference in prices at points where production is taking place to cause goods to move across national frontiers.

TRADE BALANCES

When trade is conducted on purely commercial principles by innumerable independent entrepreneurs (including merchants and dealers) all over the world, not paying attention to national interests, but each seeking profit where he may, the pattern of trade, when looked at from a national point of view, emerges as a by-product of their activities. When the accounts are cast up for say, a year, some national economies will be found to have had an excess of value of exports of goods *plus* receipts for services, tourist expenditure, etc., and receipts of interest and dividends from foreign placements over the corresponding payments for imports, etc.; that is, they have a surplus on income account; and some are in the reverse position. When transport costs are included, the positive and negaiive balances of all nations sum to zero. The manner in which countervailing payments settle the balances will be discussed later.

We can distinguish four main influences on the pattern of balances in any situation : (1) structural influences connected with demand for particular types of commodities and capital goods relatively to their relative normal prices in different countries ; (2) over-all differences in costs due to differences in wage levels relatively to productivity ; (3) over-all differences in demand due to different levels of activity in different countries ; (4) movements of exchange rates or the consequences of national policies designed to prevent them.

Examination of the last group of influences must be postponed until we have discussed international payments. We glance briefly at the first three groups as follows :

The Structural Pattern. At any moment there are different patterns of relative normal prices within different countries. The main influence on the differences of the patterns is demography — where the land-labour ratio is high, wheat, for example, is cheaper relatively to manufactures than where it is low. A second group of influences is historical — a nation which happens to have developed an industry (say, watchmaking) ahead of others has for a long time an advantage in respect to the capital equipment, know-how of entrepreneurs, skill of labour, etc., which make the commodity concerned cheaper in that country (relatively to other commodities) than it is in countries where the industry has recently been established. On the other hand, an old industry, once the technical leader in a particular line, say textiles, may have become obsolete, and its younger rivals in other countries have an advantage, because it is easier to adopt new methods of production when an investment is first made than to change over from methods which once led the world and are now being pushed into an inferior position which the producers concerned (entrepreneurs and workers alike) are reluctant to admit.

A third group of influences arises from economies of scale. Where a particular industry happens to have grown to a considerable size, the normal prices of its products (relatively to the general run of manufactures) are low, even though there is no discernible reason why the industry should flourish where it is rather than anywhere else.

When the various national price levels are translated into a common unit of account at the ruling exchange rates between currencies, the relative differences in prices within each country appear as absolute differences between countries. Thus, traders supplying a market in a country with a low land-labour ratio find wheat cheaper abroad than at home; a country with a young watch industry or an old textile industry finds watches or cloth cheaper abroad; each finds specialities produced on a large scale abroad unobtainable at home. Looking at the same thing the other way round, suppliers of wheat in a country with a high land-labour ratio find a market abroad for much more than their home market would absorb, and so forth. Trade flows around the world in such a way that when transport and selling costs have been added to production costs (including profit) the price of comparable articles is more or less the same in any one market, no matter what its point of origin.

The structure of the pattern of costs is continually changing with demographic developments, technical innovations and changes in scale, and the pattern of demand is changing with national incomes and with tastes. The underlying pattern of trade is always in course of development and actual trade is continuously adapting itself to changes in the pattern. Surpluses and deficits for particular countries emerge and shift as the process goes on. In particular, a small country highly specialised upon a narrow range of exports based on some feature of its own geography may be in a highly favourable position at one moment (when the demand for its specialities is high) and in a disastrous position at another, when tastes have changed or a rival source of supply has come into existence. A large country with a wide range of production is much less vulnerable, both because overseas markets absorb a smaller proportion of its output, and because the variety of its exportable goods is great, so that when one market fails others are likely to be growing.

The structural pattern of relative costs determines the underlying pattern of trade over which other influences play.

Over-all differences in costs. The general level of prices in each country, assuming a more or less uniform rate of profit throughout the world, depends upon the relation of output per head to wages (calculating money wages in each country in any one currency at the ruling exchange rates).

Suppose that in Alaph output per head is higher over a wide range of production than in Beth and Gimmel, and that wages are also higher. Then we can pick out a group of commodities, say, textiles, which are produced in all three countries at more or less the same normal prices because, in this particular line, at the moment, the differences in wages and in productivity just about compensate. These goods are potentially exportable, but they do not move across frontiers because the price differences are not sufficient to make trade profitable. For some commodities, say motor-cars, productivity in Alaph, relatively to that in the other two countries, is considerably higher than in textiles, while for others, say cheese, the relative advantage in productivity is less in Alaph and in Gimmel than in Beth, and in others again, say watches, the relative advantage is less in Alaph and in Beth than in Gimmel. Then at the moment, when the relative wage levels are such that no textiles are moving across frontiers, Alaph is exporting motor-cars, Beth cheese and Gimmel watches.

In each country technical progress and capital accumulation are going on and real wages are tending to rise through time. Now suppose that in Alaph accumulation, relatively to the rate of technical progress, is more sluggish than in the other two (whether because of an exceptional rapid rate of progress, or because of a weaker urge to accumulate or a more monopolistic economy). Alaph has a chronic tendency to develop a surplus of labour, and money wages relatively to output per head rise less fast than in other countries. Motor-cars are becoming progressively cheaper on world markets, and cheese and watches relatively dearer. Alaph textiles are also growing cheaper relatively to those produced in Beth and Gimmel. To simplify exposition, let us suppose that we begin from a moment when each country's trade happens to be in balance. We then have to consider, at a later date, how balances have been affected by the change in relative over-all costs that has taken place.

The physical volume of exports from Alaph of motor-cars is likely to have increased, since more will be bought abroad when they are cheaper relatively to incomes in Beth and Gimmel. Alaph traders have begun to find it possible to sell textiles abroad. The physical volume of imports of watches and cheese is likely to have declined, because home sources of supply can now compete with imports, or because demand is deflected to other commodities which are cheaper at home.

Thus there is a tendency for Alaph to develop a surplus of exports. But three factors in the situation tell the other way. First of all, the price of motor-cars has fallen in terms of cheese and watches. To simplify the argument we will suppose that exchange rates remain constant (how this may be we shall see in a moment) and that the money price of cheese and watches are constant (in Gimmel and Beth money-wage rates have risen in proportion to output per head) while the money price of motor-cars has fallen (in Alaph money wages have risen, if at all, less than output per head). The sums required to pay for Alaph's annual imports have been reduced, because the physical volume of imports has fallen, while their prices are constant. The money values of exports may have changed in either direction. It is swollen by the newly started export of textiles, but for motor-cars the fall in price may have been more than in proportion to the increase in volume of sales, so that it may well happen that the total money value of Alaph's exports has fallen, and it may have fallen by more than the value of imports.

Secondly, the state of effective demand in Alaph has altered. The motor-car and textile industries are experiencing a boom. So are home industries producing goods rival to watches and cheese (they may or may not be producing similar commodities, but in either case they are benefiting from a transfer of purchasing power from imports to home goods). On the other hand, some home industries may be suffering from the fact that purchasing power has been deflected from their products in order to buy cheese and watches (smaller quantities are being bought but at higher relative prices; the proportion of income spent upon them may have risen on balance, so that they are sucking purchasing power from other markets).

In so far as the net effect has been to increase activity in Alaph, incomes tend to be raised, and this tends to brake the physical reduction in imports.

Thirdly, the textile industries in Beth and Gimmel, as well as the special export industry of each, are suffering from a decline in output, and imports of motor-cars (greater quantities though at lower prices) may be sucking purchasing power out of the home markets for other commodities. In so far as incomes decline in Beth and Gimmel, and unemployment emerges there, the increase in physical imports of motor-cars and textiles is braked.

These influences may outweigh the tendency for Alaph to develop a surplus of exports.

It is thus impossible to generalise about the effect upon trade balances of over-all changes in the level of costs. Everything depends upon the underlying structural pattern of demand and relative costs, and on the reactions on effective demand of relative price changes. Over the long run there is a certain self-correcting tendency in the development of trade balances. When initially the relative fall in Alaph prices engenders a surplus of exports and stimulates home production in substitution for imports, the demand for labour in Alaph is raised, and the initial cause of the unbalance (too sluggish a rise in money wages in Alaph) is mitigated. When the initial effect is the other way, and Beth and Gimmel have developed trade surpluses, the situation in Alaph is exacerbated, but in Beth and Gimmel the demand for labour is raised, money wages tend to rise faster than output per head, the price of cheese and watches rises still further relatively to Alaph incomes (which themselves are lowered by the slumpy conditions following from a deficit in trade superimposed upon the initial tendency to stagnation) and at some point the physical volume of exports is likely to fall low enough to offset the rise in prices. In any given state of the structural pattern of demands and relative costs there is, in principle, some level of relative wages which would ensure balanced trade, and the development of unbalance itself sets up a movement in the direction of the levels of wages which would correct it. The movement in this direction, however, is slow and imperfect, and in a constantly changing world the corrective forces are chronically lagging behind the developments that they have to correct. In a purely logical sense we may say that there is a tendency towards the establishment of balance, but in an historical sense there is a tendency for unbalance to be the normal condition of affairs.

The Level of Activity. There is no reason to expect the investment going on in the world at any moment to be evenly spread amongst the nations, for they occupy areas in space which are quite arbitrary from an economic point of view. At any moment, the rate of investment that is going on in the world as a whole governs the demand for labour in the world as a whole : the demand for labour generated by investment is not confined to the labour force within the frontiers of the country where the investment happens to be taking place but is spread over the world in a manner depending upon the underlying structure of demands and costs. Capital goods to be set up on sites, say, in Alaph may be produced abroad, and the corresponding demand for labour is in the investment sector in Beth or Gimmel. In so far as Alaph workers are occupied with investment, commodities may be imported to supply their consumption (and the consumption of rentiers sharing in the high profits generated by the investment that is going on). Suppose that the investment sector in Alaph has absorbed labour both from the motor industry and from textiles. The price of motor-cars has risen and less are bought by Beth and Gimmel. The price of textiles in Alaph has risen sufficiently to attract imports of textiles (as well as of cheese and watches) from Beth and Gimmel. Or may be that only Gimmel can export textiles, while an absorption of labour into her textile industry out of food production creates a demand for imports of cheese from Beth.

Beth and Gimmel share in the world investment that is taking place through the surplus of exports that each is experiencing. The national accumulation of each country (the addition to wealth of its citizens) over, say, a year, is equal to net home investment carried out in the year *minus* its deficit or *plus* its surplus on income account (the difference between exports, interest receipts from foreign placements owned by

home citizens, etc. over imports, interest payments, etc.).
For simplicity, assuming that the only investment made during
a year was in Alaph, the world accumulation for that year is
the value of the addition to capital in Alaph. Alaph's national
accumulation is this value *minus* the year's deficit on income
account and the national accumulation of Beth and of Gimmel
is the year's surplus of each.[1]

The geographical distribution of investment, both over
the long run and over the course of cyclical fluctuations, is a
major influence on the pattern of trade balances, and would
be at work even in a world where all nations were more or
less alike from a structural point of view, so that if investments
were evenly spread amongst them (and relative wage levels were
in line with relative productivity) there would be no trade at all.

BALANCES OF PAYMENTS IN A PERFECT CAPITAL MARKET

Transactions between citizens of different nations, as well
as payments for imports and receipts for exports of goods and
services, include payments of interest from entrepreneurs in
one country to rentiers in others, and they include purchases
of second-hand placements between rentiers of different
nations, loans from rentiers in one country to entrepreneurs
in others [2] and finance provided by parent firms in one country
for subsidiaries set up in another. The whole mass of ingoing

[1] To bring out the point let us suppose that only Beth can produce
capital equipment and only Alaph can use it, while only in Gimmel is there
an excess of income over consumption (rentier saving and undistributed
profits). In Alaph the whole labour force is occupied in producing for
home consumption and equipment is being imported (we abstract from
local investment). Alaph has an annual import surplus equal to her annual
home investment, and from a national point of view her net rate of
accumulation is zero. In Beth part of the labour force is in the investment
sector (producing equipment to be exported to Alaph), but consumption
is equal to net income. Imports of commodities from Gimmel make up
the difference between net income and home production of commodities.
For Beth trade is in balance and national accumulation zero. Gimmel is
running an export surplus of commodities (to supply the demand generated
in Beth by the employment in her investment sector) and is making national
accumulation equal to the value of the capital goods being erected on sites
in Alaph.

[2] Deposits in foreign banks may be included under this heading.

and outgoing transactions of all kinds, over, say, a year, makes up the balance of payments of any one nation.

When there is a perfectly unified world capital market, and rentiers have no national prejudices (either way) in respect to the placements that they hold, the balances of payments automatically adjust themselves to the balances of trade.

The accumulation of capital made over a year by the citizens of a nation, taken as a whole, is the excess of the year's net income over expenditure on consumption, and this is equal to the net investment made during the year, *plus* or *minus* the balance on income account. It is matched by rentier saving and undistributed profits. New wealth, requiring some placements in which to be held, then exceeds or falls short of the finance absorbed by home investment during the year, and there is an excess or deficiency of demand for placements equal to the year's surplus (positive or negative) on income account. When, for instance, Alaph has had an import surplus over the year, the finance which has been used during the year for home investment has exceeded the addition to wealth made during the year by Alaph citizens; new Alaph securities have been sold to finance investment (or transfers have been made from foreign associates) in excess of the savings of Alaph rentiers and undistributed profits of Alaph firms. In a perfect world capital market a small rise in the yield of Alaph securities is sufficient to make them attractive to foreign rentiers; the excess of supply over home demand has caused a small rise in yield and attracted purchases from abroad; there has accordingly been a balance of borrowing from abroad that just makes up the deficit in home saving. Or when Beth is running an export surplus, a year's addition to wealth in Beth exceeds the year's borrowing and self-financing by Beth entrepreneurs, and a small fall in the yield of Beth securities is sufficient to cause foreign securities to be bought to the extent required to fill the gap.

For international transactions to be possible there must be some internationally acceptable medium of exchange to bridge any temporary gap in payments from day to day, but, over the course of a year, in these conditions, the demand of foreigners for each country's currency (required to pay for its exports and to make placements in it) is matched by the demand of the home citizens of each for foreign currency (to pay for imports and make placements abroad) and there is no net movement of balances.

THE FOREIGN EXCHANGES

When the world capital market is not perfect small changes in relative yields are insufficient to bring the flow of capital transactions into line with the flow of trade. The automatic adjustment of demand and supply for each currency fails to operate, and the only-too-familiar problem of an exchange crisis is liable to present itself.

When, say, Beth rentiers prefer Alaph securities to their own, the demand for Alaph currency (being purchased in order to make placements in Alaph) may exceed, to any extent, the supply provided by the current surplus of exports from Beth. The yield of Alaph securities tends to fall, but there is no reason to expect the fall to go far enough to choke off the demand of Beth rentiers. First of all, they may have some strong reason for preferring Alaph securities, so that the fall in yield required to discourage them would be very great and, secondly, Alaph owners of securities are likely to have a view about what level of yields is normal, and when the price rises somewhat they are ready to sell them to Beth rentiers and hold money balances for a time, expecting the price of Alaph securities to relapse again in the near future. The rise in price of Alaph securities is thus braked below the point at which demand coming from Beth would be choked off. The excess demand for Alaph currency coming from Beth then fails to correct itself and Beth currency tends to depreciate on the exchanges.

When there are speculators operating in world currencies who believe that the depreciation is temporary they buy Beth currency (drawing upon reserves of Alaph and Gimmel currencies that they have been holding for the purpose of operations of this kind) and so bridge the gap in the balance of payments. But if they expect the depreciation to go further, they operate the other way.

Since the world capital market is not in fact perfect, since speculators (very reasonably) have not in general faith in the exchange rates that happen to be ruling at any moment and since fluctuating exchange rates are a great nuisance to traders and to rentiers who hold foreign placements, it is necessary for the monetary authorities of the various nations to operate schemes to preserve stability. The gold standard was such a scheme, though it came into being by a process of evolution rather than as a conscious plan to control exchange rates.

Once the authorities have come into the picture they cannot fail to take a view as to what exchange rate they want to see ruling, and thus national exchange-rate policies come into operation as an independent influence on the pattern of trade.

The problems of exchange-rate policy are both intricate and familiar, and we shall not embark upon a discussion of them here. They may be summed up by saying that where there is an excess of home demand for foreign currency the authorities have, in general, a choice between raising home interest rates (in order to check the excess demand for foreign placements) and allowing a fall in the exchange rate. The first course tends to restrict home investment and so brings into play the consequences of a lower level of activity at home. The second operates on relative prices of home and foreign goods and brings into play the consequences of a fall in the over-all level of costs.[1] International monetary policy, therefore, is an independent influence on the pattern of trade balances which operates through the channels of the influences that we have already discussed.

National authorities also operate on the pattern of trade through commercial policy (tariffs, etc.) whether designed for piecemeal objectives — to favour some particular influential group of entrepreneurs, or to protect some group of workers from the consequences of a change in demand ; or for over-all objectives — to operate upon the balance of trade or the level of home employment. This also is a subject only too painfully

---

[1] As we have seen, this may be the reverse of what is required, for a fall in costs may reduce the balance of trade. But it is never easy for the authorities to diagnose the situation and they may allow the exchange rate to fall in circumstances when it does more harm than good.

familiar both in real life and in economic literature, and since we have not introduced government action into our model it would be inappropriate to discuss it here.

WORLD ACCUMULATION

There is a considerable difference between international investment that comes about in a rather accidental way as a result of the pattern into which trade balances happen to have fallen through the interplay of the four groups of influences discussed above and the external investment of the capitalist sector as a whole in non-capitalist areas. When investment is being made to develop sources of raw materials or exotic commodities, a demand for the product of the new capital installations already exists and (apart from unforeseen obsolescence and short-period fluctuations) there is no problem of finding a market for it. Profits on the investment are provided by the sale of the produce in the capitalist sector and the resulting export surplus of the colonial territory automatically services its debts.

When one capitalist country has been importing capital from others (by running an import surplus matched by sales of placements) it has piled up obligations to pay interest without necessarily having increased its capacity to export. It may then run into difficulties with its balance of payments. This is particularly likely to happen if its import of capital was due to a structural disadvantage in trade or to maladjustment of wage rates to productivity, for its borrowing from abroad then has no connection with any superior profit opportunities represented by investment in its industries (rather the reverse). Even if its deficit was due to high home investment, there is no particular reason to expect the future product of the new capital installations to be readily saleable abroad so as to service the debts to foreign rentiers that have been incurred while the investment was going on. The world as a whole is richer by the investment made in Alaph, and world real income, taken as a whole, is greater by the enhanced productivity of Alaph labour, but the world may not want to consume its extra income in the form of Alaph goods.

Every phase of world investment is creating a fresh situation and requiring a changed pattern of trade balances without any particular tendency to alter the structure of demands and costs in such a way as to bring the required change of pattern into being.

The existence of nations each with its own labour force and its own geographical and historical peculiarities introduces great complexity into the process of accumulation and makes the chance of the conditions of a golden age ever being realised remote indeed.

CONCLUSION

THE reader must draw his conclusions for himself. On parting
I only beg him to glance back to Chapter 2 and recall that the
outputs that we have been discussing all this time are outputs
of saleable goods; they are not co-extensive with economic
wealth, let alone with the basis of human welfare.

NOTES ON VARIOUS TOPICS

NOTES ON VARIOUS TOPICS

WELFARE ECONOMICS

THE analysis going under the title of Welfare Economics was evolved when habits of thought prevailed which are now discredited, though we have by no means succeeded in freeing ourselves from them. The pioneers of the theory, if challenged, would have repudiated the idea that they thought of *utility* as a kind of juice contained in commodities (like phlogiston in combustibles), but they can best be understood if we read them as though they were thinking in some such terms. Latter-day economists are careful to avoid this *naïveté*. They treat utility as an ordinal, not a cardinal quantity (and many refine it still further), that is to say, they regard the consumer as putting commodities through a competitive examination, and choosing those that score the best marks.

But they are still pursuing a will-o'-the-wisp. Consumers can be observed from the outside to choose what they choose; but each of us knows from his inner experience that a consumer, even in such a prosaic act as buying a pound of tea, is reacting to a whole complicated social situation, not to its strictly economic aspects only. We know that he is influenced by moods, so that his conduct is not consistent from day to day, and that he is influenced by motives of which he is himself unconscious ('I can't think what it was that made me buy that hat'). We know (or at least salesmen believe) that he is influenced by appeals to fear and snobbishness that advertisers cunningly trail before him. We know that his consumption is a complicated intertwining pattern of goods and services so that the idea of putting any one pair of items, or any one item and purchasing power in general, through a competitive examination is a very misleading metaphor to apply to it. We know that his pattern of consumption is much influenced by the habits of his forebears (brought up in a tea-drinking country, he drinks tea). We know that he often buys things he does not particularly enjoy consuming in order to produce an impression on the Joneses, or avoids things that he would enjoy for fear of being thought common.

If we look within, we are led into misty speculations about the relation of wealth to welfare. If we look without we can observe, through trade figures and family budget studies, what it is that buyers buy. If we want to form an opinion on the economic well-being of a community, we look to such things as the food consumed, the conditions of housing and work-places, the variety of different kinds of goods being consumed (for we know that with rising wealth families purchase more kinds rather than greater quantities of goods). We look to such phenomena as the infant death rate for pointers to the effect of the level of consumption on the health of the community, and to such phenomena as the prevalence of alcoholism and neurosis to judge how great a strain the rules of the game that they are playing put upon human nature.

The contribution made by so-called Welfare Economics to all this is a great elaboration and refinement of the theory of index numbers. But there is no golden rule for index numbers. When it comes to the point, we have to judge as best we may the relevance of any particular method of measuring wealth to the problem in hand, and its success in yielding results that are conformable to common sense.

THE NEO-CLASSICAL THEORY OF WAGES AND PROFITS

The theory of wages and profits which forms the background of neo-classical economic doctrine is somewhat hazy because, first, the main emphasis of the theory is on relative prices, so that problems of output as a whole are little discussed and ill defined; secondly, the strict logic of the theory applies to stationary states while the argument based on it is largely concerned with accumulation,[1] so that it is often hard to know what question is being treated.

So far as it is possible to make it out, the theory appears to have two branches, one developed by Marshall and the other by Wicksell.

According to the Marshallian version[2] there is a certain rate of profit (which governs the rates of interest) representing the supply price of capital. The stock of capital, relative to the supply of labour, tends to be such as to establish this rate of profit. A chance fall in the rate of profit below this level would cause capitalists to consume more than current profits, thus failing to maintain

---

[1] Marshall is quite candid on this point. See *Principles* (7th ed.), p. 460 and Appendix H.

[2] Most clearly stated by Pigou, *The Economics of Stationary States*.

the stock of capital goods by renewals of those wearing out. The consequent fall in the ratio of capital to labour would lower real wages and raise the rate of profit. Conversely, a chance rise in the rate of profit would lead to accumulation, raise the ratio of capital to labour and so depress the rate of profit. Thus, given the available supply of labour and the state of technical knowledge, the stock of capital in equilibrium is such as to establish the required rate of profit. The technique of production is then determined, and total real wages (though this is never stated in so many words) is the residual when the required profit has been subtracted from total output.

According to the version developed by Wicksell the value of the stock of capital in terms of commodities is simply given. The amount of employment offered by a given value of capital depends upon the real-wage rate. At a lower wage rate there is a smaller value of a given type of machine (only Wicksell makes this point clearly and it does not seem to have been properly digested into the teaching of the neo-classical doctrine) [1] and at the same time machines are designed for a less-mechanised technique and embody less capital per unit of labour at a given wage rate. In equilibrium the wage level is such that the value of capital per man is such that the whole available labour force is employed by the given value of capital.

Both versions of the static equilibrium theory are frequently called into play to support the argument that an arbitrary rise in wage rates would cause unemployment, by reducing the total of capital in existence (depressing the rate of profit below the supply price of capital) and by causing what remains to be embodied in forms offering less employment. [2]

A serious difficulty about this argument is that wage bargains are necessarily made in terms of money (generalised purchasing power) and it is not obvious how the real-wage rate can be affected by them under conditions of perfect competition. Before Keynes' *General Theory* it was common simply to take for granted without argument that the wage bargain determines the real-wage rate [3] (this was strikingly inconsistent with the rest of the neo-classical theory, according to which the money prices of commodities are determined by money costs of production and the level of demand

---

[1] For my part, I only became aware that Wicksell had made the point after I had stumbled upon it myself. It is mentioned by C. G. Uhr ('Knut Wicksell, A Centennial Evaluation', *American Economic Review* (December 1951), who calls it the *Wicksell effect*.

[2] For a recent restatement of this point of view see D. H. Robertson, *Wages*, Stamp Memorial Lecture, 1954.

[3] See, *e.g.*, J. R. Hicks, *Theory of Wages*.

in terms of money expenditure).[1] Nowadays it is more usual to insert the assumption that the banking system operates in such a way as to keep the total of money incomes constant when money-wage rates alter.[2] This requires the banking system to raise the rate of interest so as to discourage gross investment and create unemployment when the money-wage rate rises. When the number of workers employed is reduced, the money demand for commodities is raised in a smaller proportion than the money wage per worker; therefore prices rise in a smaller proportion than wage rates, and the real-wage rate is raised. But now the theory seems to have got into a tangle, for the rate of interest has been raised, which is encouraging to saving, while what the argument required was that consumption of capital should be set in train. The attempt to deal with short-period problems on the basis of static equilibrium theory is bound to lead to trouble.

The true meaning of the neo-classical theory seems rather to be that the level of real wages is determined by the conditions of supply of capital and that it cannot be influenced by the wage bargain.

Wicksell's version of the theory has been incorporated into our analysis of golden ages, but there is nothing in our argument to correspond to Marshall's supply price of capital. The notion of supply price belongs to the rentier aspect of capital. The alleged reason why the stock of capital begins to dwindle when the rate of profit falls below the critical level is that capitalists, who 'discount the future', are unwilling to own so much capital when the 'reward of waiting' has been reduced. They are conceived as looking at capital from a rentier point of view, as a source of consumable income, and when income per unit of capital falls they consume part of the pre-existing stock by refraining from replacing worn-out capital goods with new ones of the same value in terms of commodities.

In our argument the entrepreneurial aspect of capital is dominant, and profit is desired mainly as a means of accumulating capital, rather than capital being desired mainly as a means of consuming profit.

It is hard to believe that if the rentier aspect of capitalism had been dominant over the entrepreneurial aspect the system would have been tolerated so long or flourished so well as in fact has been the case.[3]

---

[1] The point is not cleared up in the latest restatement of the theory in Robertson's Stamp Lecture (see above, p. 391, note).

[2] See A. C. Pigou, *Lapses from Full Employment*, and D. H. Robertson, *op. cit.*

[3] Cf. Keynes, *The Economic Consequences of the Peace*, p. 16.

INCOME FROM PROPERTY AS THE REWARD OF WAITING

A large part of political life consists in struggles to get the rules of the game altered in ways which favour one group rather than another, and there has always been going on a great debate (growing violent and embittered in our own day) as to whether, as a whole, the socialist rules or the capitalist rules are to be preferred, on economic grounds (which provides the better fit with the technical possibilities of production) or on moral grounds (which tends to develop the less disagreeable type of human personality). Economists are much concerned with this debate and the presentation of economic theory is coloured (often unconsciously) by political sentiments, which show themselves in the use of language. This is particularly marked in connection with the concept of income from property. The labourer is worthy of his hire. What is it that the owner of property is worthy of?

To suggest an answer, income from property is described as 'the reward of abstinence' or 'the reward of waiting',[1] in reference to the fact that property gives its owner a right to consuming power, so that if he continues to own property he is *abstaining* from using that power. This is often mixed up with the 'reward of saving'. By saving, that is refraining from consuming his current income, an individual can increase his stock of wealth. The 'reward of saving' is an addition to wealth, which, indeed, may carry with it an expectation of additional future income. Present income from property might, perhaps, be described as the reward of having saved in the past, but the saving need not have been performed by the present owner; he may have 'obtained the *de facto* possession of property by inheritance or by any other means moral or immoral, legal or illegal'.[2] Moreover, since saving is mainly out of profit, and real wages tend to be lower the higher the rate of profit, the abstinence associated with saving is mainly done by the workers, who do not receive any share in the 'reward'.

There is a more subtle and elusive notion bound up with the concept of *waiting*. An individual who has lent to a safe debtor has merely to allow time to pass to gather in his agreed interest. Does this correspond to a technical productiveness of the passage of time? Where natural processes are at work, as in the maturing of wine or the growth of trees, production takes place through time, without any expenditure of labour. If all production were of this kind we should be in the land of Cockaigne. Generally production

---

[1] Marshall, *Principles* (7th ed.), p. 233.
[2] *Ibid.* (1st ed.), p. 614.

requires work to be done; work takes time, but time does not do work. It is necessary, where the means of production (space, equipment and materials) are not so abundant as to meet all possible demands for them, that there should be property in them in order that they may be used in an effective manner. If the rules of the game exclude collective property then there must be private property. It is the scarcity of capital goods, not the productiveness of time, which makes income from property possible.[1]

There is, however, a technical sense, independent of the rules of the game, in which investment may be said to be productive. By using labour and means of production in the present to produce equipment it is possible to make a permanent net increase in output per man in the future — that is to say, the excess of the output of a given number of men employed in the future when using the additional equipment, over what it would have been without it, is sufficient to provide for the renewal of the equipment when it wears out and something extra as well. This extra rate of output over the indefinite future is the productivity of the investment.[2] The corresponding future rate of profit is the 'reward' of investment. Since it lies in the future, it can only be estimated, and the estimate may be mistaken. Moreover, additional quasi-rent to one capitalist may be largely or wholly at the expense of others — the new equipment produces a commodity coloured green which drives the pink variety out of the market and deprives old equipment of its earning power. Nevertheless there is, in general, sufficient correspondence between expected additional profit and actual additional output to give meaning (though not precision) to the concept of the social productivity of investment.

In a hazy sort of way the ownership of capital is mixed up with the idea of increasing the stock of capital, so that the moral approbation generally granted to the activities of saving and investing casts a pleasing glow over the activity of receiving interest.

Another strand of thought in this confusing complex is the idea that the rate of interest measures the rate of *discount of the future*. Everyone, it is argued, prefers consumption now to the prospect of consumption at a future date, partly on the rational ground that he may be dead before the date comes and partly from an irrational or weak-minded failure to value the future consumption now at what its true worth to him will turn out to be. Therefore, it is argued, people will not refrain from using purchasing power which they command unless they are assured

[1] Keynes, *General Theory*, p. 213
[2] Cf. above, p. 307.

of more consumption in the future for every bit forgone in the present.

The notion that human beings discount the future certainly seems to correspond to everyone's subjective experience, but the conclusion drawn from it is a *non sequitur*, for most people have enough sense to want to be able to exercise consuming power as long as fate permits, and many people are in the situation of having a higher income in the present than they expect in the future (salary earners will have to retire, business may be better now than it seems likely to be later, etc.), many are in the situation where their need for consuming power will be greater in the future (when their children have to be educated, etc.) and many look beyond their own lifetime and wish to leave consuming power to their heirs. Thus a great many, at any moment, are not only willing to own wealth without consuming it, but are saving in order to increase their wealth [1] and are eagerly looking round for a reliable vehicle to carry purchasing power into the future. Others, indeed, may be consuming wealth, or getting into debt, by overspending their incomes. It is impossible to say what price would rule if there were a market for present *versus* future purchasing power, unaffected by any other influence except the desires of individuals about the time-pattern of their consumption. It might well be that such a market would normally yield a negative rate of discount — the savers predominating over the dissavers, and being willing to sacrifice (if need be) more consumption now for less in the future.[2]

The rate of interest is normally positive for a quite different reason. Present purchasing power is valuable partly because, under the capitalist rules of the game, it permits its owner (directly or by lending to a business concern) to employ labour and undertake production which will yield a surplus of receipts over costs. In an economy in which the rate of profit is expected to be positive, the rate of interest is positive. A positive rate of interest being established, for every individual owner of wealth the present value of purchasing power exceeds its future value to the corresponding extent. It is then proper to arrive at the present value of expected future income by discounting it at the appropriate rate of interest. This has nothing whatever to do with the subjective *rate of discount of the future* of the individual concerned, though it is true that a comparison between his subjective discount rate and the rate of interest obtainable may be said (if he knows how to express himself in such terms) to influence his saving habits.

---

[1] Cf. R. F. Harrod, *Towards a Dynamic Economics*, p. 39.
[2] Cf. above, p. 288, note.

WICKSELL ON CAPITAL

Wicksell's article on Dr. Åkerman's problem [1] is not at all easy reading and the appearance of an English translation of *Value Capital and Rent* calls back to notice a simpler exposition which helps to make clear both the penetrating nature of Wicksell's contribution to the theory of capital and its limitations.

Wicksell follows Böhm-Bawerk in using the *length of the period of production* to stand for what we have called the *degree of mechanisation*. Even when he brings fixed capital into the argument, in the example of axes, he thinks of a rise in the real-capital ratio as being due only to investing in *more durable* axes.[2] This is not a point of major importance; an increase in the length of the period of production or in durability of plant are special cases of an increase in the degree of mechanisation, and Wicksell uses them only as a simple illustration of the general case.

Wicksell points out that the length of the period of production does not by itself determine the ratio of capital to labour, because the value of capital required for a given method of production depends on the real-wage rate.[3] This is a much more fundamental criticism of Böhm-Bawerk's theory than the objection that the length of the period of production is an over-simplified way of representing the real-capital ratio. As we have seen, this point of Wicksell's is the key to the whole theory of accumulation and of the determination of wages and profits.

On the other hand, Wicksell's account, in his *Lectures* [4] of the manner in which a rise in the real-wage rate leads to a lengthening of the period of production (a rise in the degree of mechanisation) is somewhat mystifying; and in *Value Capital and Rent* [5] it seems to be erroneous; for there he makes it turn on the fact that, because interest enters into the cost of capital goods, 'the price of machines can consequently never rise in the same proportion as wages'. This is a red herring. Even if the price (in terms of product) of each type of machine rises fully in proportion to the real-wage rate (as in our simplified numerical illustration, page 107, note) it is still true that the rate of profit falls by less, when wages rise, for machines that yield a higher, than for those that yield a lower, rate of output per man employed. The reason is simply that profit per man employed is the difference between proceeds and wages per man,

---

[1] 'Real Capital and Interest', included in Vol. I of *Lectures*, English ed.
[2] *Lectures*, Vol. I, p. 276.
[3] *Value Capital and Rent*, English ed., p. 137, and *Lectures*, Vol. I, p.148 and p. 268.
[4] P. 162.

and a given rise in wages reduces the difference in a greater proportion where proceeds per man are less.

Wicksell (as is natural in path-breaking work) leaves his model in a somewhat disjointed condition. He divides the whole stock of capital in a static state into durable equipment which is given and fixed, item by item, and a quantity of capital given in terms of product, which can be invested in different forms. This is admittedly quite arbitrary, and it is perfectly clear what it means so long as the product retains its physical identity — a quantity of corn which is eaten and reproduced from year to year. But he jumps too fast over the problem of what the given *quantity* of capital means when there are two commodities (corn and linen) whose prices vary in terms of each other.[1] He does not explain how or why a group of capitalists who, at one moment, command a quantity of capital given in terms of linen keep their capital constant in terms of corn when the corn-linen price alters.

The main difficulty presented by Wicksell's analysis is that he seems to be discussing in the same breath a comparison between static states with different quantities of capital and a process of accumulation going on through time As we have found, his fundamental proposition is equally important in both branches of the argument, but it cannot be well understood unless they are kept separate.

THE NATURAL RATE OF INTEREST

In a golden age the concept of the 'natural rate of interest' (as we find it in Marshall and Wicksell)[2] comes back into its own. The 'natural rate of interest' is the rate of profit on capital[3] and in a golden age the rate of profit has a definite and unambiguous meaning.

In a golden age the level of interest rates is governed by the rate of profit; given the rate of profit appropriate to a particular golden age there is only one level of interest rates that can obtain without destroying the golden-age conditions, for if interest were too low excess-investment (financed by external borrowing) would

---

[1] *Ibid.* p. 153.

[2] Marshall's views are scattered over the evidence to several Royal Commissions (*Official Papers*). Wicksell's position is stated in *Interest and Prices*.

[3] 'The average rate of discount is determined by the average level of interest [the average over the long run of rates ruling at different times], in my opinion, and that is determined exclusively by the profitableness of business.' Marshall, Minutes of Evidence before the Gold and Silver Commission, *Official Papers*, p. 41.

be stimulated so much as to create inflation, and if it were too high investment would be brought to a halt. Unfortunately this provides only a theory of what the level of interest rates would have to be to satisfy the conditions of a golden age, not a theory of what it is likely to be in the far from golden age in which we live.

A great part of Keynes's argument in the *General Theory* was concerned with showing that interest rates may get stuck at too high a level, and to persuading people that it is then both possible and desirable to get them down.

This, though it required a great deal of argument to break through received ideas, was a relatively superficial layer in his diagnosis of the causes of unemployment. Far more important is the fact that the maintenance of full employment requires a sufficient urge to keep investment going, and that the influence of the rate of interest (even if it were managed with the greatest possible skill and wisdom by the monetary authorities) is not strong enough to govern the rate of investment when that urge is lacking. We cannot turn our age into a golden one merely by controlling interest rates.

The objection to Keynes's treatment is that it seems to leave no place for the influence upon interest rates of the 'fundamental phenomena of Productivity and Thrift'.[1] Productivity is a characteristic of a stock of physical resources already in being, while thrift is connected with increases in the stock of capital in terms of value, so that it is hard to bring them to bear upon each other. But in a certain sense the productivity of investment is governed by the potential growth ratio of an economy.[2] If productivity may be taken to mean the growth ratio of a golden-age economy, then productivity and thrift may be said to determine the golden-age rate of profit. When there is a hundred per cent saving of profits (as in our first model) the rate of profit is equal to the growth ratio, and the growth ratio is determined by the fundamental phenomena of population growth and technical progress combined with the phenomenon of entrepreneurs who accumulate at the appropriate rate. When there is consumption out of profits, the rate of profit in a golden age of a given growth ratio is higher the greater the proportion of profits consumed. The less thrifty are the capitalists (entrepreneurs and rentiers combined) the higher is the rate of profit at which the rate of saving appropriate to the growth ratio is forthcoming. Given thrift, the required rate of profit is higher the higher the growth ratio.

If we imagine that the tranquillity of a golden age is perfect,

[1] D. H. Robertson, *Essays in Monetary Theory*, p. 25.
[2] See p. 173.

not only in the large but for every individual, we must suppose
that there is no liquidity preference. The supply price of loans
would then be equal to the discount rate which covers the expenses
of the banks in their capacity as providers of a medium of exchange.
But this rate of interest would be, in general, much below the
rate of profit, and could not be allowed to rule for fear of inflation.
The authorities would have to set the rate of interest at the level
at which entrepreneurs are just willing to do an amount of outside
borrowing which corresponds to the rate of outside 'saving that is
forthcoming when income is running at the golden-age level.[1] This
fully satisfies the requirements of a theory based on productivity
and thrift (with the amendment suggested above as the meaning
of productivity).

In a golden age which is somewhat untranquil from the point
of view of individuals though tranquil in the large, rentiers would
desire to keep some part of their wealth in the form of bank deposits,
in order to be able to meet sudden calls for unusual expenditure
without having to sell placements (this is what Keynes calls the
precautionary motive for holding money). This demand for
deposits would be influenced to some extent by the level of yields
of placements (the sacrifice of income for the sake of convenience
being greater the higher the level), but it is unlikely to vary very
much over any reasonable range of rates of interest. It is the
business of the banks to see to it that there is a total amount of
deposits that will satisfy this demand at the level of interest rates
required by the golden-age conditions.

At any particular moment, that level of interest rates has been
steady ever since the golden age set in, and is expected to last. It
therefore maintains itself from day to day, for any chance divergence
upwards would lead rentiers to turn bullish and buy placements
with their precautionary balances (in the expectation of a quick
capital profit when the rates relapse to their former level) and a
chance fall would be prevented by bearish sales of placements (this
is what Keynes calls the speculative element in liquidity preference).

In an untranquil world there is, at any moment, a low level
of interest such that, if it obtained, inflation would set in (though
in depressed conditions this may be much lower than any possible
actual level; it might require a subsidy in the form of negative
interest to get entrepreneurs to take the risks of investment to an extent
sufficient to generate an excess demand for labour) and a high level
such that if it obtained it would be regarded as intolerable and
some kind of reaction would set in to get it brought down. These

---

[1] Lenders then enjoy an 'economic rent' — an excess of receipts over
the supply prices of the loans that they provide.

two levels, which are governed, roughly speaking, by the prospect of profit on investment, are all that remains of the 'natural rate of interest' in an untranquil world.

Actual interest rates must be somewhere between these two levels. Where they lie (within the possible range) is governed by interactions between liquidity preference and monetary policy, and liquidity preference in turn is governed by expectations about what those interactions are believed likely to be.

Looking at the matter in a philosophical light, the reason why there is a demand for loans at a positive rate of interest is that there is a rate of profit on investment; the supply price of loans of good security is governed by the yield of existing placements, and the yield of placements is positive because the relation between liquidity preference and the supply of money is such as to keep it so.

SAVINGS AND INVESTMENT

There has been a great deal of confused controversy about the proposition that the rate of saving is equal to the rate of investment. If total income, over any arbitrary period of time, considered from the point of view of how it is earned, is divided exhaustively into that which is derived from outlay on consumption and that from outlay on investment; and, looked at from the point of view of how it is used, into that which is spent on consumption and that which is saved, then for any period the saving is equal to the investment. There is a great deal of room for dispute about the most useful definitions of the words *income, consumption, saving* and *investment,* and it is possible to define income in such a way that it would not be true to say (when using the word in that sense) that saving and investment are equal. This concerns the dictionary.

Now comes an argument. *A* says that a decision to save at a higher rate on the part of the public (the rate of investment remaining constant) will cause saving to exceed investment and that consequently the rate of interest will fall. *B* replies that this is an error because (on his definition) savings are necessarily equal to investment. *A* points out that this is a *non sequitur,* for the definitions of words cannot tell us anything about how the economic system behaves. *A* then concludes that, since his critic is at fault, therefore his original proposition was correct. This also is a *non sequitur.*

The point underlying all the verbal cross-purposes is whether decisions to invest govern the rate at which saving takes place, or whether decisions on the part of individuals to refrain from consumption in order to save govern the rate of investment. According to the capitalist rules of the game it is the business of entrepreneurs to take the initiative in organising investment; at the same time it is obvious that there is, at any moment, an absolute upper limit to the possible rate of investment set by the gap between maximum possible total output and the level to which consumption can be squeezed down. The more thrifty the community is, the bigger the gap, or the smaller the pressure required to produce a given gap. Experience shows that it is only rarely (say, in war time) that the gap is approximately filled in capitalist economies (it is rare for the economy to be continually pressing up to the inflation barrier).[1] Thus it is normally true to say that if the rate of investment decided upon by entrepreneurs were higher, income (on any reasonable definition of income) would be higher and the rate of saving (on any reasonable definition of saving) would be greater. This is not a tautological statement. If it is to be attacked, it must be attacked for lack of relevance, not lack of logic.

The mistake seems to have arisen from the view that entrepreneurs are closely limited, in their investment plans, by the supply of finance (which is a logical possibility but does not appear to be in fact the case) and that refraining from consumption provides finance, which seems to be a pure confusion.[2]

So far as the dictionary is concerned, there is a lot to be said for returning to the usage of the *Treatise on Money* and defining terms in such a way that there may be differences between the saving made in any arbitrary period (say a year) and the value of investment made in that period. Income, as we have seen, is a highly ambiguous concept, but receipts during a period of time are much less so. Let us draw a clear line between firms (entrepreneurs) and members of the public (workers, rentiers and the professions), and a clear line between outlay on investment and outlay on consumption goods (border-line cases such as an individual having a private house built for himself may be placed on either side provided that it is done in a consistent manner). Saving may then be defined as the difference between receipts and outlay for the public (excluding firms). The outlay of firms (costs of production, payments of interest, rent, etc., and distribution of profits) is the receipts of the public. The outlay of the public (purchases of consumption goods) is the receipts of the firms. The outlay of the public in any period (say a year) is normally less than their receipts, because they are saving, and the outlay of the firms is normally greater than their receipts because they are investing in excess of their retained profits. They are compensated for this excess by the value of the capital goods acquired. An excess of saving over the value of

[1] It is less rare for a particular country to be suffering from balance of payments difficulties. See above, p. 53.   [2] See below, p. 403.

A.C.—O

investment is therefore a loss to firms (or an over-distribution of profits relatively to earnings), matched by an increase in outside obligations relatively the value of assets, and an excess of investment over saving is an undistributed profit to the firms, matched by an increase in assets relatively to obligations.

THE SUPPLY OF LOANABLE FUNDS

The supply of finance available at any moment cannot be given a definite quantitative meaning. It would be possible to define it in an economy where there was a definite set of individuals endowed with the character of entrepreneurs, who alone plan and organise schemes of investment, and where each one of them, at a given moment, had command of a definite quantity of uncommitted purchasing power (liquid reserves) and a definite schedule of borrowing power, including in that conception his power to market new issues of shares. There would then be a definite but extremely complicated multi-dimensional function relating the supply of finance to a complex of rates of interest for different borrowers, similar to the supply curve of a commodity produced under conditions of imperfect competition.

Credit (borrowing power), however, is in reality very amorphous, and anyone who commands wealth is a potential entrepreneur, so that no such definite account of the conditions of supply of finance can be given.

It is possible to talk, however, of greater or less ease in the supply of finance, meaning, in a short-period sense, a better or worse state of confidence, making borrowing easier or harder, or in a long-period sense, a better or worse organisation of the financial system, improving or impairing the access of potential entrepreneurs to potential lenders.

The expression the 'supply of loanable funds' as we find it in recent literature [1] does not seem to be referring to anything like the above. It sometimes appears to mean the real resources available for investment, that is, roughly, the excess of the total supply of labour over the part engaged in producing for consumption; sometimes to mean the total amount of funds available for holding debts and shares — that is, the total of private wealth *minus* the value of land and the supply of gold. (Currency notes and bank deposits represent holdings of debt at second hand. The owner is the creditor of a bank which in turn is the creditor of government

[1] D. H. Robertson, *Essays on Monetary Theory*; A. Hansen, *A Guide to Keynes*, chapter 7; W. Fellner, *Monetary Policies and Full Employment*, pp. 140 *et seq.*

or industry.) And sometimes to mean the total of funds available for holding debts and shares outside the banking system, that is the total of wealth *minus* land and the supply of money. Moreover, sometimes it appears to mean a stock of something in existence at a moment of time and sometimes a flow of something coming forward through time. In short, its meanings are so various and confusing that all you can do, as Gogol says, is spit and cross your self.

THE QUANTITY THEORY OF MONEY

The point of the Quantity Theory as we find it, for instance, in Hume,[1] was to combat vulgarised mercantilism and to show that money is not wealth : Double the quantity of money, and you only double prices ; no one is really any the richer.

When turned round into a positive theory of the determination of the price level, it exhibits an interesting and instructive example of wrong methodology.

In its simplest form, $MV = PT$, T is an index of the transactions taking place in a period of time, P an index of prices, M a quantity of money, and V the average number of times a unit of that money enters into transactions during the period.

We ask : What is money, in the relevant sense ? Answer : Legal tender money and bank deposits. We ask : Does it include time deposits or only current accounts ? What is the difference between drawing a cheque on a bank account and drawing a bill of exchange ? Answer : This is mere logic chopping. All economic categories are to some extent arbitrary. Let us agree to call money whatever in fact is used as a medium of exchange in making transactions. Then it is obvious that the formula is correct.

Certainly, but then it has no causal significance whatever. On the other hand, if we define M as the quantity of any particular type of medium of exchange (say, notes, coins and deposits with banks of a specified type), then we must define V by means of the equation $PT/M = V$. If for any reason PT increases, while M on our definition remains constant, then V has risen. But this is a completely hollow statement. First, more transactions than formerly may have been settled through media other than our M (say, by transferring accounts by book entries between businesses, or by exchanging goods of all kinds for cigarettes). Second, even if we know for a fact that all transactions in both the periods being compared were made with our M, still the statement that V has increased is of very limited significance (and what significance it has is connected with the money market and the rate of interest rather than

[1] 'Of Money', *Essays Moral, Political and Literary.*

the price level); it merely shows that some M formerly lying in an inactive account (where it represented the title to someone's quasi-permanent wealth) has moved into an active account (where it represents a temporary balance lodged for a short period between the receipt of income and its disbursement).

Alternately, if we define V so that it stands upon its own legs, as the average number of transactions in a period made by a unit of whatever media are used for transactions, we have to define M by the equation $PT/V = M$. The supply of money then cannot be tied down to any particular category of titles to wealth, but covers everything entering into the transactions included in T.

The formula seems to tell us that PT cannot increase unless either there is an increase in the supply of some specified media of exchange, or a change in the habits governing the rate of circulation of some type of medium of exchange. But it does not tell us this; for, if we define M, V breaks loose and becomes undefinable (except as a residual quantity making the equation formally correct) or if we define V, then M breaks loose and becomes undefinable.

The all-too-common methodological trap that the argument has fallen into is to provide definitions for words more exact than the facts to which they correspond, and then to seek for light on causal relations not from the facts but from the words.

MR. HARROD'S DYNAMICS

Our analysis of accumulation in the long run is largely an elaboration of R. F. Harrod's model,[1] yet we have nowhere come across his central problem. It is interesting to inquire why this should be.

Harrod's problem, if I have understood him, is as follows: Given the ratio of saving to income, there is, at any moment, a rate of investment which will ensure a sufficient level of demand to 'leave producers content with what they have done'.[2] Exactly how this rate of investment is determined is not very clear, but we may take it to be one which generates just such a degree of seller's market as to make entrepreneurs want to continue investing. That is to say, it is sufficient to absorb the rate of saving which corresponds to the level of income that obtains when output is running well up to capacity. This rate of investment, if undertaken, causes the stock of capital to increase at a certain rate. Given the ratio of capital to income, this causes income to grow at a certain rate. This is the *warranted rate of growth* — the rate of growth of income warranted by the thriftiness of the economy. Given the capital ratio, it is higher the higher the ratio of savings to income.

[1] *Towards a Dynamic Economics.* [2] *Op. Cit.* p. 86.

The maximum possible long-run rate of growth, which Harrod calls the *natural rate*, is dictated by population growth and technical progress (which is assumed neutral and proceeding at a steady foreseen rate). This rate of growth requires a certain rate of investment to implement it.

Harrod's problem is that these two rates of investment are determined by quite different causes (the one by thriftiness and the other by technical conditions) and there is no reason to expect them to coincide. They could be equal only by a fluke and when they are not equal the economy is continually tormented by the conflict between them.

The natural rate is what we have called the potential growth ratio of a golden-age economy. We have argued that, provided (1) that the basic conditions of a golden age — neutrality of technical progress, constancy of the savings ratio, etc. — are fulfilled, (2) that the growth ratio does not require a rate of investment which, together with the concomitant consumption out of profits, absorbs more than the whole surplus of production over what is accepted as a tolerable rate of real wages and (3) that entrepreneurs have been consistently carrying it out in the past so that the stock of capital is adjusted to it, and are continuing to carry it out in the present, a golden age is, in principle, possible, and we have had no trouble from a warranted rate independently determined.

Harrod agrees pretty well with our provisos. He postulates neutral technical progress and a constant saving ratio. He admits the possibility that the warranted rate may be too low to permit the natural rate to be realised. (This he regards as a problem for backward economies.) He pays great attention to the third proviso. A large part of his argument is concerned with the fact that, if entrepreneurs are investing at less than the warranted rate, effective demand is too low to keep them content and the economy falls into a slump, while if they invest at a greater rate they create boom conditions which cannot last. But for him a problem remains when the three provisos are fulfilled.

What difference between our argument and his accounts for the fact that no such problem appears in our model?

The difference is concerned with the determination of Harrod's two basic ratios, the ratio of saving to income and the ratio of income to capital.

We have treated the ratio of saving to income as determined by (1) saving out of profits and saving out of wages (2) the distribution of income between profits and wages. We have assumed for simplicity zero saving out of wages. But this is not essential. If workers and rentiers families were equally thrifty it would still be true that the ratio of consumption to income would be considerably higher in respect to wages than in respect to profits, for the rentiers do not receive the whole of profits. A substantial proportion of profits is retained by entrepreneurs to build up reserves and to finance investment.

Given the propensity to save of each class taken separately, a higher share of wages, which entails a lower share of profit, in total income means a higher proportion of total consumption to total income. The amount of saving forthcoming from a given total income is less, in any given state of technique, the higher the real-wage rate.

The amount of investment required to implement the potential growth ratio is also influenced by the real-wage rate. The cost of a machine of a given type in terms of money of a constant purchasing power over commodities may be higher or lower at a higher wage rate. However, when the cost of the machine is lower at a higher than at a lower wage rate, because of the influence of the correspondingly lower notional interest rate on its cost in terms of labour time, the share of profit is all the lower (at a higher wage rate) and the effect upon saving all the stronger.

Thus, with a given degree of mechanisation, the amount of saving forthcoming is less relatively to the amount of investment required to maintain growth, at a higher real-wage rate, even when the ratio of value of capital to income is less.

Introducing the spectrum of techniques into the argument is a complication. A higher real-wage rate entails a higher degree of mechanisation, and this may (though it need not) mean a larger share of profits in the value of output (more capital per head outweighing a lower rate of profit per unit of capital), but at the same time it makes the amount of investment required to implement the potential growth ratio greater. The proportionate rise in the capital ratio exceeds the proportionate rise in the share of profit. Thus the latter effect must outweigh the former.

Therefore, subject to the three provisos being fulfilled, there is a possible golden age corresponding to any combination of propensities to save with technical conditions. In a golden age the actual rate of growth and the natural rate of growth are equal to each other, and the warranted rate of growth has accommodated itself to them. The relation between the propensities to save and the technical conditions determine the rate of profit at which the natural rate of growth of the economy can be realised.

The important distinction is that between the *actual* and the *natural* rate of growth when the third proviso is not fulfilled.

INNOVATIONS UNDER MONOPOLY
AND COMPETITION

In a competitive industry operating at capacity with subjective normal prices ruling, progressive firms instal Beta technique during the lifetime of Beta-minus capital goods. An entrepreneur with part-worn Beta-minus plant has to accept quasi-rents which yield a lower rate of profit on the historic cost of his plant than that being enjoyed by the progressive firms, whose costs are lower. It does not pay him to scrap the plant so long as it yields any quasi-rent at all (any excess of annual proceeds over annual prime cost excluding user-cost). When the price of the commodity concerned falls to prime cost per unit of output he must instal new plant or go out of business. Other entrepreneurs, whose Beta-minus plant has reached the end of its life, instal Beta technique, and the price of the commodity gradually falls. If the subjective-normal price (which covers total average cost and an allowance for profit on the cost of investment at the ruling expected rate) with Beta technique is less than prime cost with Beta-minus, prices fall to Beta-minus prime cost during the process of diffusion of the new technique, and some Beta-minus plant is scrapped before the end of its physical life.

It is sometimes argued that a monopolist presented with the blue-prints of a new technique would act on the same principle, installing new plant if average cost per unit of his monopolised commodity with the new technique is less than the prime cost with his existing plant. This argument appears to be fallacious. The monopolist is not obliged to lower his price because a lower-cost technique has been invented. The criterion for him is that the saving of prime cost on a year's output (due to using Beta instead of Beta-minus technique) should yield a rate of profit on the new investment as great as he can get in any other way. If he is confined for some reason to producing only this commodity, then he would find it worth while to make the substitution provided that average cost with the new technique, including interest on the finance required, is less than prime cost with the old; but in the normal way a monopolist can keep his old plant going and make any new investment that he wants to in something else. Only if cost saving for this commodity is the most attractive investment open to him will he scrap his plant before its physical life is over. For this reason the view that monopoly does not tend to retard the diffusion of innovations seems ill founded.

DIAGRAMS

DIAGRAMS

THE following diagrams illustrate those parts of the foregoing analysis that can be expressed in two dimensions. It is impossible to illustrate in one plane both relations (such as the ratio of capital to labour) and movements through time (such as the accumulation of capital). Relations can be illustrated in terms of comparisons of static positions. For this purpose we imagine that we are comparing positions in each of which the stock of capital goods is being maintained, item by item, and the flow of output is being consumed. Differences in annual profits are accounted for by differences in the expenditure of rentiers. Output consists of commodities produced in fixed proportions, and is measured in units of a composite commodity consisting of a representative sample of production.

THE TECHNICAL FRONTIER

The basic diagram to illustrate the relations of labour and capital is adapted from that used by Wicksell.[1] The vertical axis represents output per annum measured in units of the composite commodity. The horizontal axis represents stocks of capital goods measured in terms of the labour time required to produce them, reckoned at a given notional rate of interest. The amount of labour currently employed is taken to be constant, so that the vertical axis represents output per man-year and the horizontal axis represents the real-capital ratio. In a given static position with a given rate of profit which has long been ruling and is expected to rule in the future, we may represent the spectrum of known techniques in terms of output per head and the real-capital ratio, when the notional rate of interest entering into the cost of capital goods is equal to the rate of profit. OA is the output per man-year produced when all workers are employed with Alpha technique ; OB the output with Beta technique, OC the output with Gamma technique and OD with Delta technique. Ob is the cost in terms of labour time, at a notional rate of interest equal to the ruling rate of profit, of an outfit of capital goods which employs a man with Beta technique. Between Oc and Ob lie stocks of capital goods with a rising

[1] *Value Capital and Rent*, p. 122.

proportion of Beta outfits to Gamma outfits, so that *CB* represents the difference in output per man due to using Beta rather than Gamma technique, and *cb* represents the increase in the real-capital ratio involved by that difference. The curve $\delta\gamma\beta\alpha$ is a *productivity curve* showing the relation between output and the real-capital ratio when capital is reckoned at the given notional interest rate.

In the situation illustrated in Fig. 1 the real-wage rate is such that Gamma and Beta technique yield the same rate of profit. The wage rate, which is represented by *OW*, is what we have called Gamma-Beta wage rate. *WC* represents annual profit per man employed when only Gamma technique is in use, and *WB* when only Beta is in use. The value of capital per man in terms of product for Gamma technique is *OW.Oc* and the rate of profit is *WC/OW.Oc*. For Beta technique the value of capital per man is

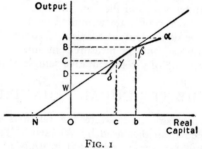

FIG. 1

OW.Ob and the rate of profit *OB/OW.Ob*. Since *OW* is the wage rate at which these two rates of profit are equal, the slope of *Wγ* and *Wβ* are the same, and *Wγβ* lies on a straight line.

As the real-capital ratio increases from *Oc* to *Ob* profit increases proportionately (from *WC* to *WB*) and the rate of profit is constant. A higher real-capital ratio would require a switch to Alpha technique and at the wage *OW* profit would increase less than in proportion to the value of capital. A lower ratio, requiring Delta technique, would reduce profit more than in proportion to the reduction in value of capital. At the wage rate *OW* Gamma and Beta technique are indifferent to the individual entrepreneur and Alpha and Delta are not eligible.

The slope of the line *Wγβ* (*WC/Oc*) represents the Gamma-Beta marginal product of investment. The rate of profit is the marginal product of investment divided by the real-wage rate.

βW is produced to cut the horizontal axis in *N*. It can be shown that the rate of profit corresponding to the wage *OW* is represented by 1/*ON*. When output is *OC*, profit is *WC*, the value of capital

is $OW.Oc$ and the rate of profit is $WC/OW.Oc$.   Since OW/ON
is equal to WC/Oc, $WC/OW.Oc = 1/ON$.

In our first model we assumed no consumption out of profits,
and the level of profits was accounted for by the rate of accumulation.   We are now illustrating static states and accounting for
profit by the consumption of rentiers.   For the economy to be in
static equilibrium with the real-capital ratio shown by Ob, there has
to be a rate of consumption per annum by rentiers per man employed shown by WB.   Similarly when the real-capital ratio is
Oc rentiers' consumption per man employed is WC.

This diagram shows the possible positions of static equilibrium
compatible with the wage rate OW.   We can now proceed to compare positions with different wage rates.   The technical conditions
are constant.   The rate of output corresponding to each technique
is the same irrespective of the wage rate, and the outfits of capital

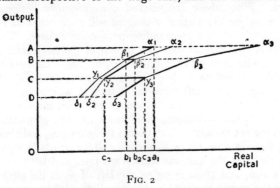

FIG. 2

goods required for each technique are the same from an engineering
point of view.   But if a different wage rate is (and long has been)
ruling there is a different rate of profit and therefore a different
notional interest rate.   The productivity curve therefore has to be
redrawn for each rate of profit to exhibit the difference in the
real-capital ratio due to a different element of interest in the cost
in terms of labour time of a given outfit of capital goods.

In Fig. 2 there are three productivity curves corresponding to
three rates of profit, the curves for lower rates of profit lying to
the left of those for higher rates.   The difference between the real-
capital ratio required for Beta technique when the rate of profit is
that consonant with the Gamma-Beta wage rate and when it is that
consonant with the Beta-Alpha wage rate is $Ob_2 - Ob_1$ or $\beta_1\beta_2$.
Similarly the real-capital ratio for Gamma technique at the Gamma-
Beta wage rate is Oc_2 and at the Delta-Gamma wage rate is Oc_3,
the difference being $\gamma_2\gamma_3$.   The thick line represents all the positions

of static equilibrium which are possible in the given technical conditions with a range of wage rates from the Delta-Gamma wage rate to one somewhat above the Beta-Alpha wage rate. This may be called a real-capital-ratio curve.[1]

Given the technical conditions, depicted in a family of productivity curves each corresponding to a different notional interest rate, the real-capital-ratio curve can be constructed as follows. Take any value of ON (as in Fig. 1) and select the productivity curve appropriate to the rate of interest $1/ON$. Draw a tangent from N to that curve. Any point lying both on the tangent and the curve represents a possible position of equilibrium which could obtain when the wage rate is such as to make the rate of profit equal to $1/ON$. By continuously varying the value of $'ON$ from zero to infinity the real-capital-ratio curve can be traced from the position at which wages are zero to the position at which profits are zero. When there are marked discontinuities between techniques, as in our illustration, a tangent will most often be found to touch an angle in its corresponding productivity curve. The point of potential equilibrium then lies in one of the horizontal bars on the real-capital ratio curve, such as $\gamma_3\gamma_2$ or $\beta_2\beta_1$. Between any pair of equilibrium points with different ordinates (showing different rates of output per man) there lies a tangent which coincides with a stretch of its corresponding productivity curve, indicating a wage rate at which two techniques yield the same rate of profit. Thus between the set of equilibrium points lying on $\gamma_3\gamma_2$ and those lying on $\beta_2\beta_1$ there is a stretch, $\gamma_2\beta_2$ showing all the points of equilibrium compatible with the Gamma-Beta wage rate, and between the set lying on $\beta_2\beta_1$ and those lying to the left of α_1 is the stretch, $\beta_1\alpha_1$ showing the points compatible with the Beta-Alpha wage rate.

[1] The traditional 'production function' shows output as a function of labour and 'capital' without specifying the units in which 'capital' is measured. It purports to exhibit the purely technical relations between labour, capital and output. Technical relations are shown by any one of our productivity curves. But the 'production function' also purports to show the relation between wages and profits which gives equilibrium in a given state of technical knowledge. This cannot be deduced from a productivity curve, for each curve is drawn for a particular rate of interest. Given the technical conditions, we have to know the real-wage rate (or the rate of profit) as a separate datum (dependent in a static state on the thriftiness of rentiers) in order to determine within what range of real-capital ratios the possible positions of equilibrium lie. When the steps in the hierarchy of techniques are very small the range of positions compatible with a given wage rate is very narrow. We may then say that the technical conditions and the wage rate determine the equilibrium position. Or if we know the equilibrium position, the wage rate is determined. The basic fallacy on which the 'production function' is erected is the idea that the marginal product of labour determines the wage rate.

Substituting consumption by rentiers for the wages of men employed on net investment, we can use this diagram to illustrate the comparisons of golden-age economies set out in Chapter 12.

Alaph lies to the left of the point α_1. Alaph-Beth and Beth Alaph lie on the line $\beta_1\alpha_1$, towards the upper and lower ends respectively. Upper Beth lies a little to the right of β_1 and Lower Beth a little to left of β_2, Gimmel lies between γ_2 and γ_3.

Fig. 3 shows the relationship between the real-capital ratio and the ratio of capital in terms of value to labour. In the upper half of the diagram the horizontal axis represents real-capital and in the lower half value of capital in terms of commodities. $OW_{\beta\alpha}$

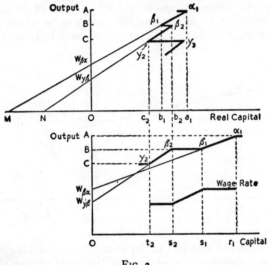

FIG. 3

is the Beta-Alpha wage rate, and $OW_{\gamma\beta}$ the Gamma-Beta wage rate. $1/OM$ and $1/ON$ are the corresponding rates of profit. Oc_2 is the real-capital ratio when all labour is employed with Gamma technique and Ot_2 is the corresponding value of capital in terms of commodities. Similarly Ob_2 and Os_2 correspond to Beta technique. We take the distance $OW_{\gamma\beta}$ as the unit for capital in terms of value on the lower axis and use a scale which makes the distance Ob_2 equal to Os_2 and therefore Oc_2 equal to Ot_2. The two straight lines $\gamma_2\beta_2$ are then identical.

The difference in the value of capital between γ_2 and β_2 (represented by t_2s_2) is accounted for by the difference between the outfits of capital goods required for Gamma and Beta technique. The difference between the value of capital at β_2 and β_1 (s_2s_1) is accounted for by the higher wage rate combined with the lower notional interest rate consonant with it.

A two-dimensional diagram cannot illustrate changes in relations taking place in time, but by mentally projecting it into a three-dimensional construction with time at right angles to the page we can visualise a movement from a position vertically behind a point in the diagram to a position vertically in front of another point, the distance between the two points in the dimension at right angles to the page representing the time taken by the transition from one point to another.

The output axis in our diagrams is measured in units of commodities and cannot represent changing ratios of investment to consumption. We can imagine investment to be taking place, so to say, off-stage while the diagram depicts output per head in terms

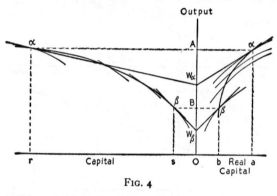

FIG. 4

of commodities of that part of the labour force which is engaged in producing a flow of output of commodities while keeping the corresponding stock of capital goods intact. On this basis we may use the above diagram to illustrate the argument of Chapter 14. The movement from Ot_2 to Os_2 represents the Gamma-Beta period of accumulation at a constant wage rate and the movement from Os_2 to Os_1 represents the Beta period with the wage rate rising from $W_{\gamma\beta}$ to $W_{\beta\alpha}$ and the rate of profit falling from $1/ON$ to $1/OM$.

When the hierarchy of techniques is very dense, so that the degree of mechanisation can change by very small steps the angularities of the curves corresponding to changes in the rate of profit are smoothed out. Both the productivity curves and the real-capital-ratio curve can then be drawn as smooth continuous curves, as in Fig. 4. The output OB, OA, etc., and the potential equilibrium positions β, α, etc., then do not represent adjacent techniques.

Between each pair of positions marked in the diagram there is a range of possible positions corresponding to intermediate rates of profit. We represent real capital in the right-hand part of the diagram and value of capital in the left hand.

Corresponding to each of the family of productivity curves on the right hand is what we may call a pseudo-productivity curve on the left hand, showing what the value of capital per man would be if the wage rate were that which is compatible with the rate of interest used in drawing the corresponding productivity curve. Each pseudo-productivity curve has a meaning only in the neighbourhood of the point of equilibrium corresponding to the wage rate on the basis of which it is drawn.

The real-capital-ratio curve cuts the family of productivity

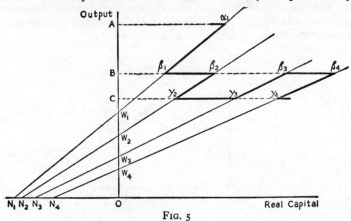

FIG. 5

curves from below as it rises. The value-capital-ratio curve cuts the pseudo-productivity curves from above.

The point β on each curve corresponds to the output OB. Draw a tangent to the productivity curve through β. Its intercept on the product axis, OW_β, is the wage rate at which the corresponding technique will be in use. As before, we take OW_β as the unit for the value of capital axis, so that the tangent to the pseudo-productivity curve through β on the value-capital-ratio curve is drawn as identical with that to the productivity curve through β on the real-capital-ratio curve. The elasticity of the tangent, $W_\beta B/OB$, is the ratio of profit to output, or relative share of capital in product.

Similarly, draw tangents at α. The elasticity of the pair of tangents is the same, the greater distance to the left of the left-hand position of α compensating for the smaller slope of the tangent.

The slope of the tangent on the left ($W_\alpha A/A\alpha$) is the rate of profit on capital.

Fig. 5 illustrates a real-capital-ratio curve containing a 'perverse' relationship in which a lower rate of profit corresponds to a less mechanised technique. As the real-wage rate rises from OW_4 to OW_1 and the rate of profit falls from $1/ON_4$ to $1/ON_1$, the system moves from a position where Gamma and Beta techniques are equally profitable and accumulation is raising the degree of mechanisation from Gamma to Beta, passes through a range over which Beta technique alone is used, and then comes into a range where once more Beta and Gamma are equally profitable, but the degree of mechanisation is falling from Beta to Gamma. For rates of wages higher than OW_3 (with rates of profit lower thán $1/ON_3$) the relations are 'normal', and at OW_2 the degree of mechanisation begins to rise again. With discontinuities smoothed out the real-capital-ratio curve would appear as in Fig. 6.

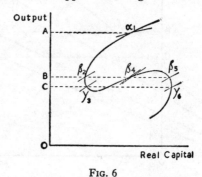

FIG. 6

TECHNICAL PROGRESS

Using once more the device of projecting a plane diagram into three dimensions with time at right angles to the page, we can illustrate the development of a golden-age economy with neutral technical progress. In Fig. 7 the productivity curve through β belongs to the state of technical knowledge at a particular date. The rate of profit is $1/ON$ and the real-capital ratio is OF. The three higher productivity curves represent a superior state of technical knowledge, obtaining at a later date. The curve through β_+ is drawn on the basis of a notional interest rate equal to the rate of profit $1/ON$, the curve through γ_+ for a higher rate of profit and that through α_+ for a lower rate of profit. The relations between the β and β_+ productivity curves show that technical progress has been neutral. β_+ technique is that which is chosen (in the later situation) at the β rate of profit $(1/ON)$ and this technique requires the same real-capital ratio (OF). This may be expressed by saying that the tangents to the β and the β_+ productivity curves have equal elasticities at the same real-capital ratio. $(W_\beta B/OB$ is equal to $W_{\beta_+}B_+/OB_+)$. The rise in real wages (from OW_β to OW_{β_+}) is in the same proportion as the increase in output per head (from OB to OB_+) at the real factor ratio OF.

If the real-wage rate had risen in a smaller proportion (which implies a rate of accumulation too slow to keep up with technical progress) the economy would be off the line of a golden age and would have moved in the direction β to γ_+. If the wage rate had risen in a greater proportion, the economy would have moved in the direction β to a_+.

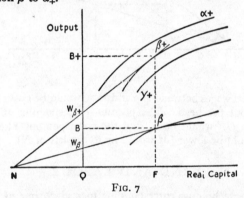

Fig. 7

Fig. 8 represents technical progress with a capital-using bias. This is shown by the fact that the real-capital ratio corresponding to a constant rate of profit $(1/ON)$ has been raised from OF to OG. The elasticity of the tangent at β_+ (the point which represents the technique that would be chosen in the new conditions at the old rate of profit) is greater than that at β $(W_{\beta_+}B_+/OB_+$ is greater than $W_\beta B/OB)$. With the new technique and the old real-capital ratio (OF) the economy would be at γ_+ and the rate of profit would have risen to $1/OQ$.

To have maintained a quasi-golden age (with a constant rate of profit) accumulation must have been sufficient to increase the real-capital ratio from OF to OG. The real-wage rate has then risen from OW_β to OW_{β_+}, while output per head has risen from OB to OB_+. The proportionate rise in the wage rate $(W_\beta W_{\beta_+}/OW_\beta)$ is less than the proportionate rise in output (BB_+/OB).

With a capital-saving bias in technical progress the real-capital ratio corresponding to a constant rate of profit is reduced and the rate of profit at a constant real-capital ratio raised. In the diagram β_+ would lie to the left of β and G to the left of F. The proportion-

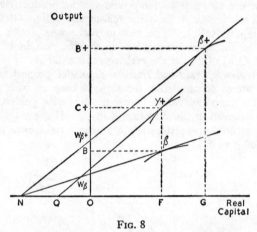

FIG. 8

ate rise in real wages between W_β and $W_{\beta+}$ would be greater than the rise in output per head. The position corresponding to the real-capital ratio OF would be α_+ and the corresponding rate of profit ($1/OM$) would be lower (M would lie to the left of N).

LAND AND LABOUR

With the techniques corresponding to a given rate of profit the relation of the marginal product of land to that of labour can be exhibited as in Fig. 9. The vertical axis represents man-years of employment and the horizontal axis acres of land. The curve passing through β represents combinations of land and labour that may be used to produce a given rate of output of commodities in conditions of static equilibrium with the techniques (and the appropriate capital goods) that would be used when a Beta rate of profit is ruling.

The slope of this curve at any point shows the increase in the quantity of labour required to keep output constant (at the land-labour ratio corresponding to that point) when land is reduced by one unit. The loss of output due to having one less acre of land is the marginal product of land. The increase in the number of men that would be required to make up a unit loss of output is the inverse of the marginal product of labour. The slope of the curve is therefore the ratio of the marginal product of land to the marginal product of labour. A tangent cutting the labour axis in R and the land axis in W shows the ratio of the marginal product of land to the marginal product of labour as OR/OW.

Where there is a marked gap between the factor ratio required for Beta-R techniques (which use a higher ratio of land to labour than exists in the economy as a whole) and for Beta-W techniques (which use a lower ratio) there is a range of ratios of land to labour, shown as the segment of the curve, such as *ma*, over which the ratio of the marginal products is constant and output would be maintained (in face of a change in the factor ratio) by switching between Beta-R and Beta-W techniques. Over such a range the tangent and the curve coincide; to the left of *m* the ratio of land to labour falls below that at which all labour could be employed with Beta-W techniques, and for any further reduction in the ratio of land to labour the ratio of the marginal product of land to that of labour would be higher and the slope of the tangent great. The ratio of rent to wages would rise and a new pair of Beta-R and Beta-W techniques would become eligible. Conversely, to the right of *a* the slope of the curve is less. The general shape of the curve, therefore, is convex to the origin.

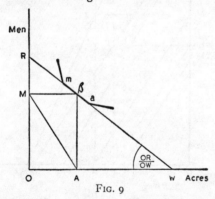

Fig. 9

In the diagram the ratio of land to labour in the economy as a whole is shown as OA/OM and the economy is in equilibrium at β when (with a Beta rate of profit ruling) the ratio of rent per acre to wage per man is OR/OW.

In Fig. 10 three positions are shown with the same ratio of land to labour $(OA_1/OM_1 = OA_2/OM_2 = OA_3/OM_3)$ representing equilibrium with Gamma, Beta and Alpha rates of profit. The same output is being produced in each position and the superiority of a higher degree of mechanisation shows itself in the reduction in the quantity of factors required to produce it. In the case illustrated

OR_β/OW_β is less than OR_γ/OW_γ, showing that Beta technique has a land-saving bias compared to Gamma; OR_α/OW_α is greater than OR_β/OW_β, showing that Alpha technique has a labour-saving bias compared to Beta. If accumulation raises the degree of

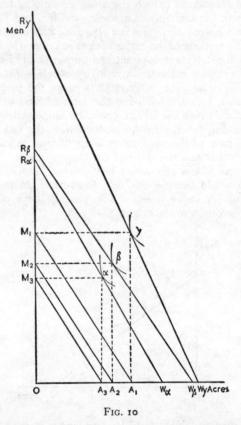

FIG. 10

mechanisation from Gamma to Beta to Alpha, wages and rents taken together rise (as the rate of profit falls). From Gamma to Beta rents rise by less than wages (and may even fall); from Beta to Alpha wages rise by less than rents (and may even fall).

THE VALUE OF INVESTED CAPITAL

With some drastic simplifying assumptions it is possible to construct a geometrical illustration of the cost of an outfit of capital goods.[1] The assumptions are : (1) a uniform rate of profit rules throughout the system, has long ruled and is confidently expected to continue to rule ; (2) capital goods can be used at full efficiency for a definite period of time and then become useless, with no scrap value ;[2] (3) there is no overlap between the period of gestation and the period of use of capital goods ; (4) during the gestation period a given labour force is employed continuously for a definite time. There is no cost other than wages and interest.

The wages cost of production of an outfit of capital goods is incurred over the gestation period. It can be represented as in Fig. 11. Wages are paid at intervals of t and the whole gestation period, T, is made up, in the case illustrated of $7t$. The whole wages bill, wT, is $7w$. The first period's work is advanced by the workers to the entrepreneur and paid at the end of $t1$. The finance invested in the first wage payment is outstanding for $6t$, the second for $5t$, etc. Thus the pile of blocks represents the finance expended

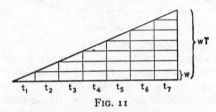

FIG. 11

weighted by the time that it is outstanding. The investment on which interest cost is incurred, including (though they do not receive it) interest on the finance advanced in kind by the workers, is the area of the triangle, which is $\frac{1}{2}wT^2$.

Fig. 12 represents the investment including the first two rounds of compound interest on the finance. The notional interest rate is the rate of profit ruling in the tranquil static economy and since profit accrues continuously the notional interest is best represented by the instantaneous rate of interest, r. The finance on which interest has to be reckoned rises from zero at the beginning of the gestation period to wT at the end. At the last moment, when the whole wages bill has been paid simple interest on the finance is being incurred at the rate rwT. The area of the thin shaded triangle, representing simple interest, is therefore $\frac{1}{2}rwT^2$. Simple interest on this rises from zero to a rate of $\frac{1}{2}r^2wT^2$. The weighted average

[1] This section illustrates the note by D. G. Champernowne and R. F. Kahn which follows (pp. 431 ff.), and has been compiled with their help.

[2] This has been called the 'one-horse shay' assumption. See Eric Schiff, 'A Note on Depreciation and Growth', *Reveiw of Economics and Statistics* (February 1954).

time for which the finance entailed by simple interest on the wages bill is outstanding is $\frac{1}{3}T$. The thin white strip, representing the second round of compound interest, therefore has an area equal to $\frac{1}{6}r^2wT^3$.

The cost of the outfit of capital goods including the first two rounds of interest is thus $wT + \frac{1}{2}rwT^2 + \frac{1}{6}r^2wT^3$.

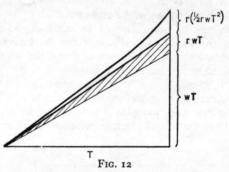

$r(\frac{1}{2}rwT^2)$
rwT
wT

T
FIG. 12

This is an approximation to K, the cost of the investment up to the moment when the capital goods are ready for use.

We now turn to the period of use of the capital goods. They will earn quasi-rent over a period which we may again call T. What return must they yield in order to make this investment eligible when the rate of profit obtainable on investment in general is r?

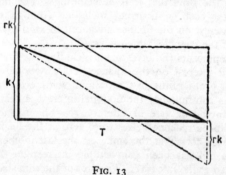

rk
k
T
rk

FIG. 13

The first requirement is that quasi-rent should yield the repayment of K over the period T. Quasi-rent must therefore be at a rate at least equal to K/T so that at the end of T the finance is available for reinvestment. The finance requires a total sum of interest over the period of commitment of $\frac{1}{2}rKT$, and the amortisation fund also yields $\frac{1}{2}rKT$ over the period. In Fig. 13 the left-hand triangle represents finance committed and the right hand represents receipts. Since the period of commitment precedes the period of receipts, interest must be earned on the interval between them to make the investment eligible. In Fig. 14 T, the life of the capital goods, is represented by the distance OR. OQ is $\frac{1}{2}T$. At the date Q an amortisation fund accumulated at the rate K/T has amassed half the initial cost, K. If quasi-rent were no more than $K/T+\frac{1}{2}rK$, the triangle OPQ (equal to $\frac{1}{8}rTK$) would represent an excess of

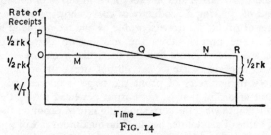

FIG. 14

interest payments over receipts and the triangle QRS (which is equal to OPQ) would represent receipts of interest in the amortisation fund in excess of payments. OM is $\frac{1}{3}OQ$, representing the centre of gravity of the triangle OPQ. Similarly QN is $\frac{2}{3}QR$. The weighted average time over which payments precede receipts is MN, which is equal to $\frac{2}{3}T$. Simple interest on the excess of payments over receipts is therefore

$$r \left(\frac{2T}{3} \times \frac{rTK}{8} \right),$$

which is equal to $r^2T^2K/12$. This represents an approximation to the extra quasi-rent required to provide interest on the interest involved in the investment. For the investment to be eligible the quasi-rent must therefore be (including only the first round of compound interest)

$$\frac{K}{T} + \frac{1}{2}rK + \frac{r^2TK}{12}.$$

Capital goods yielding quasi-rent at this rate have a capital value of

$$\frac{K}{2}\left(1 + \frac{rT}{6} \right).$$

POSTSCRIPT

An alternative form of the foregoing diagrams, which may be easier to follow, has been developed from the analysis of Piero Sraffa's *Production of Commodities by Means of Commodities*.[1] As before, the illustrations are confined to stationary states, so that net output consists of commodities. All values are reckoned in terms of commodities.

Instead of drawing a productivity curve showing all techniques at one rate of profit, we draw a profile of one technique at all rates of profit. The profile shows the relationship between the real wage and the rate of profit for the particular technique. At zero profits, the wage is equal to net output per unit of labour. At successively higher rates of profit the wage is successively lower, the amount of profit, that is, net output per head minus the wage, being sufficient to yield the corresponding rate of profit on the corresponding value of capital per head. The maximum rate of profit that the technique can yield obtains at zero wages;[2] it is the ratio of net output to the value of capital which is appropriate to that rate of profit.

If, within a particular technique, the value of capital per unit of labour employed were uniform for all capital goods and commodities at any one rate of profit, it would be so at all and the value of capital in terms of commodities would be independent of the rate of profit. The profile in such a case would be a straight line.

When the value of capital per unit of labour employed is greater (at all rates of profit) in the production of commodities than in the production of capital goods, a lower rate of profit (and higher wage) is associated with a greater value of capital, Figure I illustrates such a case :

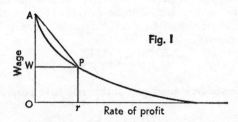

Fig. I

[1] See 'The Badly Behaved Production Function' by Joan Robinson and K. A. Naqvi, *Quarterly Journal of Economics*, November 1967. This discussion owes a great deal to Dr. Piero Garegnani and to Dr. Amit Bhaduri.

[2] On page 414 above it is implied that, when wages are zero, the rate of profit is infinite. This is an error that was pointed out by Sraffa, *op. cit.* p. 94.

OA is the output of commodities per unit of labour employed (including the labour required to keep capital intact). At the wage OW, profit is AW; the rate of profit is Or (WP) and the value of capital is shown by the slope of the cord AP, that is, AW/WP — the amount of profit divided by the rate of profit.

In Wicksell's examples the relation between the rate of profit and the value of capital are of this form. (The *rise* of the value of capital with a *rise* of real wages has been called 'the Wicksell effect'.[1]) Some passages in Chapter 10 above suggest that it is to be taken as the general case, but this is an unnecessary limitation on the argument. Cases where the value of capital for a particular technique falls as the real-wage rate rises ('negative Wicksell effect') must not be excluded (some profiles of this type appear in Figures II, III and IV below). The most general case is that in which the value of capital, for a particular technique, falls over some ranges and rises over others, so that the profile is inflected. (A rise or fall in this sense, of course, is not a process taking place through time; it is merely a convenient way of expressing a comparison of differences.)

Now, on the same axes, draw the profiles for two techniques, one, Alpha, having a higher net output per man than the other, Beta, and therefore a higher amount of profit at each wage rate.

A wage rate at which the two techniques are equally profitable (an Alpha-Beta or Beta-Alpha wage rate) is one at which the ratio of the value of capital for Alpha to that for Beta is equal to the ratio of their amounts of profit. This is shown in the old diagram by both techniques lying on the same tangent from the wage rate to the productivity curve corresponding to the rate of profit; in the new, by an intersection of the profiles at a switching point.

We may call a *forward* switch one where a slightly lower wage would make the Beta technique eligible. A *backward* switch is one where a slightly lower wage would make Alpha eligible. In Chapter 10 above a backward switch was treated as a curiosum, which unduly depreciated its importance in the analysis. A forward switch occurs where a small reduction in the wage rate, which reduces the ratio of the amount of profit for Alpha to that for Beta, raises the ratio of the values of capital, so that the Alpha technique, which has the higher value of capital at the switch point, ceases to be eligible; a backward switch occurs when the ratio of the values of capital falls by more than the ratio of the amounts of profit; that is to say, that technique Beta, with the lower amount of profit, ceases to be eligible because the value of capital rises too fast (or falls too slowly) when the wage is reduced.

[1] Cf. p. 391.

A backward switch means that the Alpha technique, which was eligible at the highest wage rates, becomes eligible again at some lower wage rate.

Alpha is called 'more mechanised' than Beta because it has a higher net output per unit of labour, not because it has a higher value of capital. At wages some way above a forward switch or below a backward switch it may well have a lower value of capital than Beta.

The following figures, combining the two types of diagram, show technical frontiers each composed of a pair of techniques.

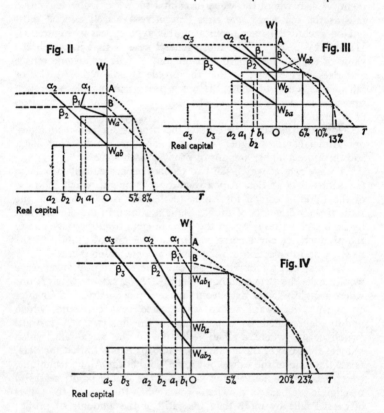

In each diagram the vertical axis represents net output per unit of labour. The right-hand horizontal axis is the rate of profit and the left-hand real capital, that is, the value of capital in terms of commodities divided by the real-wage rate. The labour force being given, *OA* is the output of the Alpha technique and *OB* of the Beta technique. *OWa* is a wage at which Alpha is eligible; at *OWb*, Beta is eligible. At *OWab* there is a forward switch and at *OWba* a backward switch. The value of capital for Alpha at the wage *OWab* is *OWab . a_1*; for Beta *OWab . b_1*, and so forth. $a_1\beta_1$, etc. are the corresponding productivity curves.

In Figure II the Beta technique has a constant value of capital shown by a straight line in the right-hand diagram. For Alpha the value of capital falls as the real-wage rate rises, shown by a curve that is convex outwards. The value of capital is less for Alpha than for Beta at low rates of profit. In Figure III Alpha has a constant value of capital and for Beta the value of capital falls as the real-wage rate rises. In Figure IV both techniques have a falling value of capital, the convexities of the curves varying relatively to each other so as to give a backward switch between two forward ones.

By including the profile for every technique that is eligible at least one wage rate we can exhibit all the relations shown in the old diagrams by the real-capital ratio curve.

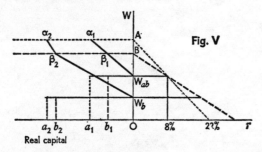

Figure V, in which each technique has a value of capital that does not vary with the rate of profit, exhibits the basis of the 'well-behaved production function' of neo-neoclassical theory, in which the technique that is eligible at a higher wage rate always has a higher net output per unit of labour and a higher value of capital.

It must be repeated that this whole argument is concerned with comparisons of equilibrium positions at different rates of profit, not with a process of accumulation or with changes taking place at a point in time.

THE VALUE OF INVESTED CAPITAL

BY

D. G. CHAMPERNOWNE AND R. F. KAHN

THE VALUE OF INVESTED CAPITAL

1. THIS Note will discuss the effect of the rate of interest on the value of capital involved in the use of a given technique of production under equilibrium conditions. It is confined to a consideration of the relationship between the value of a set of equipment of balanced age-composition and the cost of a brand-new set of equipment. This latter cost will itself include an element due to interest, depending on the time pattern of production of the equipment: the manner of that dependence is a matter for separate investigation and will not be discussed here.

To simplify the argument we shall assume an equilibrium such that: (1) the balanced age distribution of finished equipment is uniform from age o to age T years (this implies equilibrium without growth); (2) during the life of T years, each item of equipment is of constant efficiency, and at the end of its life it becomes valueless; (3) risk and uncertainty are absent.

In the absence of interest the value of an item of finished equipment would be proportional to its unexpired life, and hence the value of finished equipment of balanced age-composition would be exactly half the value of the equipment when new. The remainder of this Note considers how this argument must be modified to allow for: (1) the rate of interest, (2) unfinished equipment.

2. We shall examine two cases, the disintegrated case and the integrated case. The latter is relevant when a cross-section of the whole economy is to be considered.

Interest is at the instantaneous rate of r per annum, and the suffixes r and 0 will be used according to whether the rate of interest is or is not taken into account. We shall work throughout in terms of quantities measured per unit of finished equipment.

In the disintegrated case, the employer replaces each item of equipment, at the end of its life of T years, by buying new equipment at a cost K_r: his rate of expenditure on replacement of a balanced equipment is then K_r/T per annum.

In the integrated case, the employer manufactures his own equipment at a cost K_0 (excluding interest). His outlay on a balanced equipment for purposes of replacement is then K_0/T per annum, in the form of factor-payments.

Let C_r be the value of equipment of balanced age-composition in the disintegrated case. Then in the integrated case, the balanced set of equipment will in addition include some unfinished equipment in course of being produced : hence if C'_r denotes in this case the value of all equipment, C'_r will exceed C_r because of the inclusion of unfinished equipment. In fact, the difference between C_r and C'_r is the capital employed in the disintegrated case by the manufacturer of equipment. This is the capitalised value of the interest payments included in the value of the new equipment supplied by way of renewals, *i.e.* it is the capitalised value of $K_r/T - K_0/T$; and $C'_r - C_r$ is, therefore, equal to

$$\frac{K_r - K_0}{rT}.$$

Our object is to derive expressions for C_r/K_r and C'_r/K_r, thus generalising our knowledge that $C_0/K_0 = \frac{1}{2}$ when there is a zero rate of interest.

3. The required expressions can be obtained in a large variety of ways, but the following argument seems the most direct.

Imagine that an employer purchasing a set of equipment has the choice of buying a completely new equipment or an equipment of a balanced age-structure. In the former case he will have to put down K_r now and an equal sum every time the equipment needs replacement, *i.e.* at intervals of T years. In the latter case he will start straight away spending money on renewals and will continue to do so at a steady rate for an infinite period. Otherwise the two cases will produce the same results — the costs of production, apart from renewals, will be the same and so will the sale proceeds. The employer should therefore be indifferent between the following three alternatives :

   (i) To pay out K_r at times o, T, $2T$, . . . for sets of new equipment ;
   (ii) To pay out C_r at once (for a balanced set of finished equipment), and a constant flow at the rate of K_r/T per annum on replacements (disintegrated case) ;
   (iii) To pay out C'_r at once (for a balanced set of equipment with the pipe-line of equipment under production), and a constant flow at the rate of K_0/T per annum towards replacements (integrated case).

The present values of these three sets of payments are :

$$K_r\{1 + e^{-rT} + \dots \} = \frac{K_r}{1 - e^{-rT}}, \tag{i}$$

$$C_r + \frac{K_r}{rT} \quad \cdot \quad \cdot \quad \cdot \quad \cdot \quad \text{(ii)}$$

$$C'_r + \frac{K_0}{rT} \quad \cdot \quad \cdot \quad \cdot \quad \cdot \quad \text{(iii)}$$

(r being the rate of interest). These must all be equal. Hence

$$\frac{C_r}{K_r} = \frac{1}{1 - e^{-rT}} - \frac{1}{rT} \qquad \text{by equating (i) and (ii),} \quad \cdot \quad \text{(1)}$$

$$\frac{C'_r}{K_r} = \frac{1}{1 - e^{-rT}} - \frac{K_0}{rTK_r} \qquad \text{by equating (i) and (iii)} \quad \cdot \quad \text{(2}$$

or $\qquad C'_r = \frac{K_r}{1 - e^{-rT}} - \frac{K_0}{rT} \quad \cdot \quad \cdot \quad \cdot \quad \cdot \quad \cdot \quad \cdot \quad \cdot \quad$ (2a)

It will be seen that, as indicated at the end of Section 2,

$$C'_r - C_r = \frac{K_r - K_0}{rT}.$$

Looked at in this way, the capital, C_r, invested in a balanced equipment, is the difference between two perpetual annuities, each at the rate of K_r/T per annum, but in one case the payments being made at discrete intervals of T and in the other case the payments being made continuously. The argument amounts to this :

Let a be the advantage of having a new equipment K_r instead of an equivalent amount C_r of balanced equipment.

Then a consists of the fact that if we set aside K_r/T every year, as amortisation fund, we have at the end of T years the accrued interest on the amortisation fund to play with : moreover, we then have the same advantage a again. Since a capital of K_r/rT would yield the funds required for the amortisation fund, the accrued value of the fund after T years will be

$$\frac{K_r}{rT} (e^{rT} - 1),$$

and the accrued interest will thus be :

$$\frac{K_r}{rT} (e^{rT} - 1) - K_r.$$

The present value of this is

$$\frac{K_r}{rT} (1 - e^{-rT}) - K_r e^{-rT}.$$

Hence
$$a = \frac{K_r}{rT}(1 - e^{-rT}) + e^{-rT}(a - K_r),$$

$$\therefore \ a = K_r \left\{ \frac{1}{rT} - \frac{1}{e^{rT} - 1} \right\},$$

$$\therefore \ C_r = K_r - a = K_r \left\{ \frac{1}{1 - e^{-rT}} - \frac{1}{rT} \right\}.$$

4. The following alternative approach may commend itself to some readers. Under equilibrium conditions the demand-value of any piece of equipment must at all times equal its cost-value, and we may speak unambiguously of its value under these conditions.

Let the value of a piece of equipment of age t be $K_r(t)$. This value, viewed from the side of demand, is due to the prospect of its providing $(T - t)$ years of service. It follows that $K_r(t)$ is the value of a certain annuity of unexpired life, $(T - t)$ years.

Now the value of an annuity of unexpired life $(T - t)$ is

$$A(T - t) = \left\{ 1 - e^{-r(T - t)} \right\} A(\infty),$$

where $A(\infty)$ is the corresponding permanent annuity.   Hence

$$\frac{K_r(t)}{K_r} = \frac{1 - e^{-r(T - t)}}{1 - e^{-rT}}.$$

Now C_r, the value of a balanced equipment, is equal to the average value of $K_r(t)$ over $t = 0$ to $t = T$.   Hence

$$C_r = \frac{1 - qe^{-rT}}{1 - e^{-rT}} K_r,$$

where q is the average value of e^{rt} over $t = 0$ to $t = T$. .   . (3)

q may be evaluated by integral calculus, or as follows: consider £1 accruing at interest r compound over T years; its average value is q, and the accrued interest is $e^{rT} - 1$.   Hence

$$rTq = e^{rT} - 1, \quad \text{and} \quad q = \frac{e^{rT} - 1}{rT}.$$

Substituting in (3), $C_r = \left\{ \frac{1}{1 - e^{-rT}} - \frac{1}{rT} \right\} K_r.$

5. If we regard capital-value as due to cost, the formula is slightly more difficult to obtain.

Let D represent the gross earnings of an item of equipment costing K_r.

Then the cost after t years is reduced to

$$K_r - (Dt + D') = K_r(t),$$

where D' represents the accrued interest on earnings. Now $Dt + D'$ may be regarded as the accrued interest, at rate of interest r, after t years on a capital of D/r. Hence

$$Dt + D' = \frac{D}{r}(e^{rt} - 1).$$

$$\therefore K_r(t) = K_r - \frac{D}{r}(e^{rt} - 1).$$

But if the rate of interest is such as to provide equilibrium, the cost of capital of age T must be zero ;

$$\therefore K_r - \frac{D(e^{rT} - 1)}{r} = 0,$$

$$\therefore D = \frac{rK_r}{e^{rT} - 1},$$

$$\therefore K_r(t) = \left\{ 1 - \frac{e^{rt} - 1}{e^{rT} - 1} \right\} K_r = \left\{ \frac{1 - e^{r(t - T)}}{1 - e^{-rT}} \right\} K_r.$$

Hence, as in Section 4, we again obtain

$$C_r = \left\{ \frac{1}{1 - e^{-rT}} - \frac{1}{rT} \right\} K_r.$$

6. It is a matter of some interest that good approximations to this expression can be obtained, as

$$\frac{C_r}{K_r} = 1 - \frac{1}{rT} \text{ for } rT > 4 ; \quad \cdot \quad \cdot \quad \cdot \quad \cdot \quad \cdot \quad \cdot \quad (4)$$

$$\frac{C_r}{K_r} = \frac{1}{2} + \frac{rT}{12} - \frac{r^3 T^3}{720} \text{ for } rT < 4 ; \quad \cdot \quad \cdot \quad \cdot \quad \cdot \quad (5)$$

$$\frac{C_r}{K_r} = \frac{1}{2} + \frac{rT}{12} \text{ for } rT < 2 \text{ (a rougher approximation than (5))} \quad (6)$$

These formulae are the best obtainable approximations to (1), expressible as the sum of two or three terms involving powers of $1/rT$ and of rT respectively.

It is only for values of rT in the neighbourhood of four that either result (4) (for rates of interest or lives of equipment sufficiently large to compensate for any smallness of the other) or result (5) (for low rates of interest or short lives of equipment) does not give a very good approximation.

7. It is interesting to regard approximation (4) from the following intuitive approach. If the equipment has an infinite life, the value of the capital invested is clearly equal to the cost of the equipment when new. The ratio C_r/K_r is then unity, which is its limiting value at the upper end. This value of unity for the ratio in the limiting case can be regarded as made up of two equal parts — $\frac{1}{2}$, which arises without interest being brought in, and again $\frac{1}{2}$, through the operation of interest. If the life of equipment, though not infinite, is long (without the rate of interest being correspondingly low) the ratio is pulled down below the limiting value of unity in the manner shown by approximation (4).

Approximations (5) and (6) show how the ratio C_r/K_r is raised above the value of one-half, which is the limiting value at the lower end, when the rate of interest, without actually being zero, is low (without the life of equipment being correspondingly high).

8. The entry of the fraction $\frac{1}{3}$ into approximations (5) and (6) (disguised as $\frac{1}{12}$) is reminiscent of Wicksell's reference to the distance of the centre of gravity of a triangle from its base.[1] The reference occurs in the course of 'A Mathematical Analysis of Dr. Åkerman's Problem', some of which bears on the subject-matter of this Note, and for this reason a direct demonstration of approximation (6) may be of interest.

We can imagine that the capital cost K_r of a new equipment is made up of two parts, C_r and $K_r - C_r$. C_r receives a normal profit under equilibrium conditions from the earnings of the equipment after deduction as an amortisation allowance of K_r/T per annum. Since K_r/T per annum is needed to replace the equipment after T years, it follows that the interest on the amortisation fund over the life of the equipment is equal to the interest on $K_r - C_r$ over the same period.

We first calculate the former. The simple interest obtained by the end of the period T years consists of the successive elements of the annuity,

$$\frac{K_r}{T}\, rT, \; \frac{K_r}{T}\, r\, (T-1), \; \text{etc.,}$$

and therefore adds up to $\frac{1}{2}K_r rT$. This simple interest earns the first order of compound interest for a weighted average period $\frac{1}{3}T$, and the first order of compound interest therefore comes to $\frac{1}{6}K_r r^2 T^2$.

Now we must to the same degree of approximation calculate

[1] Wicksell, *loc. cit.* p. 283.

the interest at the end of T years on an initial sum $K_r - C_r$. The simple interest amounts to $(K_r - C_r)rT$. It earns the first order of compound interest for an average period $\frac{1}{2}T$, and the first order of compound interest therefore comes to $\frac{1}{2}(K_r - C_r)r^2T^2$. Hence

$$K_r(\tfrac{1}{2}rT + \tfrac{1}{6}r^2T^2) = (K_r - C_r)(rT + \tfrac{1}{2}r^2T^2).$$

It follows that
$$\frac{C_r}{K_r} = \frac{1}{2}\frac{1 + \frac{2}{3}rT}{1 + \frac{1}{2}rT}.$$

If second and higher orders of rT are neglected, this comes to

$$\frac{C_r}{K_r} = \frac{1}{2} + \frac{rT}{12}.$$

INDEX

Accumulation, 55-6, 83-4, 244
 and trade cycle, 213-16
 synopsis, 173-6
 with given knowledge, 139-48
 world, 384-5
Advertisement, 18, 92, 251, 262,
 339, 389
Amortisation, 5, 67, 90, 104-5, 163

Balance of payments, 53, 237 n.,
 280-3
Balogh, T., 137 n.
Bank deposits, 31, 234
 notes, 31, 226
Banks, 10, 225, 227, 236
 profits of, 228, 249
Bensusan-Butt, D., viii
Bentley, N. C., 335 n.
Bliss, 83, 99, 151, 218
Blyth, C. A., vii
Böhm-Bawerk, 396
Bonds, 7, 229-31
Boom, 78, 91, 98, 198-202, 264-6.
 See also Seller's market
Boulding, K. E., 18 n.
Brumberg, R., 251 n.
Building, 47, 200 n., 270
Buyer's market 189
 wages in, 196

Capacity, 51, 119, 184
 bottleneck, 51, 200
Capital :
 measurements of, 103 5, 117-23,
 127, 143, 144, 146, 396, 422-5,
 431-9. *See also* Real-capital
 ratio
Champernowne, D. G., vii, xi,
 105 n., 144 n., 301 n., 312 n.,
 423 n.
Clapham, J. H. v
Clemens, E. W., 185 n.
Cohen, Ruth, viii, 109 n.
Commodity, 17

'Concertina effect', 203-4
Consumption, 16, 18, 24, 34, 41
 biased, 358-60
 of profits, 249, 257, 265-73
 of rent, 296-7
Costs, 38
 marginal, 184
 overhead, 183
 prime, 183
 user, 183
Cycle, trade, 208-12, 213
 and trend, 215, 269
 theory of, 211-12

Definitions, viii, 9, 313
Demand, particular, 250, 253-6
Depression, 209, 268-9. *See also*
 Buyer's market *and* Stagnation
Diminishing returns, law of :
 simple, 284-6, 329, 341
 sophisticated, 305, 321, 341
Duesenberry, J., 251 n., 262 n.

Economic theory, v, 63
Economies of scale. *See* Scale
 of uniformity, 339
Entrepreneur, 5-6, 39-40, 68, 73,
 257
Equilibrium, 57-9. *See also*
 Tranquillity
Euler's Theorem, 285 n.
Excess-investment, 229

Fellner, W., 402 n.
Finance, 5, 9-10, 50, 110, 230,
 243, 275, 278, 289, 291, 402
Foreign trade. *See* Balance of
 payments
Foresight, 66
Frontiersman, 283, 330-1, 332,
 368
'Full cost', 186 n.
Full employment, 49

441